Administering Exchange 2000 Server

Mitch Tulloch

McGraw-Hill
New York Chicago San Francisco Lisbon London
Madrid Mexico City Milan New Delhi San Juan
Seoul Singapore Sydney Toronto

McGraw-Hill

A Division of The ***McGraw-Hill*** *Companies*

1 2 3 4 5 6 7 8 9 0 DOC/DOC 0 5 4 3 2 1

ISBN 0-07-212708-2

The sponsoring editor for this book was Michael Sprague and the production supervisor was Daina Penikas. It was set in New Century Schoolbook by Patricia Wallenburg.

Printed and bound by R.R. Donnelley & Sons.

This book is printed on recycled, acid-free paper containing a minimum of 50% recycled, de-inked fiber.

Contents

INTRODUCTION

Welcome to *Administering Exchange 2000 Server!* My name is Mitch Tulloch and I have written a number of best-selling computer books including *Administering IIS4*, *Administering IIS5* (with Patrick Santry), and *Administering Exchange Server* published by Osborne/McGraw-Hill, as well as several Nutshell books published by O'Reilly & Associates and the best-selling *Microsoft Encyclopedia of Networking* published by Microsoft Press.

So much for my literary credentials. You probably want to know what this book is about!

One-Minute Summary (Read This!)

My previous book, *Administering Exchange Server* (McGraw-Hill, 1999), was very popular and reached the number 1 position on the Microsoft Exchange bestsellers list on Amazon. What readers liked best about the book was that *it made Exchange 5.5 simple!* With dozens of hands-on walkthroughs, I led readers through all aspects of administering messaging systems based on Microsoft Exchange 5.5.

The present book is the sequel to the previous one. It is not a revision but *a complete rewrite*. This was obviously necessary because of the many and fundamental differences between Exchange 2000 and earlier versions of the product.

The focus of this book is on *day-to-day administration of Exchange 2000*. The book is organized in 25 chapters that gradually lead the reader from simpler topics (pure installations, recipients, address lists, and recipient policies) to more complex ones (administrative and routing groups, storage architecture, connectors, upgrades, monitoring, and maintenance).

These chapters contain more than *150 hands-on walkthroughs* that cover a multitude of tasks that competent Exchange 2000 administrators should be able to perform. Readers can use the various walkthroughs on their own testbed systems similar to the one described in the book. Numerous screenshots make this book an excellent learning tool even for readers who cannot set up their own testbed systems. This book also includes notes, tips, background information, and under-the-hood looks at how Exchange 2000 operates.

Anyone who needs to learn how to perform day-to-day administration of Exchange 2000 will find this book an excellent learning tool and valuable reference guide. Corporations can use it to train junior administrators, and technical schools can use it in the classroom. Individuals intending to take the Exchange 2000 examinations as part of their MCSE certification will find this book an excellent tool for gaining the hands-on experience that is always the most valuable key for success.

Experienced administrators who are familiar with previous versions of Exchange will find this book a quick and easy introduction to the new version of the product. The focus of this book centers on core administration tasks, so readers seeking in-depth treatment of how to migrate large-scale Exchange 5.5 organizations to Exchange 2000 will need to consult other sources such as the *Microsoft Exchange 2000 Server Resource Kit* from Microsoft Press. And even though some troubleshooting information is included, this book is not intended as an in-depth guide for troubleshooting Exchange migration, connectivity, or disaster recovery.

Chapter Titles

To give you a quick idea of the topics discussed in this book, here is a list of the different chapter titles:

1. Installation
2. Administration Tools
3. Users
4. Contacts
5. Groups
6. Outlook
7. Address Lists
8. Offline Folders and Address Lists
9. System Manager
10. Recipients Revisited
11. Recipient Policies

Walkthroughs

More than 150 hands-on walkthroughs form the core of this book. These walkthroughs can be performed by readers on their own testbed systems if they have the necessary hardware and software. All that is needed are several Pentium II machines networked together and the following software: Windows 2000 Advanced Server, Exchange 2000 Server or Enterprise Server, and Outlook 2000. Whether you plan to perform these walkthroughs yourself or just do them in your head with the help of the numerous screenshots provided, you'll learn a lot about administering Exchange 2000. To show you what you'll learn, here is a quick list of the walkthroughs included in this book:

- Installing the first Exchange server
- Installing subsequent Exchange servers
- Installing the Exchange administration Tools on a Windows 2000 Professional client machine
- Creating custom MMC for administering Exchange
- Using terminal services to administer Exchange
- Creating a mailbox-enabled user
- Configuring and testing mailbox-enabled users
- Creating a mail-enabled user

- Changing a user from mail- to mailbox-enabled
- Deleting a mailbox-enabled user
- Copying a mailbox-enabled user
- Creating a mail-enabled contact
- Configuring a mail-enabled contact
- Mail-enabling an existing contact
- Creating a mail-enabled security group
- Configuring a mail-enabled security group
- Disabling a mail-enabled security group
- Mail-enabling a standard security group
- Hiding and displaying membership of a mail-enabled security group
- Creating a mail-enabled distribution group
- Installing Outlook
- Configuring Outlook for Exchange
- Using Outlook
- Creating a new address list
- Updating address lists across an enterprise or domain
- Rebuilding an address list
- Modifying an address list
- Configuring Outlook to use address lists
- Configuring offline folders
- Synchronizing offline folders
- Configuring Outlook to use an offline address list
- Creating and configuring offline address lists
- Exploring the Exchange organization hierarchy
- Displaying the Exchange Advanced Tab
- Configuring the Exchange Advanced tab for mailbox-enabled users
- Configuring the Exchange Advanced tab for mail-enabled users
- Configuring the Exchange Advanced tab for mail-enabled contacts
- Configuring the Exchange Advanced tab for mail-enabled groups
- Creating, modifying, and removing users with LDIFDE
- Modifying the default Recipient Policy
- Creating a new recipient policy
- Modifying a recipient policy
- Setting the priority of recipient policies
- Forcing recipient-policy updates
- Overriding recipient policies
- Enable support for administrative groups
- Change the operations mode
- Rename the default First Administrative Group
- Create a new administrative group

- Install an Exchange server into an administrative group
- Add a container to an Administrative Group
- Move an object between administrative groups
- Copy an object between administrative groups
- Delete an administrative group
- Delegating control over the entire Exchange organization
- Delegating control over administrative groups
- Delegating rnlic folder using a network share
- Configuring replication settings for a public-folder store
- Replicating public folders
- Viewing replication status
- Verifying public-folder replication
- Adding and removing public-folder replicas
- Configuring age limits for replicas
- Copying and moving public folders
- Propagating public-folder settings
- Modifying email addresses for public folders
- Configuring administrative and directory permissions for managing public folders
- Configuring client permissions for controlling access to public folders
- Specifying indexing priority for a server
- Creating a full-text index
- Populating a new index
- Viewing indexing statistics
- Scheduling indexing
- Rebuilding a corrupt index
- Other indexing tasks
- Creating a server policy
- Creating a mailbox-store policy
- Creating a public-store policy
- Adding items to a policy
- Applying a policy
- Modifying a policy
- Enabling routing groups
- Creating a routing-group container
- Creating a new routing group
- Renaming a routing group
- Moving servers between routing groups
- Designating routing-group masters
- Connecting routing groups
- Deleting a routing group

- Installing routing-group connectors
- Testing routing-group connectors
- Configuring common settings for connectors
- Configuring routing-group connectors
- Removing routing-group connectors
- Installing SMTP connectors
- Configuring SMTP connectors
- Starting, stopping, and pausing virtual servers
- Specifying a unique identity for a virtual server
- Controlling inbound connections for virtual servers
- Creating a new virtual server
- Configuring the default SMTP virtual server
- Display current sessions for a virtual server
- Terminating current sessions for a virtual server
- Configuring a front-end server
- Viewing server and connector status
- Enabling and configuring monitors
- Enabling and configuring notifications
- Enabling and configuring protocol logging
- Enabling and configuring diagnostic logging
- Enabling and configuring message tracking
- Managing SMTP queues
- Backing up Exchange
- Upgrading Exchange 5.5 to Windows 2000
- Installing the Active Directory connector (ADC)
- Preparing the forest using FORESTPREP
- Configuring connection agreements
- Preparing the domain using DOMAINPREP
- Upgrading Exchange 5.5 to Exchange 2000

Acknowledgments

Credit shall be given where credit is due! Thanks tremendously to the following people and companies for their continued help and support:

- Ingrid Tulloch, Vice President of MTIT Enterprises, for her valuable advice and assistance during the writing of this book. She's a great wife but a terrific Vice President! :-)

- Michael Sprague, my long-time editor at Osborne/McGraw-Hill, for his helpful advice and constant nagging to meet the deadlines.
- David L. Rogelberg, outstanding literary agent (www.studiob.com), for his generous encouragement and support. Thanks also to all the other great people at Studio B: Sherry, Neil, Kristin, Stacey, Craig, David Talbott, and others for the terrific job they do.
- Steve Wynkoop, founder of Swynk (www.swynk.com), fellow columnists in my Exchange and Windows 2000 sections on Swynk (www.swynk.com/mitch), and our 65,000 terrific Swynk readers for their continued support, advice, and encouragement.
- MTS Communications Inc. (www.mts.mb.ca) for generously providing me with Internet services and for hosting my company Web site (www.mtit.com).
- Valerie Anne-Owen, gracious proprietor of Le Beaujolais Restaurant (www.lebeaujolais.com), whose outstanding cuisine enabled my wife and I to reward ourselves when various milestones in writing this book were achieved.
- John Beaudry of Beaudry's Hairstyling, whose talent for styling hair and beards has kept me from looking like most computer nerds I know (we're bums, one and all).
- Ken and Bonnie Lewis, our long-time friends, who let us hang out with them when working on this book left me worn-out and exhausted. Thanks also to their kids, Karina, Alana, Sherri, and Vanessa, who have enriched our lives tremendously.

And, finally, let me express my heartfelt thanks to you, *my readers*, who have read (and bought!) my previous books in pleasantly agreeable numbers and have often provided me with helpful feedback that has made me a more knowledgeable IT professional and a better writer.

Disclaimer

Although I've tried hard in good faith to make this work as accurate and reliable as possible, neither myself (the author) nor the publisher (Osborne/McGraw-Hill) assume any liability or responsibility whatsoever for any loss or damage arising from the information presented in this book. In other words, the information provided in this book is presented on an "as is" basis. The author recommends strongly that you test all procedures and suggestions outlined in this book in a test environment before implementing them in a production environment, and that you refer to Microsoft's official documentation on Exchange 2000 as the authoritative guide to configuring and using the product.

Mitch Tulloch, MCT, MCSE, B.Sc., Cert.Ed.
www.mtit.com
www.swynk.com/mitch

CHAPTER 1

Installation

This chapter covers the basics of installing the Exchange 2000 Server. The planning and design issues associated with upgrading to Exchange 2000 will be covered in Chapter 25. We'll begin by installing Exchange on a couple of Windows 2000 machines in a simple testbed environment. This will give us the opportunity to learn Exchange from the ground up and prevent us from getting bogged down in the nitty-gritty details of planning, upgrading, and migration, which we'll deal with in Chpater 25.

For the record, the Windows 2000 forest we're going to use as our testbed consists of two machines running Windows 2000 Advanced Server. One of these machines is a domain controller and the other is a member server. The domain controller is the forest root domain controller and has the DNS name mtit.com (the domain name for my company, MTIT Enterprises). As we progress, we'll add more domains, Exchange servers, and client computers as the need arises. Figure 1.1 shows the initial deployment in our testbed environment.

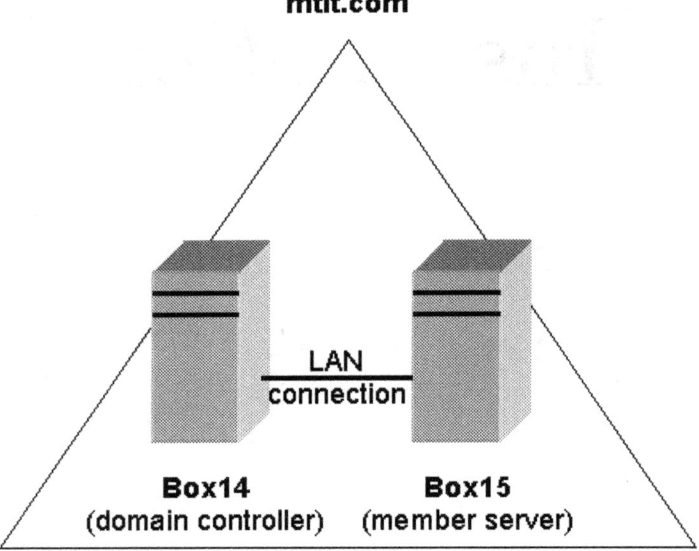

Figure 1.1 Initial Windows 2000 testbed environment.

The topics we'll cover in this chapter include Exchange hardware and software requirements, how to install the first Exchange server in your organization, installing subsequent Exchange servers in your organization, troubleshooting installation problems, and much more.

There are two walkthroughs in this chapter:

- Installing the first Exchange server
- Installing subsequent Exchange servers

NOTE

Most of the walkthroughs in this book can be performed in a testbed environment consisting of no more than three computers, provided you're willing to reinstall and reconfigure these machines several times. However, you have half a dozen computers to play with, you can perform the walkthroughs without performing any reinstallations.

Installing Exchange

Installing Exchange 2000 on a fresh system as part of a new messaging system deployment is relatively straightforward with few pitfalls. It's quite a different story if you want to upgrade an existing Exchange 5.5 messaging system with its various sites and servers (upgrading from Exchange 5.5 and migrating third-party mail systems to Exchange is covered later in this book).

Hardware Requirements

The minimum and recommended hardware requirements for installing the Exchange 2000 Server and the Exchange 2000 Enterprise Server are shown in Table 1.1. These requirements are essentially the same as those for installing Exchange 5.5; in other words, the more powerful the machine the better. In addition to the requirements listed, a CD-ROM is required for installation, unless you are performing the installation from a distribution point (shared folder containing the Exchange CD source files) over the network.

You also want to ensure that you have a reliable connection with the Internet before installing Exchange. Otherwise you will be able to send and receive mail only within your organization over the LAN—not a very exciting scenario from a business point of view. You want to ensure you have a properly configured firewall to protect your LAN from the Internet and have the firewall configured to pass traffic over port 25, the port for SMTP communications.

TABLE 1.1 Hardware requirements for the Exchange 2000 Server and the Exchange 2000 Enterprise Server.

Component	Minimum	Recommended
Processor	Pentium 133	Pentium II or higher
Memory	128 MB	256 MB or higher
Disk	200 MB on the system drive and 500 MB on the drive on which Exchange is installed	RAID and disk mirroring

NOTE

You should always meet or exceed the recommended requirements for an installation; minimal requirements are only acceptable when testing in an informal environment, such as learning Exchange at home to prepare for a Microsoft Certified Professional (MCP) exam. In a production environment, you would probably use symmetric multiprocessing (SMP) machines with 512 MB or more RAM for improved performance and RAID and disk mirroring to provide greater reliability and fault tolerance for your Exchange servers. We'll talk about disk subsystems for Exchange servers when we discuss storage groups in a later chapter.

Software Requirements

Exchange 2000 can only be installed on Windows 2000 and not on Windows NT. Specifically, Exchange 2000 can be installed on:

- Windows 2000 Server
- Windows 2000 Advanced Server
- Windows 2000 Datacenter Server

For small companies, Windows 2000 Server may be sufficient; larger companies will require the fault-tolerant clustering services of Windows 2000 Advanced Server to ensure full 24 × 7 availability for their Exchange-based messaging system.

In addition, the Windows 2000 machine on which you install Exchange on must belong to an Active Directory domain (a Windows 2000 domain)—it cannot belong to a workgroup. You must have Active Directory installed and working on your network before installing your first Exchange server, and you should test thoroughly to make sure your implementation of Active Directory is functioning properly before deploying Exchange because Exchange makes changes to the schema of Active Directory when the Exchange server is first installed, and these changes cannot easily be undone without completely reinstalling Active Directory.

Exchange cannot be installed on a machine unless the Global Catalog server in the local domain can be contacted during Setup. The Global Catalog server is typically the first Windows 2000 domain controller you install in your domain, but you may have moved this role to another domain controller and you must ensure that domain controller is running when you install Exchange.

Active Directory uses the *domain name system* (DNS) as its name resolution protocol, and you must ensure that DNS is set up and functioning properly before installing Exchange.

You must have Internet Information Services (IIS) running on the server on which you plan to install Exchange because Exchange uses IIS as its protocol engine and cannot function without it. Fortunately, IIS is installed by default when you install any version of Windows 2000 Server on a machine.

To enable public folder support on Exchange, you also need to make sure that IIS is installed with the optional Network News Transfer Protocol (NNTP) service (this is not installed by default during a typical Windows 2000 Server installation, so do a custom install instead and make sure NNTP service is installed as part of IIS).

NOTE

If you plan to upgrade an existing Exchange 5.5 system, you also need the Exchange Active Directory Connector (ADC) to be installed and running first (this is covered later in the book when we talk about upgrading from earlier versions of Exchange).

Installing the First Exchange Server

Walkthrough

There are important differences between the first Exchange 2000 Server and subsequent Exchange servers that you install in your organization. With the first Exchange server, the Setup process modifies the schema of Active Directory to support new classes, objects, and attributes required by Exchange.

In addition, with the first installation of the Exchange server, you need to specify the name of your new Exchange organization; with subsequent installations, servers automatically join the existing organization.

Finally, if you have created new administrative and routing groups (in addition to the existing default ones created during the first Exchange installation), then you will need to select the specific administrative and routing groups you want your subsequent Exchange servers to join when Setup is run for these servers. We'll talk about these two kinds of Exchange groups in Chapters 12 and 21.

Let's begin. We'll perform a CD installation of Exchange 2000 Enterprise Server as the first Exchange server in our company MTIT Enterprises. The identity of the system it will be installed on is as follows:

- Computer name: Box14
- Operating system: Windows 2000 Advanced Server with Windows 2000 Service Pack 1 applied
- DNS and Windows 2000 testbed domain name: mtit.com
- Role: root domain controller in the testbed domain
- Domain mode: Native mode

NOTE

Microsoft strongly recommends that you install Windows 2000 Service Pack 1 (SP1) before installing Exchange 2000. This applies to installing Exchange on both domain controllers and member servers. SP1 fixes a number of issues that cause problems with Exchange, so this is a necessity.

In addition, make sure your Windows 2000 Server page file is set to at least twice the installed RAM before installing Exchange. Naturally, Exchange can only be installed on an NTFS partition.

Finally, a domain controller must be available on the network when you install Exchange. You can install Exchange on either a domain controller or a member server; it doesn't matter as long as Exchange can communicate with Active Directory during the installation process.

In our testbed setup we're installing our first Exchange server on the forest root domain controller. In a production environment, this would be a bad idea for several reasons: the forest root domain controller has special single-operation master roles by default and thus has a heavier operational load than other domain controllers, and the first Exchange server in a forest performs certain special operations in the Exchange organization. Thus, if you followed the above scenario in a production environment and this machine went down, you could be in trouble while you configure other domain controllers and Exchange servers to assume these special roles. But in a small testbed environment like the one we're describing in this book, the choice we've made is OK.

Log on to the machine using an enterprisewide administrator account to perform the installation (you can use the default Administrator account in the forest root domain of your enterprise). Make sure you are logged on to the domain and not the computer before running Setup (this is not an issue on domain controllers, only member servers). To check this, examine the Log On To box in the Log On To Windows dialog box and see whether the name of the domain or of the computer is currently displayed.

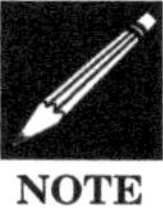
NOTE

The user account you use to install the first Exchange server in your forest must be a member of three built-in groups: Schema Admins, Enterprise Admins, and Domain Admins. User accounts you use to install subsequent Exchange servers need only be members of Enterprise Admins and Domain Admins and do not need to belong to Schema Admins.

IIS 5.0 is installed by default during a typical installation of Windows 2000 Server. Verify that the following IIS components are installed and running: SMTP service and NNTP service. If these are not installed, use Add/Remove Programs in the Control Panel to install them because they are needed by Exchange.

Also make sure that a domain controller and a DNS name server are available before installing Exchange (in this case, we are installing Exchange on the root domain controller in the domain, and it is also a DNS server, but if this is not the case, make sure that these machines are running and available on the network).

Inserting the Exchange CD brings up the splash screen followed by a welcome screen, after which you must accept the EULA and enter your CD key. At this point the Component Selection screen is displayed (Figure 1.2). We'll accept the default settings and do a typical installation of the Microsoft Exchange Messaging and Collaboration Services and the Microsoft Exchange System Management Tools. Note the installation path and disk space requirements for this installation choice.

The next screen offers the choice of either creating a new Exchange 2000 organization or joining an existing Exchange 5.5 organization. Because we're focusing on a new Exchange deployment, we'll accept the default setting (new organization).

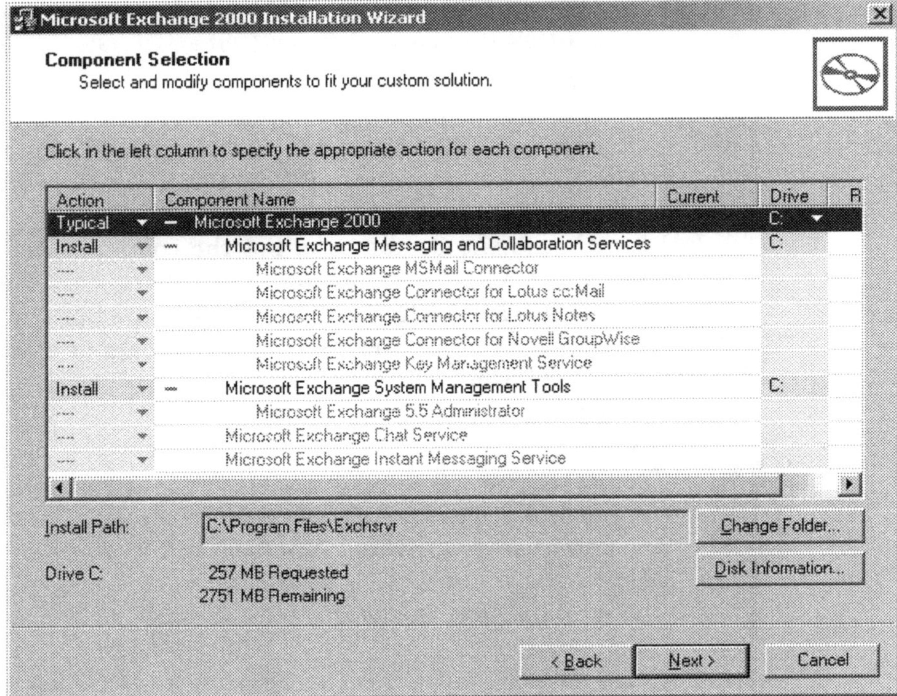

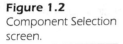

Figure 1.2 Component Selection screen.

The next screen requests us to specify a name for our new Exchange organization (Figure 1.3). This name can contain embedded spaces and hyphens but cannot contain any of the following special characters: ~`!@#$%^&*()_+={[}] | \:;'"<,>.?/

The next screen requests us to confirm that we will abide by the licensing agreement for this product. Exchange only supports Per Seat licensing, not Per Server licensing, so you must purchase a Client Access License (CAL) for every messaging client that will access your Exchange server, regardless of whether these clients are Microsoft products like Outlook or Outlook Express, third-party mail clients, or freeware.

Licensing is an important issue for administrators in today's business environment because they may be held responsible for use of products that are not properly licensed. See the Resources section at the end of this chapter for links to more information on licensing Microsoft products such as Exchange.

The next screen requests us to confirm our selection of components to install. At this point proper installation begins, and services are stopped while files for Exchange messaging and collaboration services are copied to your system. Because this is the first Exchange server in our Win-

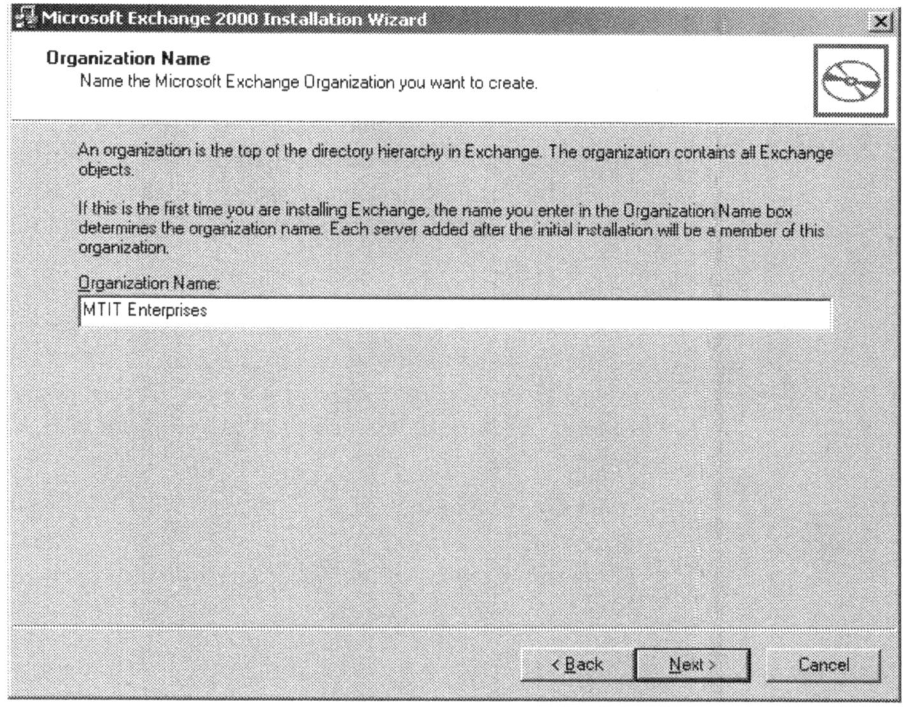

Figure 1.3 Organization Name screen.

dows 2000 domain, the Active Directory schema is also modified, which may take a while. Additional files are then copied, registry keys created, Exchange services added, Active Directory objects created, and services started. We're done.

No reboot is necessary. That's a nice surprise!

Postinstallation Features

Installing Exchange on a Windows 2000 system makes a number of changes to that system:

- New services
- New directories
- New shares
- New tools
- New groups
- New Active Directory system objects

New Services

A number of new services are installed when you install Exchange on a system. The exact number of new services depends on whether you elected to install additional optional components such as messaging connectors or the Microsoft Exchange Chat Service component. Table 1.2 describes the services installed during a typical installation of Exchange.

NOTE

You can see how tightly Exchange 2000 is integrated with IIS by examining the names of the executables associated with Exchange services. You can do this by using the Services node in Computer Management. The following Exchange services are part of the IIS main IIS executable `inetinfo.exe`*:*

- *Microsoft Exchange IMAP4 service*
- *Microsoft Exchange POP3 service*
- *Microsoft Exchange Routing Engine service*

TABLE 1.2

Exchange 2000 services installed during a typical installation.

Service name	Display name	Description	Startup type
MSExchangeES	Microsoft Exchange Event	Monitors folders and fires events for Exchange 5.5–compatible server applications	Manual
IMAP4Svc	Microsoft Exchange IMAP4	Provides Internet Message Access Protocol version 4 (IMAP4) services	Automatic
MSExchangeIS	Microsoft Exchange Information Store	Manages information storage	Automatic
MSExchangeMTA	Microsoft Exchange MTA Stacks	Provides X.400 services	Automatic
POP3Svc	Microsoft Exchange POP3	Provides Post Office Protocol version 3 (POP3) services	Automatic
RESvc	Microsoft Exchange Routing Engine	Processes routing information	Automatic
MSExchangeSRS	Microsoft Exchange Site Replication Service	Provides directory services to legacy Exchange 5.5 and earlier servers	Disabled

continued on next page

TABLE 1.2 Exchange 2000 services installed during a typical installation (continued).

Service name	Display name	Description	Startup type
MSExchangeSA	Microsoft Exchange System Attendant	Provides system-related services for Microsoft Exchange	Automatic
MSSEARCH	Microsoft Search	Creates full-text indexes on content and properties of structured and semistructured data to allow fast linguistic searches	Automatic

New Directories

Exchange 2000 Setup creates a new directory structure whose root folder is called Exchsrvr. By default the path for this folder is C:\Program Files\Exchsrvr unless otherwise specified during Setup. Table 1.3 describes the subdirectories of the Exchsrvr directory that are created during a typical installation.

TABLE 1.3 Subdirectories of the Exchsrvr directory that are created during a typical installation of Exchange.

Directory	Description
Address	Contains email address generators (proxy DLLs) for Lotus cc:Mail, Novell Groupwise, Microsoft Mail, Lotus Notes, SMTP, and X.400.
Bin	Microsoft Exchange binary files and administrative tools
<servername>.log	Formerly the Tracking.log
Conndata	Routing information
ExchangeServer_<servername>	Configuration files
Exchweb	Outlook Web Access (OWA) files
Mailroot	Messaging queues
Mdbdata	Information Store files
Mtsdata	Configuration, template database, and log files for the MTA
Res	DLLs for Event viewer and performance
Schema	OLEEDB schema
Srsdata	Site replication service files

New Shares

During a typical installation two Exchange-related shares are created: Address and <server_name>.log. The first share, Address, provides access to Exchange address objects over the network. The folder that is shared is \Exchsrvr\Address and the default shared folder permissions are as follows:

- The Administrators group has full control.
- The Exchange Site Services account has full control.
- The Everyone special identity has Read access.

See the following note for an explanation of the Site Services account.

The second share, <server_name>.log, provides access to the Exchange message tracking logs. In our earlier walkthrough, this file would be named Box14.log because the name of the computer on which we installed Exchange was Box14. The folder that is shared is \Exchsrvr\<server_name>.log and the shared folder permissions are the same as those for Address.

The permissions on these shares should not be changed or Exchange may not work properly.

NOTE

What Happened to the Exchange Service Account?

Previous versions of Exchange used a special user account called the Exchange Service account (or Site Service account). This special user account needed to be created before the first Exchange server was installed and was used by Exchange servers to authenticate with each other for purposes of message transfer and directory replication between sites. It was also needed whenever a new Exchange server was added to a site or a new site to an organization.

In a pure Exchange 2000 environment, however, the Exchange Service account is no longer needed. Instead, all Exchange operations now run in the context of the Local System account on each server. Another name for this account is the Machine account (or Computer account). The advantage is that you can't bring down an Exchange organization by accidentally renaming the Exchange Service account or changing its password. Another advantage is that it is more secure because the operating system automatically changes the password for the Machine account every 7 days with the use of a complex, randomly generated password (in contrast, Exchange 5.5 administrators usually never bother changing the password of their Exchange Service accounts).

You can see how Exchange uses these Machine accounts by examining the membership of the Exchange Domain Servers global group using Active Directory Users and Computers. This global group, created when the first Exchange server is installed, has as its members the Machine accounts of all Exchange servers in the domain. Also, when you uninstall Exchange from a machine, the account for that machine is removed from the global group.

New Tools

Installing Exchange on a system adds a number of new tools used for administering Exchange. Some of these tools will be covered in detail in Chapters 2 and 9, but Table 1.4 provides a quick summary.

TABLE 1.4 Tools for administering Exchange installed during a typical installation.

Tool	Start → Programs →	Description
Exchange System Manager	Microsoft Exchange	Manages Exchange configuration settings, recipient policies, address lists, storage groups, connectors, and just about everything else
Active Directory users and computers	Microsoft Exchange or Administrative Tools	Creates and configures mailboxes, establishes email addresses, and enables Instant Messaging for users
Active Directory Cleanup Wizard	Microsoft Exchange	Identifies and merges multiple mail accounts in Active Directory that refer to the same user
Migration Wizard	Microsoft Exchange	Migrates mailboxes from third-party mail systems

New Groups

Installing Exchange creates two new group objects in the Users container in Active Directory and populates these groups with members as follows:

Exchange Domain Servers (Security Group with Global Scope)

Membership in this group includes the computer accounts of all Exchange 2000 Servers in the domain. In our walkthrough, this means that the Computer account Box14 found in the Domain Controllers Organization Unit in domain mtit.com is the only member of this group at this point. You can verify this using the Active Directory Users and Computers console. This group is used to control access to directories and shares for Exchange servers within the forest.

Exchange Enterprise Servers (Security Group with Domain Local Scope)

Membership of this group includes the Exchange Domain Servers global groups from each domain in the forest.

You should not modify the memberships of these groups but let Exchange handle this task.

New Active Directory System Objects

By selecting View → Advanced Features in the Active Directory Users and Computers console, you can display hidden Active Directory containers and objects. Once you have installed your first Exchange server in your domain, there is a new container called Microsoft Exchange System Objects Present. This contains hidden public folders for address books, event storage, free/busy information, and other important under-the-hood Exchange stuff. You should not move or modify any of these objects unless instructed to do so by Microsoft Technical Support. Most of these objects can be safely managed by using Exchange System Manager.

Troubleshooting Installation Problems

There are a few common mistakes that can cause problems when you are trying to install Exchange:

- You need to be logged on to the domain in order to run Setup. You cannot install Exchange on a member server when you are logged on locally to the member server. With domain controllers this is not an issue because you cannot log on locally to a domain controller (all logons to domain controllers are domain logons, not local logons—logging on to the domain means being authenticated by Active Directory on a domain controller, and logging on locally means being authenticated by the local security database of the member server). Clearly this also means that, if you are installing Exchange on a member server, there must be a domain controller available on the network.

- Your domain account should be an administrator account that belongs to the Domain Admins, Enterprise Admins, and Schema Admins groups for installing Exchange.

The following are some additional issues associated with Exchange installations. This list is by no means comprehensive. Check the *knowledge base* (KB) on Microsoft TechNet for the latest information on installing Exchange.

Exchange Server Setup Progress Log File

When you install Exchange on a machine, a log file called Exchange Server Setup Progress.log is created and saved in the root of your system drive (usually the C:\drive). You can examine this log for more information when you have problems with your installation.

Exchange and MP3

Don't install third-party MP3 music software on an Exchange server, because both MP3 music files and Exchange streaming database files use the same extension, .stm. It won't affect the running of your Exchange server, but if you double-click on an Exchange streaming database file like Priv1.stm or Pub1.stm, your MP3 application will try to open the file and play it like a music file! For more information, see KB article Q257875.

Uninstalling Exchange

If you uninstall Exchange and then try to reinstall it on the same machine, you will get an error if any files were left behind in the /mdbdata folder from the first installation. Delete these files before reinstalling Exchange. For more information, see KB article Q256618.

Installing on a Member Server

If you try installing Exchange on a member server, make sure the "Append parent suffixes of the primary DNS suffix" check box is selected on the DNS Property page under Advanced TCP/IP Settings of Internet Protocol (TCP/IP) Properties. For more information, see KB article Q258967.

Using More Than 1 GB of RAM

To install Exchange on a Windows 2000 Advanced Server machine having more than 1 GB of RAM, you need to reconfigure virtual memory first by adding the /3GB parameter to the startup line in the boot.ini file on the machine. For example, change the line

```
multi(0)disk(0)rdisk(0)partition(2)\WINNT="Microsoft Windows 2000
Server" /fastdetect
```

to

```
multi(0)disk(0)rdisk(0)partition(2)\WINNT="Microsoft Windows 2000
Server" /fastdetect /3GB
```

For more information, see KB article Q266096.

SMTP Domains

If you've configured SMTP domains using the SMTP Service of IIS5, these domains will be deleted when you install Exchange on the same machine. You will need to re-create these domains manually afterward. For more information, see KB article Q251620.

Installing Subsequent Exchange Servers

Walkthrough

As mentioned earlier in this chapter, there are differences between installing the first Exchange 2000 Server and subsequent Exchange servers in your organization. This section walks through the process of installing a second Exchange server in the Exchange organization MTIT Enterprises.

We'll perform a network installation of Exchange 2000 Enterprise Server as the second Exchange server in the existing Exchange organization MTIT Enterprises. The system it will be installed on has the following characteristics:

- Computer name: Box15
- Windows 2000 domain: mtit.com
- Role: Member server

Log on to the machine using an enterprisewide Administrator account to perform the installation (you can use the default Administrator account in the forest root domain of your enterprise). Make sure you are logged on to the domain and to the member server using the local Administrator account before running Setup.

Connect to the network distribution point where the Exchange installation files are located and run `\Setup\I386\Setup.exe`. The Installation Wizard leads you through a process similar to the first Exchange installation, except that you are not prompted to create a new Exchange 2000 organization or join an existing Exchange 5.5 organization because Setup queries Active Directory and detects that an Exchange 2000 organization already exists in the forest. Because there can be only one Exchange 2000 organization per Windows 2000 forest, this has to be the one to join.

The rest of the installation process is similar to the first Exchange server installed. If you open Exchange System Manager (discussed in Chapter 9). you should find objects representing both Exchange servers in the Servers container.

NOTE

Subsequent Exchange installations are much faster than the first installation because the schema of the Active Directory had to be modified, which takes a fair amount of time. There is a way to perform this modification before installing the first Exchange server, which will be discussed in Chapter 25.

Setup Switches

There are a number of optional switches that can be used when Setup.exe is run from the command line for installing Exchange. Table 1.5 describes these switches and their use.

TABLE 1.5 Command line switches for Exchange Setup.exe.

Switch	Description
/?	Lists the different switches and briefly describes them
/All	Enables all components for installing, upgrading, or reinstalling Exchange 2000
/CreateUnattend <filename>.ini	Creates the specified answer file for performing unattended installations of Exchange 2000
/DisasterRecovery	Allows recovery of an Exchange 2000 server after the server configuration has been restored from backup
/DomainPrep	Prepares the current domain for first installation of Exchange 2000
/EncryptedMode	If used with /CreateUnattend, then the answer file created will be encrypted
/ForestPrep	Prepares the forest for first installation of Exchange 2000
/NoErrorLog	Suppresses error logging during installation
/NoEventLog	Suppresses event logging during installation
/Password <password>	Provides autologon password for current user
/ShowUI	If used with /UnattendFile, then UI will be displayed during an unattended installation
/UnattendFile <filename>.ini	Performs an unattended installation using the specified answer file

Unattended Installations

Installations of Exchange can be performed with the same unattended installation method as that supported by Windows. Exchange makes this easy by providing a setup switch that creates the necessary answer (initialization, or .ini) file by walking through a wizard. The wizard creates an answer file that is then used to respond to the prompts that appear during a normal installation, thereby allowing Exchange to be installed without user intervention.

The process of creating an answer file is simple:

- Insert the Exchange CD.
- Open a command prompt and change to the \Setup\I386 directory.
- Type setup /CreateUnattend <filename>.ini, where <filename> is the name of the answer file you wish to create, which should include the absolute path to where the file will be saved. You can use the additional switches /Encryptedmode and /ShowUI to customize the answer file creation process.
- The Exchange Installation Wizard then starts. Just follow the prompts to select the components and provide the information required. The wizard is a bit disconcerting because it doesn't indicate that it is creating an answer file until it's finished.
- Once the answer file is created, you can run Setup on the target server and use the /UnattendFile switch to perform the unattended installation of Exchange.

NOTE

You can open and view an answer file using Notepad, but you should be cautious about editing an answer file directly unless you understand its syntax.

Clustered Installations

You can install Exchange in a clustered configuration using the Cluster Service of Windows 2000 Advanced Server. This provides increased reliability for mission-critical deployments of Exchange in enterprise environments. For more information, see KB article Q263272 on Microsoft TechNet: "XADM: How to Set Up Exchange 2000 Server on a Windows Cluster."

Summary

In this chapter we've looked at installing Exchange 2000 Server and some of the associated issues. We've focused on the fresh deployment of Exchange.

In the next chapter, we'll look at the Exchange server administration tools and how to use them.

CHAPTER 2

Administration Tools

Although machines running Exchange server can be administered by running Exchange administration tools from the local console of each machine, there are other ways Exchange servers can be managed. The usual way is to install the Exchange administration tools on an administrator's Windows 2000 Professional client machine and administer the servers from the administrator's office instead of the room where the servers themselves are located.

It's also possible to administer Exchange servers from downlevel desktop clients running Windows 95, Windows 98, Windows NT 4.0 Workstation, or even Windows for Workgroups 3.11. This can be done by using the Terminal Services feature of Windows 2000 Server/Advanced Server.

Both of these methods of administering Exchange are covered in this chapter. Also discussed is how to create custom Microsoft Management Consoles (MMC) for administering Exchange servers.

There are three walkthroughs in this chapter:

- Installing the Exchange administration tools on a Windows 2000 Professional client machine
- Creating custom MMC for administering Exchange
- Using Terminal Services to administer Exchange

Exchange Administration Tools

The tools for administering Exchange Server are integrated into the same interface used for administering the Windows 2000 platform, namely the MMC. Installing Exchange on a machine installs a number of new stand-alone and extension snap-ins that can be added to new or existing consoles to create custom tools for administering Exchange. A new console called System Manager is also created with these Exchange snap-ins, and this console together with several other tools are added to a new program group called Microsoft Exchange.

Although these Exchange administration tools can be run directly from the local console of an Exchange server, it is more typical to install these tools on an administrator's client machine running Windows 2000 Professional. The main reason is that dedicated servers are typically located in a secured, air-conditioned back room, and it's more comfortable and convenient for administrators to manage these servers from their offices instead of standing in the server room listening to the overpowering sound of the air conditioning.

Let's now look at how to set up the Exchange administration tools on a Windows 2000 client.

Installing the Exchange Administration Tools on a Windows 2000 Professional Client Machine

Walkthrough

The procedure for installing the Exchange administration tools on a Windows 2000 Professional client machine is straightforward and involves four steps:

- Log on to the machine as an Enterprise administrator
- Install the Windows 2000 Server/Advanced Server administration tools
- Upgrade to Windows 2000 Service Pack 1 (SP1)
- Install the Exchange administration tools

Let's walk through these steps in detail. Start by logging on to the client machine using an administrator account that is a member of both the Domain Admins and Enterprise Admins groups. To run Exchange Setup, you must have enterprisewide administration privileges.

Next install the Windows 2000 administration tools from the Windows 2000 Server/Advanced Server compact disk or from a network distribution point (shared folder) containing these source files. The Windows 2000 Server administration tools must be installed on the client machine before installing the Exchange administration tools because the primary tool used for creating and managing Exchange users (mailboxes) is the Active Directory Users and Computers console. Because the snap-in for this console is not included with Windows 2000 Professional, the entire set of snap-ins for Windows 2000 Server/Advanced Server must be installed on the client machine first. Of course, if you are already using the client machine for administering Windows 2000 Servers on your network, then you already have these tools installed.

To install the Windows 2000 Server administration tools, open the Add/Remove Programs utility from the Control Panel. Select Add New Programs and insert the Windows 2000 Server/Advanced Server CD or browse to the network distribution point. The file you need to install is \I386\Adminpak.msi, a Windows Installer Package that installs the additional snap-ins needed to administer Windows 2000 Servers from a Windows 2000 Professional machine. Add this package to install the tools (Figure 2.1).

Figure 2.1 Installing \I386\Adminpak.msi from the Windows 2000 Server/Advanced server CD.

Once these tools are installed, try opening the Active Directory Users and Computers console from the Administrative Tools program group to see if you can connect to a domain controller and view objects in the domain.

If you are new to Windows 2000 Professional, you may be wondering where the Administrative Tools program group is located. This program group has been hidden away in the Control Panel and by default is not present under Programs in the Start menu. You can make it appear there by right-clicking on the Taskbar at the bottom of your screen, selecting the Advanced tab of the Task and Start Menu Properties sheet, and selecting Display Administrative Tools under Start Menu Settings.

Next install Windows 2000 SP1, which changes a few settings needed by Exchange Setup. At the very least, you need to install the Exchange 2000 hot fixes for Windows 2000, which are described in KB article

Q262259 on Microsoft TechNet, but it's better to apply the full-service pack instead (the hot fixes were sufficient for RC2 but are not enough for the final version of Exchange, for which SP1 is required). Applying SP1 or the hot fix collection requires a reboot.

Finally, install the Exchange server System Management tools by running Setup from the Exchange CD (or from a distribution point where these setup files are located). The process is similar to installing Exchange as described in Chapter 1, with this exception: when you get to the Component Selection screen (Figure 2.2), make sure you select only the following items:

- Microsoft Exchange 2000 (first item at top): select Custom
- Microsoft Exchange System Management tools: select Install

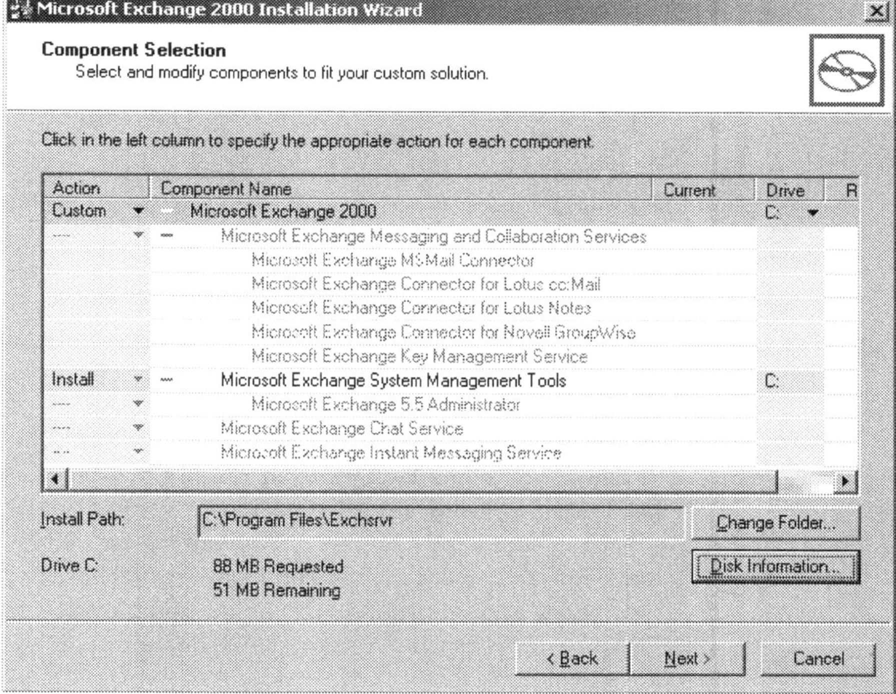

Figure 2.2
Installing the Microsoft Exchange System Management tools.

You'll need about 58 MB of free space to install these components, and no reboot is required. Once installation is complete, exit the Exchange Setup screen and check whether the installation works by clicking Start → Programs → Microsoft Exchange and selecting a tool to see if it opens correctly. You can now administer Exchange servers in your enterprise from your Windows 2000 Professional administrator's client machine.

Customizing the MMC

One of the great things about the Microsoft Management Console in Windows 2000 is that you can customize consoles to meet your administrative needs. You can add additional snap-ins to existing consoles or create a custom console from scratch. Let's take a moment to see how this is done and what kind of custom console we can create for administering Exchange.

Creating Custom MMCs for Administering Exchange

Walkthrough

We'll create a new console from scratch for administering Exchange. This console will have virtually everything we need to administer Exchange in a single console tree, which is probably not a good idea because it overwhelms the user with functionality (but it's fun to do anyway).

Click Start → Run, type mmc, and click OK. This opens a blank MMC (one with no snap-ins installed and thus no administrative functionality). Select Add/Remove Snap-in from the Console menu to open the Add/Remove Snap-in box. Click Add to open the Add Standalone Snap-in dialog box to display a list of snap-ins available for installing into the console.

Select Exchange System from the list of snap-ins and click Add. The Exchange System snap-in enables day-to-day management of most aspects of Exchange servers in the enterprise. When you click Add, you are requested to specify which domain controller the snap-in should connect to for administration (Exchange configuration information is stored in Active Directory on Windows 2000 domain controllers). You can specify a particular domain controller or just leave it at the default setting, which is Any Writable Domain Controller. Click OK and the snap-in is installed.

Repeat this procedure with the following additional snap-ins:

- Exchange Message Tracking Center for tracking messages.
- Exchange Advanced Security for sending encrypted and digitally signed messages.

- Active Directory Users and Computers for managing mailboxes for users and groups.
- Event Viewer for monitoring event logs to check problems; here you'll have to specify on which Exchange server machine you want to manage event logs.
- ActiveX Control—Select the System Monitor Control for monitoring performance logs on the machine.

Once you've added these various snap-ins, click Close to return to the Add/Remove Snap-ins box to review your selections (Figure 2.3). If you like, you can use the Extensions tab of this box to review the extension snap-ins that will be installed.

NOTE

A stand-alone snap-in provides some basic administrative functionality to an MMC. An extension snap-in adds additional, installed stand-alone snap-ins and is dependent on them. You should generally not make any changes to the default selection of extension snap-ins, which will be installed when you are creating a custom MMC.

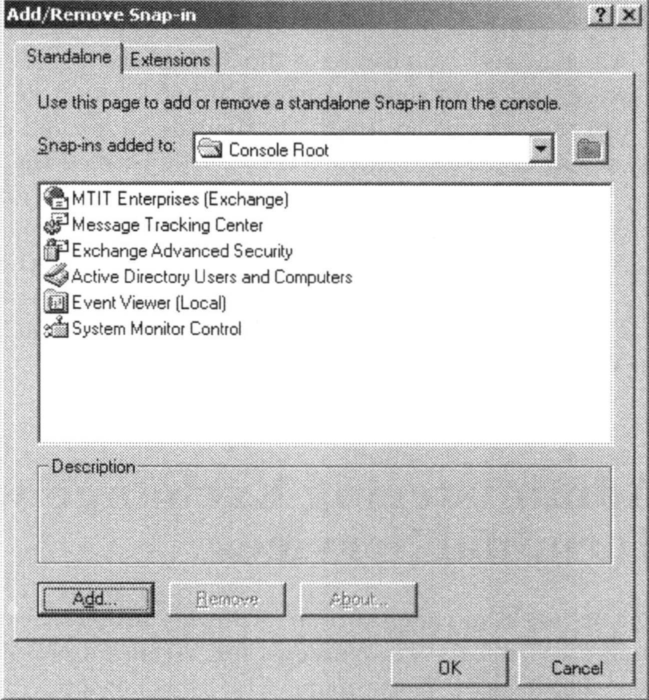

Figure 2.3 Installing stand-alone snap-ins for administering Exchange.

Once you've finished reviewing your selection, click OK and your custom console is finished. Maximize the child window in the console and further customize your console at will (Figure 2.4). Then save your console with a descriptive title such as Exchange Mega-Console. This saves the configuration of the console in an .msc file. You could save your console in one of two ways:

- The Administrative Tools folder in the user profile of the currently logged-on user (this is the default choice). In other words, you will be able to access the console by Start → Programs → Administrative Tools → Exchange Mega-Console. Be aware that if you do this, your console will only be available from your own Start menu, other users (even administrators) who log on to the same machine will not see this console in their Start menus.
- If you want any user who logs on to your computer to be able to access the console from the Start Menu (for example, if several administrators share the same workstation), save the .msc file to the following path:

```
\Documents and Settings\All Users\Start Menu\
Programs\Administrative Tools
```

- Alternatively, you can save the .msc file to a shared folder on the network and point administrators to its location on the network. They can then download the file to their desktops and double-click on it to open the console, provided they have installed the Exchange administration tools as in the previous walkthrough in this chapter. Or you could email them the file as an attachment, or publish its location in Active Directory, or mail it on a floppy disk. There are many options.

For more information about customizing the MMC, see any good book on Windows 2000 administration.

Administering Exchange with Terminal Services

If your desktop computers are running a downlevel operating system such as Windows 95, Windows 98, Windows NT Workstation 4.0, or even windows for Workgroups 3.11, all is not lost. You can use Windows

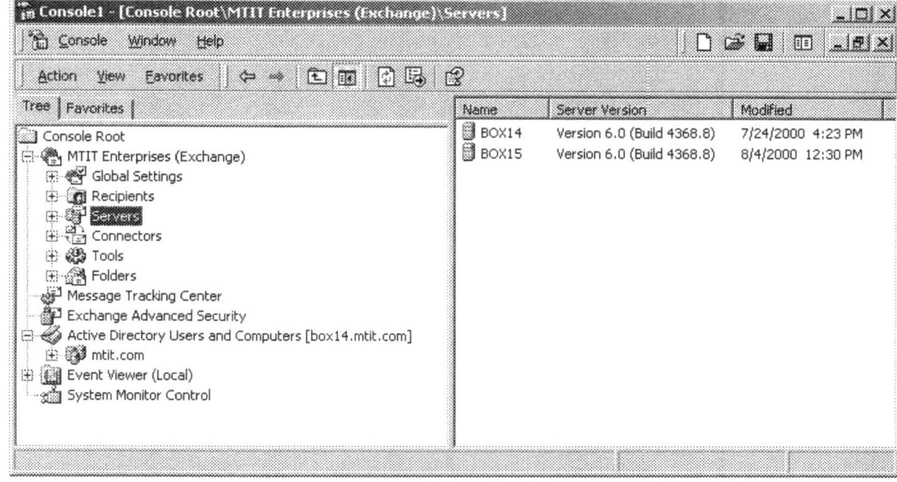

Figure 2.4 Custom MMC for administering Exchange.

2000 Terminal Services to administer Exchange from any of these machines provided the appropriate Terminal Services client is installed on them. This is a boon for remote administration because, as an administrator, you are often not in your office but somewhere else on site when suddenly something happens that needs your attention. You may have a Windows 2000 Professional workstation set up in your office for administering Exchange, but what do you do if you only have an employee's Windows 98 workstation nearby? Provided you've set up Terminal Services on a computer running Exchange, you can quickly install Terminal Services client on the employee's workstation and then connect to the server and administer it.

Let's see how this works in practice.

Using Terminal Services to Administer Exchange

Walkthrough

To administer Exchange using Terminal Services, you need to do two things:

- Install Terminal Services on an Exchange machine so it can function as a Terminal server.
- Install the appropriate Terminal Services client on the administration workstation.

Let's install Terminal Services on Box15, the second Exchange server in our testbed domain mtit.com. Log on to the local console of the Exchange server using a Domain Admins account, open Control Panel, and start the Add/Remove Programs utility. Select Add/Remove Windows Components to start the Windows Components Wizard and choose the Terminal Services component in the Windows Components screen of the wizard.

This choice will install and enable Box15 to run as a terminal server and create installation disks for installing Terminal Services Client on client workstations. However, to use Box15 as a terminal server, you will also need to install the Terminal Services Licensing component.

The problem is, you cannot install the Terminal Services Licensing component on a member server such as Box15 that belongs to a domain—you can install the licensing component on either a domain controller or a stand-alone server. Now we chose to install Terminal Services on Box15 (a member server running Exchange) instead of Box14 (a domain controller running Exchange) because installing Terminal Services on a domain controller requires extra resources on an already overloaded machine. Therefore, we'll install Terminal Services on Box15, our member server, and Terminal Services Licensing on Box14, our domain controller (just to make things a bit complicated!).

To continue the installation of Terminal Services on Box14, click Next and make sure Remote Administration mode is selected. Click Next and accept the default licensing role and license database path. Click Next and insert the Windows 2000 Server/Advanced Server CD when prompted to complete the installation. You'll need to reboot afterward.

Now reinstall Windows 2000 SP1 or the Exchange 2000 hot fix package as described earlier in this chapter (you must reinstall service packs/hot fixes after you install new components of Windows 2000 on your machine). Another reboot is required.

Now go to Box14 and install the Terminal Services Licensing component using Add/Remove Programs in the Control Panel. You'll be asked to specify the role of the license server and the location of the licensing database. Leave the defaults, which sets Box14 as the licensing server for the mtit.com domain, and finish the wizard and reapply SP1.

The result of these steps is that there are new Start menu shortcuts in the Administrative Tools program group on each machine as follows:

- Box14 has Terminal Services Licensing
- Box15 has Terminal Services Client Creator, Terminal Services Configuration, and Terminal Services Manager

We won't go into all the details of running Terminal Services (see any good Windows 2000 administration book for such information) but will focus on our goal of being able to manage Exchange from a Windows 98 workstation.

NOTE

Strictly speaking, we didn't need to install Terminal Services Licensing on Box14 because Terminal Services Licensing is only required if you are running terminal servers in Application Server mode. But we have chosen for Box15, our terminal server, to run in Remote Administration mode instead, and this mode does not require special licensing. I went through the extra steps just to illustrate a more general installation of Terminal Services.

Start Terminal Services Client Creator and select the option to create a set of disks for installing the 32-bit Terminal Services Client software (Figure 2.5). You will need two blank formatted floppies (or you can choose the option to format if required). Label your floppies "32-bit Windows 2000 Terminal Services Client Installation Disk" numbers 1 and 2.

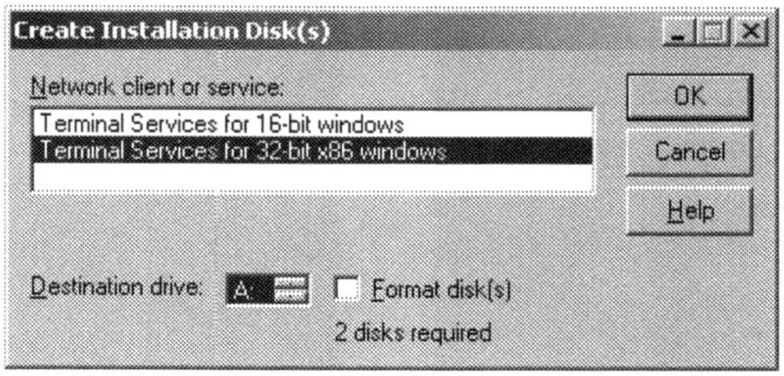

Figure 2.5 Creating an installation disk set for 32-bit Terminal Services Client.

Now use these disks to install the Terminal Services Client on a machine running Windows 98 called Desk94 that is part of the mtit.com domain. Note that the machine on which you are installing the Terminal Services Client must be part of the domain where the terminal server is located.

To install the client software, simply log on as an administrator, insert the first disk, click Start → Run → A:\Setup.exe, and press OK. When prompted, enter your name and organization, accept the licensing agreement and default installation location, and specify whether the Terminal Services Client will be used by all users who have access to this computer or only by the current user.

TIP

Another way of installing Terminal Services Client is from a shared folder on the network, called a distribution point. Simply share the following folder on your Terminal Server machine (in this case, Box15):

```
\Winnt\System32\Clients\Tsclient
```

Users can then connect to this share file, select the appropriate subfolder (win16 or win32 depending on which client you want to install, the 16-bit or 32-bit one), and run `Setup.exe` *from that subfolder.*

Once the Terminal Service Client software is installed on the workstation, log on as an administrator and start the client with Start → Programs → Terminal Services Client → Terminal Services Client. This opens the Terminal Services Client dialog box (Figure 2.6).

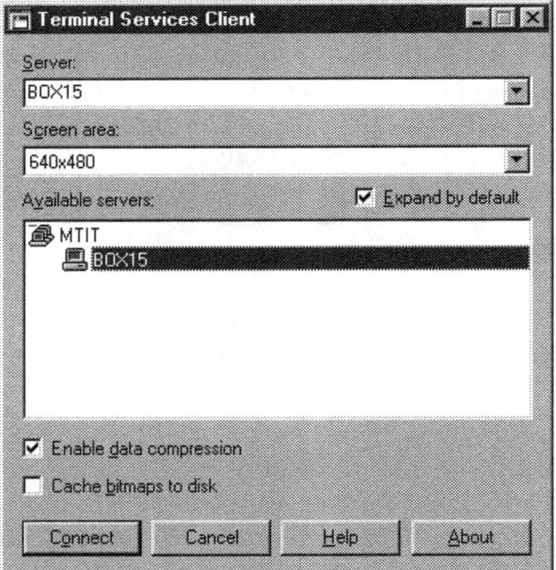

Figure 2.6 Starting Terminal Services Client on the Windows 98 workstation.

In the listbox showing the available terminal servers in the domain, select Box15, the Exchange Server on which we installed Terminal Services.

Select a screen area for the Terminal Services Client window that will open up on the workstation. This will typically be one level down from the screen resolution of the workstation. In this case, the screen resolution on the workstation is set to 800 × 600 so we select 640 × 480 as the size of the Terminal Services Client window that will open on the workstation.

In addition, selecting data compression and bitmap caching can improve performance of the Terminal Services session you are going to open.

After you click Connect, the Terminal Services Client tries to establish a session with the Exchange server running Terminal Services. A terminal window will then open on the client and a Log On To Windows dialog box will appear within the terminal window (Figure 2.7).

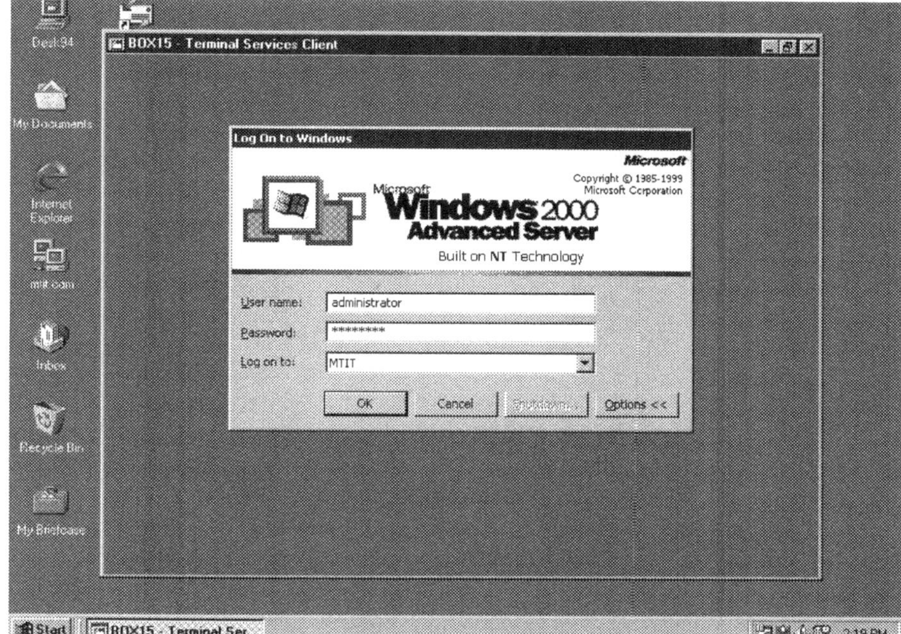

Figure 2.7 Establishing a terminal session by logging on to the terminal server.

After proper credentials have been entered, the logon box will disappear and the terminal window will display a desktop for the remote Exchange server, in this case, the credentials of the administrator who will be managing the remote Exchange server (by default, all users are allowed to logon to terminal servers (see the Terminal Services Profile tab of the properties sheet for user accounts in the Active Directory Users and Computers console).

To test the remote administration capabilities of running Terminal Services, open the Exchange System Manager console in the terminal window by clicking Start → Programs → Microsoft Exchange → System Manager (Figure 2.8). An MMC should open within the terminal window, displaying the Exchange organization console tree (Figure 2.9). You can now perform any administration tasks on the Exchange server just as if you were logged on locally to the console of the server.

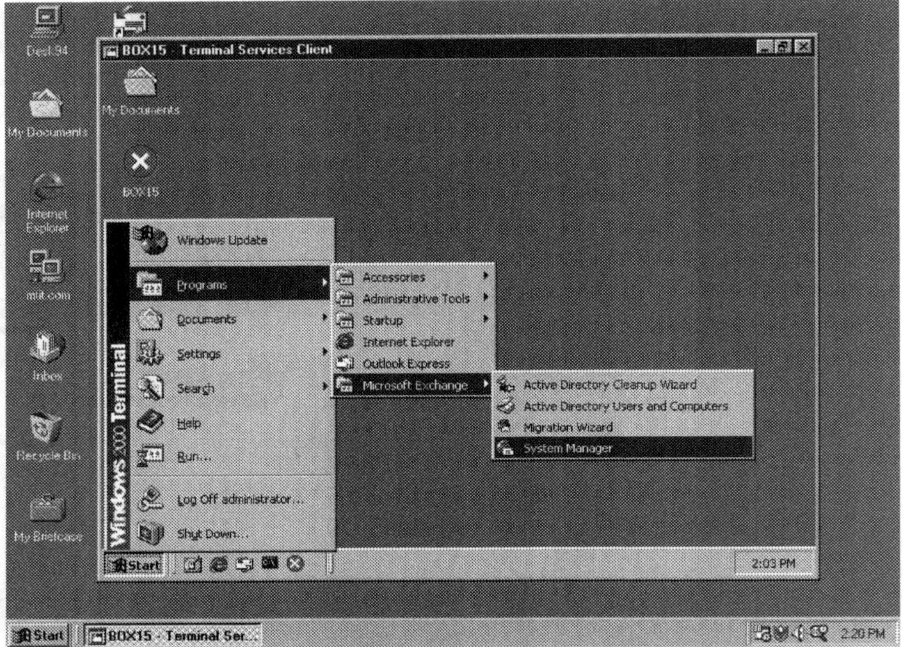

Figure 2.8
Remotely starting Exchange System Manager in a terminal window.

Summary

In this chapter we've looked at preparing to use the Exchange administration tools for administering an Exchange organization. We've seen how to install these tools on an administrator's Windows 2000 Professional workstation, how to customize an MMC to create a custom tool for administering Exchange, and how to remotely manage Exchange servers using Windows 2000 Terminal Services.

In the next chapter, we'll consider the administration of *mailbox-* and *mail-enabled users* in Exchange, and how to create and configure them.

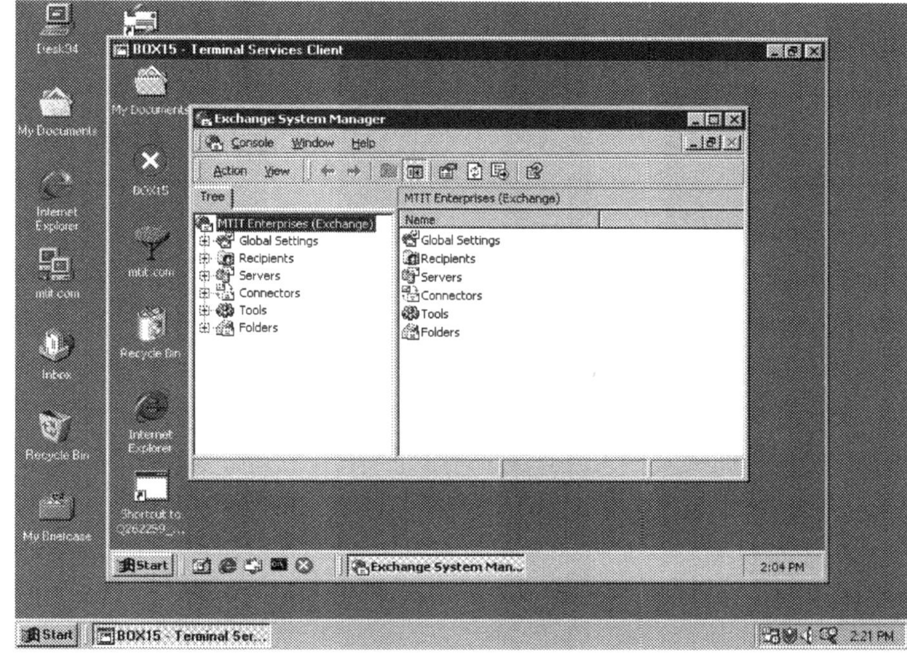

Figure 2.9 Exchange System Manager running in a terminal window.

CHAPTER 3

Users

A big part of administering messaging systems is managing users and their associated mailboxes and email addresses. This chapter looks at the steps involved in managing users in an Exchange 2000 Server environment. We'll look at how to create and manage mail- and mailbox-enabled users and test them by sending messages using Outlook Web Access (OWA), a component of Exchange that allows users to access their mailbox folders using a standard Web browser like Internet Explorer.

There are six walkthroughs in this chapter:

- Creating a mailbox-enabled user
- Configuring and testing mailbox-enabled users
- Creating a mail-enabled user
- Changing a user from mail- to mailbox-enabled
- Deleting a mailbox-enabled user
- Copying a mailbox-enabled user

Active Directory Users and Computers

The primary tool for administering users and their associated mailboxes and email addresses is the Windows 2000 administrative tool called Active Directory Users and Computers (ADUC; Figure 3.1). ADUC is the standard Windows 2000 tool used for administering User objects, Group objects, Computer objects, and other kinds of objects within Active Directory.

When you install Exchange, ADUC is enhanced with extensions to enable administrators to create and configure mailboxes and email addresses for users, groups, and contacts. This chapter assumes that you already have some basic familiarity with using ADUC (if not, consult any standard book on basic Windows 2000 administration).

Mail-enabled versus Mailbox-enabled

To borrow terminology from previous versions of Exchange, a recipient is an entity that can receive mail. Recipients include users, groups, con-

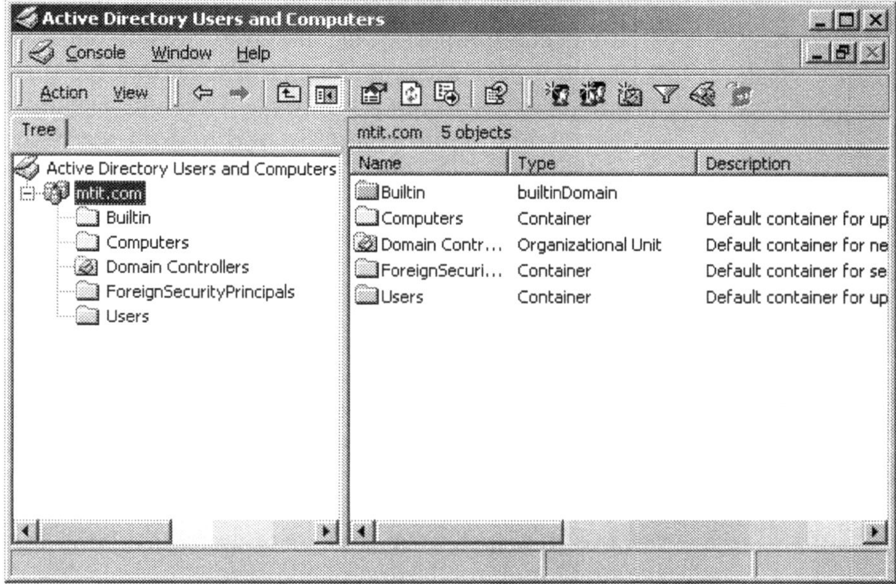

Figure 3.1
The Active Directory Users and Computers console.

tacts, and other objects such as meeting rooms that can be booked using mail messages.

In Exchange 2000 recipients can be either mail-enabled or mailbox-enabled. It's important to understand the difference between these two terms.

- A *mailbox-enabled user* has both an email address and a mailbox. The email address is stored in Active Directory, and the user's messages are stored in the Web Store, the Exchange 2000 component that replaces the Information Store database in previous versions of Exchange. Having an email address allows other users to send mail to the user, and having a mailbox allows the user to receive such mail. In other words, mailbox-enabled users can send and receive email. This sounds like the normal situation, and it is—most ordinary users in the Windows 2000 enterprise will probably be mailbox-enabled under normal circumstances.
- A *mail-enabled user* has an email address but no mailbox. In other words, having an email address allows other users to send mail to a mail-enabled user, but without an Exchange mailbox, a mail-enabled user can only receive email if the user has a mailbox configured on some other messaging system. A typical scenario where you might create and configure a mail-enabled user would be for a consultant

who is going to be temporarily working at your company. The consultant needs temporary logon rights to your network; hence, you would create a user account instead of a contact for the consultant. But the consultant typically already has an email account on a messaging system at his or her company and doesn't want to have to check two mailboxes every day. Hence, you would mail-enable the consultant's user account instead of mailbox-enabling it and have the consultant's email address point to their mailbox back at the consulting company.

NOTE

Exchange 2000 also supports another type of recipient called a contact. Contacts can be mail-enabled but cannot be mailbox-enabled, and you cannot log on to the network as a contact—only users can do this. Contacts are thus like the custom recipients of earlier versions of Exchange. We'll look at contacts in more detail in Chapter 4.

Let's now look at a number of tasks involving creating and configuring mail- and mailbox-enabled users.

Creating a Mailbox-Enabled User

Walkthrough

We'll start by creating a new user account in our testbed mtit.com domain. This new user will be mailbox-enabled and capable of sending and receiving mail using Exchange. The user will be Jane Smith, a member of the marketing department of MTIT Enterprises.

Because we're going to create a number of users in marketing, we'll start by opening ADUC and creating a new *organizational unit* (OU) that will contain our new user accounts. This new OU will be called Marketing Users (see the Backgrounder for more information about organizational units).

To create the new OU, right-click on the mtit.com domain node in the console tree shown in Figure 3.1 and select New → Organizational Unit, type Marketing Users in the Name textbox, and click OK. The new OU should now be visible in the console tree of ADUC.

BACKGROUNDER

Organizational Units

Organizational units are containers in Active Directory that can be used to group together objects such as users, groups, contacts, printers, and so on. Objects contained in an OU can be administered collectively by using the Delegation of Control Wizard and by assigning Group Policies to the OU. In this sense, OUs form administrative boundaries similar to domains but without having the resource overhead of domains. Instead of structuring a network as a tree of domains, an enterprise could structure it as a single domain containing a tree of OUs. There are advantages and disadvantages to doing this, but to discuss this is beyond the scope of this book; see any good book on Active Directory planning and design for further information.

When you run `dcpromo` *to create your first Windows 2000 domain on a network, Active Directory is configured with a number of default containers: Built-in, Computers, Domain Controllers, and Users. These default containers are intended to be used for upgrading from Windows NT–based networks to Windows 2000. For example, when a Windows NT member server joins a Windows 2000 domain, a computer account for the member server is created within the Computers container. Or when you upgrade a Windows NT domain controller to Windows 2000, the user accounts formerly in the SAM database are migrated to the Users container in Active Directory.*

If you are building a new Windows 2000–based network instead of upgrading an existing one, you could simply use these default containers and create your new user accounts within the Users container, leave the computer accounts for your member servers and workstations in the Computers container, leave the computer accounts for your domain controllers in the Domain Controllers container, and so on. But you would only do this in a simple, small network with a limited number of users and computers. In a larger enterprise, it is advantageous to create new accounts and move existing ones where possible to OUs you create to facilitate delegation of administrative authority and application of Group Policy to these objects.

Now right-click on the Marketing Users OU and select New → User to open the New Object-User dialog box (Figure 3.2). Enter the First Name and Last Name for the user Jane Smith; notice that the Full Name field is generated automatically from these. The Full Name field represents the user's display name in Exchange and is used for creating the user's X.400 and (where required) cc:Mail email addresses, as we'll see later. The Full Name must be 64 characters or less, must be unique in the domain, and can be edited if desired (for example, to remove an initial if you entered one).

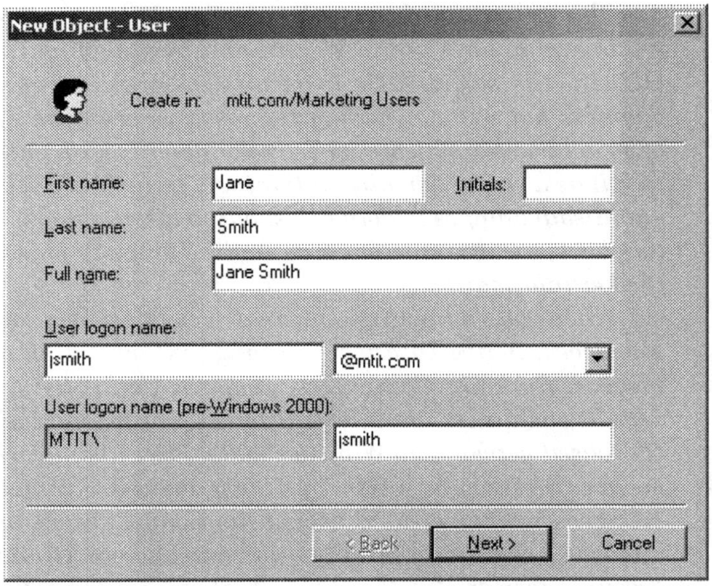

Figure 3.2 Creating a new user in ADUC.

Tab to the User Logon Name field and enter the logon name for the user. The logon name is used for logging on to the network and consists of two portions: a user-specific prefix and a domain suffix. A suitable prefix portion for Jane Smith could be any of the following:

- jsmith (most typical choice, consists of first initial and surname)
- janes (alternative choice, consists of first name and last initial)
- js (initials only, suitable for small companies only)
- jane (if she's the boss!)

It's best to be consistent in defining user logon names—we'll use the first initial and the surname (jsmith). In a multiple-domain network, you could then choose a domain suffix from the drop-down listbox, but in our testbed environment we have only @mtit.com. Jane's full user logon name is thus jsmith@mtit.com, and she can logon to the network using this name. When you specify the user logon name, it is automatically used as the pre–Windows 2000 user logon name (actually only the first 20 characters are used).

Click Next and specify a password for the user and any password options you wish to select.

Click Next and you'll see the user's default Exchange settings (Figure 3.3). If you don't see this screen, see the following Tip. By default, the

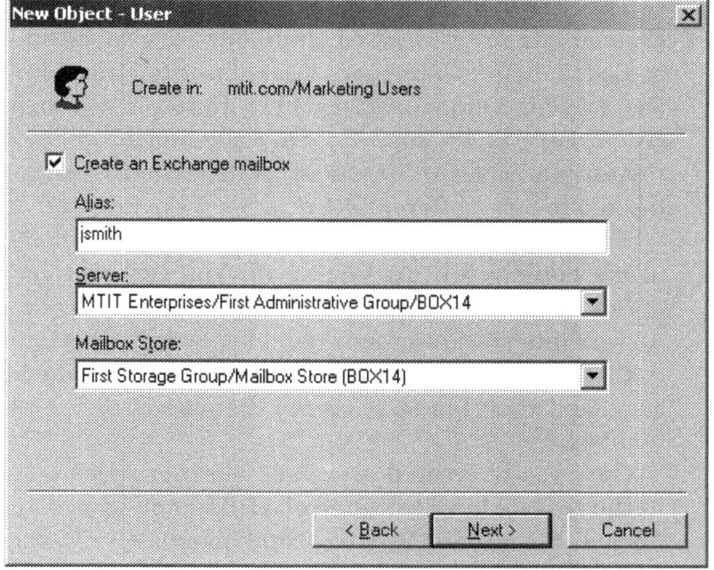

Figure 3.3 Specifying the Exchange settings for a new user.

checkbox Create an Exchange Mailbox is selected, which means we are creating a mailbox-enabled user that can send and receive mail.

By default, the Exchange *alias* for the user is the same as the user-specific portion of the user's logon name (in this case jsmith), but it can be edited if desired. The alias is used for three purposes:

- To automatically generate SMTP and (where required) MS Mail addresses for the user.
- To provide an easy way for other users to send mail by simply typing an alias such as jsmith into the To box of the mail client (Active Directory resolves the alias into the user's email address to properly address the message).
- The Exchange alias is also used as the name for the user's Exchange mailbox within Active Directory.

TIP

Was the Exchange screen (Figure 3.3) missing when you created the new user using ADUC? You may be working from a domain controller that doesn't have Exchange installed on it or from a workstation with the standard Windows 2000 administration tools (`adminpak.msi`*) installed but not the Exchange snap-in extensions (see Chapter 2).*

The server drop-down listbox lets you select which Exchange server the mailbox will be located on. In our case, we could choose either Box14 or Box15, both of which are located in the First Administrative Group of the Exchange organization MTIT Enterprises (we'll cover Administrative Groups in Chapter 12). Only Exchange servers that are configured to host mailboxes will show up in this list (Exchange servers can be configured to have different roles, as we'll see later).

The Mailbox Store listbox lets you select which Mailbox Store the user's mailbox will be located in. You can configure multiple mailbox stores on a single Exchange server and can group stores on different servers into storage groups (more on these topics later).

Click Next, verify the information you entered and change it if necessary, and click Finish to create the user Jane Smith and her Exchange mailbox.

Once you've created user Jane Smith, select the Marketing Users OU in the console tree (left pane of ADUC) and look at the various fields displayed in the details pane (right pane). The Exchange extensions for ADUC cause additional fields to be displayed in the details pane, and for user Jane Smith these should look something like the following:

- Name: Jane Smith (this is the user's display name in Exchange)
- Type: User
- Description: (blank)
- E-Mail Address: jsmith@mtit.com
- Exchange Alias: jsmith
- Exchange Mailbox Store: CN=Mailbox Store(BOX14),CN=First Storage Group,CN=Information Store,CN=BOX14,CN=Servers,CN-First Administrative group,CN=Administrative Groups,CN=MTIT Enterprises,CN=Microsoft Exchange,CN=Services,CN=Configuration, DC=mtit,DC=com
- Modified: (today's date)

TIP

If you create a new mailbox-enabled user and the email address for the user isn't visible in the E-Mail Address column in the details pane, press F5 to refresh the ADUC console.

It's handy to be able to see users' email addresses from the details pane, and by selecting View → Choose Columns you can hide information you don't want (like the distinguished name of the mailbox store where the user's mailbox is located; see the Backgrounder).

BACKGROUNDER

Distinguished Names

Every object in Active Directory is uniquely identified by a distinguished name or DN (objects must have names that can "distinguish" them from other objects in the directory). DNs are read right-to-left starting with the domain containers (DC), any OU containers, and other containers (CN) in which the object is located. In the example of user Jane Smith, the mailbox store directory object (not the mailbox store itself, just the directory object that contains the properties and settings of the mailbox store) that contains her mailbox is found in the mtit.com domain, in the Configuration container of Active Directory, in the Services subcontainer, under Microsoft Exchange, in the container representing the specific Exchange organization called MTIT Enterprises, in the administrative group called First Administrative Group, in BOX14 under the Servers container, in the First Storage Group within the Information Store of Box14, in the particular mailbox store named Mailbox Store (Box14). Whew!

Configuring a Mailbox-enabled User

Creating a new mailbox-enabled user isn't really enough—you also need to further configure the user. Let's start by verifying the email addresses created for our user Jane Smith in the previous walkthrough. We'll look at the three Exchange-related tabs on the properties sheet for a user in ADUC, namely the Exchange General, Exchange Features, and E-mail Addresses tabs.

NOTE

There is one more Exchange-related tab on users' properties sheets, but it normally isn't displayed. If you select View → Advanced Features from the menu in ADUC, you'll see some extra tabs on users' properties sheets, including an Exchange Advanced tab. We'll talk about that in Chapter 10.

Select the Marketing Users OU in the console tree, right-click on user Jane Smith in the details pane, and select Properties. Select the E-mail Addresses tab of the Jane Smith Properties sheet (Figure 3.4).

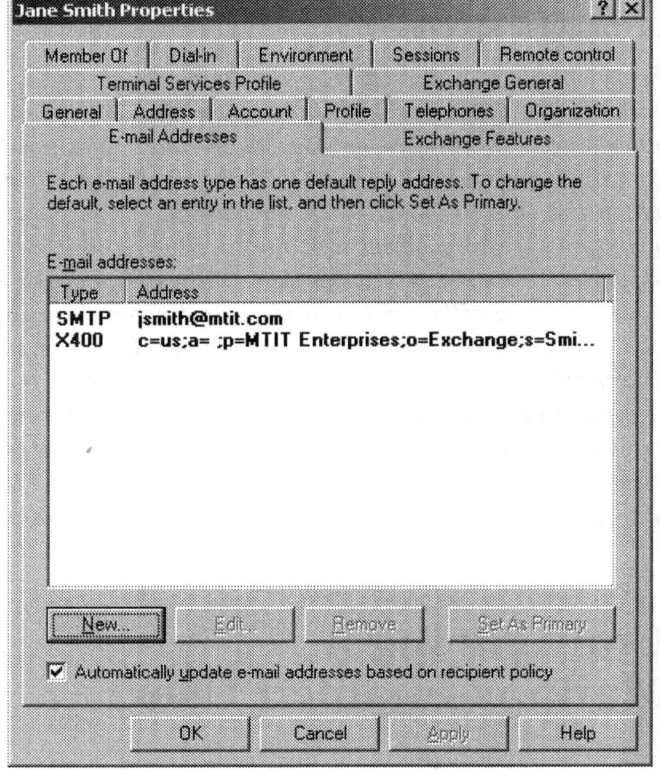

Figure 3.4
The E-mail Addresses tab of the Properties sheet for mailbox-enabled user Jane Smith.

By default, Exchange automatically creates two types of addresses for every new mail- or mailbox-enabled user, namely the SMTP (Internet) and X.400 addresses. If, in addition, we had an MS Mail or cc:Mail connector installed in our Exchange organization, addresses for these messaging systems would have been automatically created for the new user as well. We'll see how to create additional and modify existing email addresses for users later on in this chapter.

UNDER THE HOOD

Exchange 2000 and SMTP

In previous versions of Exchange, the X.400 Connector was sometimes used as an alternative to the Site Connector to provide messaging connectivity between different sites within an Exchange organization, whereas the Internet Mail Service was used to provide connectivity with external SMTP hosts on the Internet. In Exchange 2000, SMTP has become the default messaging transport protocol. X.400 connectors are used either to connect with foreign X.400 mail systems or for controlling the bandwidth on low-speed dedicated links between Exchange routing groups. In this book we'll focus mainly on SMTP as our messaging transport because it is used by default in Exchange 2000 and because the rapidly increasing popularity of the Internet in recent years has been sending X.400 into eclipse as a messaging standard. For more information on X.400 addressing, see my previous book Administering Exchange Server *from McGraw-Hill.*

Select the Exchange Features tab of the Properties sheet. Here you can enable or disable special features such as Instant Messaging.

Select the Exchange General tab (Figure 3.5). Here we can view which mailbox store the user's mailbox is located in, change the Exchange alias for the user if desired, and configure user-specific delivery restrictions, deliver options, and storage limits. Figure 3.5 shows these last three options in detail.

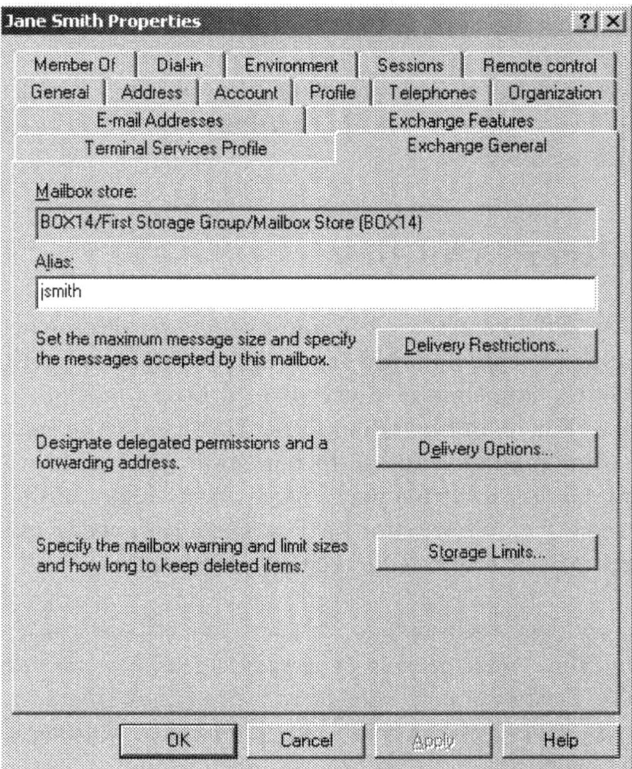

Figure 3.5 The Exchange General tab of the Properties sheet for mailbox-enabled user Jane Smith.

Delivery Restrictions

These settings are used to specify the maximum message size the user can send or receive and from whom the user is allowed to receive messages. The settings specified here apply only to the user selected (see the following Note for how to globally configure delivery restrictions for all users). The default (global) size restrictions configured for your Exchange organization are used, and messages are accepted from everyone. You can filter which users, groups, or contacts a user is allowed to receive messages from, but only for recipients within the global address book of your Exchange organization. If a message exceeds the maximum specified message size, a *nondelivery report* (NDR) will be sent to the sender.

NOTE

You specify global delivery restrictions for all users using System Manager. This tool is covered in Chapter 9, but if you're eager to peek ahead, just click Start → Programs → Microsoft Exchange → System Manager → expand the root node of the console tree → expand Global Settings → right-click Message Delivery → select Properties → select the Defaults and Filters tabs.

Any delivery restrictions or other settings configured for individual mailboxes override similar settings configured at the global level on mailbox stores.

Delivery Options

These settings are used to allow others to access the user's mailbox and to automatically forward incoming messages to another mailbox.

Giving someone else access to a user's mailbox is a common occurrence. For example, when Jane Smith is going on vacation, you could give her manager access to her mailbox to handle important business mail. Giving multiple users access to a single mailbox is also important in scenarios where you have a special-purpose mailbox such as support@mtit.com to handle tech support inquiries.

NOTE

A mailbox must always be associated with a user account in Exchange 2000. To create a special-purpose mailbox like support@mtit.com, you could create a user account with a complex, random name and assign the user account a (different) complex, random password and document these items carefully. Change the alias of the user to support and configure the email address as support@mtit.com. Then grant access for this mailbox to the appropriate users.

Giving a user access to another user's mailbox is called granting Send On Behalf permission, and means the given user can read items in the other user's mailbox and also send messages on behalf of the mailbox owner.

An alternative method of dealing with users going on vacation is to have messages sent to the user's mailbox automatically forwarded to the mailbox of their manager or some other responsible person. You also have the option of keeping a copy of the forwarded message in the user's mailbox so that when they return they can see the messages that arrived in their absence but which were forwarded to their manager.

Another use for this forwarding feature is when a user is traveling without a laptop and needs to access his or her mail from a public Internet terminal. In this case, you could configure the mailbox to automatically forward all incoming mail to the user's Hotmail account but keep a copy of the messages in case the user is unable to access Hotmail during the trip.

You can also use the Delivery Options screen to specify the maximum number of recipients to whom the mailbox-enabled user can send messages. There is also a global version of this setting in the Message Delivery settings under Global Settings in System Manager. The default global setting is a maximum of 5,000 recipients, which means that a user cannot send a single message that is addressed to more than 5,000 recipients. This is essentially an anti-spam kind of feature.

TIP

What if you have two mailbox-enabled users and you configure each to forward mail to the other and to keep a copy of the forwarded mail? Try it out, but only on a tested system!

Storage Limits

These settings are used to place restrictions on the maximum size of a mailbox and how long deleted items are retained before being permanently removed. There are default values for these settings which are configured at the global level (see the following Note).

NOTE

If you want to peek ahead, here's how you use System Manager to globally configure storage limits and deleted-item retention time for all mailbox-enabled users in your organization: click Start → Programs → Microsoft Exchange → System Manager → expand the root node of the console tree → expand the Servers container → expand Box14 → expand First Storage Group → right-click on Mailbox Store (BOX14) → select Properties → select the Limits tab.

Storage limits are specified in kilobytes. There are three kinds of storage limits you can configure for a mailbox:

- *Issue Warning At.* When the mailbox exceeds this limit, a warning message is sent to the user to clear the mailbox of old, unwanted messages. By default, these warning messages are sent each night at midnight, but you can change this in System Manager (see the Note). The main point is that generating these warning messages is a CPU-intensive activity for Exchange servers and so should be scheduled to occur during off-hours.
- *Prohibit Send At.* Once this limit is reached, the user is prevented from sending any more messages until the mailbox is empty.
- *Prohibit Send And Receive At.* If the mailbox size reaches this limit, the user won't be able to send or receive messages until the mailbox is cleared out to a size beneath this limit. You should use caution enabling this setting, because it may cause users to lose important incoming messages. It's generally best to configure only the first two settings and leave this one unspecified (by default, the global settings leave all three unspecified).

NOTE

Mailbox storage limits only apply to server-based mailboxes, not to personal folders stored on users' workstations.

Deleted-item retention is a feature of Exchange that allows deleted messages to be retained in case users made a mistake in deleting them and need to undelete them. When a user deletes a message from his or her mailbox, it is marked hidden instead of being deleted and is retained for a period called the deleted-item retention period. Once this period has expired, the message is permanently deleted from the mailbox store and is unrecoverable. The default global value for this setting as configured in System Manager is 0 day, which means that deleted items are permanently deleted right away. You can override the global settings on a per-mailbox basis and have the option of specifying that deleted items should not be permanently removed until the mailbox store has been backed up.

TIP

A typical value you might set for a deleted-item recovery period is 7 or 14 days.

Additional User Configuration Settings

In addition to configuring Exchange-specific settings on the E-mail Addresses, Exchange Features, and Exchange General tabs of a mailbox-enabled user's properties sheet, you should also configure the user contact information on the General, Address, Telephones, and Organization tabs. This information is useful in a large enterprise, where there are many users, because it allows users to search for recipients within Active Directory by specifying their title, department, office, city, and so on. It's a lot of work to enter this information, but that's what a directory is for! Specifying the user's email address and home page URL on the General tab allows administrators to send a message to the user or open the user's home page by right-clicking on the user in ADUC.

Other tabs on users' properties sheets allow you to configure users' group membership, grant them dial-in access, configure logon hour restrictions, change password options, enable Terminal Services access, and a whole host of other settings that are beyond the scope of this book and are covered in any good book on Windows 2000 administration.

Configuring and Testing Mailbox-enabled Users

Walkthrough

In addition to Jane Smith in the previous walkthrough, create two more mailbox-enabled users, Fred Jones and Henry Lee, within the Marketing Users OU in mtit.com. Use the same email-address and alias conventions you used for Jane, and leave all other mailbox configurations at their default settings.

BACKGROUNDER

Local Security Policy

The Local Security Policy for a machine determines password settings, user rights assignment, audit policy, and so on. The effective policy settings on a machine, however, are a cumulative result of domain, OU, and local Group Policy settings.

To see how this works, let's enable ordinary users to log on to a domain controller (Box14), something that by default the Local Security Policy on such machines prohibits. On Box14 click Start → Programs → Administrative Tools → Local Security Policy. This displays the Local Security Policy (and effective policy settings) for the local machine, that is, for the Computer object Box14 in Active Directory. Then expand Security Settings → expand Local Policies → select User Rights Assignment in the console tree → double-click the Log On Locally policy setting in the details pane. Notice that the effective policy setting for the Users group is unchecked, that is, members of this group are not allowed to log on locally to the machine. The local policy setting for users is checked (enabled), however, which means that some group policy setting higher up in the chain of authority, such as for the OU or the domain, must be unchecked (disabled).

To see this, click Start → Programs → Administrative Tools → Domain Controller Security Policy. This displays the security settings portion of the Group Policy Object (GPO) linked to the default Domain Controllers OU in the current domain. (You can display the full GPO for the Domain Controllers OU by right-clicking on the OU in ADUC → select Properties → select Group Policy tab → select Default Domain Controllers Policy → click Edit. If the Group Policy tab is not visible on the Domain Controllers Properties sheet, select View → Advanced Features first in ADUC.) Then expand Security Settings → expand Local Policies → select User Rights Assignment in the console tree → double-click the Log On Locally policy setting in the details pane → click Add → type Users (or browse for it) → click OK twice. Now wait a few minutes for the policy change to take effect and then log off as Administrator and try logging on to Box14 as jsmith@mtit.com.

Of course, you wouldn't want to enable ordinary users to log on to domain controllers in a production environment, but this discussion gives you some idea of how policy settings are applied and modified.

Now logoff as Administrator and logon as jsmith@mtit.com using whatever password you assigned this user. If you get a message saying "The local policy of this machine does not permit you to log on interactively", it's because you're working at a domain controller (Box14) and the Group Policy settings only allow administrators to log on interactively to domain controllers. Switch to the member server (Box15) and you should be able to log on. If you do want to allow ordinary users to log on to your domain controller, see the Backgrounder.

In case you haven't realized it, there are two ways a user like Jane Smith (jsmith) in domain mtit.com (pre–Windows 2000 domain name MTIT) can log on using the Log On To Windows box that appears when you press Ctrl+Alt+Delete in Windows 2000. First, she could specify her user name as jsmith, enter her password, click the Options button, and select MTIT from the drop-down listbox. This is the way you logged on in Windows NT. The newer alternative is for her to just enter jsmith@mtit.com as her user name and specify her password.

While logged on as Jane Smith, click Start → Run and enter the URL http://localhost/exchange and press OK. Surprise! Outlook Web Access (OWA), an Active Server Pages application that allows users to send and receive their email using only a simple Web browser like Internet Explorer, is installed by default with Exchange 2000. OWA may be all the mail client your users need in your enterprise, in which case no more deployment of Microsoft Outlook may be needed. The initial OWA screen is shown in Figure 3.6.

OWA looks best when the screen resolution on users' machines is 1024 x 768 or higher. In this book I've used 800 x 600 resolution to show greater detail.

Let's walk through the process of Jane Smith sending a message to Henry Lee. Click the New button on the OWA toolbar to open an Untitled Message window. Jane could type Henry's email address directly into the To field in this window, but it's more likely she would simply find his address in the directory, that is, in Active Directory. So click the To button to open the Find Names window (these windows, believe it or not, are all Internet Explorer browser windows). Type Lee in the Last Name field and click the Find button to find all users in the directory who have the surname Lee; only Henry's name turns up (Figure 3.7). Select Henry Lee in the listbox and click the To button at the bottom to add Henry to the list of recipients for your message. Then close the Find Names window (it doesn't close automatically).

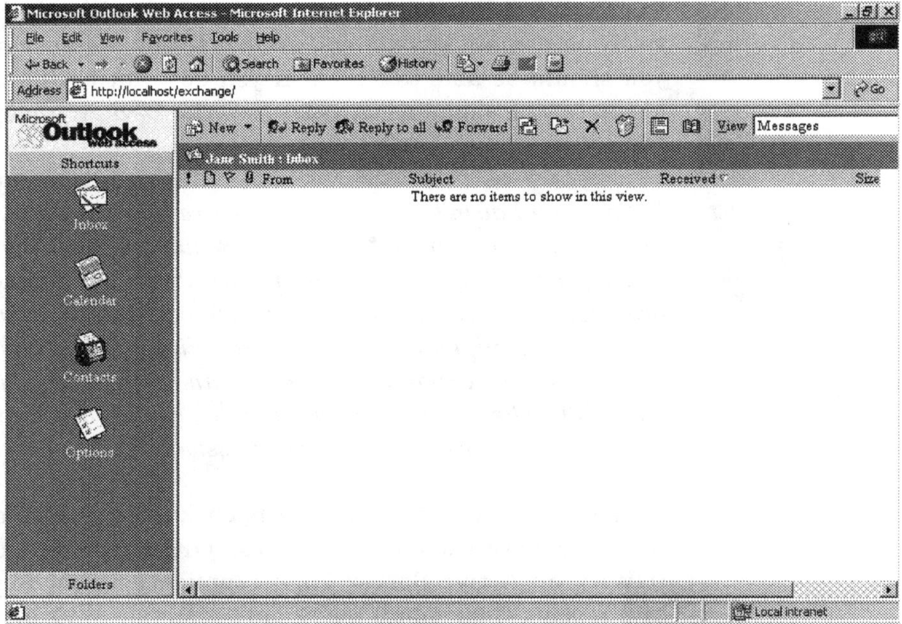

Figure 3.6
Outlook Web Access.

NOTE

If a user logs on to the computer and uses Internet Explorer (IE) to open the URL http://<server_name>/exchange, where <server_name> is the name of the Exchange server, OWA will open and the user will immediately be able to read his or her mail. If the computer is running Netscape Navigator, a dialog box will appear requiring the user to enter his or her network credentials before using OWA.

When working in an intranet environment (users are connected to the LAN where the Exchange server resides), users can just use the name of the Exchange server to use OWA to access their mail, for example, http://box14/exchange. If users need to use OWA from outside the LAN (that is, over the Internet), then they will need to use the fully qualified domain name of the Exchange server to access it with OWA, for example, http://box14.mtit.com/exchange.

Add a subject and message body and then click Send on the toolbar of the Untitled Message window to send your message. Now close OWA, log off as Jane Smith, log on as Henry Lee, and start OWA again. The message from Jane should be visible in Henry's Inbox. Double-click on the message to read it.

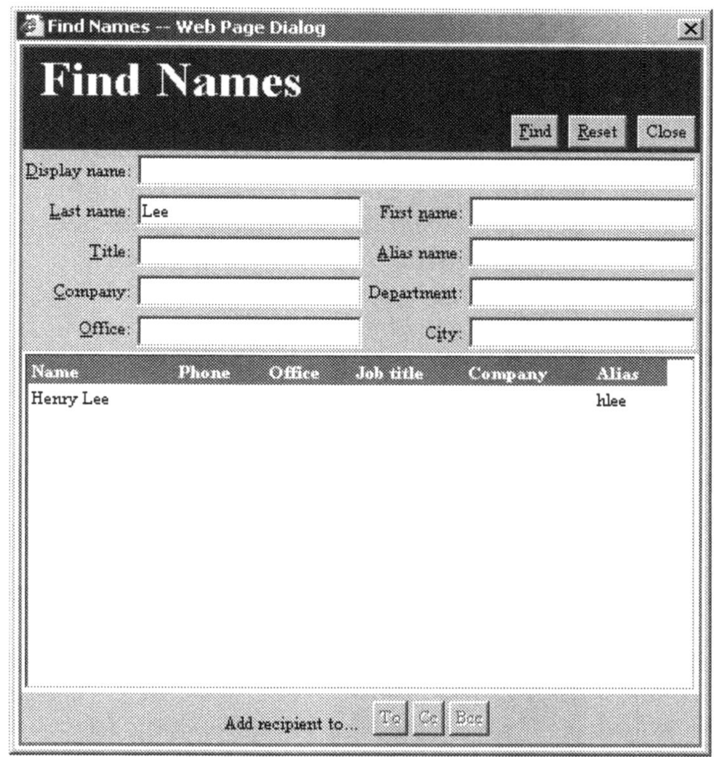

Figure 3.7 Searching for a recipient in the directory.

TIP

To make OWA easier to use in our testbed environment, for each logged-on user create a shortcut whose target is http://localhost/exchange and with the name OWA, and then drag the shortcut onto the Start menu for that user. If you have a Windows 2000 Professional workstation set up and registered with Dynamic DNS, you can specify the shortcut target instead as http://box14.mtit.com/exchange.

There are many ways to show how OWA works, but our focus is on Exchange, and most features of OWA are fairly obvious to anyone who has ever worked with Microsoft Outlook. Take some time later to explore the OWA interface, especially the Options shortcut in the left-hand bar. Click the Help icon at the top right of the screen for more information about features you are examining, and read the Backgrounder in this chapter on OWA for further information.

Outlook Web Access

OWA is an Active Server Pages (ASP) application that runs on IIS and enables users to access their Exchange mailboxes with a standard Web browser. In previous versions of Exchange, OWA was an optional component, but in Exchange 2000, it is installed by default, which is one reason Exchange requires that IIS be previously installed.

OWA can be useful as a mail client for users whose workstations run a different operating system than Windows (such as UNIX workstations), for users whose machines that have insufficient hardware resources to support the full Microsoft Outlook mail and collaboration client, and for users who do not have their own client computer (such as temporary employees who share a common computer).

The version of OWA included with Exchange 2000 requires that client machines use a Web browser that fully supports HTML 3.2 and ECMA scripting standards, which basically means you need Microsoft Internet Explorer (IE) 4.0 or higher or Netscape Navigator 4.0 or higher. However, using IE 5.0 as your client brings some special benefits because of its support of DHTML. Specifically, IE 5.0 users can display the public folder hierarchy and navigate it easily, can drag and drop items between folders, and have a rich-text editing environment for composing messages. In addition, IE 5.0 can perform some processing locally, thereby reducing the processing load on the Exchange server and enabling it to support more clients. The downside of this increased functionality is that IE 5.0 requires machines with more processing power than IE 4.0 or Netscape Navigator 4.0; don't install IE 5.0 on an old machine or it will crawl!

Although OWA has many functional similarities to the standard Outlook client, it lacks some Outlook features, specifically tasks, journaling, Outlook rules, offline folders, copying items between public folders and personal mailbox folders, printing templates, spell-checking, certain delivery options, calendar reminders, and so on. For the best user experience, use Outlook 2000 as the messaging and collaboration client in your enterprise; for cheap and easy deployment, however, OWA can't be beat.

Here's a tip on administering OWA within your organization. Although OWA is installed by default when you install Exchange and you can't prevent this, you can disable OWA for specific users if you need to. Simply start ADUC and select View → Advanced Features. Then open the Properties Sheet for the user, switch to the Exchange Advanced tab, click Protocol Settings, and double-click on HTTP within the Protocols dialog box. Clear the checkbox labeled Enable For Mailbox to disable OWA for the user.

A few tips on using OWA: if you have several users sharing a computer that uses OWA to send and receive their mail, be sure to configure the Web browser on the machine so that client-side caching of Web pages is disabled; otherwise, a smart user will be able to read the other users' mail. Disabling caching will slow down OWA, however, so make sure the machine is up to snuff in its hardware and has a 100-Mbp network card. If you're running IE 5.0, disable the Save Password feature as well. Also, educate users to close their Web browser at the end of each OWA session to protect their privacy or, even better, to log off the machine when they're finished their session.

Let's try out a few more scenarios. Fred Jones will be taking on the responsibility of handling all general marketing inquiries for MTIT Enterprises, so we want to assign Fred a second email address, namely marketing@mtit.com. Log on as Administrator and open ADUC, right-click on Fred Jones in the marketing OU, and select the E-mail Addresses tab on Fred's Properties Sheet. To add a new email address for Fred, click the New button. A dialog box opens asking you to select which type of email address you want to create (Figure 3.8).

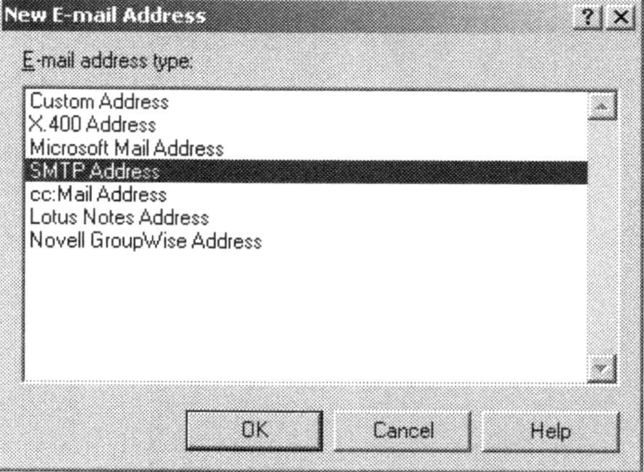

Figure 3.8
Select the type of email address to create.

Select SMTP Address and click OK in the dialog box. A new Internet Address Properties box appears asking you to type the new SMTP address you want to create for the current user. Type marketing@mtit.com into this box and click OK to return to the Properties Sheet for Fred. There are now two SMTP addresses specified for Fred (Figure 3.9); his old address (fjones@mtit.com) is in boldface font and the new one (marketing@mtit.com) is in normal font. When there are two or more addresses of a given type for a user, the one in boldface is the primary address of that type, which means that this is the default reply address that is added in the From field for outgoing mail sent by the user. So if you selected the new address marketing@mtit.com and clicked the Set As Primary button, any mail sent by Fred would have its reply address set as marketing@mtit.com.

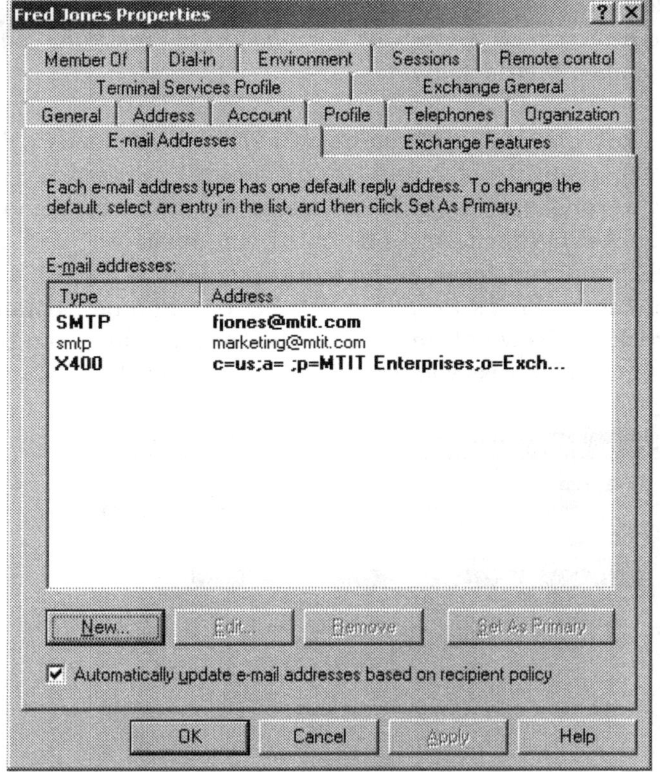

Figure 3.9 User with two SMTP addresses, the one in boldface font being the default reply address for SMTP mail.

Now close Fred's Property Sheet, log off as Administrator, log on as Henry, and send a message to marketing@mtit.com (type this address into the To field of the Untitled Message window in OWA). Then log on as Fred and you should receive the message.

NOTE

You can add, remove, and edit email addresses for users, but you cannot remove the user's last SMTP address. If you try, you will receive an error saying "This is the primary SMTP email address of this recipient, it can-

not be removed" because Exchange uses SMTP by default for routing messages, so there must be at least one SMTP address for every user.

Next, let's change the display name and alias of Henry Lee, who has decided he would prefer to be called by his Chinese name Zhonghua Lee. Log on as Administrator, open Henry's Properties Sheet in ADUC, and change the:

- General tab: change first name to Zhonghua, change display name to Zhonghua Lee, and change the email field to zlee@mtit.com
- Exchange General tab: change alias to zlee

Now click the Apply button and switch to the E-mail Addresses tab. Note that the email address still reads hlee@mtit.com. Depending on whether Henry has just joined the company or has been there a while, you can click either Edit to change his email address to zlee@mtit.com or New to create a new email address, zlee@mtit.com, and set the new address as his primary one (and then delete the old one a few months later). A change in the primary SMTP email address is automatically reflected in the E-mail field on the General tab as well. Don't forget to update the user's X.400 address information also.

NOTE

When you display user objects in the Details pane of ADUC, the first field is Name. This is the name of the object in Active Directory and is not the same as the display name for the user. Even though we changed Henry's first name to Zhonghua and his display name to Zhonghua Lee on the General tab of his Properties Sheet, this change is not reflected in the details pane. To see why, select View → Advanced Features from the ADUC menu bar to show additional details of objects in Active Directory and then open Zhonghua's Properties Sheet and select the Object tab, which is now visible. Note that the fully qualified domain name of this user object in AD is still

```
mtit.com/Marketing Users/Henry Lee
```

Internally Active Directory still calls this user Henry Lee despite our changes. The simplest way to work around this is to add an additional field to the Details pane of ADUC by selecting View → Choose Columns → select Display Address under Hidden Columns → Add → Move Up, so it follows Name. Of course, this doesn't really solve our problems because if

Henry is changing his name for Exchange he probably wants to change his logon name from hlee@mtit.com to zlee@mtit.com.

What we really need to do is to first rename his user account in Active Directory before we change his Exchange information. To do this, right-click on Henry Lee in the marketing OU in ADUC and select Rename. Type "Zhonghua Lee" (without quotes) and press ENTER and a dialog box appears to confirm the name change and to allow additional changes. In this dialog box, change the first name to Zhonghua, the display name to Zhonghua Lee, and the two user logon names to zlee and click OK. This will change the fully qualified domain name of this user object in AD to:

```
mtit.com/Marketing Users/Zhonghua Lee
```

but it does nothing about his email address, so now open the Properties Sheet for the user, select the Exchange General tab, change his email alias to zlee, and then switch to the E-mail Addresses tab and change his SMTP address to zlee@mtit.com. The change is now complete.

Finally, Jane is headed away on holidays and needs to give Fred access to her email while she's gone, but she would like to retain any incoming messages so she can review them later. We need to configure delivery options for Jane, so log on as Administrator, open her Properties Sheet in ADUC, select the Exchange General tab, and click Delivery Options. Click the Forward To option button and click Modify to select Fred Jones from Active Directory. Select the checkbox that allows messages to be both forwarded and copied to Jane's mailbox (Figure 3.10). Click OK twice.

Now log on as Zhonghua (Henry) and send a message to Jane, saying "I hear you're going on vacation". Then log on as Fred to see if he received a forwarded copy of Henry's message. Click Reply and reply to the message saying, "This is Fred—yes, she already is on vacation." Log on as Zhonghua to read the reply; note that the reply appears in Zhonghua's Inbox as having come from Fred. Remove the delivery options once you've finished the exercise.

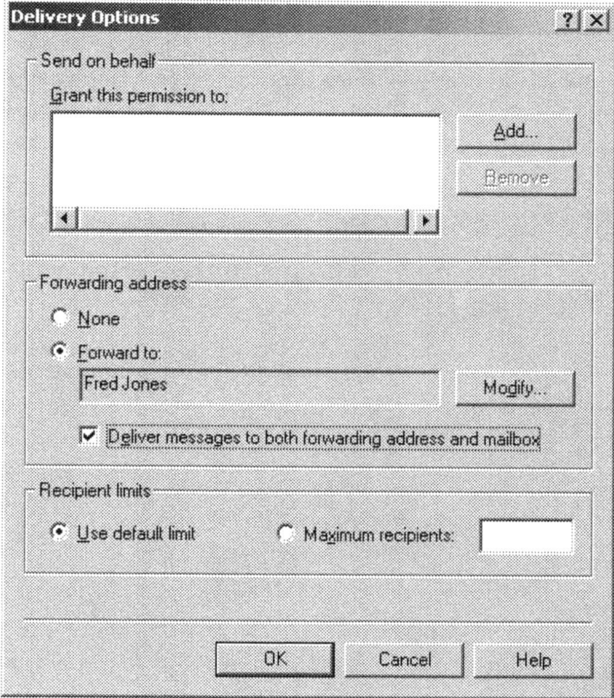

Figure 3.10 Forwarding Jane's mail to Fred.

Creating a Mail-enabled User

Walkthrough

Let's create a mail-enabled user account for Jack Fontaine, who is a consultant with a different company and is coming to work with MTIT Enterprises temporarily for a few weeks. Jack wants to be able to log on to our network and send and receive mail with other users in our company, but doesn't want a mailbox with our company as he already has one with his own company.

Log on as Administrator, start ADUC, create a new OU called Consultants, and right-click on this OU to select New → User. Enter his first and last names into the New Object User box, specify his user logon name as jfontaine, and click Next. Specify password information and click Next. Now here's the key to creating a mail-enabled user instead of a mailbox-enabled user: clear the Create An Exchange Mailbox checkbox here (see Figure 3.3) and click Next and then Finish. When you create a user in this fashion, an email address is not automatically generated for the user (as in when we create a mailbox-enabled user) because Exchange has no idea of what messaging system this user already belongs to. So we've simply create a new user that is neither mail- nor mailbox-enabled at this point, and next we need to mail-enable the user.

To mail-enable user Jack Fontaine, right-click on this user in ADUC and select Exchange Tasks. This opens the Exchange Task Wizard (Figure 3.11), something we haven't seen before.

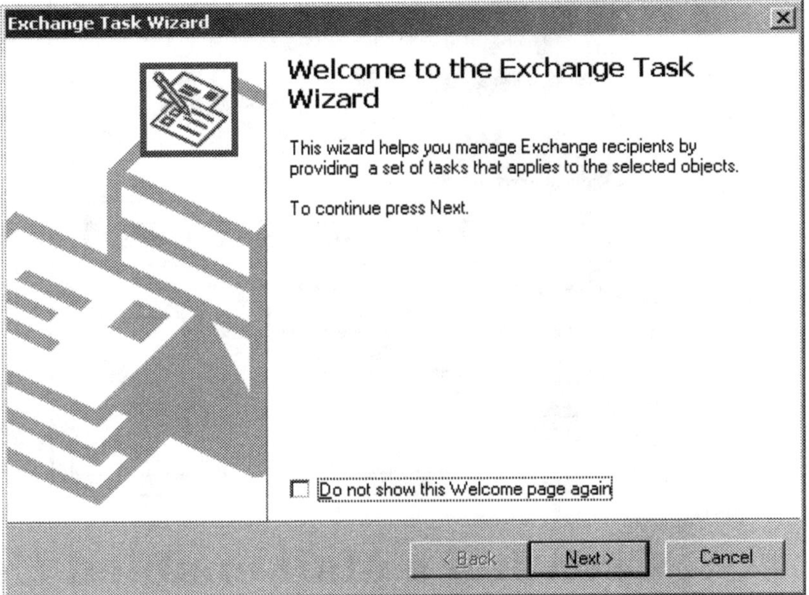

Figure 3.11 The Exchange Task Wizard.

Clicking Next shows that there are three tasks we can perform on the selected user account:

- Create Mailbox, which turns the user into a mailbox-enabled user
- Establish email addresses, which turns the user into a mail-enabled user
- Enable Instant Messaging, which enables the user to participate in Exchange instant messaging

We want the second option, so select it and click Next. The alias jfontaine is suggested for Jack's directory entry in Active Directory, which is fine because it conforms with our company policy. Click Modify to specify Jack's external SMTP address as jack@fictitiousdomain.com, and leave Jack associated with the First Administrative Group (Figure 3.12). Click Next and then Finished to complete the wizard.

User Jack Fontaine is now mail-enabled. To test this, open OWA and click the Address Book icon on the toolbar to open the Find Names window. Type “J” (no quotes) in the Display Name field, click Find, and Jack Fontaine should be one of the users who come up as potential mail recipients.

Figure 3.12 *Specifying an external email address for a user.*

Exchange Task Wizard

Establish e-mail addresses
Establish e-mail addresses for the selected recipients to include them in the Exchange address list.

Type an alias for this recipient and press Modify to enter the external e-mail address.

Alias:
jfontaine

External E-mail Address:
SMTP:jack@fictitiousdomain.com
Modify ...

Associated Administrative Group:
MTIT Enterprises/First Administrative Group

< Back | Next > | Cancel

Changing a User from Mail- to Mailbox-enabled

Walkthrough

It should be pretty obvious how to do this by now. Jack Fontaine is currently mail-enabled, so simply right-click on this user in ADUC, select Exchange Tasks, and click Next. However, the Create Mailbox option we saw earlier is no longer here, so we have to select the Delete Email Address option instead, which un–mail-enables the user; then restart the wizard and select Create Mailbox, this time to make the user mailbox-enabled. The steps are straightforward.

To change Jack back into a mail-enabled user, use the wizard to first delete Jack’s mailbox and then a second time to associate an external email address with his account.

Deleting a Mailbox-enabled User

Walkthrough

What happens to a user's mailbox when you delete the associated user account? Let's try it. Jack Fontaine is finished his consulting work and is leaving the company. Right-click on his account in ADUC and select Delete. A dialog box appears informing us that there is an associated object (a mailbox) for this user object in AD and that if we delete the user then the mailbox will be deleted also. There's a checkbox where we can reverse this action, but it's ghosted and can't be selected. In other words, Exchange won't let us create orphaned mailboxes by deleting user accounts but not their mailboxes.

What should you do? After all, Jack might still receive important mail after he leaves the company. The simplest thing to do is to first configure his delivery options to forward mail to the person who managed him while he was at MTIT Enterprises, and then disable (not delete!) his user account in Active Directory. Disabling an account prevents it from being used for logging on to the network but does not prevent it from receiving mail in its associated mailbox. Test this by sending Jack a message while his account is disabled and then enable his account and see if he received it.

TIP

Here are a few more tips on using OWA. As an administrator, you can use OWA to access other users' mailboxes if you know their user credentials including their password. Simply use the URL:

```
http://<exhange_server_name>/exchange/<user_name>.
```

For example, to access Jack Fontaine's mailbox after he's left the company, open the URL:

```
http://box14/exchange/jfontaine
```

while logged on locally to the Exchange server. This opens a dialog box requesting the user name, password, and domain for the user whose mailbox you are trying to access. Enter Jack's credentials and you can access his mailbox (his account must be enabled).

The issue of employee privacy is a serious one. Except in very high-security environments, you will generally set a user's initial password to password *and force them to change this to a password of their own choice when they first log on to the network. In this way users are responsible for their passwords and administrators are checked from looking in users' folders and mailboxes, which is the way things should be. You should be sure that your company has formulated clear policies with management on such issues.*

You can even go straight to Jack's calendar by using the URL: http://box14/exchange/jfontaine/calendar

To access a public folder called Projects, you could use the URL: http://box14/public/projects

And to access the root of the public folder tree, use: http://box14/public

Cool, huh?

Copying a Mailbox-enabled User

If you are going to create a number of users who all belong to the same department and have similar user account requirements, you can speed the process by creating one user and then using this user as a template for creating the others. You do this by simply copying the first user to create the other users. When you copy a user, most of the user environment settings are copied except those settings that should be unique to every user such as name, password, and so on.

Let's try it out. Open the Properties Sheet for Fred Jones, fill in all of the information fields (description, title, department, and so on) on the various tabs, and change some of the default settings (account expiry date, logon script name, remote access permission, startup environment, group membership, and so on). Include not just general account settings but also Exchange settings such as delivery restrictions, storage limits, and so on. This will help us learn what settings are copied and which are not.

Now right-click on Fred Jones in ADUC and select All Tasks → Copy. The Copy Object User dialog box opens, which is similar to the New Object-User box shown in Figure 3.2. Enter the following information:

- First name: Donna
- Initials: P
- Last name: MacKenzie
- User logon name: dmackenzie

Click Next and note that the password is unspecified but the password options are the same as those for the template account Fred Jones. Enter a password and click Next; click Next again to create an Exchange mailbox for Donna using the default settings (similar to Fred's) and click Finish to create the new mailbox-enabled user.

TIP

You can simultaneously open several Properties Sheets for different users in ADUC, a nice feature of Windows 2000. This helps you compare the copied user with the template.

Now open the Properties Sheet for Donna MacKenzie and examine which settings have been copied from Fred and which have not. Table 3.1 shows a quick summary of the settings that are copied when you copy an account.

TABLE 3.1

Settings copied when a mailbox-enabled user is copied.

Tab	Settings copied
General	None; these settings are unique to each user
Address	All except street
Account	All except user logon names
Profile	All if <username> is the replaceable variable in the home folder path
Telephones	None
Organization	None; these settings are unique to each user
E-mail Addresses	None; these settings are unique to each user
Exchange Features	None; these settings are unique to each user
Terminal Services Profile	None; these settings are unique to each user
Exchange General	All except Exchange alias
Member Of	All
Dial-in	None; these settings are unique to each user
Environment	None; these settings are unique to each user
Sessions	None; these settings are unique to each user
Remote Control	None; these settings are unique to each use

Summary

In this chapter we've covered the basics of creating and configuring mail- and mailbox-enabled users in Exchange using the ADUC console, a Windows 2000 administration tool that is enhanced by installing Exchange. We've also looked at how OWA can be used as a messaging client for Exchange.

In the next chapter, we'll look at how to create and manage another type of Exchange recipient, the *mail-enabled contact*.

CHAPTER 4

Contacts

Another type of recipient that Exchange administrators must manage are contacts. This chapter looks at contacts and how to administer them, and includes the following three walkthroughs:

- Creating a mail-enabled contact
- Configuring a mail-enabled contact
- Mail-enabling an existing contact

Standard and Mail-enabled Contacts

A contact is someone with whom people in your organization need to communicate but who belongs to a different company. Windows 2000 allows you to create contacts in Active Directory (AD) and configure various personal and business information regarding these contacts such as name, address, title, company, and so on.

Exchange 2000 adds the functionality of allowing contacts in AD to have email addresses associated with them. Users can then look up addresses for contacts the same way they do with mail- and mailbox-enabled users within your organization.

The main differences between users and contacts are:

- Users can log onto your network; contacts can't.
- Users can have mailboxes in your Exchange organization; contacts, if they have mailboxes at all, have them with a different company's messaging system.
- Contacts have fewer configurable properties than users (because they have no mailboxes, logon names, home folders, user profiles, and so on).

The main advantage of populating AD with contacts is saving users the effort of maintaining their own (redundant and overlapping) contact lists and reducing the time users spend entering one-off addresses in the To field of their outgoing mail.

Contacts are simple to create and manage, and you'll learn how to do this in this chapter.

TIP

Remember, mail-enabled contacts and mail-enabled users are both generally used for persons external to your company to whom your employees frequently need to send mail, which is why you want them included in AD. The difference is that users can also log on to your network, whereas contacts can't.

Creating a Mail-enabled Contact

Walkthrough

Zyllian Zbignowski is a marketing consultant for Fictitious Corp and frequently does contract work for MTIT Enterprises, so to make life easier for our own marketing department, we'll create a mail-enabled contact for her in AD.

Log on as Administration, open ADUC, and start by creating a new OU within the mtit.com domain. Give this new OU the name Marketing Contacts. Once this OU is created, right-click on the OU, and select New → Contact to open the New Object Contact dialog box. Enter Zyllian's first and last names, and specify her display name as Zyllian Zbignowski (Figure 4.1).

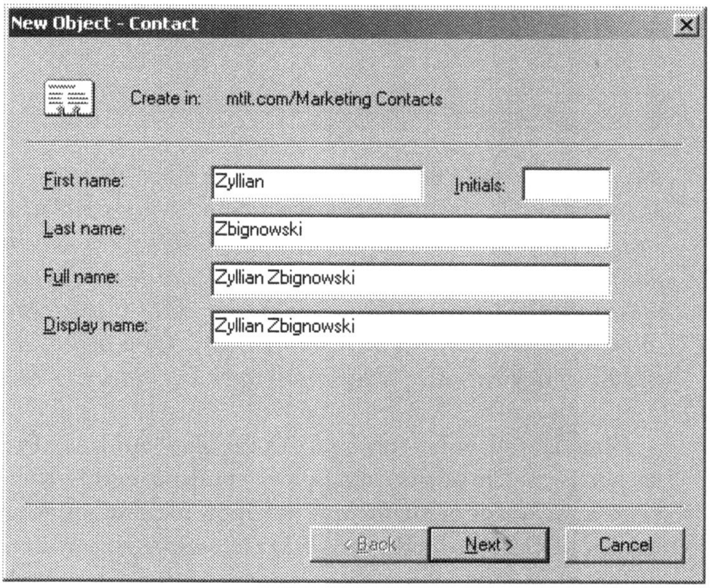

Figure 4.1
Creating a new mail-enabled contact.

Click Next and leave the checkbox selected to create a new Exchange email address for Zyllian. Change the alias to "ZZ" (no quotes) and click Modify to specify her external email address. Select SMTP Address as the type of address to create for her (Zyllian uses the messaging system hosted by her company's Internet service provider). On the General tab of the Internet Address Properties dialog box, type her email address as zz@fictitionsdomain.com (Figure 4.2).

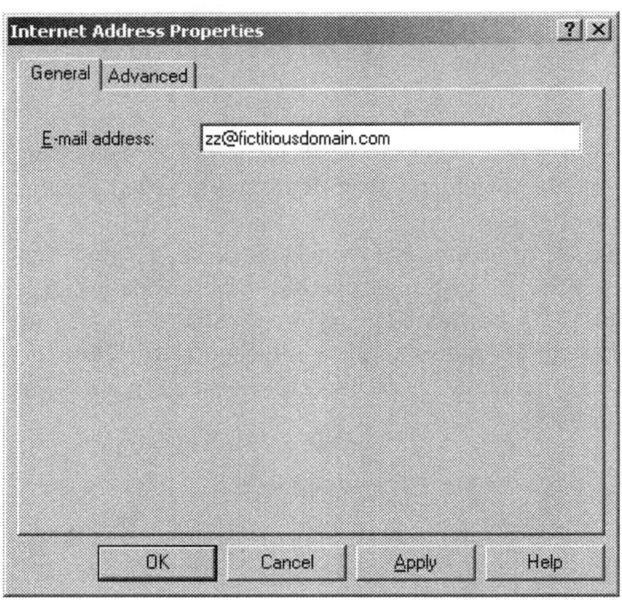

Figure 4.2
Specifying an external email address for a new mail-enabled contact.

NOTE

If the external recipient belonged to a company that used an X.400 messaging system, you would create an X.400 rather than an SMTP address for the mail-enabled contact. Unlike mail- and mailbox-enabled users, who must always have at least one SMTP address defined for them, mail-enabled contacts can have any type of email address, not just SMTP. They can also have more than one address, as we will see later.

Click the Advanced tab of the Internet Address Properties box to view its settings. These settings allow you to override the default SMTP message and attachment format settings for Exchange to meet the requirements of the contact's own SMTP messaging system, which may have different requirements from yours. Configuring these settings should be done in consultation with the SMTP provider for the external contact, but the default settings usually work fine in most cases.

Click OK to close the dialog box and return to the New Object Contact box (Figure 4.3). Leave the associated administrative group listbox set to First Administrative Group for now (we'll look at administrative groups in Chapter 12).

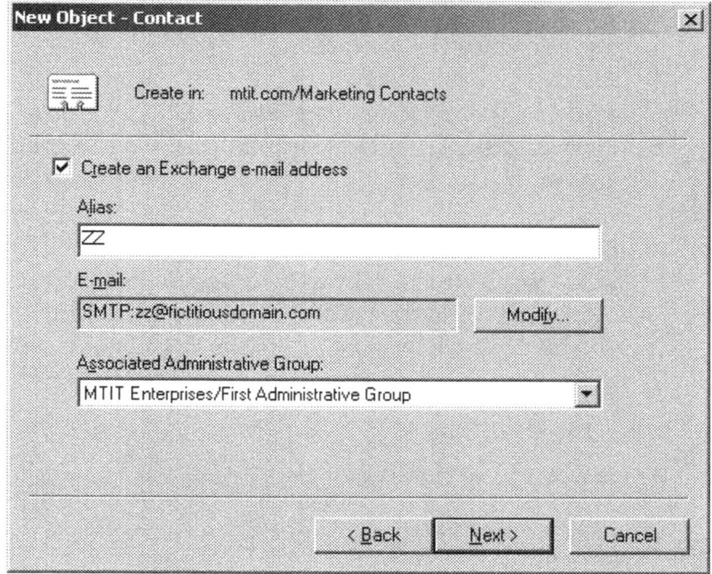

Figure 4.3 Specifying addressing information for a new mail-enabled contact.

Click Next and then Finish to create the new mail-enabled contact. Now that the contact has been created, it needs to be configured properly.

Configuring a Mail-enabled Contact

Walkthrough

To configure our new contact, double-click on it in ADUC to open its Properties Sheet. Compared to the large number of tabs present on user objects, contacts are a breeze to configure!

Start by supplying the necessary business information for the contact telephone number, Web page, company, address, title, department, and so on. The more information you specify, the more useful this contact object will be to your users because it will enable them to search AD more easily.

Switch to the E-mail Addresses tab. Note that this is the same as that of mail-enabled users as discussed in the previous chapter (see Figure 3.4). You can use this tab to add new email addresses for the contact, specify a primary address when there is more than one address of a given type, edit existing addresses, and remove unnecessary ones.

Switch to the Exchange General tab now (Figure 4.4). Here you can further configure the contact by:

- Changing the alias for the contact
- Modifying the primary email address for the contact or create a new address
- Specify a maximum size for incoming messages or use the default limit set in Server Manager
- Decide whether the contact will be allowed to receive email from anyone or only from specified users in your Exchange organization (you can list those users from whom the contact either can or cannot receive email).

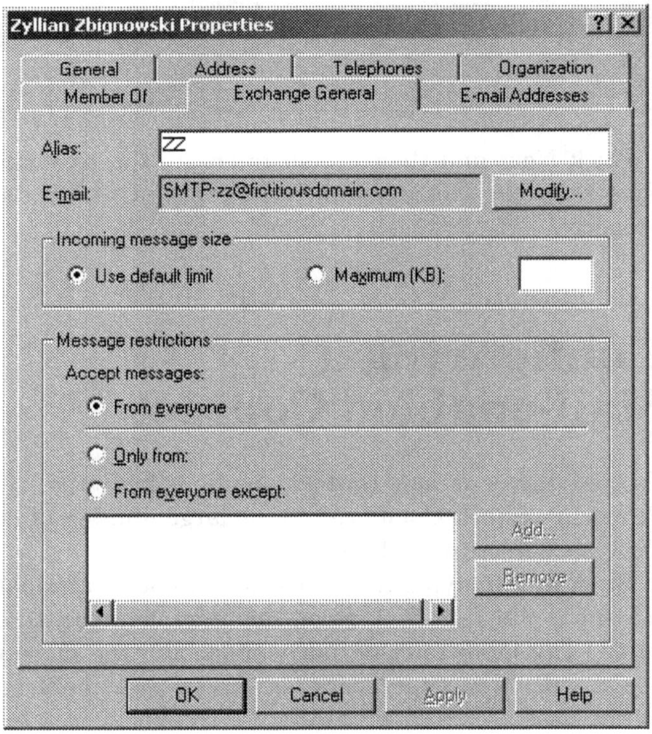

Figure 4.4 Configuring Exchange settings for a mail-enabled contact.

If you now open Outlook Web Access, you'll find that you can click To and search AD for the contact Zyllian Zbignowski, but if you send mail to her it will bounce back to you unless her email address is a real one and your Exchange server is connected to the Internet (which is not the case in our testbed environment).

Mail-Enabling a Standard Contact

If you have already created contacts in AD before installing Exchange, these contacts are not automatically mail-enabled during Setup. So you may want to mail-enable these contacts manually afterward, and this is how to do it.

If you don't have any standard contacts, first create one like this: right-click on the OU where you want the contact to reside, select New → Contact, specify the name of the contact, click Next, clear the checkbox (see Figure 4.3) so that the contact does not become mail-enabled for Exchange, click Next, and then click Finish.

Now you can manually mail-enable your standard contact by right-clicking on it and selecting Exchange Tasks to start the Exchange Tasks Wizard. The only task you can select in the wizard is the one you want: Establish email address. The steps are straightforward. You can similarly use the wizard to change a mail-enabled contact back into a standard one.

Summary

This chapter looked at how to create and configure mail-enabled contacts for recipients external to your Exchange organization. In the next chapter, we will see how to *mail-enable groups* in Exchange, a feature that enables you to perform simultaneous mass mailings.

CHAPTER 5

Groups

In addition to users and contacts discussed in the previous two chapters, a third kind of Exchange recipient is groups. In previous versions of Exchange, mail was sent simultaneously to multiple users by using *distribution lists* (DLs). In Exchange 2000, DLs are replaced by mail-enabled groups.

This chapter has six walkthroughs:

- Creating a mail-enabled security group
- Configuring a mail-enabled security group
- Disabling a mail-enabled security group
- Mail-enabling a standard security group
- Hiding and displaying membership of a mail-enabled security group
- Creating a mail-enabled distribution group

Note that this chapter is not about administrative groups or routing groups, which are not recipients and are discussed in Chapter 21.

Groups in Windows 2000

Before explaining how to mail-enable groups for mass distribution of email, we'll take a moment to talk about groups in Windows 2000 and review how they've changed since Windows NT.

Windows NT had two types of groups: global and local. This in itself was enough to confuse most people! Both groups were used to contain user accounts, but each type of group had a different purpose:

- *Global groups* were used to group together users according to function, location, or some similar criteria. All marketing users might be members of the Marketing global group, for example, because they have similar network and resource access needs.
- *Local groups* were used to provide users with controlled access to network resources, such as shared folders and printers. For example, to control access to a company's color laser printer, a local group called ColorLaserPrinter would be created and granted Print permission for the printer. Marketing users could then be granted access to the printer by making the Marketing global group a member of the ColorLaserPrinter local group.

Groups in Windows NT were confusing because there were so many different ways of granting users access to resources. For example, to allow Bob, a user in the marketing department, the ability to print to the color laser printer, you could:

1. Grant Print permission for the printer directly to Bob's user account.
2. Make sure Bob was a member of the Marketing global group and then grant Print permission for the printer directly to the Marketing global group.
3. Grant Print permission for the printer to the ColorLaserPrinter local group and then make the Marketing global group (of which Bob is a member) a member of this local group.

All three methods worked, but, although Microsoft recommended the third method, many administrators used the second method because it eliminated the bother of creating an additional local group (the first method is too much work—what if you have hundreds of users who need access to the printer?). The real advantage of using local groups only became evident when the enterprise was large and needed several Windows NT domains. In this case, using local groups reduced the amount of administration required in managing users' access to resources.

NOTE

There is another type of group in Windows NT (and Windows 2000) called the local group, but this exists only on stand-alone Windows 2000 Servers or on Windows 2000 Professional machines that are configured to belong to a workgroup instead of a domain. We won't cover local groups here because they have limited usefulness in a domain-based enterprise.

The Scope of Things

Groups are even more flexible (read: complicated!) in Windows 2000. Groups now operate at three instead of two levels (scopes):

- *Domain local groups* can be used for controlling access to resources within a single domain, but they can contain members from any domain in the forest. They correspond to the local groups of Windows NT.

- *Global groups* can be used for controlling access to resources anywhere in the forest, but they can contain members only from their own domain, They correspond to the global groups of Windows NT.
- *Universal groups* can be used for controlling access to resources anywhere in the forest, and they also can contain members from any domain in the forest. Universal groups have no counterpart in Windows NT.

TIP

Universal groups aren't particularly useful unless your company has implemented a forest with multiple domains. If you have only one domain, use global and domain local groups only.

To make things even more complex, the membership rules for these three types of groups depend on whether your Windows 2000 network is running in mixed mode or native mode. In mixed mode Windows 2000 interoperates with existing Windows NT domain controllers; in native mode all domain controllers are running Windows 2000. Table 5.1 outlines the membership rules for each group scope in Windows 2000.

NOTE

You need to be aware that the terms mixed mode *and* native mode *refer to two different things when discussing Windows 2000 and Exchange 2000. In Windows 2000* mode *refers to whether the Windows 2000 domain controllers are backward-compatible with downlevel Windows NT domain controllers. In Exchange 2000* mode *refers to whether the Exchange 2000 servers are backward-compatible with downlevel Exchange 5.5 servers. We'll discuss this further in Chapter 25, but it's unfortunate that Microsoft chose the same terminology for both platforms, both with a different meaning.*

TABLE 5.1

Group scopes and membership rules in Windows 2000.

Scope	Membership in mixed mode	Membership in native mode
Domain Local	Accounts from any domain Global groups from any domain	Accounts from any domain Global groups from any domain Universal groups from any domain Domain local groups from the same domain
Global	Accounts from the same domain	Accounts from the same domain Global groups from the same domain

continued on next page

TABLE 5.1

Group scopes and membership rules in Windows 2000 (continued).

Scope	Membership in mixed mode	Membership in native mode
Universal	Not available	Accounts from any domain Domain local groups from any domain Global groups from any domain Universal groups from any domain

Types of Groups

We've used the words *scope* and *type* interchangeably in our discussion of these groups, but in Windows 2000 these terms have precise and different meanings:

- *Scope* refers to where members of the group can be taken from (from the local domain or the entire forest) and where the group can be used to grant permissions for control of resources (in the local domain or the entire forest).
- *Type* refers to whether the group can be used for controlling access to network resources or not.

There are two types of groups in Windows 2000:

- *Security groups* can be used for controlling access to resources but can also be mail-enabled for sending mail simultaneously to groups of mail- or mailbox-enabled users and contacts.
- *Distribution groups* cannot be used for controlling access to resources. They can only be used for sending mail simultaneously to groups of mail- or mailbox-enabled users and contacts.

Windows NT only had one type of group, that is, security, although it wasn't named as such. Furthermore, you couldn't mail-enable the group for mass mailings to users. That's why earlier versions of Exchange added the DL, which corresponds to the mail-enabled distribution groups of Windows 2000. This actually made life more difficult for administrators, because they had to maintain two kinds of groups.

For example, in Windows NT, if you had a marketing department, you would create a Marketing global group to group all members of that department together for granting them access to network resources they might need. Then to send mail to all marketing employees, you would have to create and populate a marketing distribution list with the mailboxes of the members of the department. If a new employee joined the department, you would have to add a new NT user account to the global group and his or her Exchange 5.5 mailbox to the distribution list. In contrast, Exchange 2000 makes things simpler by the way its mailing lists are integrated with the group types and scopes of Windows 2000, as we will see later in this chapter.

Using Groups in Exchange

Before we actually start working with groups in Exchange, let's discuss some of the strategies involved for effectively using them. We'll consider how best to use the different types and scopes of Windows 2000 groups with Exchange.

Group Types and Exchange

Because you can mail-enable both security and distribution groups in Exchange, you'll probably want to use mail-enabled security groups mainly for internal mail and mail-enabled distribution groups for external mail.

For example, you could create a global or universal group called Finance for the accounting department (depending on whether you have a single- or multidomain enterprise and how members of this department are administered and geographically distributed) and then mail-enable the Finance group to be able to simultaneously send mail to all employees within this department. Or you could mail-enable the Backup Operators built-in group to be able to send mail simultaneously to all backup operators in your domain.

In contrast, if your marketing department periodically sends mass mailings to mail-enabled contacts in different companies, you could create a Marketing Contacts distribution group and populate it with these contacts.

Group Scopes and Exchange

Different group scopes can be mail-enabled for managing mass mailings to different groups of users within your organization. For example:

- Domain local groups might be used for grouping users in the same department or office together. Mail-enabling these groups lets you mass mail to everyone in the department or office.
- Global groups might be used for grouping together users in the same geographic location or organizational unit. Mail-enabling these groups lets you mass mail to everyone at the location or in the same OU.
- Universal groups might be used for grouping users that have similar business functions across several domains. Mail-enabling these groups lets you mass mail to everyone having that function in the enterprise.

In addition, you can create both mail-enabled security and mail-enabled distribution groups of different scopes for sending mass mail to users according to their: department, role, geographic location, project involvement, and so on.

Plan your groups carefully before you deploy Windows 2000 in your enterprise so that they can be used effectively for both controlling access to network resources and mass-mail distribution within and beyond your organization. In addition, mail-enable existing security groups wherever possible before creating new security or distribution groups for mass-mailing purposes.

Working with Groups

We'll now look at the steps involved for creating and managing mail-enabled groups in Exchange. These procedures are quite straightforward to implement, and we'll use the testbed environment described in Chapter 1.

Creating a Mail-enabled Security Group

Walkthrough

Let's create a Marketing global group, mail-enable it, and populate it with all users we previously created in our Marketing Users OU.

Open ADUC on the Exchange server or a workstation running the Exchange administration tools, right-click on the Marketing Users OU, and select New → Group. This opens the New Object Group dialog box. Type *marketing* as the group name (this is automatically copied as the pre–Windows 2000 group name as well) and leave the default settings as Global Scope and Security Type (Figure 5.1).

NOTE

The option to create a universal scope group is available, meaning that our Windows 2000 domain, mtit.com, has been changed from mixed mode to native mode (a one-time process that can't be reversed), which we did previously because there are no Windows NT domain controllers in our testbed environment. One advantage of running in native mode, which we didn't mention previously, is that you can change global and domain local groups into universal ones after you create them, if you need to.

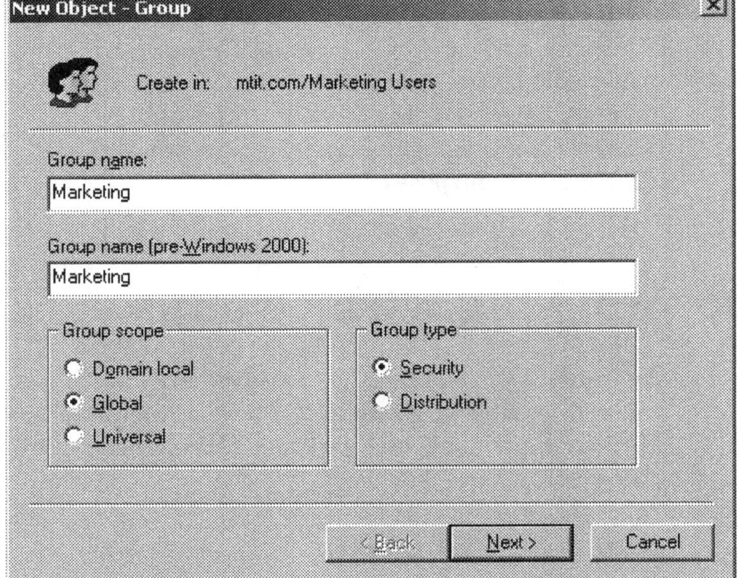

Figure 5.1 Creating a new Marketing global group.

In the next dialog box, note that the option to create an Exchange email address for the new group is cleared by default, so you have to select the checkbox to mail-enable the new group. The suggested alias is Marketing, the same as the name of the group, and the new group will be created in the default First Administrative Group of our organization MTIT Enterprises, which we'll accept (Figure 5.2).

NOTE

Actually, the checkbox to create an Exchange email address is cleared only if you selected either global or domain local as the scope of the group you wanted to create; if you selected universal for the scope, the checkbox is selected by default because mail-enabled universal groups are easier to use than mail-enabled global or domain local groups when Exchange is implemented in a forest with multiple domains and domain trees.

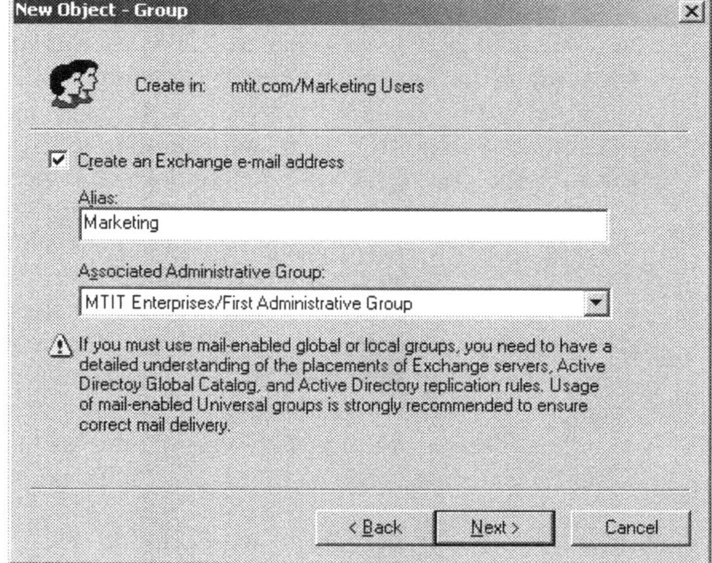

Figure 5.2 Mail-enabling the new Marketing global group.

Click Next and then Finish to create the new mail-enabled group. We'll test it in a moment.

Configuring a Mail-enabled Security Group

Walkthrough

Right-click on the Marketing group in ADUC and select Properties to open the Properties Sheet for the new group. Let's look at some of the tabs of this Properties Sheet.

- *General tab.* The email address that was automatically generated for the group is marketing2@mtit.com rather than the expected, marketing@mtit.com (Figure 5.3). Why is the address different than expected? In Chapter 3, we created the additional email address marketing@mtit.com for user Fred Jones because the company decided it was Fred's job to handle general marketing inquiries from users outside the company. Because the address marketing@mtit.com was already in use for this purpose, Exchange assigned our new mail-enabled group the address marketing2@mtit.com instead. We can fix this, if we want, by deleting Fred's second address and then changing the address for the Marketing group on the General tab.

- *Members tab*. Click Add to add the users in the Marketing OU to the mail-enabled group. An easier way of doing this might be to select all the users in the OU, right-click, select "Add members to a group," and specify that they be added to the Marketing group.
- *Exchange General tab*. Here we can change the display name and alias for the group, specify a maximum message size (usually a good idea when using a group to perform mass mailings), and configure message restrictions (who can use the group's address for performing mass mailings to the group). If you want to allow a free-for-all discussion, leave the message restrictions at their default setting (accept messages from everyone). If you only want the manager of the department to be able to send mass mail to the group, select Only From and specify the manager's user account.
- *E-mail Addresses tab*. If you change an address here or on the General tab, it is updated on the other tab automatically.

TIP

It's a good idea to set message restrictions carefully on all mail-enabled groups in your enterprise. Otherwise, people from outside your company may be able to use them to spam your users. For example, to allow marketing users to use marketing@mtit.com for discussing issues among themselves, you would configure the Marketing group to accept messages only from the members of the Marketing group itself (you can specify the Marketing group here instead of selecting every single marketing user account from the list).

This can create a small problem if users sometimes travel or work from home and use a personal (noncompany) email account when they do so. You could create a separate distribution group called MarketingOffsite, create mail-enabled contacts with the personal email addresses of such users, add these contacts to your MarketingOffsite group, and then add the MarketingOffsite group to your mail-enabled Marketing group. Windows 2000 allows more flexibility than Windows NT in nesting groups, especially when it is running in native mode; see any good book on Windows 2000 administration for more information.

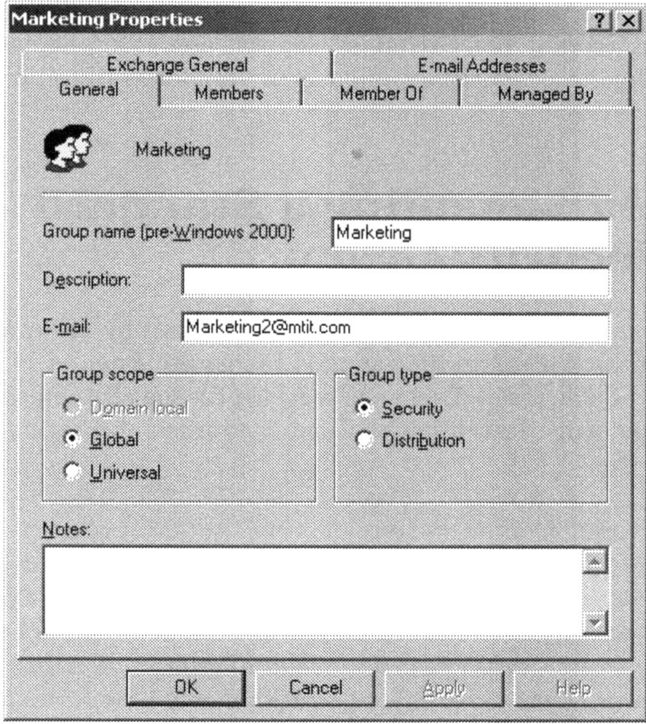

Figure 5.3 Configuring the Exchange settings for the Marketing global group.

Finally, test that you can send mail to the group. Logon as marketing user Jane Smith, open OWA, and send a message to marketing. Then log on as a different marketing user to check if the message came through.

Disabling a Mail-enabled Security Group

If we change our mind later and decide that we won't be sending mass mail to marketing-department employees (we'll be inviting them to the coffee room for meetings instead), then we can change the mail-enabled group to a standard group. To do this, right-click on the Marketing group in ADUC and select Exchange Tasks to start the Exchange Task Wizard. From the list of available tasks, select Delete E-Mail Addresses and finish the wizard.

Now open the Properties Sheet for the Marketing group and you'll notice that the Exchange General and E-mail Addresses tabs are no longer present—the group is now standard rather than mail-enabled.

Mail-enabling a Standard Security Group

Walkthrough

Reenable the Marketing group for mail by rerunning the Exchange Tasks Wizard and selecting Establish An Email Address from the list of available tasks. Exchange will suggest the alias Marketing for the group and will reestablish the email address marketing@mtit.com for the group.

TIP

You can also mail-enable built-in groups such as the built-in global groups Domain Admins, Enterprise Admins, and Domain Users and the built-in local groups Administrators, Users, Backup Operators, Account Operators, and so on. Built-in local groups are found in the Buildin container of the domain, and built-in global groups are located in the Users container.

Hiding and Displaying Membership of a Mail-enabled Security Group

Walkthrough

By default, the membership of a mail-enabled group is visible to users in OWA. You can hide group membership from users by running the Exchange Task Wizard for a mail-enabled group and selecting the Hide Membership option from the list of available tasks. This changes the security descriptor of the selected group to prevent viewing of the group's membership by users.

To display hidden membership for a group, rerun the Exchange Tasks Wizard and select Unhide Membership.

Creating a Mail-enabled Distribution Group

Working with distribution groups is similar to working with security groups. We'll create a Marketing Contacts distribution group to contain the contacts within the Marketing Contacts OU created in Chapter 4.

Right-click on the Marketing Contacts OU in ADUC and select New → Group to open the New Object Group box. Type Marketing Contacts (with a space between the words) for the group name and specify Universal for the scope and Distribution for the type.

In the next box you'll see that the suggested alias for the new mail-enabled distribution group will be MarketingContacts (no space between words). The reason is that space characters are not allowed in SMTP addresses, and Exchange uses SMTP as its underlying message transport.

Once you create the new mail-enabled distribution group, you can open its Properties Sheet to configure it in various ways. For example, you could:

- Change the scope of the group to global or domain local
- Change the type of the group to security
- Change the default email address or add additional ones
- Configure message size limits and message restrictions
- Add or remove members from the group

Summary

In this chapter, we looked at how to create and configure new mail-enabled groups and to mail-enable existing groups. In the next chapter, we'll look at using Microsoft Outlook 2000 as a client for Exchange 2000.

CHAPTER 6

Outlook

So far we've looked at various types of Exchange recipients and have tested sending and receiving mail using OWA, a component of Exchange that is installed by default. OWA is a lightweight mail client, however, and many companies prefer the full functionality of Microsoft Outlook as their messaging client.

This chapter looks at the basics of installing, configuring, and using Outlook 2000 as a client for Microsoft Exchange. It includes the following walkthroughs:

- Installing Outlook
- Configuring Outlook for Exchange
- Using Outlook

Exchange Clients

Messaging systems are more than just backend servers—you also need to consider what client software your users will be using for sending and receiving mail or otherwise collaborating with each other. Generally speaking, the more recent the version of your client software, the more functionality your users will enjoy.

Although you may have hundreds of times more client machines than mail servers, client machines are generally easier to upgrade than servers for two reasons:

- Tools like Microsoft Systems Management Server (SMS) 2.0 make the deployment, configuration, and maintenance of software on client machines relatively easy (once you've mastered the intricacies of SMS).
- If something goes wrong with a client machine, it's easy to wipe it clean and start over. Failure during a server upgrade is a far more serious matter because it may lead to lost data and affect the life of everyone who uses it.

The downside of client applications is that there are so many of them and so many different versions, and maintaining more than one application or version on your network can be a real headache.

With Microsoft Exchange, there are many options in choosing your primary messaging client:

- Microsoft Outlook 2000
- Earlier versions of Outlook such as Outlook 98 and Outlook 97
- Microsoft OWA
- Microsoft Outlook Express (OE)
- Third-party Internet mail client software

There are advantages and disadvantages in using these different clients:

- *Outlook 2000* offers users the greatest number of features for both messaging and collaboration and is designed specifically to work with Exchange on the backend and the Microsoft Office 2000 suite of applications on the client site. Deploying Outlook 2000 is relatively straightforward, but the hidden cost is that of training your users to use such a powerful client effectively (unless you are upgrading from an earlier version of Outlook they are already familiar with). Generally speaking, however, Outlook 2000 is the preferred client for desktop users in a company that uses Exchange 2000.
- *OWA* simplifies deployment considerably because it enables users to access many Outlook functions such as messaging, scheduling, and contacts with the use of a standard Web browser. The full functionality of the version of OWA included with Exchange 2000 is only realized if you have Microsoft Internet Explorer 5.0 or higher installed on users' desktops. OWA also lacks some of the functionality of the true Outlook client, but may be sufficient for some companies that can be satisfied with a more lightweight client. OWA is probably better suited as a client for traveling employees who need to be able to access their email and schedule from any machine connected to the Internet such as an Internet terminal. We looked at OWA in Chapter 3.
- *OE* is another lightweight client that is suited best to employees who travel or work offsite. OE is fine for Internet mail but lacks the scheduling features supported by Outlook and OWA.

Let's look at how to install and configure Outlook 2000, the client that supports the greatest number of features for Exchange and is generally used as the default desktop messaging and collaboration client for companies that deploy Exchange.

Installing Outlook

Walkthrough

To install Outlook 2000 on a client machine, log on with an account that has privileges for installing software and run setup.exe from the compact disk or from a distribution point (a shared folder on the network where the Outlook installation files are stored). This starts the Welcome to Microsoft Outlook 2000 Wizard (Figure 6.1).

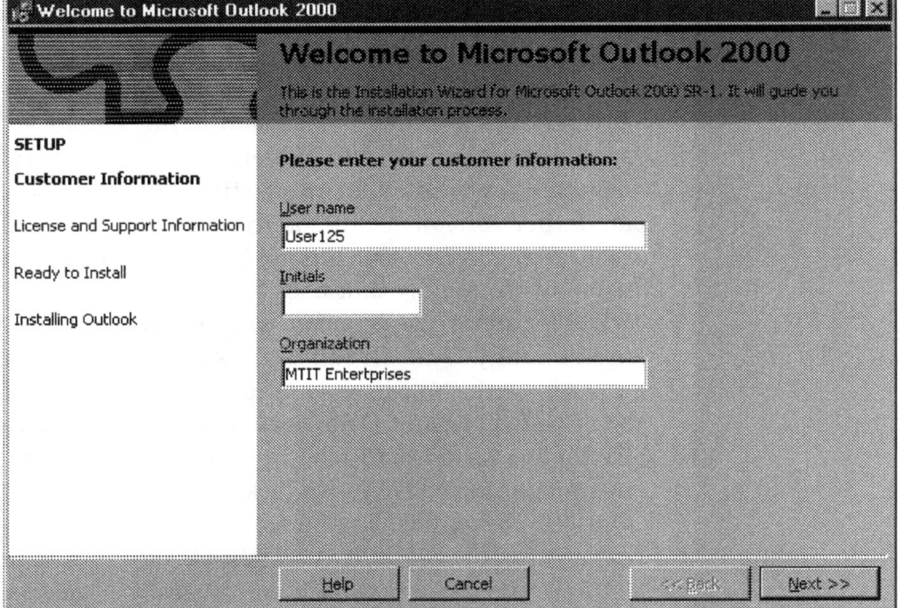

Figure 6.1
Running setup.exe to install Outlook 2000.

TIP

You can also perform unattended installations of Microsoft Outlook using answer files or automatically deploy Outlook using software such as Microsoft SMS. These deployment scenarios are beyond the scope of this book because our primary focus is on Exchange.

Specify your user name and organization and client Next. Then read the EULA, accept it, and click Next. You now have a choice of either accepting the default installation options by clicking Install Now or choosing to customize the installation by specifying which components you want to install and where to install them by selecting Customize (Figure 6.2). We'll chose the default option Install Now and proceed.

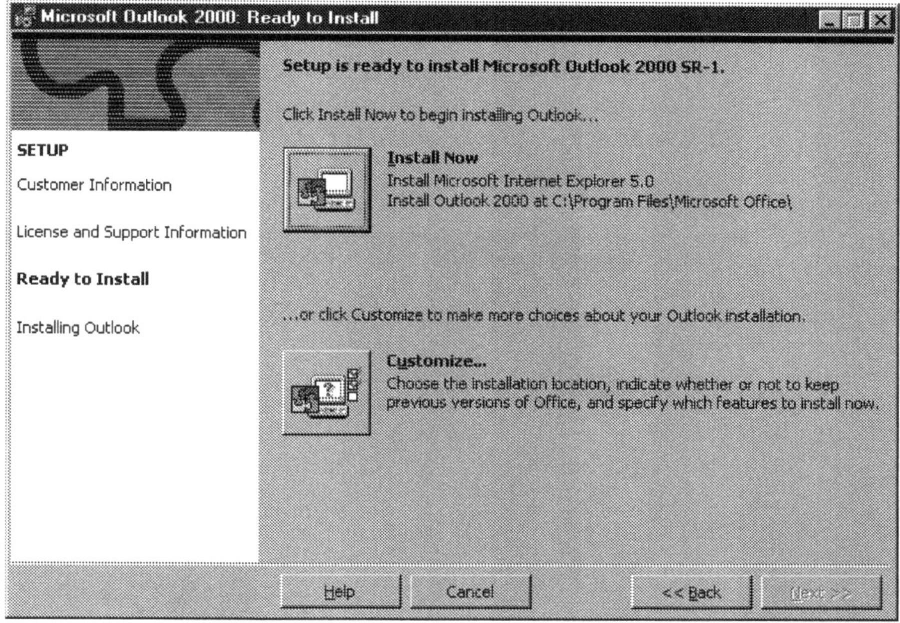

Figure 6.2
Choosing a typical or custom installation

Windows Installer will then proceed to install and configure Outlook on the client computer. Once this is finished, Outlook will be installed but is not specifically configured for the user who will be using it—we'll look at that next.

NOTE

In our walkthrough, we are installing and configuring Outlook 2000 as a new mail client; there are no previous mail clients on the machine. If there is an existing mail client, Outlook offers the option of importing the mail, list of contacts, and other information from the existing client into Outlook.

Configuring Outlook for Exchange

Walkthrough

Having installed Outlook on a user's client machine, we still have to configure it to connect with the user's mailbox on the appropriate Exchange server on our network. Let's assume this particular client machine (desk125.mtit.com) is used primarily by Jane Smith (jsmith@mtit.com) of the marketing department of MTIT Enterprises.

Log on as Jane Smith and double-click on the Microsoft Outlook icon on the desktop to begin the configuration process. Windows Installer starts and a moment later the Outlook 2000 Startup Wizard appears (Figure 6.3).

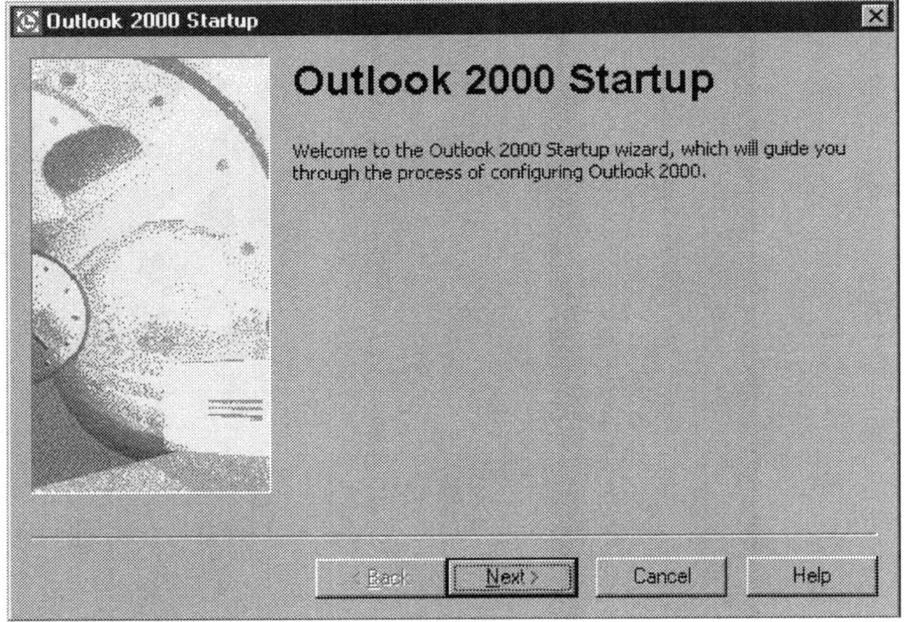

Figure 6.3 Configuring Outlook for a specific user

The next screen offers a choice of three different ways to configure Outlook with regard to the backend messaging service it will use (Figure 6.4).

- *Internet Only* is intended mainly for users who work from home and connect to a mail server using standard Internet protocols such as SMTP, POP3, and IMAP4. Selecting this option starts the Internet Connection Wizard that lets you specify the DNS names of the mail servers you want to connect to and your Internet mail account information (username and password for each mail server). These mail servers could be Exchange servers, UNIX Sendmail servers or some other kind of Internet messaging servers. If you are deploying Outlook in a corporate setting with Exchange, you will want to use the Corporate or Workgroup option, which is discussed next.

- *Corporate or Workgroup* lets you connect your Outlook client machines directly to your Exchange server and is the best choice for clients that have direct LAN or high-speed dedicated WAN connections with your Exchange servers. This is the service option we will choose in our walkthrough as we continue below.
- *No E-mail* is an option provided for users who plan to use Outlook as a stand-alone scheduling client on machines not networked or connected to the Internet. Or you could use it if you already had some other mail client on your machine and wanted to keep it and use Outlook only for scheduling and other purposes.

As mentioned above, we'll select Corporate or Workgroup as our mail service option and click Next to continue configuring Outlook.

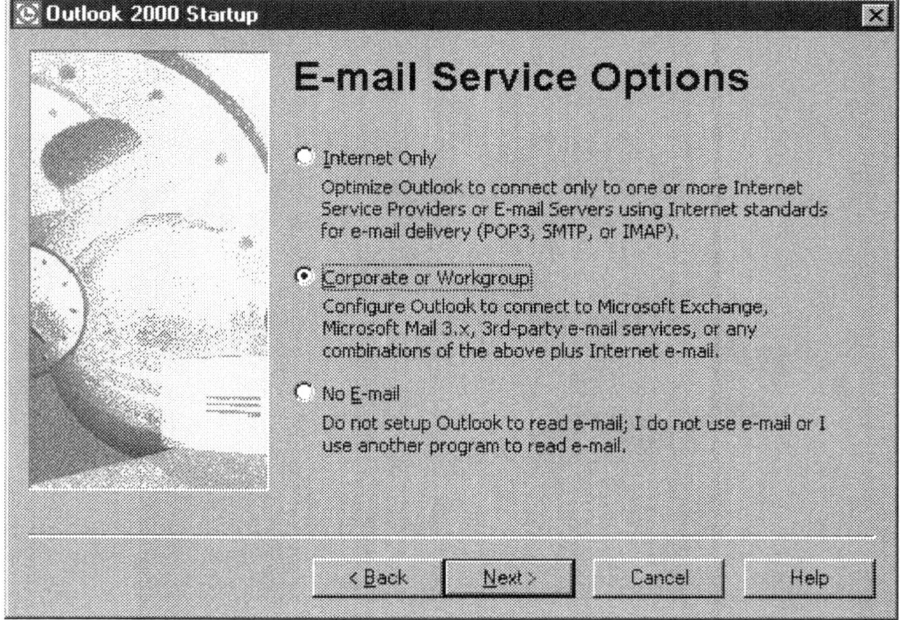

Figure 6.4 Specifying your back-end messaging service

The wizard now asks you to specify whether to connect your Outlook client to an Exchange server, to a messaging service on the Internet, or both (Figure 6.5). We'll select only Exchange Server here. If the user had additional (noncompany) Internet mail accounts, you could select the Internet E-mail option as well for configuring these.

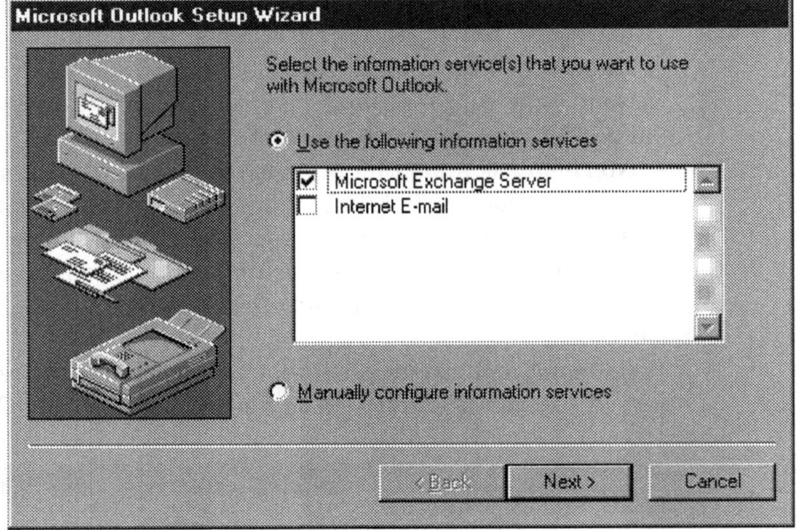

Figure 6.5 Selecting Microsoft Exchange Server as your information service

Next (Figure 6.6) enter the name of the Exchange server that the user's mailbox has been created on (in this case, Box14) and the name of the mailbox belonging to the user, which is just the alias of the user (in this case, jsmith for Jane Smith).

TIP

If you can't remember on which Exchange server you created a user's mailbox, start ADUC, open the Properties Sheet for the user, switch to the Exchange General tab, and look at the Exchange server specified within the Mailbox Store textbox.

Next you'll be asked whether the user travels with the computer. Select No for desktop machines that are permanently connected to the Exchange server through the LAN.

You'll now be presented with summary information telling you that Microsoft Outlook will be configured with the following two services: Microsoft Exchange Server and Outlook Address Book.

Outlook will now start (Figure 6.7). Notice the striking similarity between the Outlook 2000 interface and the Exchange 2000 version of OWA shown in Figure 3.6. Notice also the differences: Outlook 2000 includes Tasks and Notes views, and OWA does not.

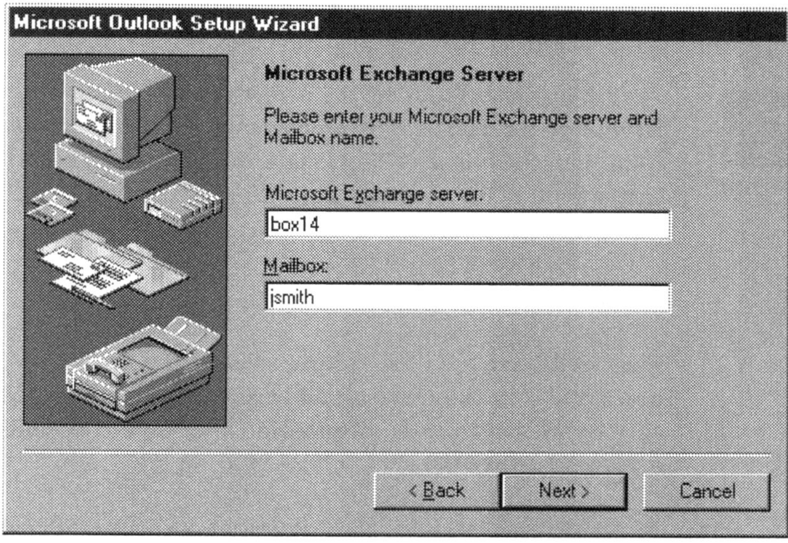

Figure 6.6
Specifying the user's mailbox and the Exchange server on which it is located.

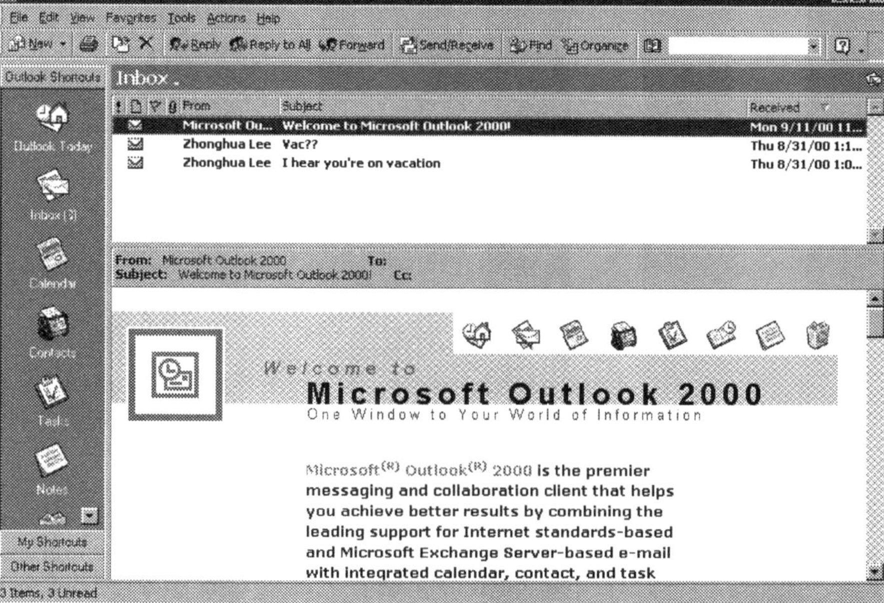

Figure 6.7
The Outlook 2000 user interface.

Using Outlook

Walkthrough

Let's play with Outlook for a few minutes to see how it interacts with Exchange as a backend information service. This is not meant to be a complete overview of Outlook's many features; see any good book on Outlook 2000 for more information.

Address Book

First of all, click on the Address Book icon on the toolbar to open it. Figure 6.8 shows the Outlook address book, which by default in the Corporate or Workgroup configuration displays the contents of the Global Address List (GAL).

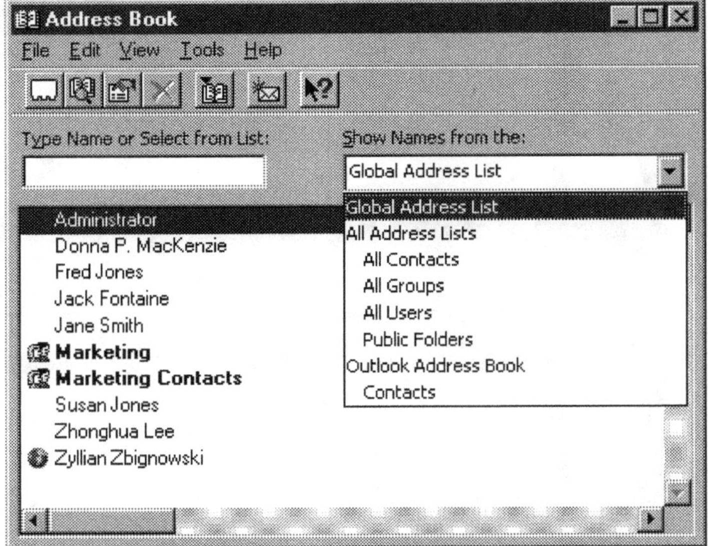

Figure 6.8 The Outlook address book displaying the GAL and other address lists.

Figure 6.8 actually shows the Show Names drop-down listbox so you can see the various address lists available. If you select the All Groups address list, for instance, the address book will display only mail-enabled groups like Marketing and Marketing Contacts and hide everything else. You can also create custom address lists in Exchange to make it easier for users to browse the GAL when it contains thousands of recipients. We'll cover address lists in more detail in Chapter 7.

The GAL is a list of all mailbox- and mail-enabled users, mail-enabled contacts, and mail-enabled security and distribution groups in your Exchange organization. In other words, it's a list of everything in AD that can receive mail (you can, of course, send mail to users and other objects that are not listed in AD simply by entering a one-off, or one-time email address for the recipient in the To box of the Untitled-Message window in Outlook). There are other kinds of address lists besides the GAL, including default ones and ones you create. This is covered in Chapter 7.

Let's see what information we can display in Outlook for Fred Jones, another employee in the marketing division of MTIT Enterprises. Having the address book open, you could simply double-click on Fred Jones as displayed; but if you had thousands of recipients, you would first have to find his name. The easiest way to do that is to type Fred into the Find a Contact box (just to the right of the Address Book icon on the toolbar) and press Enter, and Outlook will search AD to find information on all users whose name begins with Fred (you should type at least three letters into the Find a Contact box to speed the search process). Once you've found the correct Fred, you can double-click on his name to open his Outlook Property Sheet (Figure 6.9).

Figure 6.9 Information on Exchange recipient Fred Jones as displayed in Outlook.

Note the various types of information displayed concerning Fred, including his address and telephone information, group membership, email address, and so on.

By clicking the Add to Personal Address Book button, you can add Fred as a contact within the local list of Outlook contacts the user can maintain on the client machine. These local (client-side) contacts can be displayed in the address book by selecting Contacts under Outlook Address Book, shown in Figure 6.8.

Groups and Group Membership

You can also display information about mail-enabled groups in Outlook. To do this for the Marketing group, which we created in Chapter 5, open the address book, select All Groups in the Show Names listbox, and double-click on Marketing. This opens the Marketing Properties box (Figure 6.10), which displays the membership of the group (in this case, four mailbox-enabled users), which other groups Marketing itself belongs to, and the email addresses for the group. Once again you can add this group to your local machine's address book, if desired.

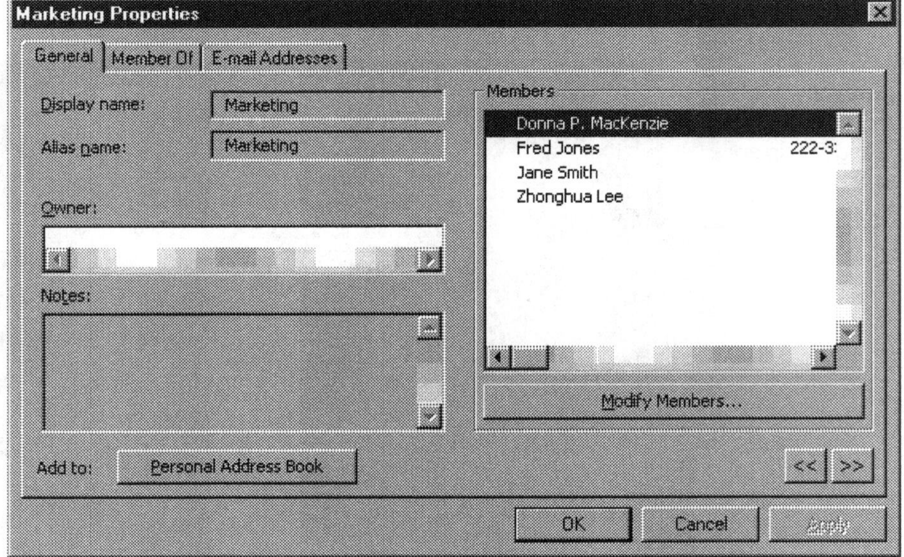

Figure 6.10 Displaying the members of a mail-enabled group.

There's something more we need to say about the list of members displayed on the General tab shown in Figure 6.10. Recall from the previous chapter, that when you run the Exchange Tasks Wizard on a mail-enabled group, one of the options you can select from the list of available tasks is Hide Membership. This option hides the membership of a group from users' address books. You can test this by opening ADUC, right-clicking on the Marketing group object within the Marketing Users OU, selecting Exchange Tasks from the shortcut menu, and selecting Hide Membership from the list of available tasks in the wizard. Now open the Properties Sheet for the Marketing group from the Outlook address book and notice that the list of members that was visible (Figure 6.10) is now empty. Rerun the Exchange Tasks Wizard and select Unhide Membership to undo your actions. These changes take effect immediately and do not require the Outlook user to log on or off.

Open the Marketing Properties box shown in Figure 6.10 on the client and click Modify Members. Try to remove a user from the group and you'll discover (if you're logged on as ordinary user Jane Smith) that you can't—you have insufficient permission to perform this action. We'll look at permissions in Chapter 13 and see how to rectify this problem.

Configuring Delivery Services

When you choose the Corporate or Workgroup option for configuring Outlook, you are automatically choosing to have users' mail delivered and stored in their mailboxes, which are located on your Exchange servers. There are other delivery options you can configure for users' mail.

Personal Folders

In this scenario mail is stored in a special file located on the user's client computer. This file has the extension .pst and is generally referred to as a Personal Folders, or PST, file. PST files are commonly used when the Internet Only option was selected instead of the Corporate or Workgroup option. This allows users to connect to their Internet mail server and download their mail to their local machine so that they can read and reply to it while disconnected from the Internet, thus saving connection time charges. However, PST files are not a good idea in the corporate environment because it means that users' mail is stored on their local machines, which are not as secure as backend servers and are generally not backed up regularly. Furthermore, PST files tend to get corrupted from time to time and need to be repaired using the Inbox Repair Tool scanpst.exe.

TIP

To determine if a particular machine with Outlook installed is configured to use PST files, select View → Folder List to see if there is a node labeled Personal Folders in the folders tree. Alternatively, select Tools → Services to see if Personal Folders is listed as an installed information service.

Offline Folders

This delivery option causes mail to be stored in the user's mailbox on the Exchange server but also synchronized with (copied to) a special Offline Folders, or OST, file having the extension .ost and located on the client computer. This allows users to view their mail and compose new messages and replies while disconnected from the Exchange server. This is a good option to implement if your users travel a lot and have Outlook installed on their laptops.

To change the delivery options for Outlook mail and perform other advanced configuration of messaging services, either

- Select Tools → Services from the Outlook menu bar
- Right-click on the Microsoft Outlook icon on the desktop and select Properties

Either method opens the MS Exchange Settings Properties box (Figure 6.11). The Services tab that is displayed by default lists the different information services (message delivery services) currently configured on the client machine. In a default Corporate or Workgroup installation, the two services that are installed are Microsoft Exchange Server and Outlook Address Book, but by clicking Add you can add and configure any of the following additional information services:

- Internet E-mail
- Microsoft LDAP Directory
- Microsoft Mail
- Microsoft Outlook Support for Lotus cc:Mail
- Personal Address Book
- Personal Folders

The Delivery tab (Figure 6.12) indicates where incoming mail is currently delivered to, which in this case is Jane Smith's mailbox. Here we can verify our earlier statement that the default delivery setting for Outlook when configured with the Corporate or Workgroup option, is server-based mailboxes.

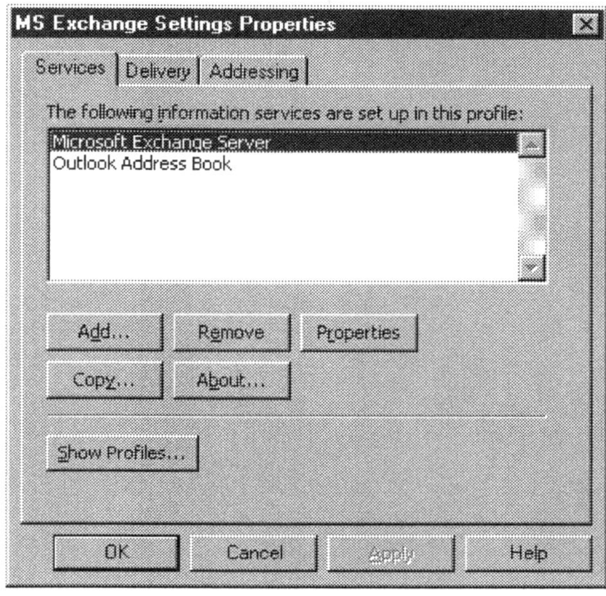

Figure 6.11 Services tab of the MS Exchange Settings Properties box.

If, in addition, you had PST files configured on the client, you could select from the deliver New Mail drop-down listbox whether incoming mail should be delivered to the server-based mailbox on the Exchange server or to the Inbox folder located within the local PST file on the client machine.

The processing order displayed in the second listbox deserves some attention. There are two information services currently configured to deliver mail to the Outlook client: Microsoft Exchange Transport and Microsoft Exchange Remote Transport. The first of these is the normal connection-based LAN messaging transport, which delivers mail immediately to the client when connected to the Exchange server through the LAN. The second transport is when Outlook is configured to access the Exchange server using Remote Mail, an option that allows Outlook to use a dial-up networking (DUN) connection. Remote Mail, when configured, enables Outlook to automatically connect according to a predefined schedule over a phone line to a remote Exchange server, collect mail, and hang up. This can be useful in small remote branch offices or for users working from home or traveling.

By default, Outlook tries for a direct (LAN) connection to the Exchange server first; if this fails, it attempts a remote mail connection (if configured). You would change the order of these transports if Remote Mail was your main delivery option.

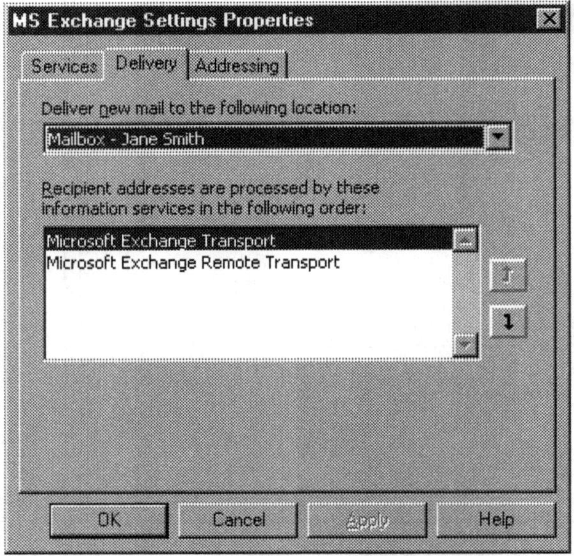

Figure 6.12 Delivery tab of the MS Exchange Settings Properties box.

The final Addressing tab (Figure 6.13) of the MS Exchange Settings Properties box lets you specify the address list displayed in the Outlook address book when Outlook starts up. By default, this is the GAL discussed previously, but this is usually overkill in a large company because it contains too many users. To see how this works, select All Groups in the Show This Address List First listbox, click OK to close the dialog box, then start Outlook and open the address book from the toolbar to see which address list it now uses by default.

The Addressing tab also displays where users' personal contacts are stored (in Outlook's Contacts folder) and the order in which names are checked against address lists when sending mail to recipients (first the GAL on the Exchange server, then, if necessary, the user's local Outlook Contacts list). These settings should normally be left as they are.

Returning to the Services tab, select the Microsoft Exchange Server information service and click Properties. This opens a new Microsoft Exchange Server dialog box (Figure 6.14) that allows advanced configuration of the Exchange Server information service. Here we can see the specific mailbox (jsmith) and Exchange server (Box14) used by Outlook for this user. By selecting Manual Control Connection State and Work Offline and Use Dial-up Networking, you can configure your client to use Remote Mail. Other tabs allow further configuration of how your Outlook client interacts with the Exchange server, but further configuring of Remote Mail is beyond the scope of this book.

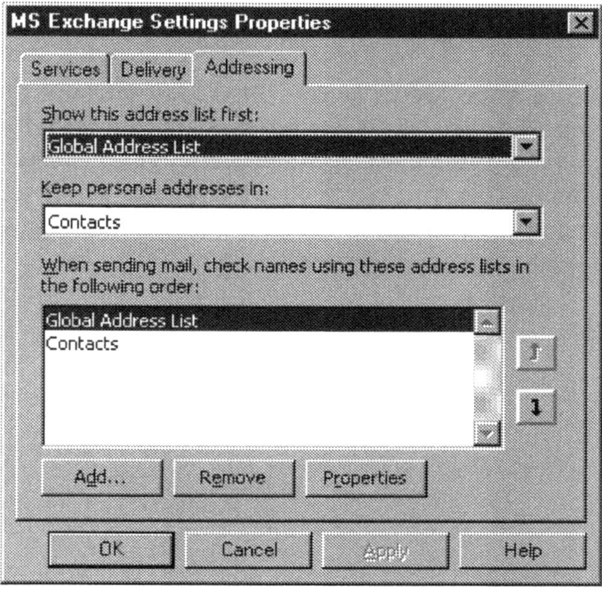

Figure 6.13 Addressing tab of the MS Exchange Settings Properties box.

Figure 6.14 Configuring the Microsoft Exchange Server information service.

Summary

In this chapter, we've looked at using Outlook 2000 as a client for Exchange. Outlook 2000 has many advanced features that makes it the client of choice for most organizations, but it can be complex to deploy, use, and maintain. In the next chapter, we'll look at a feature of Exchange called *address lists* that makes it simpler for Outlook users to address messages to recipients.

CHAPTER 7

Address Lists

In the previous chapter we looked at Outlook as an Exchange client and showed how the Outlook address book displays the contents of the GAL and other default address lists. We mentioned that it's usual in a large company to create custom address lists to make things easier for users when they are browsing the address book for a recipient. In this chapter we examine more closely the idea of address lists and how to manage and create them.

There are five walkthroughs in this chapter:

- Creating a new address list
- Updating address lists across an enterprise or domain
- Rebuilding an address list
- Modifying an address list
- Configuring Outlook to use address lists

During our discussion of address lists we will also explain the function of the Recipient Update Service and how to manage it.

Address Lists

Address lists are a way of logically grouping recipients together so that they display as one collection in client address books. The goal is to make it simpler for users to find recipients in their address books, particularly in a large company when there may be thousands of recipients to choose from.

There are many different criteria you might choose for grouping recipients together, for example:

- *By location.* For example, you might create one address list for employees in Vancouver, another for those in Seattle, and so on. This makes it simpler for employees to find recipients in their own location to send them mail.
- *By department.* Create one address list for the accounting department, one for marketing, and so on.
- *By business function.* Create one list for managers, one for temporary employees, and so on.
- **By type.** Create one list for users, one for meeting rooms, and so on.

Default Address Lists

When you install Exchange in an enterprise, several default address lists are created to make life easier for you. These include:

- *Global address list.* This is the master list containing all mail-enabled users, groups, and contacts within your Exchange organization.
- *Offline address list.* This is a master list of addresses that can be downloaded to Microsoft Outlook clients that have been configured to use offline folders.
- *All users.* A list of all mailbox- and mail-enabled users in your Exchange organization.
- *All groups.* A list of all mail-enabled security and distribution groups in your organization.
- *All contacts.* A list of all mail-enabled contacts in your organization.
- *Public folders.* A list of all public folders in your organization.

If you look back for a moment to Figure 6.8 you can see the address book open in Outlook 2000 and the various default address lists displayed within it.

Custom Address Lists

If these default address lists are insufficient for your purposes (and they usually are), you can easily create your own custom address lists. You can configure Outlook to use these address lists in various ways, edit lists, and perform other administrative actions with regard to them. The remainder of this chapter will walk you through some of these procedures.

NOTE

Offline address books are covered in Chapter 8, entitled Offline Folders.

Create a New Address List

Walkthrough

It's time to take another peek at System Manager, one of the two Exchange administration tools most used in daily administration of Exchange (the other being ADUC, which was introduced in Chapter 3). We'll cover the general details of System Manager in Chapter 9, but for now we'll just use it to create and manage address lists.

Start System Manager by selecting Start → Programs → Microsoft Exchange → System Manager. In the console tree (left pane), expand Recipients node and select the All Address Lists node (Figure 7.1).

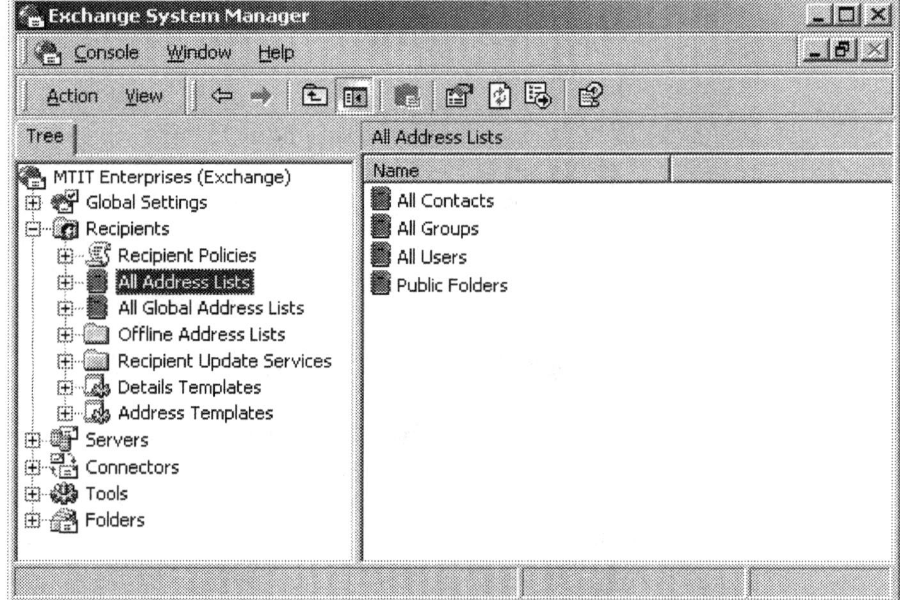

Figure 7.1 Displaying address lists using System Manager.

Right-click on All Address Lists and select New → Address List to display the Create Exchange Address List dialog box. We'll create a new address list called Marketing Department to which we'll add all our mailbox-enabled marketing employees, so type Marketing Department into the text box (Figure 7.2).

Now we need to set filter rules so that our address list will display only the recipients we desire. Click the Filter Rules button to open the Find Exchange Recipients dialog box. Note that this box is the same Find box you can use with ADUC to search Active Directory for user and group objects, computers, printers, and other types of directory objects.

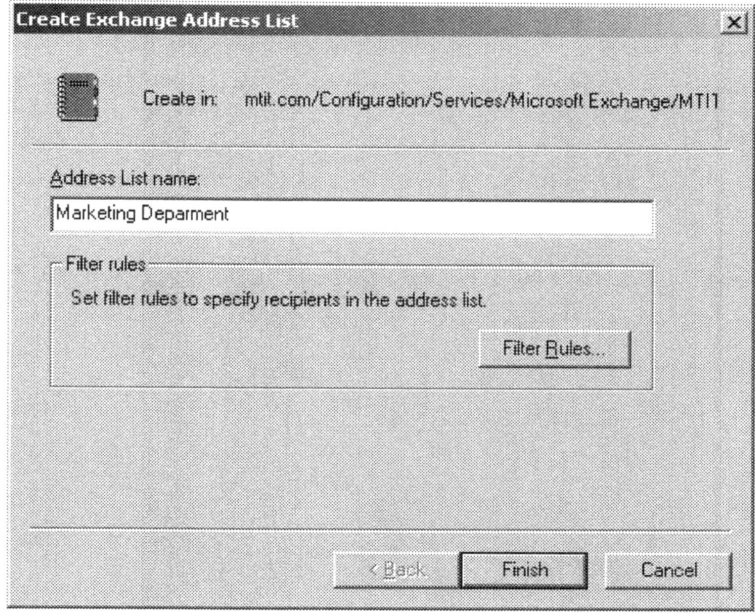

Figure 7.2 Creating an address list for the Marketing department.

In other words, installing Exchange has simply enhanced this tool by providing an additional Find function for finding directory objects that are Exchange recipients.

Leave the Find listbox set to Exchange Recipients and also leave the In listbox set to the domain mtit.com (because there is only one domain in our testbed forest). On the General tab, deselect all the checkboxes except the first one, Users With Exchange Mailbox, because we plan to have only marketing-department employees in our address list and all these employees are mailbox-enabled users (Figure 7.3). Note that public folders can also be included in address lists because they are another form of recipient (you can post messages to them).

Select the Storage tab next (Figure 7.4). This tab gives you the option of specifying which Exchange servers or mailbox stores you choose your address list recipients from. You can select one of the following options:

- *Mailboxes on any server.* This is the default setting and searches all Exchange servers in your organization for recipients that have the criteria specified on the other two tabs.
- *Mailboxes on this server.* If you have only one Exchange server in a particular location and are creating address lists based on location, choose this option to search the specified server for the desired recipi-

ents. Only one Exchange server can be selected here, so it's either all or one as far as address lists are concerned.

- *Mailboxes in this mailbox store.* If you have several mailbox stores configured on your Exchange servers, you can select a specific mailbox store to populate your address list with recipients. All mailbox stores on all servers within your organization are displayed, but only one store can be selected for populating your list.

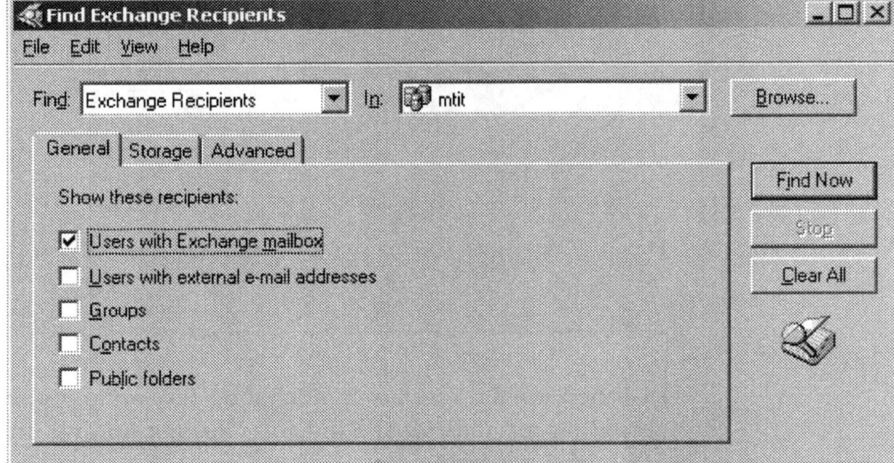

Figure 7.3 Specifying the type of recipients for the new address list.

We'll leave the Storage tab at its default setting (I've previously created several more mailbox-enabled Marketing users on the second Exchange server Box15 and want to be able to include these recipients in my Marketing Department address list).

The Advanced tab is where the fun begins. Because we want to include only users who belong to the marketing department in our address list, we need to specify this condition here. If you open a user's Properties Sheet for a moment, you'll see that a user's department attribution is specified on the Organization tab, so it goes without saying that the Department field on the Organization tab must contain the word *marketing* for every marketing employee if we are to successfully create our address list filter. This is another reason it is always good to insert the various information fields on users' Properties Sheets soon after you create those users.

Select the Field control on the Advanced tab to display a drop-down menu of recipient object types. Select User and then Department from this menu. This inserts with the word *department* into the textbox below the Field control.

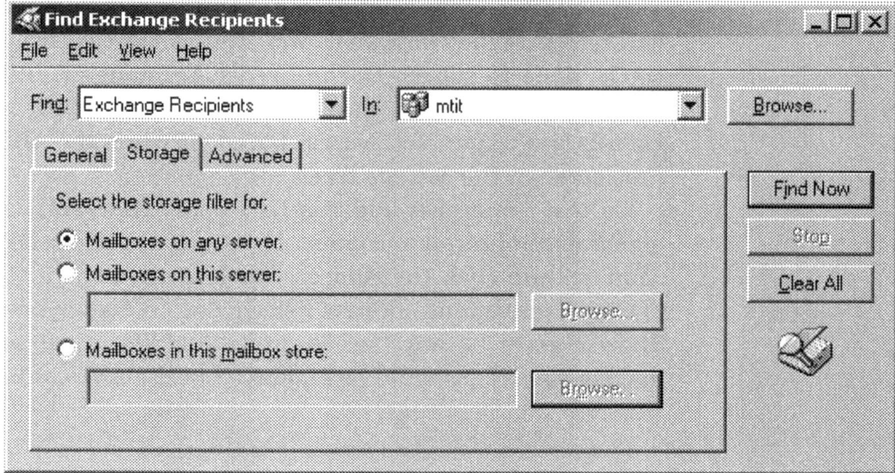

Figure 7.4
Specifying the source of address list recipients.

Change the Condition field to Is (Exactly) and type "Marketing" (no quotes) into the Value field beside it. We haven't created our filter criteria yet—click Add to add our condition to the filter criteria list shown in (Figure 7.5).

If you make a mistake in creating a filter criterion on the Advanced tab, double-click on the criterion and edit it, and then add it again to the list. You can add as many criteria as you like on the Advanced tab, but it's best to keep things simple.

Figure 7.5
Creating filter criteria.

If you like, click Find Now to display the recipients that your filter will select. Make changes to your filter, if necessary, and click OK when you're done to return to the Create Exchange Address List box. Then click Finish to create your new address list, which will show up in the Details (right) pane of System Manager when the All Address Lists node is selected in the console tree.

To test your new address list, open Microsoft Outlook on a client machine configured to connect to your Exchange server (see the previous chapter) and click the Address Book icon on the toolbar. The new Marketing Department address list should be displayed when you click the Show Names listbox (see Figure 6.8). When you select this list only, marketing users should be displayed in the address book.

Updating Address Lists Across an Enterprise or Domain

Walkthrough

If you have a number of Exchange servers in a large domain or a forest of several domains, changes to an address list may not be updated immediately across the organization. This means users who connect to certain Exchange servers for their mail may not immediately see the changes in the version of the address list used by their local server.

There are two ways you can deal with this: wait for the update process to occur naturally or force it manually. Updating of Exchange address lists across a domain or organization is handled by the Recipient Update Service (see the Backgrounder).

To update address list information manually across a domain, select the Recipient Update Services node under the Recipients container in System Manager and right-click on the instance of the Recipient Update Service for the desired domain and select Update Now (Figure 7.6). A background process starts the update process.

To update address list information across the entire enterprise, right-click on Recipient Update Service (Enterprise Configuration) and select Update Now.

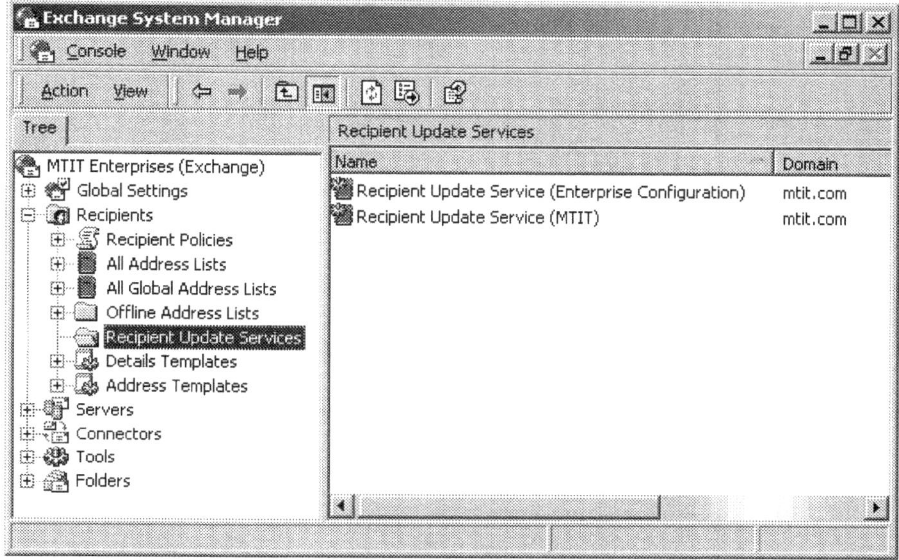

Figure 7.6 Managing the Recipient Update Service.

BACKGROUNDER

Recipient Update Service

The Recipient Update Service *is an Exchange service that updates recipient objects in a domain with specific kinds of information. The service is used by Exchange to replicate address list membership and email addresses across an organization so that all Exchange servers have the most current information. There is one instance of the service governing replication across the whole enterprise, and separate instances for each domain within which Exchange servers are installed. You can view these services by expanding the Recipients container in System Manager and selecting Recipient Update Services in the console tree.*

Exchange administrators can schedule when this service operates to handle traffic generated by this service. To see how to do this, right-click on an instance of the Recipient Update Service and select Properties and change the Update Interval on the General tab from its default value of Always Run to a different schedule (or create a custom schedule). If you have large address lists and many recipients in your organization, make sure the update schedule you specify ensures that all updates can be completed before the next update cycle begins.

There are other ways you can manage the Recipient Update Service. Using the General tab of the Properties Sheet for the service, you can specify a different Exchange server and domain controller to be used by the service for a particular domain. The domain listed on the General tab is the domain serviced by the selected instance of the service, the Exchange server listed is the server that generates and updates address lists for that domain, and the domain controller listed is the domain controller which the Exchange server connects to in order to generate and update address lists. To move the selected service to a different Exchange server or specify a new domain controller, you should first disable the service by selecting Never Run for the Update Interval. Make sure you change it from Never Run to some other update interval when you have finished the process or your address lists will never be updated in the selected domain. It's generally best if the service is run on an Exchange server that is also a domain controller within the selected domain in order to minimize network traffic.

You must have one instance of the Recipient Update Service configured for every domain in your enterprise that has recipients, even domains that have no Exchange server in them. To create a new Recipient Update Service for a domain, first run setup.exe for Exchange using the `/domainprep` *switch on a Windows 2000 server in the domain where there is no Exchange server (the DomainPrep utility is discussed in Chapter 25). Then right-click the Recipient Update Services container in System Manager and select New → Recipient Update Service. Specify the domain you want the service to manage, the Exchange server that it will run on, and the domain controller the Exchange server will connect to for recipient information.*

By the way, if you're wondering how the Recipient Update Service can be an Exchange service but not be visible in the Services node of Computer Management, the Recipient Update Service is actually a part of the Microsoft Exchange System Attendant service, an umbrella service for a number of Exchange-related automated self-management tasks.

Rebuilding an Address List

Walkthrough

Membership in address lists can sometimes get out of sync in a large organization. This typically happens when many changes have been made to the list from different locations. If necessary, you can rebuild address list membership across a domain or the entire enterprise by right-clicking on the appropriate instance of the Recipient Update Service and selecting Rebuild. You should do this during off-peak hours because the rebuild process is time and resource intensive.

Modifying an Address List

There are several specific tasks you can perform on a selected address list. We'll illustrate this using the Marketing Department list we created earlier.

Select the All Address Lists node in the Recipients container of System Manager, right-click on the Marketing Department list, and select Properties. The General tab displays in a condensed logical notation the filter you have configured for this list. Click Modify to change your filter or Preview to display the list membership based on the currently configured filter. Remove deletes your current filter if you need to reconfigure the list from scratch.

The Security tab lets you manage the permissions associated with the list. We'll cover permissions in more detail in Chapter 13, but for now just select Authenticated Users in the top listbox and note that these users have List Contents permission for the address list, enabling them to view the contents of the list. The grayed-out checkbox indicates that this permission is inherited rather than directly applied to the object. Click Advanced and you'll see that the permissions for Authenticated Users are actually more detailed.

Other tasks you can perform on address lists using System Manager are renaming a list and deleting it.

Configuring Outlook to Use Address Lists

Once address lists are created and configured on the server side, they also need to be configured on the client side. If you are using Microsoft Outlook configured to run in Corporate or Workgroup Users mode, your users can have access to the various address lists you create on your Exchange servers.

Start Outlook and select Tools → Services to open the Services dialog box (see Figure 6.13). Using this dialog box, you can specify the following client-side address settings:

- *Show this address list first.* By default, the GAL is the first one displayed for Outlook users. Users can select a different address list from the drop-down list, if desired.

- *Keep personal addresses in.* This is the personal address book that users can store their personal address in, which by default is the Contacts folder in Outlook.
- *When sending mail, check names using these address lists in the following order.* If a user simply types a name or nickname into the To field when sending a new message, this listbox specifies the order in which address lists are checked to resolve the name of the recipient into its associated email address. You should leave the GAL at the top of the list because users sometimes add the addresses of internal recipients to their Contacts folder and then send mail using this address. If the recipient changes department or location in the company, the new address will be updated in the GAL on the servers but the user may not be aware of this and so will not update the Contacts folder. The result is that mail sent to the recipient will bounce back.

Summary

In this chapter, we've looked at how to create and manage address lists, a feature of Exchange that makes it simpler for Outlook clients to address mail to recipients. We have covered only online address lists. In Chapter 8, we'll examine *offline address lists* and provide more details about configuring Outlook for offline use.

CHAPTER 8

Offline Folders and Address Lists

In the previous chapter we looked at creating and managing address lists in Exchange. These address lists enable permanently connected Outlook clients to more easily browse logical subsets of the GAL.

But what if you have some Outlook clients configured for offline use? In this case, you need to create and manage offline address lists for these users. This chapter looks at administering offline address lists and begins with an overview of how to configure Outlook clients for offline use. There are four walkthroughs in this chapter:

- Configuring offline folders
- Synchronizing offline folders
- Configuring Outlook to use an offline address list
- Creating and configuring offline address lists

Offline Folders

Offline folders are a feature of Outlook 2000 that allows a copy of server-based mail folders to be kept on the user's client machine. Then, when the client machine is disconnected from the server (for instance, when a laptop is removed from its docking station), the user has full access to his or her mail and can read it, reply to it, compose new messages, and so on.

Offline folders were automatically configured for your machine if you answered yes to the question "Do you travel with this computer?" when you ran `Setup.exe` to install Outlook on your machine. You also have the option of enabling offline folders after installing Outlook, which is something we will do below. Once we've configured offline folders, we'll look at how to create and maintain offline address lists.

NOTE

Offline folders are included as a feature of Windows 2000, but Outlook 2000 can implement offline folders even on a machine running Windows NT 4.0. In Chapter 6, we installed Outlook 2000 on a machine called Desk125 that was running Windows NT 4.0 Workstation, and we'll use this for our walkthrough here as well.

Configuring Offline Folders

Walkthrough

We'll start by enabling and configuring offline folders on a machine running Outlook 2000. The end result will be to create an offline folder file, or OST file, having the .ost extension on the local machine.

Start Outlook 2000 and from the menu select Tools → Synchronize → Offline Folder Settings. A dialog box will appear, saying "You must configure an offline folder file before you can use this folder offline. Would you like to configure an offline folder file now?" Answer yes to continue the process. If you didn't receive this message but instead see a box like the one shown in Figure 8.2, you already have offline folders configured on your machine.

Next you'll see the Offline Folder File Settings box (Figure 8.1), which specifies the location of the OST file that will be created. You can leave this set to the default location or change it to something else, if desired (it's probably best to leave it set at the default location within the user's local profile on the machine).

By default, the OST file is compressed using Compressible encryption, a format that supports both encryption to secure the file's contents and compression to minimize disk storage space. If you want greater security because of company mail policy or multiple users having access to the client machine, choose Best Encryption instead.

Figure 8.1 Creating an offline folder (OST) file in Outlook.

Click OK and accept the prompt to create the OST file on your local machine. Once this file has been created, the Offline Folder Settings box appears (Figure 8.2), allowing you to configure how you want this feature to work on your machine.

You can select and deselect folders within your server-based mailbox to specify which folders will have their contents mirrored on the local machine using offline folders. You can also configure filters to specify criteria by which messages within a folder will be downloaded for offline viewing. By clicking the Download Options button, you can also specify message size limits for downloaded messages.

Select the checkbox that specifies that the offline address book should be downloaded. There are other options you can choose with the Settings button, but we'll do that later.

Once you're done, verify that offline folders are enabled as follows: select Tools → Services to open the Services box, select Microsoft Exchange Server and click Properties, switch to the Advanced tab, and verify that Enable Offline Use is selected.

TIP

If you need to reconfigure offline folder settings later, just select Tools → Options → to open the Options dialog box, switch to the Mail Services tab, and click the Offline Folder Settings button. You'll see the box shown in Figure 8.2.

Figure 8.2 Configuring offline folder settings.

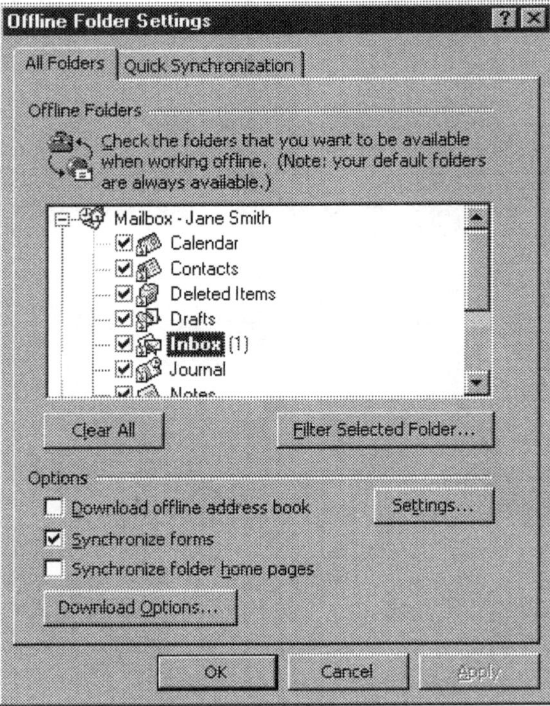

TIP

You can tell Outlook is running in offline mode when the shortcuts in the outlook bar (the bar on the left) have the up–down arrow symbol meaning "offline" superimposed on them:

Synchronizing Offline Folders

Walkthrough

Once you've enabled and configured offline folders for Outlook, you need to synchronize them with your server-based mailbox folders. You can do this either manually or automatically.

Manual synchronization can be performed by either:

- Selecting Tools → Synchronize and choosing a synchronization option.
- Pressing the F9 function key, which synchronizes all folders.

Try initiating manual synchronization now by pressing F9, and you will see the action being performed in the bottom right corner of Outlook's status bar.

Automatic synchronization is preferable, and it can be configured in several ways. Select Tools → Options to open the Options dialog box and then switch to the Mail Services tab (Figure 8.3). Make sure the option Enable Offline Access is selected (you can disable offline folders any time by deselecting this setting) and choose one or more of the following synchronization options:

- *When online, synchronize all folders upon exiting.* If you choose this option, every time you exit and log off Outlook, your offline folders are synchronized with your server-based mailbox folders.
- *When online, automatically synchronize all offline folders every n minutes.* Here you can specify a time interval for scheduling when synchronization should occur while connected to the network where your Exchange server is located.
- *When offline, automatically synchronize offline folders every n minutes.* If you are disconnected from the network where your Exchange server is located, selecting this option will cause Outlook to connect periodically to synchronize offline folders. This is useful for dial-up clients where connection charges need to be minimized.

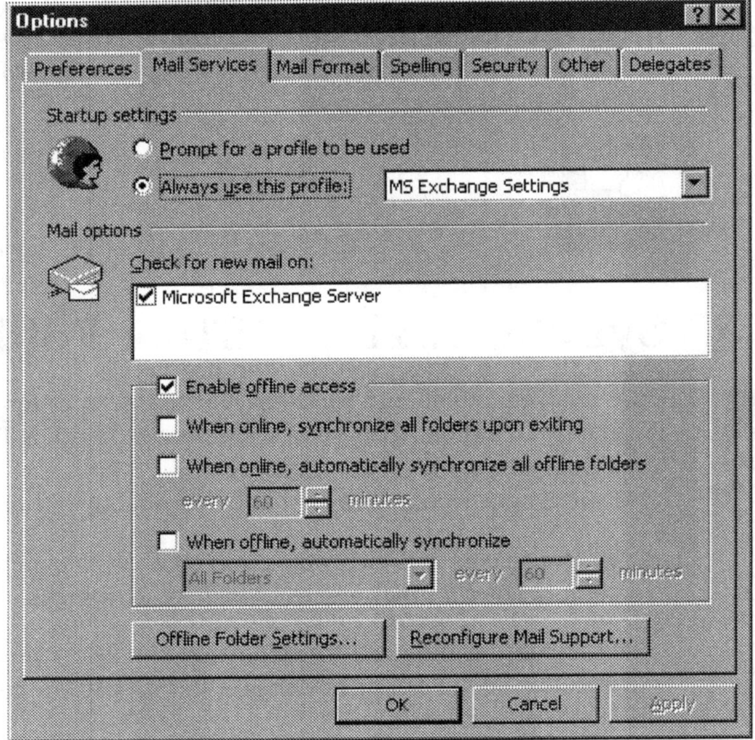

Figure 8.3 Configuring synchronization settings for offline folders.

Offline Address Lists

Exchange supports two different kinds of address lists: standard (online) and offline. In the previous chapter, we looked at how to create and manage standard address lists, which are designed to be used by Outlook clients that are permanently connected to the Exchange server by a LAN or dedicated WAN connection.

In contrast, offline address lists are designed for Outlook clients configured to use offline folders. Outlook can download offline address lists to users' client machines so that they can use these lists for finding and sending mail to recipients while disconnected from the network where Exchange resides. Offline address lists are only available to users when Outlook is configured to be used offline.

In the remainder of this chapter, we'll look at how to create and manage offline address lists in Exchange and how to download them to Outlook clients.

NOTE

It's important to know another difference between online and offline address lists: even though you can create as many offline address lists as you like in Exchange, each Outlook client can download only one offline address list, namely the one designated the default offline address list. We'll see how to do this later in this chapter.

Configuring Outlook to Use an Offline Address List

Walkthrough

Configuring an Outlook client to use an offline address list is straightforward. Open Outlook and select Tools → Options to open the Options box and select the Mail Services tab. Click the Offline Folder Settings button to open the Offline Folder Settings box and make sure that Download Offline Address Book is selected in this box. Further configure your offline address book settings by clicking the Settings button. This opens the Offline Address Book dialog box (Figure 8.4).

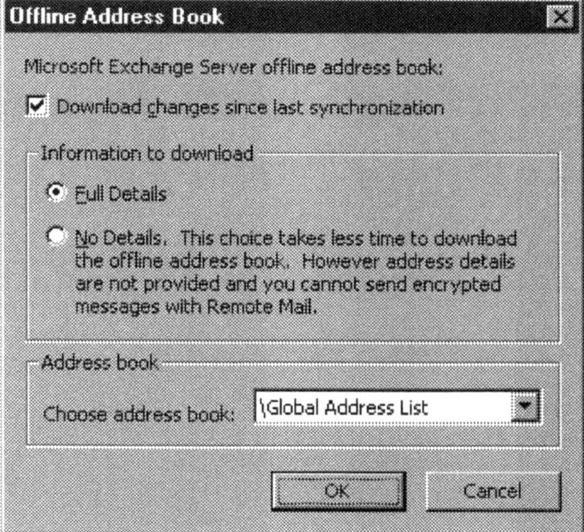

Figure 8.4 Configuring offline address book settings.

Selecting the Download Changes Since Last Synchronization checkbox causes the offline address book on the client to be updated only with changes that were made to the version on the server. Clearing this checkbox causes the entire offline address book to be downloaded from the server.

Full Details causes all address information to be downloaded for each recipient in the offline address book. No Details speeds up downloading but provides less information about recipients.

Choose Address Book lets you select which offline address list to download from the server. At this point, there is only the default offline address list on the server, and this list is the same as the GAL of all recipients, as we'll see in a moment.

Creating and Configuring Offline Address Lists

Walkthrough

You can use Server Manager, one of the Exchange administrative tools, to create and manage offline address books on your Exchange servers. To do this, log on as an administrator to a machine having the Exchange administrative tools installed and click Start → Programs → Microsoft Exchange → Server Manager. Expand the console tree and select the Offline Address Lists node within the Recipients container. The Details pane displays the Default Offline Address Book (Figure 8.5).

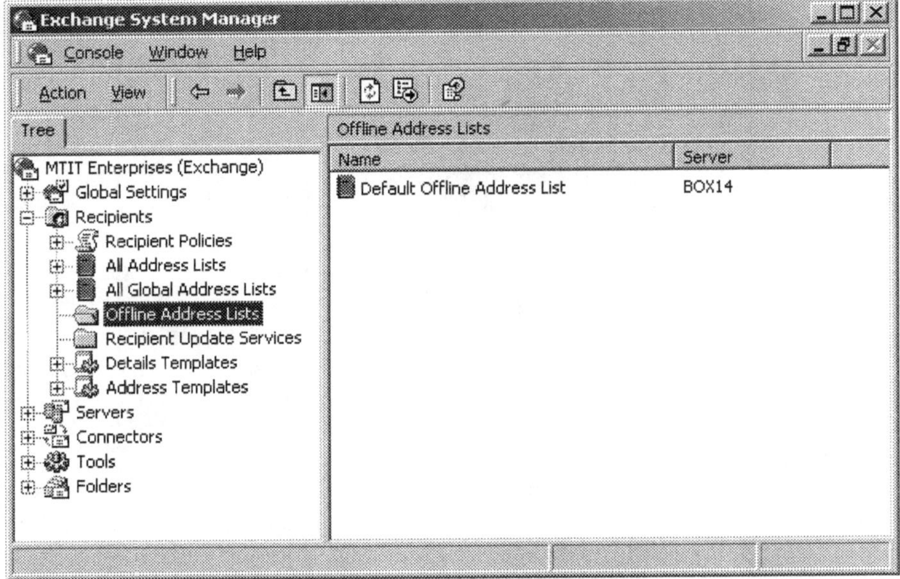

Figure 8.5 Offline address lists in Server Manager.

The Default Offline Address List

Before we create a new offline address list, let's examine this default list and see what options we have for managing it. Double-click on the Default Offline Address List node in the Details pane to open its Properties Sheet (Figure 8.6). The General tab lets you specify the offline address list server, what standard (online) address lists are mapped to the default offline address list, how the offline list is updated, and whether compatibility with earlier versions of Exchange is required. Let's look at each of these in detail:

- *Offline address list server*. This is the Exchange server that is responsible for generating and storing offline address list files. These files are stored in a hidden public folder on the server, and Outlook clients connect to this folder to download the list to their client computers. Click Browse to choose a different offline address list server from the list of available Exchange servers in your organization.
- *Address lists*. This listbox displays all the standard (online) address lists that are used to create the selected offline address list. We can see that the default offline address list is generated from the default GAL and contains the same recipients as this list, in other words, all recipients in your Exchange organization. Click Add to add other address lists (this would be superfluous here) or Remove to remove existing ones.
- *Update interval*. This specifies the time of day when the server rebuilds the offline address lists it maintains. The options are to run the update process daily at 2:00, 3:00, 4:00, or 5:00 AM, to never run it, or to choose a custom schedule you define.
- *Exchange 4.0 and 5.0 compatibility*. Select this checkbox if you still have users with mailboxes on these versions of Exchange in your organization.

TIP

If you make heavy use of offline folders in your organization, you probably want to designate a specific Exchange server for maintaining your offline address lists and providing your Outlook clients with a specific server for downloading these lists.

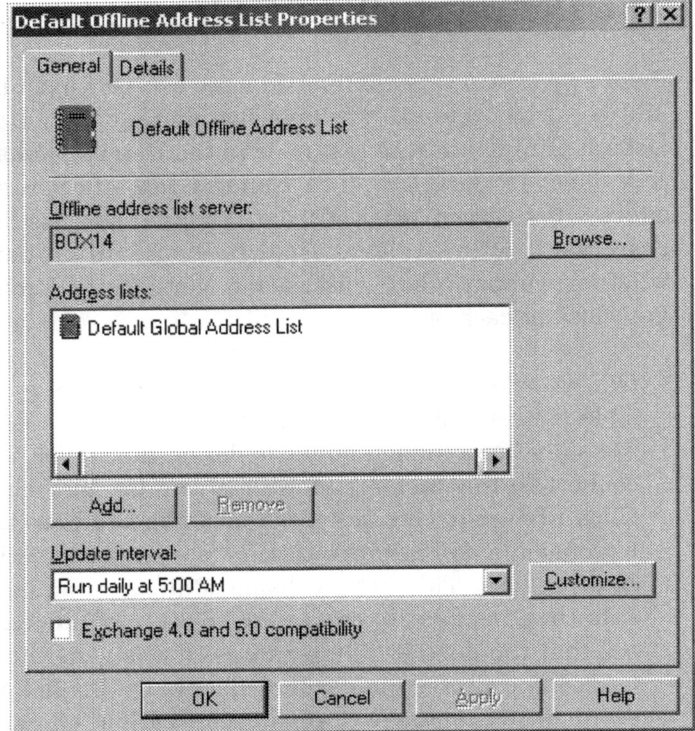

Figure 8.6 Configuring the default offline address list.

Creating a New Offline Address List

Before doing this walkthrough, create a new OU called Human Resources in the mtit.com domain and add several new mailbox-enabled users to this OU (or move some existing users to this OU, if you prefer). Also create a global group called Human Resources to contain these new users (the global group should also be located in the Human Resources OU). Make sure that the Department field on the Organization tab of each new user has Human Resources as its value. Finally, use System Manager to create a new standard (online) address list called HR for users in the human resources department. Do this by setting a filter rule to specify that the Department field is exactly Human Resources (see the previous chapter, if necessary).

Now let's create our new offline address list. Right-click on the Offline Address Lists node in the Recipients container in Server Manager and select New → Offline Address List. This opens the New Object Offline Address List wizard (it doesn't say "wizard" but this is what it is).

We'll create a new offline address list called Employees that will contain users in both the marketing and human resources departments of our company. Type Employees as the name of the new list and click Browse to specify the Exchange server Box14 as the offline address list server that maintains this list.

Click Next to specify what standard address lists will be used for generating our new offline address list. By default, the default GAL is used to generate a new list, but we want to change that, so select this list and click Remove to remove it from the Address Lists listbox.

Now click Add to display all standard address lists in AD. Double-click on the list called Marketing Department and HR lists and click OK to close the Select Address Lists box and return to the wizard (Figure 8.7).

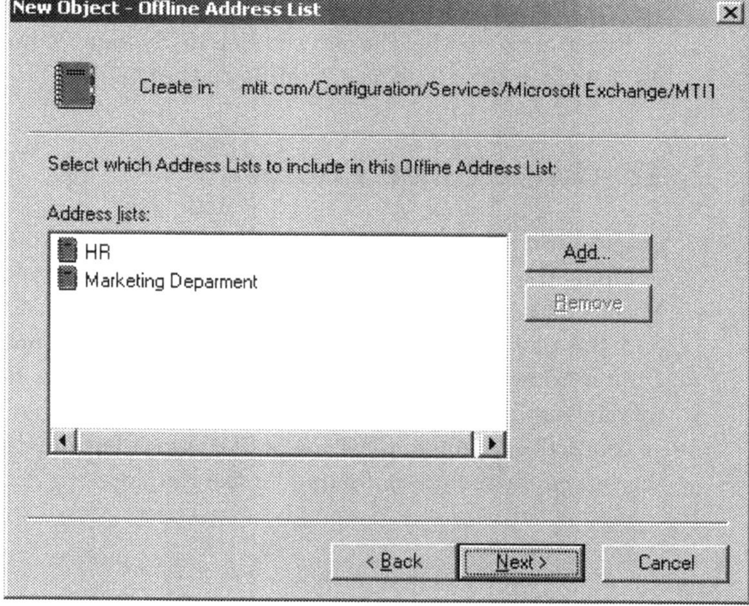

Figure 8.7 Creating a new offline address list generated from the Marketing Department standard address list.

Click Next to continue the wizard. A message will appear: "The public folder that will contain this offline address list will be created during store maintenance period on Box15. Therefore this offline address list will not be available to clients until that time." Click Next and Finish to create the new list.

Forcing a List Rebuild

The message stating that the new list wouldn't be available until store maintenance period (5:00 AM by default) can be worked around as follows. Right-click on the new Employees offline address list in System Manager and select Rebuild from the shortcut menu. Click Yes to rebuild the list immediately. If your organization has thousands of users, rebuilding a list could take some time to finish.

Specifying a Default Offline Address List

Even though you can create multiple offline address lists on your servers, Outlook clients can only download one of them when working in offline mode. Let's make our new Employees list the new default list for offline clients.

Right-click on the Employees list in System Manager and select Set As New Default. Click Yes. Simple as that.

Testing Offline Folders

Start Outlook on the client configured to use offline folders.

Open the Address Book in Outlook and select the drop-down Show Names listbox. You should have only two entries: the Offline Address Book and the user's personal Outlook Address Book (Contacts). If you select Offline Address Book you should see listed only users in the marketing and human resources departments (you should not see any mail-enabled groups or contacts or mail-enabled users like Administrator that do not belong to the two departments configured for the Employees offline address list).

Summary

We've spent some time looking at how to manage Exchange recipients and address lists. Along the way we've learned how to use the Exchange administration tool called ADUC, which is also the main Windows 2000 administration tools for administering objects in AD. We've briefly introduced another Exchange tool, *System Manager*, in our discussion of address lists. In Chapter 9, we'll take a bird's-eye view of System Manager and what it is used for.

CHAPTER 9

System Manager

In previous chapters we've looked at managing Exchange recipients using the ADUC console. We've also looked at how to manage address lists using System Manager, another Exchange administration tool. This chapter looks more deeply at the System Manager console, provides an overview of its use, and introduces a number of new concepts that will be covered in more detail later on. In other words, this chapter provides a kind of bridge between earlier material and more advanced topics on Exchange administration.

This chapter has only one walkthrough:

- Exploring the Exchange organization hierarchy

System Manager

If ADUC is the primary tool used for administering Exchange recipients (users, contacts, and groups), then System Manager is the tool used for managing almost everything else. Specifically, you use System Manager to:

- Configure global settings for all Exchange servers in your enterprise
- Create and manage address lists, address templates, and recipient policies for Exchange recipients
- Create and manage system policies for Exchange servers, mailbox stores, and public folder stores throughout your organization
- Create and configure information stores and protocols
- Configure routing of messages between different sites and routing groups
- Create and manage public folders throughout your organization
- Install and configure connectors for connecting Exchange to other mail systems

About the only things you don't use System Manager for are:

- Migrating mail accounts from other messaging system (use Migration Wizard instead)
- Identify and merge multiple accounts in AD that refer to the same user (use AD Cleanup Wizard instead)
- Back up and restore Exchange configuration information and information store data (use Backup instead)

Let's take a look at some of the information displayed in System Manager. We'll introduce a number of new Exchange concepts in this chapter, many of which we'll elaborate on in further detail in later chapters.

NOTE

System Manager in Exchange 2000 is essentially the functional equivalent of the Exchange Administrator tool in Exchange 5.5 but Exchange Administrator connects to an Exchange 5.5 server to obtain configuration information for your Exchange organization, whereas System Manager connects to a Windows 2000 domain controller to query AD for Exchange configuration information.

TIP

When System Manager starts, it connects by default to the nearest domain controller to query AD for the information it needs to build its hierarchy of Exchange objects. System Manager first tries to connect to a domain controller residing in the same subnet and, if that fails, domain controllers in the same Windows 2000 site.

It's possible also to connect System Manager to a specific domain controller. To do this, add the System Manager snap-in to a new MMC and specify the domain controller you want to connect to when prompted. One reason for doing this might be to overcome the effects of AD replication latency when changes have been made on one domain controller that have not yet been replicated to domain controllers near your Exchange servers.

Exploring the Exchange Organization Hierarchy

Walkthrough

Let's start by looking at the top-level portion of the hierarchy of an Exchange organization using System Manager. Figure 9.1 shows System Manager's console tree for our testbed deployment of Exchange.

The left-hand pane of the console window in System Manager displays the tree or hierarchy of objects in your Exchange organization. The root node of the hierarchy is the container representing the organization itself, which is labeled MTIT Enterprises (Exchange). This organization name was determined when you specified it during installation of your first Exchange server (see Chapter 1). Once the organization

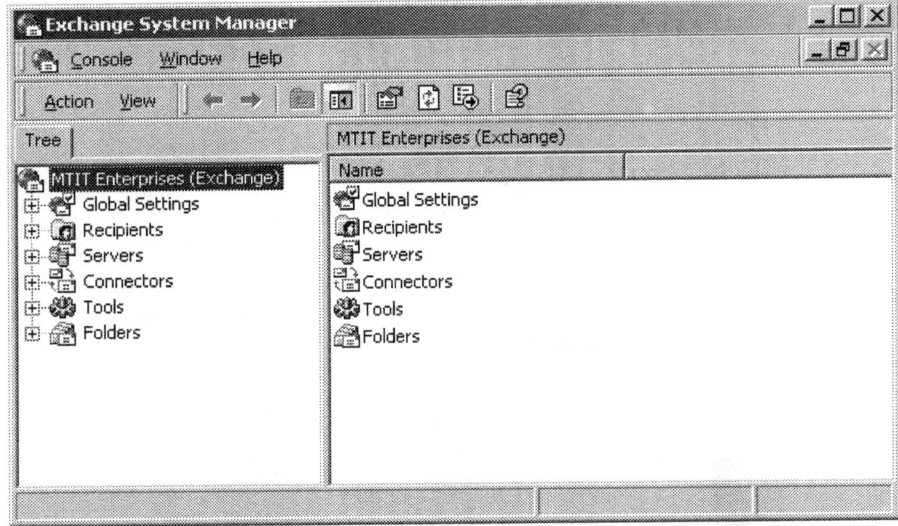

Figure 9.1 Exchange organization hierarchy for MTIT Enterprises testbed deployment.

name has been specified, it is permanent and cannot be changed afterward, so it's a good idea to decide carefully what you want the name to be before you install your first server.

Beneath the Organization node (or rather within it, because this node is a container object) are various top-level containers, each of which contain other nodes (either leaf nodes or containers) and which are used to configure various aspects of Exchange. The six top-level containers displayed in our testbed deployment are as follows:

- *Global settings*. Contains objects whose settings apply globally to all servers and recipients in your Exchange organization.
- *Recipients*. Contains objects for managing settings pertaining to recipients. Exchange recipients include mailbox- and mail-enabled users, mail-enabled contacts, and mail-enabled groups.
- *Servers*. Contains objects for configuring various aspects of Exchange servers in your organization.
- *Connectors*. Contains connectors you have installed for connecting your Exchange organization with foreign or third-party mail systems.
- *Tools*. Contains tools for monitoring various aspects of your Exchange organization.
- *Folders*. Contains objects for configuring public folder trees in your organization.

In addition to these items, System Manager's console tree may contain other top-level containers depending on how System Manager is configured. These additional containers are:

- *Administrative groups.* Contains objects that enable you to logically organize the structure of a large Exchange organization to simplify its administration.
- *Routing groups.* Contains objects that enable you to control message routing within a large Exchange organization.

Administrative and routing groups are covered in Chapters 12 and 21, so we won't go into further detail about them here. We'll finish this section by looking at how to make these additional containers visible and how to perform tasks on objects within the various containers in System Manager.

To change the way the console tree appears, try this: right-click on the root node MTIT Enterprises and select Properties to open the MTIT Enterprises Properties Sheet (Figure 9.2). Note the two checkboxes for displaying routing and administrative groups. If you select either (or both) of these and then restart System Manager, a different set of top-level containers is displayed. These differences are summarized in Table 9.1. Return your settings to the default values (unchecked) when you are finished.

TABLE 9.2

Top-level containers visible in System Manager depending on checkboxes selected on the Organization (Root Node) Properties sheet.

Container	None	Routing	Administration	Both
Global settings	✔	✔	✔	✔
Recipients	✔	✔	✔	✔
Servers	✔	✔		
Connectors	✔			
Tools	✔	✔	✔	✔
Folders	✔	✔		
Administrative groups			✔	✔
Routing groups		✔		

NOTE

We'll look at these other views of System Manager that are configured using the Organization (root node) Properties Sheet when we cover administrative and routing groups in Chapters 12 and 21. You may have also noticed the Operation Mode setting and Change Mode button; we'll

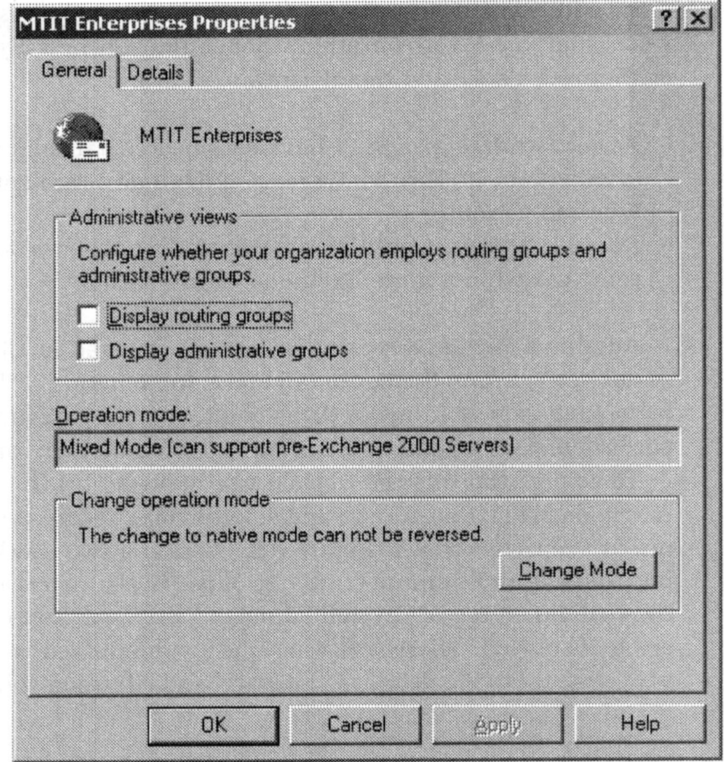

Figure 9.2 MTIT Enterprises (root or organization node) Properties Sheet.

cover these later as well. Our present goal is to gain an overview of the tool System Manager.

You probably noticed when you right-clicked on the Organization (root) node that there was an option called Delegate Control. This starts the Exchange Administration Delegation Wizard, which we'll look at in a later chapter. For now just note that to perform administrative tasks on objects in the System Manager hierarchy, you just right-click on the object and select the appropriate task from the shortcut menu. We'll summarize some of the tasks you can perform as we explore the hierarchy in the rest of this chapter.

Let's use the remainder of this chapter to become familiar with the default top-level containers. Additional details on many of the objects in these top-level containers will be provided in later chapters.

Global Settings

The top-level container called Global Settings contains objects that are used for specifying enterprisewide settings for Exchange messaging services. Figure 9.3 shows the contents of this container in our testbed deployment. Objects in this container include Internet message formats and message delivery.

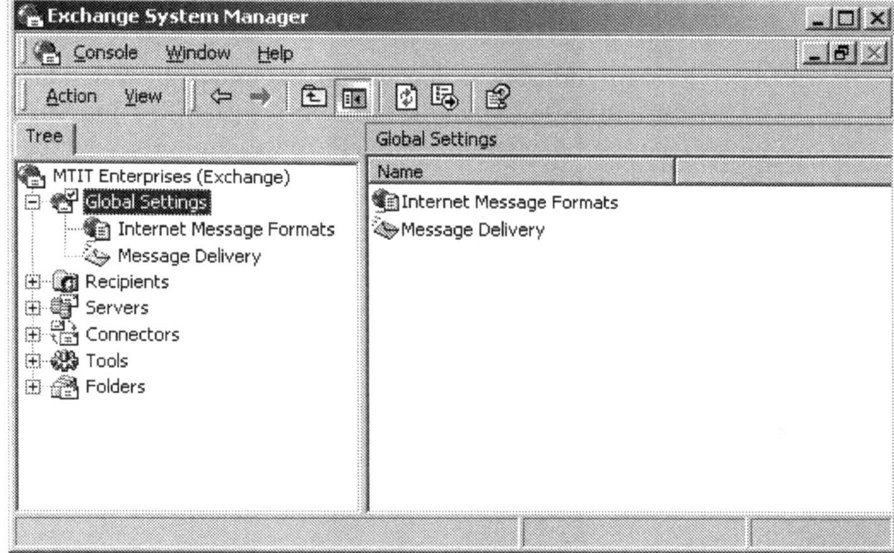

Figure 9.3 Global Settings container of Exchange organization hierarchy.

Internet Message Formats

Right-clicking on this container opens a Properties Sheet that lets you globally specify MIME content types; that is, mappings between MIME types and file extensions for mail attachments. These MIME types only apply when MAPI clients such as Outlook are sending or receiving mail with non-MAPI (Internet) clients such as Outlook Express. Within the Internet Message Formats containers you will find another object representing the default SMTP domain. The properties of this object can be used to define the type of message encoding to use when sending mail to non-MAPI (Internet) clients such as Outlook Express, what character sets to use, and when to use advanced features such as Exchange rich-text format, word wrap, automatic replies, and so on. We'll discuss these properties in Chapter 22.

Message Delivery

The Properties Sheet for this object lets you globally specify message delivery settings for all recipients in your organization. You can limit outgoing and incoming message size, specify the maximum number of recipients for a single message, and set up filters for weeding out unwanted incoming messages. This information is fairly straightforward, and we've already looked at configuring such settings on a per-user basis in Chapter 3 when we looked at the Delivery Restrictions and Delivery Options buttons on the Exchange General tab (see Figure 3.5).

In addition, if you install Exchange Instant Messaging (IM) in your organization you will have an object called Instant Messaging that can be used to configure global firewall and proxy server settings for all your IM clients.

As far as administrative tasks are concerned, most configuration of Global Settings objects is done through Properties Sheets, but you can right-click on the Internet Message Formats container to create and configure a new SMTP domain.

TIP

ADUC console, System Manager supports drag and drop, which you can use to move objects from one administrative group to another and so on.

Recipients

We've already looked at several of the nodes in the Recipients top-level container in previous chapters, so we'll summarize these and introduce the others.

Recipient Policies

These are policies that are applied to groups of Exchange recipients in your organization. Polices are a feature of Windows 2000 that simplify administration by controlling settings for groups of objects. Recipient policies are used to specify the format for the default email addresses created for recipients. We'll look at recipient policies in more detail in Chapter 11, but if you like you can right-click on the Default Policy and select Properties to see what recipient policies are all about.

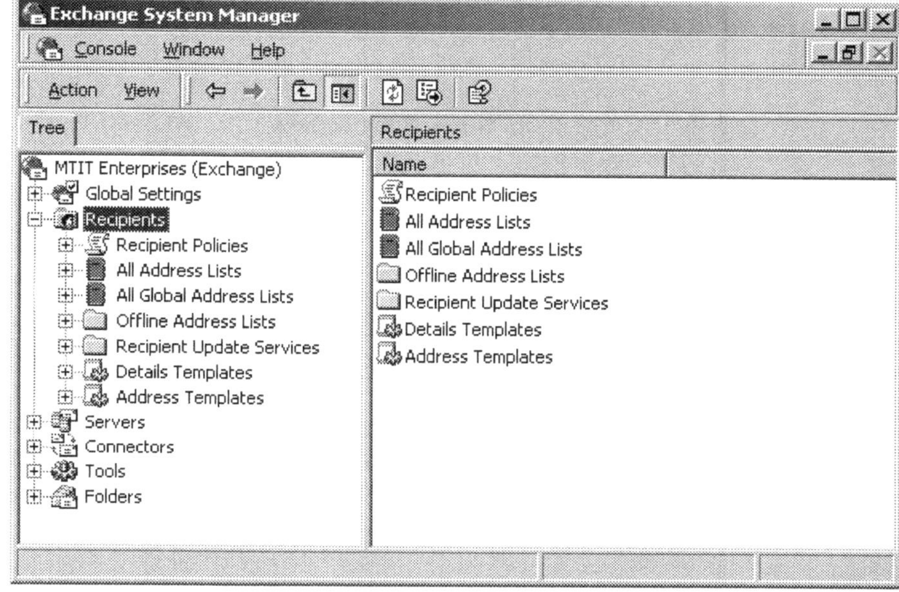

Figure 9.4 Recipients container of Exchange organization hierarchy.

All Address Lists

This contains all standard (online) address lists created for your Exchange organization. Address lists in Exchange 2000 are the equivalent of address book views in earlier versions of Exchange. We covered address lists in Chapter 7.

All Global Address Lists

This contains all GALs created for your organization. It's an interesting feature of Exchange 2000 that you can create several GALs in addition to the default GAL. One reason for replacing the default GAL with a customized one might be to restrict client access to GAL recipients in your organization (Outlook clients can view everything in the GAL so one way of preventing this is to redefine the GAL in a more restrictive way). Another reason might be hosting multiple Exchange organizations on one or more Exchange servers.

Offline Address Lists

We covered this in Chapter 8.

Recipient Update Services

We discussed this in Chapter 8.

Details Templates

Templates are used to specify how recipients are displayed in the Outlook address book. Within the Details Templates container there are individual containers for different languages. If you select the English container in the console tree, you'll see the following template objects in the Details pane: User, Group, Public Folder, Search Dialog, Mailbox Agent, and Contact. You can customize these templates to change the way they appear in the Outlook address book. For example, you could add new fields, remove existing fields, rearrange fields, add new controls, and so on. Try opening one of the templates, switching to the Templates tab (wait a moment while the schema is loaded), and click Test to display the current appearance of the template. Double-click on a control in the listbox to change its location, height, width, display name, and so on. Click Test to view your changes and then click Original to undo your changes. To make changes take effect immediately for clients, rebuild your address lists (see Chapter 7).

Address Templates

These templates are used to define the appearance of the dialog boxes used to create new email addresses for recipients. It's not likely that you would want to change these templates.

Here is a summary of administrative tasks you can perform on objects in the Recipients container by right-clicking on them and selecting the appropriate shortcut menu items:

- Create a new recipient policy using New → Recipient Policy and apply a selected recipient policy using Apply This Policy Now.
- Create a new address list using New → Address List.
- Create a new global address list using New → Global Address List.
- Create a new offline address list using New → Offline Address List, rebuild a selected offline address list using Rebuild, and specify which list is the default one using Set As New Default.
- Create a new recipient update service using New → Recipient Update Service and update or rebuild a selected recipient update service using Update Now or Rebuild.

Some of these tasks we've covered previously and others will be explained in later chapters.

Servers

The top-level container called Server contains a tree of objects for each Exchange server in your organization. These objects are used to configure various aspects of the servers.

Figure 9.5 shows that the Servers container for our testbed deployment contains two containers, Box14 and Box15, representing our two Exchange servers. If you open the Properties Sheet for Box14, you'll see various tabs for:

- Enabling message tracking
- Managing log files
- Specifying whether the server is a front-end server
- Adding a locale
- Enabling different levels of diagnostic logging
- Viewing the policies applied to the server
- Monitoring the Exchange services of the server
- Configuring resource usage for full-text indexing
- Managing permissions

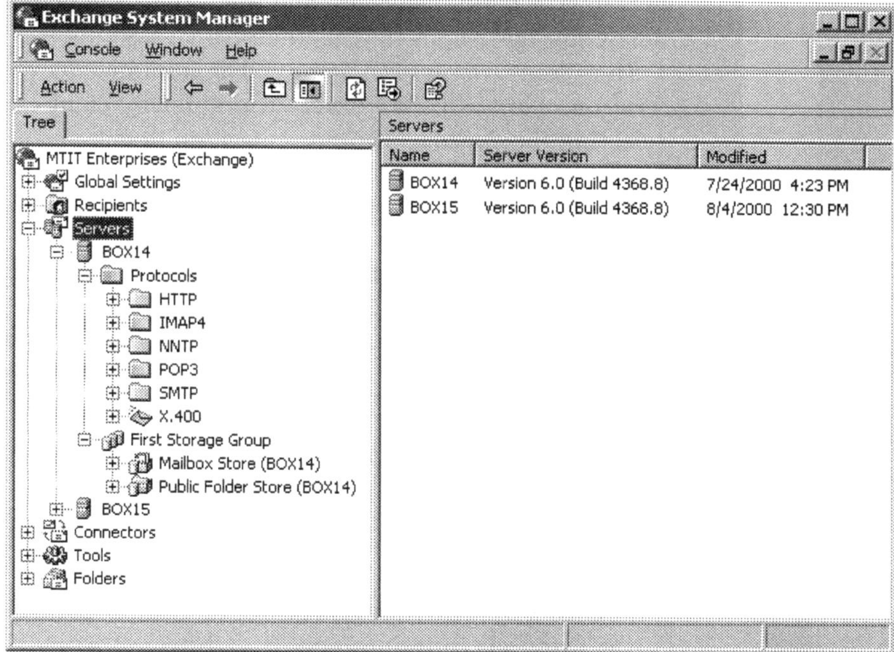

Figure 9.5 Servers container of the Exchange organization hierarchy.

These are a diverse set of management items, and we'll cover many of them in later chapters.

Figure 9.5 also shows how we've expanded the individual server container Box14 to display its contents, and you can see that individual server containers contain protocols and storage groups.

Protocols

There is one container for each protocol installed on the server, specifically HTTP, IMAP4, NNTP, POP3, SMTP, and X.400. Each of these individual protocol containers contains objects representing the virtual servers created for that protocol. We'll discuss virtual servers in Chapter 23.

Storage Groups

In each server container, a container represents each storage group that has been created on the server. Storage groups provide a method for logically grouping Exchange messaging databases together for managing them. By default, installing Exchange creates a single storage group within the server's information store, called the First Storage Group. Figure 9.5 shows that this First Storage Group contains two data stores within it, the Mailbox Store and the Public Folder Store. We'll talk more about storage groups in Chapter 14.

Here is a summary of some of the administrative tasks you can perform on objects in the Servers container by right-clicking on them and selecting the appropriate shortcut menu items:

- Remove a server by selecting it and using All Tasks → Remove Server.
- Create a new storage group by selecting a server and using New → Storage Group.
- Create a new mailbox or public store within a storage group by selecting it and using New → Mailbox Store or Public Store.
- Dismount a mailbox or public store, create a full-text index for the store, and perform other related tasks by selecting the store and using various shortcut menu options.
- Run the mailbox cleanup agent by selecting Mailboxes within a Mailbox Store of a particular Storage Group and using Run Cleanup Agent.
- Create a new virtual server by selecting a particular protocol within the Protocols container and using New → Virtual Server.

- Stop, pause, and start a virtual server by selecting it and using the appropriate option on the shortcut menu
- Terminate all sessions for SMTP, POP3, or IMAP4 protocols by selecting Current Sessions within the appropriate virtual server container and using Terminal All
- Create a new X.400 transport stack by selecting X.400 within the Protocols container and using New → Transport Stack

NOTE

This is only a small sampling of the tasks you can perform using objects in the Servers container. We'll look at many of these tasks later in this book.

Connectors

This top-level container contains any connectors you have installed in your organization. Connectors are used to establish connectivity with third-party and foreign mail systems and between different routing groups in an Exchange organization. We've omitted a screenshot here because in our testbed Exchange environment no connectors have been deployed. Exchange includes support for the following types of connectors:

- *SMTP connectors.* These can be configured to use Simple Mail Transport Protocol (SMTP) to transfer messages between Exchange and non-Exchange messaging servers, between routing groups within an Exchange organization, and between different Exchange organizations.
- *X.400 connector.* These can be configured to use the ITU's X.400 messaging protocol to transfer messages between different routing groups within an Exchange organization or between your Exchange organization and a foreign X.400 messaging system. There are several types of X.400 connectors depending on the underlying transport used.
- *Routing group connector.* These can be configured to link different routing groups together within an Exchange organization. Routing group connectors are new to Exchange 2000 (as are routing groups) and roughly correspond to the Site Connector of earlier versions of Exchange.
- *Dirsync server/requestor.* These are used to establish directory synchronization with legacy Microsoft Mail 3.x servers. MS Mail is pretty much dead overall, we won't be talking about it again in this book.

We'll talk more about connectors later on. The tasks you can perform on connectors depend on the kind of connectors installed, and we won't look at them here.

Tools

This top-level container (Figure 9.6) is used to group together various tools for monitoring Exchange services. It typically contains three objects.

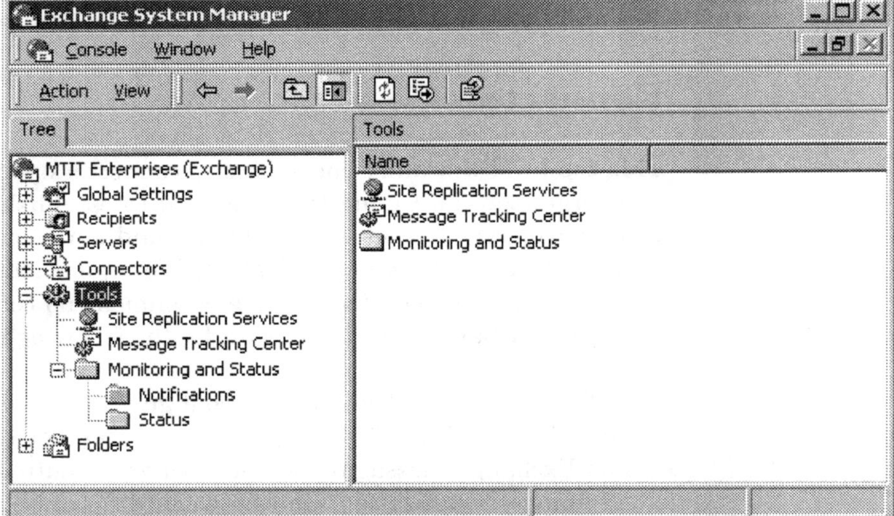

Figure 9.6 Tools container of Exchange organization hierarchy.

Site Replication Services

This object contains Site Replication Service objects you have created to establish connectivity with downlevel Exchange 5.5 servers. The Active Directory Connector must be installed before you can create these services. We'll talk more about Active Directory Connectory in Chapter 25.

Message Tracking Center

This is used to track the path messages take through your Exchange organization and is a useful troubleshooting tool when messages go astray. To track messages, you must first enable it so that your Exchange servers will generate the appropriate message tracking log files. We'll cover this in Chapter 24.

Monitoring and Status

This object contains two other containers, Notifications, which can be used to send email or run a script when an Exchange server enters a warning or critical condition, and Status, which displays the current status of your Exchange servers.

To summarize, the administrative tasks you can perform on objects in the Monitoring and Status container by right-clicking on them are:

- Creating a new email or script notification by using New → Email Notification or Script Notification.
- Connecting to a server to obtain status information by selecting the Status container and using Connect To and specifying which servers and connectors to monitor by using Custom Filter.

Folders

This top-level container displays the various public folder trees you have configured in your organization, lets you create new public folder trees, connect to a replica of a particular tree on a specified server, and create a new public folder within a specified tree. We'll cover public folders in Chapters 17 and 18.

NOTE

We'll look at the two remaining top-level containers (Administrative Groups and Routing Groups) in the chapters dealing with these topics.

Summary

In this chapter, we've surveyed the various top-level containers of System Manager and looked at their contents and some of the administrative tasks you can perform by using them. In the next chapter we will look once more at Exchange recipients and some advanced ways of managing them.

CHAPTER 10

Recipients Revisited

In previous chapters, we looked at the basic administration tasks associated with Exchange recipients—mail-enabled users, groups, and contacts. This chapter follows up on the previous ones by providing additional information about advanced properties of these recipients and bulk administration of Exchange recipients.

There are six walkthroughs in this chapter:

- Displaying the Exchange Advanced tab
- Configuring the Exchange Advanced tab for mailbox-enabled users
- Configuring the Exchange Advanced tab for mail-enabled users
- Configuring the Exchange Advanced tab for mail-enabled contacts
- Configuring the Exchange Advanced tab for mail-enabled groups
- Creating, modifying, and removing users with LDIFDE

Advanced Recipient Properties

By default, advanced properties of Exchange recipients are hidden in ADUC because these advanced settings are not needed as often as the basic settings for daily administration of recipients. We'll look first at how to display these advanced settings and then see how to configure them for mail-enabled users, groups, and contacts.

Displaying the Exchange Advanced Tab

Walkthrough

To display the advanced settings for Exchange in ADUC, select View → Advanced Features from the menu bar. This has two effects:

- The console tree now displays additional containers that were not displayed before. These containers include LostAndFound, System, and Microsoft Exchange System Objects (Figure 10.1). The first two containers are for Windows 2000 in general; the Exchange container contains hidden public folders and the System Mailbox.
- Several new tabs are added to Properties Sheets of objects displayed in ADUC. Two of these tabs are added to all objects in ADUC, namely an Object tab giving the fully qualified domain name of the object within AD, and a Security tab displaying the permissions currently

assigned to the object. Exchange recipients also have an Exchange Advanced tab added to their Properties Sheet, and we'll cover this tab in a moment.

Let's now look at what we can do with the Advanced tab for different kinds of recipients.

NOTE

You shouldn't change anything in the Microsoft Exchange System Objects container unless you really know what you're doing, and you shouldn't need to unless something goes wrong and you have to work through a troubleshooting procedure outlined in the Knowledge Base on Microsoft TechNet. For example, there is a procedure outlined in KB article Q253784 that describes how you can log on to the system mailbox to view its contents, but if you do this carelessly you may make your Exchange server become unstable, and Microsoft recommends that you do not do this unless instructed to do so in conjunction with Microsoft Product Support Services (PSS).

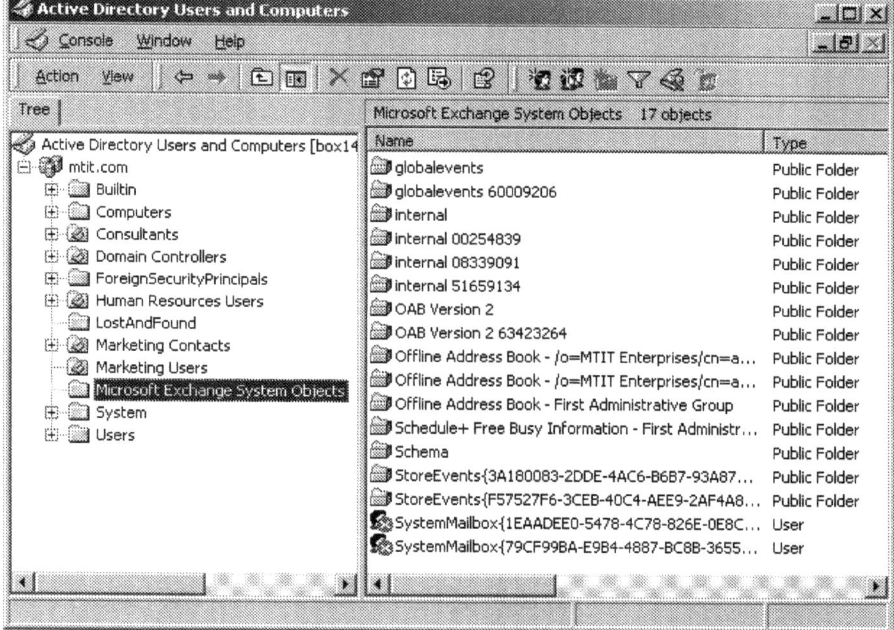

Figure 10.1 Advanced view of console tree in ADUC.

Configuring the Exchange Advanced Tab for Mailbox-enabled Users

Walkthrough

Figure 10.2 shows the Exchange Advanced tab for a mailbox-enabled user, Jane Smith. Let's briefly look at the different settings you can configure here:

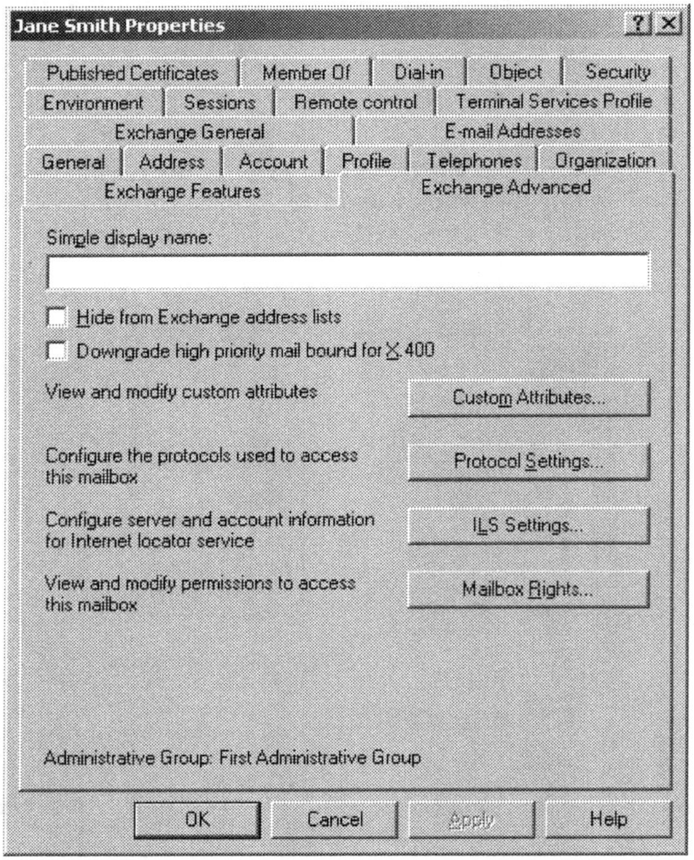

Figure 10.2 Exchange Advanced tab for mailbox-enabled users.

- *Simple display name.* Some email clients cannot read all of the characters that a normal display name in Exchange can contain. For these clients, you can configure a simple display name containing only characters they can interpret. This may be an issue, for example, when working with a foreign language that uses non-ANSI characters.

- *Hide from Exchange address lists.* You can hide this user from all address lists (including the GAL) by selecting it. Try it out by selecting the checkbox to hide recipient Jane Smith and then open Outlook on a client machine while logged on as a different mailbox-enabled user and see if Jane Smith appears under the GAL in the Outlook address book.
- *Downgrade high-priority mail bound for X.400.* If you are connecting to a foreign X.400 messaging system and have trouble with message delivery, you may need to select this option to make your outgoing mail conform to the original 1984 X.400 standard.
- *Custom attributes.* This button lets you custom define up to 15 additional attributes for your mailbox-enabled users. For example, you might want to specify an employee ID number for all your users.
- *Protocol settings.* By default, a mailbox-enabled user's settings for HTTP, POP3, and IMAP4 protocols are inherited from the virtual server on which the mailbox resides. By clicking the Protocol Settings button, you can enable or disable each of these protocols separately on a per-user basis and, for POP3 and IMAP4, can specify messaging encoding and default character set on a per-user basis. For example, to disable HTTP for the selected user (Jane Smith), click Protocol Settings → HTTP → Settings → clear the Enable For Mailbox checkbox. Disabling HTTP for Jane Smith should mean she can no longer use OWA to access her mail. Try it out—you should get an HTTP 403 Forbidden error message in your browser. You may have to wait a moment for the setting to take effect.
- *ILS settings.* This is used for configuring ILS servers for Microsoft NetMeeting clients.
- *Mailbox rights.* This opens a dialog box that allows you to view and modify the permissions for the user's mailbox. We'll cover permissions in Chapter 13.

At the bottom of the Exchange Advanced tab is the location of Jane Smith's mailbox (in this case, the First Administrative Group). This is useful information if you have created additional administrative groups in a large-scale implementation of Exchange.

Configuring the Exchange Advanced Tab for Mail-enabled Users

Advanced settings for mail-enabled users are similar to those for mailbox-enabled users. Figure 10.3 shows the Exchange Advanced tab for a mail-enabled user named Drew Michelson. The following settings were discussed in the previous walkthrough:

- Simple display name
- Custom attributes
- ILS settings

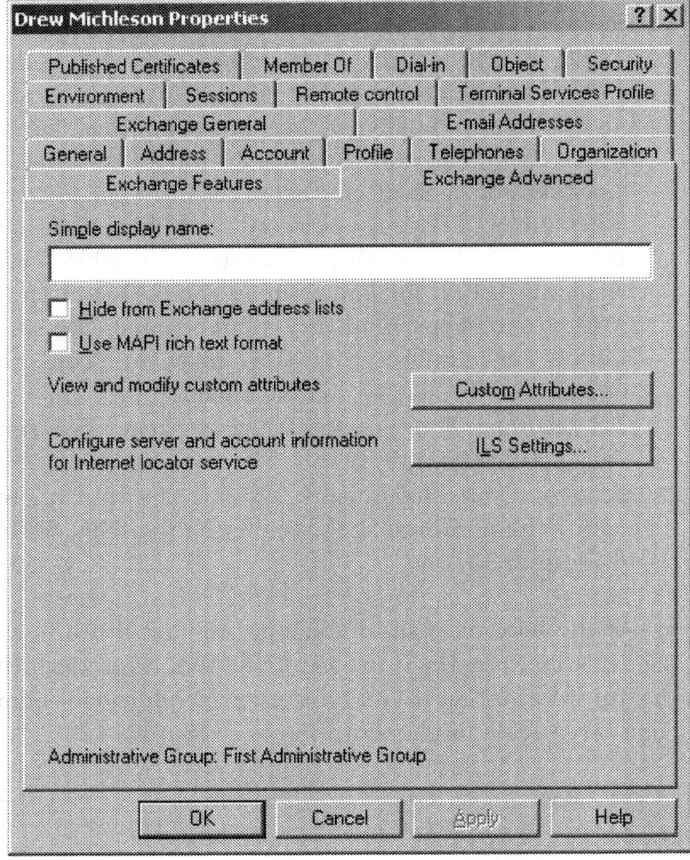

Figure 10.3 Exchange Advanced tab for mail-enabled users.

Mail-enabled users have no protocol settings or mailbox rights because they have no mailboxes on your Exchange server. There is one additional setting:

- *Use MAPI rich-text format.* This lets you use rich-text format (RTF) for sending messages to the mail-enabled user. Because mail-enabled users are usually external users with mailboxes on a different mail system, you must ensure their mail system can understand RTF before enabling this setting.

TIP

RTF is the preferred messaging format for older Exchange clients. RTF can be globally enabled or disabled for all your recipients by the following procedure: open System Manager, expand Global Settings, expand Internet Message Formats, double-click on Default (or any selected SMTP policy), select the Advanced tab, and select either Always Use or Never Use under Exchange Rich-Text Format. The default setting is Determine By Individual User Settings, which means that RTF settings are by default enabled or disabled on a per-user basis; by default, it is disabled for mail-enabled users.

Configuring the Exchange Advanced Tab for Mail-enabled Contacts

Walkthrough

The Exchange Advanced tab for mail-enabled contacts is the same as for mail-enabled users.

Configuring the Exchange Advanced Tab for Mail-enabled Groups

Walkthrough

The Exchange Advanced tab for mail-enabled groups is the same whether these are security or distribution groups. Figure 10.4 shows the Exchange Advanced tab for the mail-enabled Marketing security group

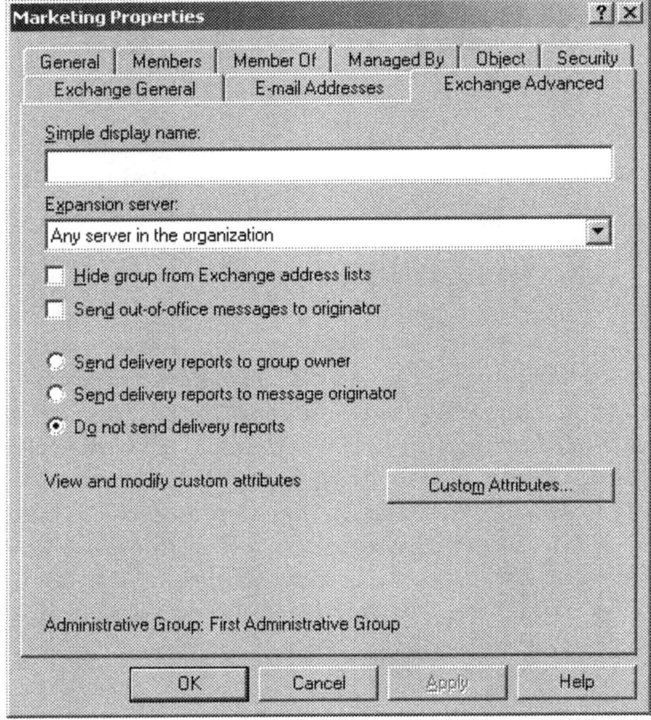

Figure 10.4
Exchange Advanced tab for mail-enabled groups.

we created in Chapter 5. We'll consider only the settings that haven't been discussed in our previous walkthroughs:

- *Expansion server*. This is an important setting to configure when implementing mail-enabled groups, especially groups that have thousands of members. The expansion server for a mail-enabled group is an Exchange server that is used to resolve the target recipient (mail-enabled group) into email addresses of its individual members so that the message can be copied to every member of the group. Expanding messages sent to mail-enabled groups that have thousands of recipients is a processor-intensive task, so if you often use large groups for mass mailings, you may want to dedicate one Exchange server in your enterprise for the role of expansion server for all your mail-enabled groups.

TIP

The most efficient way of performing expansion is to use the same Exchange server for the sender's mailbox and the expansion server. If managers are usually the ones sending out mass mailings, then place all mailboxes for managers on the same Exchange server and designate it the expansion server for the mail-enabled groups. If you are sending mass mail to a group of external users, use a bridgehead server for expansion of the group membership.

- *Send out-of-office messages to originator.* A few users in a group may be out of the office, and their mail client is configured to send out-of-office messages to anyone sending them mail. If you send mail to a group of 1,000 users and 50 of them are out of the office, selecting this option will result in 50 out-of-office reply messages filling your Inbox—no wonder this setting is disabled by default! But if you are inviting all 1,000 users to an important meeting, you may want to enable this feature and wade through your replies.
- *Do not send delivery reports.* A nondelivery report (NDR) indicates that a message could not be delivered for some reason such as nonexistent user or inability to route mail properly. Exchange is configured by default so that NDRs are not returned to the originator when sending mail to groups for reasons similar to those for receiving out-of-office replies—you're mailbox may be filled with NDRs if there is a routing problem of some kind. You can decide to have NDRs delivered to either the message originator or the group owner.

Bulk Management of Recipients

We'll conclude this chapter with a look at how you can make bulk changes to the information representing Exchange recipients in AD. The tool we'll consider is the Windows 2000 command-line utility known as LDIF Directory Exchange (ldifde.exe). LDIF Directory Exchange can be used to import data from or export data to AD and can be used to create, delete, and modify the properties of users, groups, contacts, and other objects in AD. It's a powerful tool—use it carefully!

BACKGROUNDER

LDIF

LDIF stands for LDAP Data Interchange Format and is a file format that uses Lightweight Directory Access Protocol (LDAP) for accessing and making changes to AD. An LDIF file is a text file containing LDAP commands that are used to modify the content of AD. LDAP is a stan-

dard Internet protocol for manipulating objects in directories that are based on the X.500 standard, the base of 2000's AD.

If you expanded the acronym completely, then LDIFDE would stand for Lightweight Directory Access Protocol Data Interchange Format Directory Exchange, and then it would have to be called LDAPDIFDE, which is just a bit much!

NOTE

Another command-line tool you can use to modify AD is CSV Directory Exchange (csvde.exe), which allows you to import data from or export it to comma-separated variable (.csv) files such as those used by Microsoft Excel. CSV Directory Exchange thus allows you to import data from Excel spreadsheets to create users in bulk, but it cannot be used to create contacts. CSV Directory Exchange is compatible with Exchange 5.5 bulk import/export tools and is worth looking at for these reasons. We've chosen to focus on LDIF Directory Exchange because it is a more general and powerful tool.

We'll finish this chapter with a look at LDIF Directory Exchange in action. Be aware that making changes to existing objects using LDIF Directory Exchange can be hazardous unless you follow the syntax carefully!

Creating, Modifying, and Removing Users With LDIF Directory Exchange

Walkthrough

Let's create new users in the Marketing Users OU using LDIF Directory Exchange. We first need to establish the distinguished name (DN) of the Marketing Users OU so we know where to import our users. Start ADUC and select View → Advanced Features to display advanced settings for directory objects. Open the Properties Sheet for the Marketing Users OU and select the Objects tab. The fully qualified domain name for the OU should appear as:

```
mtit.com/Marketing Users
```

This means the DN for this OU is:

```
ou=Marketing Users,dc=mtit,dc=com
```

See Chapter 3 for more on DNs. We'll need this information when we formulate our LDIF Directory Exchange command.

Before we import new users to create DNs, let's try exporting the information for the existing users in the Marketing Users OU to see what the LDIF format looks like. Log on to a domain controller using administrator credentials, open a command prompt, and type the following command:

```
ldifde -f test.txt -d "ou=Marketing Users,dc=mtit,dc=com"
```

TIP

You can also run LDIF Directory Exchange from any Windows 2000 Professional workstation by copying the file \Winnt\System32\ldifde.exe from any Windows 2000 Server machine (domain controller or member server) to the corresponding location on the workstation. Log on with administrator credentials to run the utility on the workstation.

The output of executing this command is shown in Figure 10.5.

```
Command Prompt
C:\>ldifde -f test.txt -d "ou=Marketing Users,dc=mtit,dc=com"
Connecting to "box14.mtit.com"
Logging in as current user using SSPI
Exporting directory to file test.txt
Searching for entries...
Writing out entries..........
10 entries exported

The command has completed successfully

C:\>
```

Figure 10.5 Exporting the properties of objects in the Marketing Users OU using LDIF Directory Exchange.

LDIF Directory Exchange first connects to the domain controller to query AD and writes the results of the query to the ASCII file test.txt in LDIF format. Even though there are only 10 entries exported by this operation, the exported text file is quite long and complex. Here's what the LDIF output for the single user Jane Smith looks like this (I've edited it a bit to make it more readable because some of the lines are long):

```
dn: CN=Jane Smith,OU=Marketing Users,DC=mtit,DC=com
changetype: add
homeMDB:
CN=Mailbox Store (BOX14),CN=First Storage Group,
CN=InformationStore,CN=BOX14,CN=Servers,
CN=First Administrative Group,
CN=Administrative Groups,CN=MTIT Enterprises,
CN=Microsoft Exchange,CN=Services,
CN=Configuration,DC=mtit,DC=com
memberOf: CN=Marketing,OU=Marketing Users,DC=mtit,DC=com
publicDelegatesBL: CN=Zhonghua Lee,
OU=Marketing Users,DC=mtit,DC=com
publicDelegatesBL: CN=Fred Jones,
OU=Marketing Users,DC=mtit,DC=com
accountExpires: 9223372036854775807
badPasswordTime: 0
badPwdCount: 0
codePage: 0
cn: Jane Smith
countryCode: 0
department: Marketing
displayName: Jane Smith
mail: jsmith@mtit.com
givenName: Jane
instanceType: 4
lastLogoff: 0
lastLogon: 126143834417280128
legacyExchangeDN:
     /o=MTIT Enterprises/ou=First Administrative Group
     /cn=Recipients/cn=jsmith
logonCount: 23
distinguishedName: CN=Jane Smith,OU=Marketing
Users,DC=mtit,DC=com
objectCategory: CN=Person,CN=Schema,CN=Configuration,DC=mtit,
DC=com
objectClass: user
objectGUID:: bWCiyYQ5XkGQgsMC1zpMJw==
objectSid:: AQUAAAAAAAUVAAAASyy8Ggt12XYVJa9HXgQAAA==
primaryGroupID: 513
proxyAddresses: SMTP:jsmith@mtit.com
proxyAddresses: X400:c=us;a= ;p=MTIT
Enterprises;o=Exchange;s=Smith;g=Jane;
pwdLastSet: 126120465821316144
name: Jane Smith
sAMAccountName: jsmith
sAMAccountType: 805306368
showInAddressBook:
CN=Default Global Address List,
CN=All Global Address Lists,
CN=Address Lists Container,
CN=MTIT Enterprises,CN=Microsoft Exchange,
CN=Services,CN=Configuration,DC=mtit,DC=com
showInAddressBook:
CN=All Users,CN=All Address Lists,
```

```
CN=Address Lists Container,
CN=MTIT Enterprises,CN=Microsoft Exchange,
CN=Services,CN=Configuration,DC=mtit,DC=com
showInAddressBook:
CN=Marketing Deparment,
CN=All Address Lists,
CN=Address Lists Container,
CN=MTIT Enterprises,CN=Microsoft Exchange,
CN=Services,CN=Configuration,DC=mtit,DC=com
sn: Smith
textEncodedORAddress: c=us;a= ;p=MTIT Enterprises;
o=Exchange;s=Smith;g=Jane;
userAccountControl: 66048
userPrincipalName: jsmith@mtit.com
uSNChanged: 15793
uSNCreated: 14040
whenChanged: 20000925194212.0Z
whenCreated: 20000829181621.0Z
deliverAndRedirect: FALSE
msExchHideFromAddressLists: FALSE
homeMTA:
CN=Microsoft MTA,CN=BOX14,CN=Servers,
CN=First Administrative Group,
CN=Administrative Groups,
CN=MTIT Enterprises,CN=Microsoft Exchange,
CN=Services,CN=Configuration,DC=mtit,DC=com
msExchHomeServerName:
/o=MTIT Enterprises/ou=First Administrative Group
/cn=Configuration/cn=Servers/cn=BOX14
mailNickname: jsmith
mDBUseDefaults: TRUE
protocolSettings:: SFRUUMKnMcKnMcKnwqfCp8KnwqfCpw==
securityProtocol:: AAAAAA==
msExchMailboxGuid:: tSmS9rVAu0eHPfBzNPEIXA==
msExchMailboxSecurityDescriptor::
 AQAEgHgAAACUAAAAAAAAAABQAAAAEAGQAAQAAAAACFAADAA-
IAAQEAAAAAAAAUKAAAArAMAAAgAAAAAAAAAAGAMAAAgAAAAAAAAAAHAQAAAgAAAAA
AAAAtAEAAAEAAAAAAAAAAtAEAABkAAABwAC8AQgBPAFgAMQA0AAAAAQUAAAAAAAAU
VAAAASyy8Ggt12XYVJa9H9AEAAAEFAAAAAAAFFQAAAEssvBoLddl2FSWvR/QBAA
 A=
msExchALObjectVersion: 68
msExchPoliciesIncluded:
 {7CCCFD1A-09F2-49F0-9AAF-9518E7384F70},{26491CFC-9E50-4857-861B-
0CB8DF22B5D7}
```

LDIF is a cross-platform Internet draft standard for LDAP Directory Exchange, and more documentation on it can be found in the Windows 2000 Server Resource Kit from Microsoft. The basic format can be seen from the previous example, namely that an LDIF entry for a directory object consists of the DN of the object followed by a number of attribute/value pairs representing the properties of the object in AD.

Let's try a few things with LDIF Directory Exchange. First we'll create a new user called Ralph Keaton using the LDIF file newuser.ldf:

```
dn: CN=Ralph Keaton,OU=Marketing Users,DC=mtit,DC=com
changetype: add
cn: Ralph Keaton
objectClass: user
givenName: Ralph
sAMAccountName: rkeaton
sn: Keaton
```

Note the file extension on the import file—even though it is a text (ASCII) file, be sure to use the .ldf extension. To import the object defined by this file into AD, we need to use LDIF Directory Exchange with the `-i` option, which switches from Export to Import mode. We'll also turn on Verbose Mode using `-v` to see more clearly what's happening during import.

TIP

You can find out information about the various switches supported by LDIF Directory Exchange by typing Ldifde /? at the command line.

Now let's create the new user object Ralph Keaton in AD. Copy the import file to the current directory (in this example, C:\) and type the following command at the command line:

```
ldifde -i -v -f newuser.ldf
```

Figure 10.6 shows the output of running the command. If you now open ADUC and browse to the Marketing Users OU, you'll see a new user object, Ralph Keaton. The user is currently disabled and must be enabled and then either mailbox-enabled or mail-enabled in order to use it with Exchange. It's a straightforward matter to create an import file containing thousands of new users to create.

Let's run LDIF Directory Exchange again and export the attributes of the single user object Ralph Keaton. To do this, we'll use the `-r` switch to define a filter that selects only those objects whose surname (sn attribute) is Keaton:

```
ldifde -f ralph.txt -d "ou=Marketing Users,dc=mtit,dc=com" -r
"(sn=Keaton)"
```

The contents of the export file ralph.txt look like this:

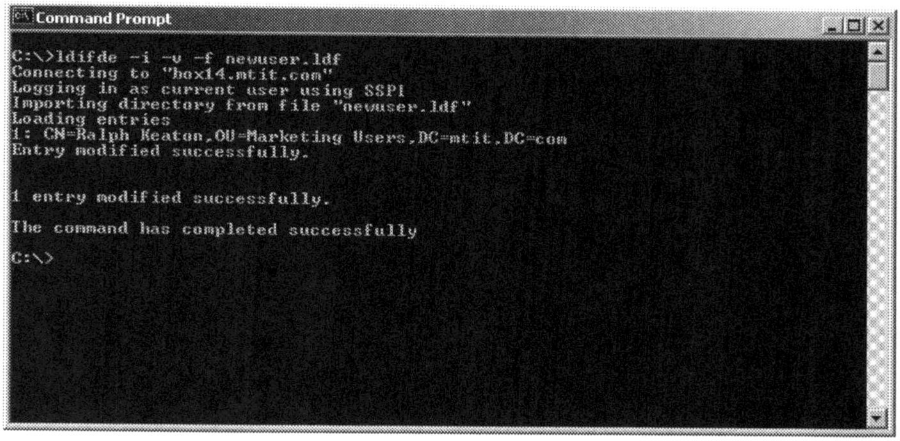

Figure 10.6 Creating a new user object using LDIF Directory Exchange.

```
C:\>ldifde -i -v -f newuser.ldf
Connecting to "box14.mtit.com"
Logging in as current user using SSPI
Importing directory from file "newuser.ldf"
Loading entries
1: CN=Ralph Keaton,OU=Marketing Users,DC=mtit,DC=com
Entry modified successfully.

1 entry modified successfully.

The command has completed successfully

C:\>
```

```
dn: CN=Ralph Keaton,OU=Marketing Users,DC=mtit,DC=com
changetype: add
accountExpires: 9223372036854775807
badPasswordTime: 0
badPwdCount: 0
codePage: 0
cn: Ralph Keaton
countryCode: 0
givenName: Ralph
instanceType: 4
lastLogoff: 0
lastLogon: 0
logonCount: 0
distinguishedName: CN=Ralph Keaton,OU=Marketing
Users,DC=mtit,DC=com
objectCategory:
CN=Person,CN=Schema,CN=Configuration,DC=mtit,DC=com
objectClass: user
objectGUID:: rZKKDxj4+EGLI37f/GqrYA==
objectSid:: AQUAAAAAAAUVAAAASyy8Ggt12XYVJa9HbQQAAA==
primaryGroupID: 513
pwdLastSet: 0
name: Ralph Keaton
sAMAccountName: rkeaton
sAMAccountType: 805306368
sn: Keaton
userAccountControl: 546
uSNChanged: 15807
uSNCreated: 15806
whenChanged: 20000926011852.0Z
whenCreated: 20000926011852.0Z
```

You can see from the output that this user object has no Exchange attributes. You can also see what a powerful tool LDIF Directory

Exchange can be for querying AD once you've become familiar with its syntax!

As another example, let's say that all the users in the Marketing Users OU have been moved to a different address as part of corporate reshuffling. The new address for these users is 11 Swyndon Way, Vancouver, BC, Canada V3W 2R7. Let's create an import file to modify the address of all marketing users. First, here's the portion of the file that will modify user Ralph Keaton:

```
dn: CN=Ralph Keaton,OU=Marketing Users,DC=mtit,DC=com
changetype: modify
replace: streetAddress
streetAddress: 11 Swyndon Way
-
replace: l
l: Vancouver
-
replace: st
st: BC
-
replace: postalCode
postalCode: V3W 2R7
-
```

The `changetype` attribute, which is `modify` in this example, is used to modify attributes of existing objects in the directory. Save this text as newaddress.ldf and import it into AD using LDIF Directory Exchange:

```
ldifde -i -f newaddress.ldf
```

Now open the Properties Sheet for Ralph Keaton in ADUC and check the Address tab to see whether it has modified the address properly. It's a straightforward matter to copy and modify this text so you can modify the addresses of thousands of users to make a large import file that is imported once using LDIF Directory Exchange to modify the addresses of all users in the OU.

Finally let's delete user Ralph Keaton from AD using LDIF Directory Exchange. Type the following text at the command line:

```
dn: CN=Ralph Keaton,OU=Marketing Users,DC=mtit,DC=com
changetype: delete
```

Save this text as deluser.ldf and import it using LDIF Directory Exchange:

```
ldifde -i -f deluser.ldf
```

With the Marketing Users OU already selected in ADUC, select Action → Refresh or press the F5 function key and you'll see that user Ralph Keaton has been removed from AD. One could similarly remove thousands of users from AD in a single stroke using LDIF Directory Exchange and a suitable import file, so be careful!

Summary

In this chapter, we've looked at some advanced administration tasks involving Exchange recipients. We've also seen how to use Windows 2000's LDIF Directory Exchange utility to perform bulk creation, modification, and deletion of recipient objects in AD. In the next chapter, we'll consider how to create and apply *recipient policies* to facilitate administration of Exchange recipients.

CHAPTER 11

Recipient Policies

In the previous chapter we looked at how to do bulk creation of users using the ldifde.exe command-line tool. Exchange 2000 also lets you use policies to manage thousands of recipients at a single stroke, and that's the focus of the present chapter.

There are six walkthroughs in this chapter:

- Modifying the default recipient policy
- Creating a new recipient policy
- Modifying a recipient policy
- Setting the priority of recipient policies
- Forcing recipient policy updates
- Overriding recipient policies

Policy-Based Management

Policy-based management is new to Exchange 2000, and it simplifies the administration of Exchange configuration settings across all or selected portions of an enterprise. By *policy* we mean a collection of settings that are applied to one or more Exchange configuration objects belonging to the same class in Active Directory. Policies can be created, applied, modified, and reapplied as desired and are a powerful tool for Exchange administration.

There are two types of policies in Exchange:

- *System policies*. These are policies that affect the configuration settings of server-side objects such as mailbox stores, public folder stores, and servers.
- *Recipient policies*. These policies affect the configuration settings of client- or user-side objects such as mail-enabled users, groups, contacts, and public folders.

In this chapter we focus only on recipient policies, and we will reserve our discussion of system policies for Chapter 20.

Recipient Policies

Recipient policies have a specific but important task in an Exchange organization: the automatic generation of email addresses for recipient objects (mail-enabled users, groups, contacts, and public folders). You can use recipient policies to:

- Define how the default email address is created for new recipients.
- Modify the default email address for existing recipients.
- Create additional email addresses for new and existing recipients.

Filtering

An LDAP-based process called *filtering* lets you specify which recipient objects a specific recipient policy affects. You can choose to apply a given recipient policy to:

- All recipients uniformly.
- Specific classes of recipients: users, groups, contacts, or public folders.
- Recipients in different departments, for example, Marketing, support, and accounting.
- Recipients in different locations, for example, Vancouver, Seattle, and New York.
- Recipient objects filtered according to any specific values of attributes you specify, including custom-defined attributes.

For example, you could create one recipient policy for all User objects in your organization and a different policy for all Group objects, or you could create one recipient policy for all recipients in Vancouver and a different one for recipients in Seattle.

NOTE

Only one recipient policy can be applied to any given Recipient object. In this regard Exchange policies are different from Windows 2000 group policies that are applied cumulatively to objects. We'll learn more about how recipient policies are applied in a moment.

Default Recipient Policy

When you install your first Exchange server, a default recipient policy is automatically created for your new organization. This default policy determines the format of the default email addresses automatically generated for Recipient objects in your organization.

The default recipient policy can be seen in the Recipient Policies container beneath the Recipients container in System Manager (Figure 11.1). The default policy applies to all recipients regardless of type (users, groups, contacts, and public folders) throughout your Exchange organization.

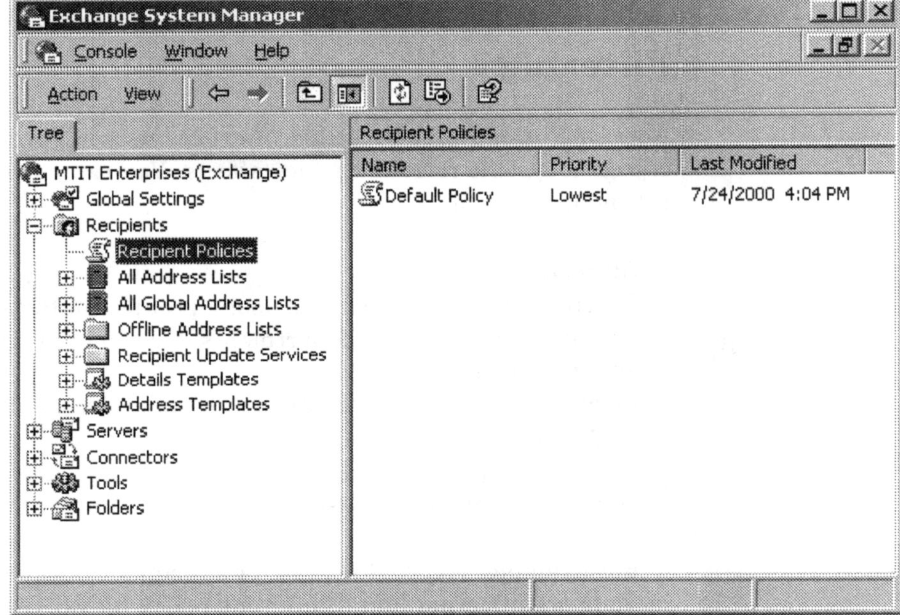

Figure 11.1
The default recipient policy in System Manager.

Let's examine the default recipient policy for our testbed deployment MTIT Enterprises. Double-click on the policy to open it (or right-click and select Properties).

The General tab displays the LDAP filter rules that define to which recipients the policy applies. Note that there is only one filter rule for the default policy: `(mailnickname=*)`.

In other words, the filter selects all recipients regardless of mail nickname (the asterisk represents the wildcard). You cannot modify or remove this rule and you cannot modify to whom the default policy applies because it uniformly applies to all recipients.

The E-mail Addresses tab shows the details of how each type of email address is generated for recipients in your organization (Figure 11.2). By default, there are only two types of email addresses generated for recipients: SMTP (Internet) email addresses and X.400 addresses.

If you have other gateways or connectors installed in your organization, other types of default addresses may be generated for recipients, including MS Mail, Lotus cc:Mail, Lotus Notes, and GroupWise.

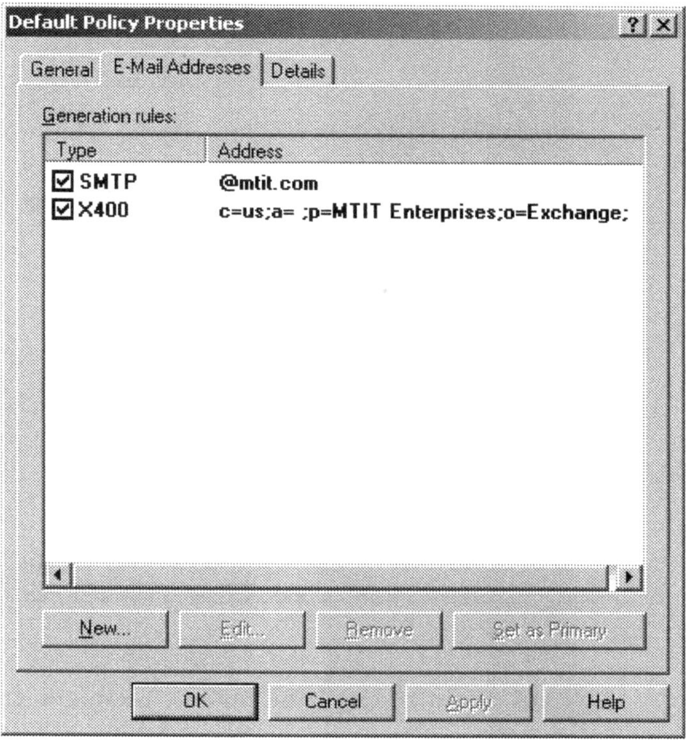

Figure 11.2 Email address types automatically generated by the default recipient policy.

Modifying the Default Recipient Policy

Walkthrough

We can modify the default recipient policy to change the way email addresses are created for all recipients in our organization. Figure 11.2 shows the X400 proxy address starts with `c=us`, meaning that the country is United States. However, our company MTIT Enterprises has its headquarters in Vancouver, Canada. To change the proxy address, double-click on the X400 proxy address shown in Figure 11.2 to open the X400 Address Properties Sheet (Figure 11.3). Change the Country/Region drop-down listbox to CA (Canada) and click OK to apply the changes and close the Properties Sheet. The X400 proxy address now starts with `c=CA`, as desired.

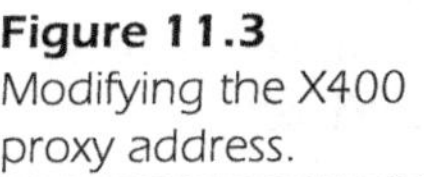

Figure 11.3 Modifying the X400 proxy address.

Click OK again to close the default recipient policy. A dialog box appears saying "The e-mail addresses of type(s) [X400] have been modified. Do you want to update all corresponding recipient e-mail addresses to match these new address(es)?" Click Yes to continue.

Let's check if the policy has been applied. Open ADUC and double-click on one of the mail-enabled recipients created in previous chapters. Switch to the E-mail Addresses tab of the Properties Sheet for the recipient. Does the X400 address for the recipient begin with `c=us` or `c=CA`? Chances are it still says `c=us` because it takes a little time (anywhere from 5 minutes to 1 hour depending on the scope of your Exchange deployment) for the addresses to be updated in Active Directory. It may also depend on how your Recipient Update Service has been configured for your domain or enterprise, as we'll see a little later in this chapter. For now just close the properties sheet for the recipient and check it again later to see whether the changes have been made.

TIP

By default, the email addresses of all recipients are automatically based on recipient policies, which means that changing the default recipient policy affects all recipients by default. You can, however, specify that selected recipients should not have their email addresses updated by policy changes. You can do this for a given recipient by selecting the E-mail Addresses tab of their properties sheet in ADUC (Figure 11.2) and clearing the checkbox at the bottom labeled "Automatically update e-mail addresses based on recipient policy." Now when you change the default policy, the email address for the selected user will not be updated automatically.

When the policy finally takes effect, your recipients have two X400 addresses, the original `c=us` and the new `c=CA`. The `c=CA` is now their primary X400 address, and the original `c=us` address has been demoted to the secondary X400 address. You can decide which is the primary address by selecting the address shown in Figure 11.2 and clicking the Set As Primary button.

NOTE

Coverage of X400 address concepts in this book is limited. For more information on how X400 messaging works and X400 address formats, see my earlier book, Administering Exchange Server, *from McGraw-Hill.*

More on Modifying the Default Recipient Policy

Besides modifying the existing SMTP or X400 proxy addresses, the default recipient policy can be used to create additional email addresses for all recipients in your organization. To do this, click the New button shown in Figure 11.2, select the type of additional address you want to create, and specify the proxy address from which the new addresses will be generated.

For example, let's say our company is in the process of changing its domain name from mtit.com to mtitworld.com. You could create a new SMTP proxy address @mtitworld.com for all recipients in your organization and, after this new domain name becomes well known with your business partners and customers, you could make mtitworld.com the default SMTP address type.

Let's do this. Click the New button, select SMTP Address, click OK, and enter the proxy address as @mtitworld.com (Figure 11.4). Click OK to define the new proxy address and return to the Default Policy Properties Sheet (Figure 11.2). Note that the new proxy address appears in the Generation Rules listbox but is unchecked, that is, not enabled until you select its checkbox. Note also that @mtit.com remains the primary SMTP address, whereas @mtitworld.com represents the secondary SMTP address, although this can be changed for all recipients by selecting @mtitworld.com and clicking the Set As Primary button.

Figure 11.4
Defining a secondary SMTP proxy address.

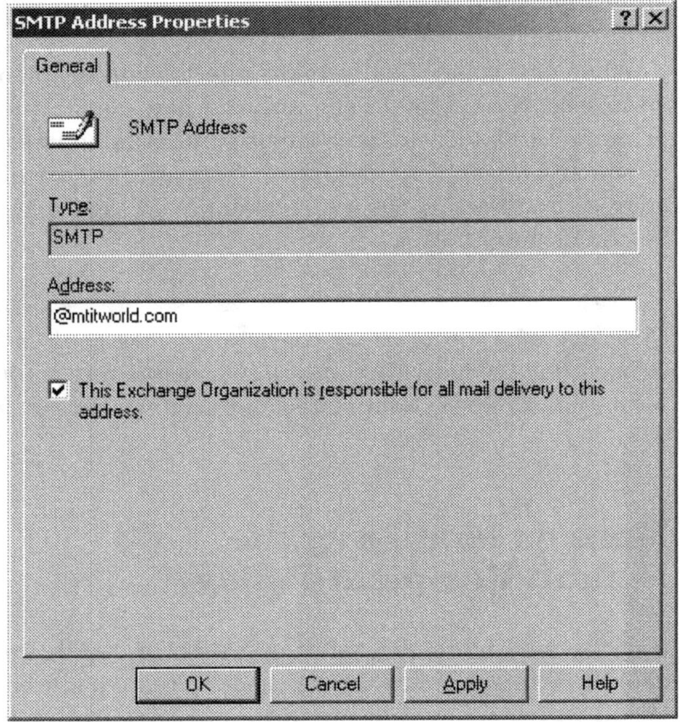

Enable the new proxy address by selecting its checkbox and click OK to apply the policy. Wait a few minutes and check the E-mail Addresses tab of a user in ADUC to see if it has been applied.

TIP

You can speed up the application of the modified default policy by right-clicking the policy in System Manager and selecting Apply This Policy Now. We'll talk about this again later in this chapter.

Creating a New Recipient Policy

Walkthrough

The default recipient policy always applies to all recipients in an Exchange organization. If you want to generate proxy addresses for only a selected portion of recipients in your organization, you have to create a new recipient policy. New policies are completely customizable, as we will now see.

Let's create a recipient policy for mailbox-enabled users in the marketing department of our testbed company MTIT Enterprises. Open System Manager, expand the Recipients container, and select the Recipients container within it. Right-click on the Recipient Policies container and select New → Recipient Policy to open a blank (unconfigured) Properties Sheet for the new policy (Figure 11.5).

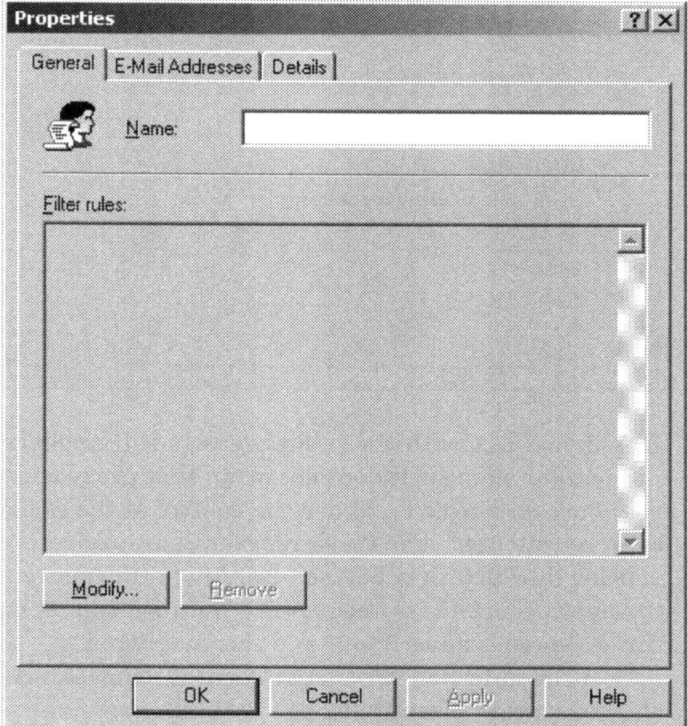

Figure 11.5
Creating a new recipient policy.

First give the new policy a name. It's a good idea to use a descriptive name, so let's call it Recipient Policy for Marketing Users.

Next we'll create a filter that selects objects of type User that have their Department attribute set to the value Marketing. Click the Modify button shown in Figure 11.5 to open the Find Exchange Recipients dialog box (Figure 11.6). We've seen this dialog box (see Figures 7.3 through 7.5) so we won't spend time discussing it now. On the General tab, clear all checkboxes except Users With Exchange Mailbox. Then switch to the Advanced tab and select Field → User → Department. Change the Condition to Is Exactly and specify the value as Marketing. Click Add to create the filter rule, click Find Now, and verify that mailbox-enabled users in your marketing department show up in the query results. Click OK to return to the Properties Sheet for the new policy you are creating.

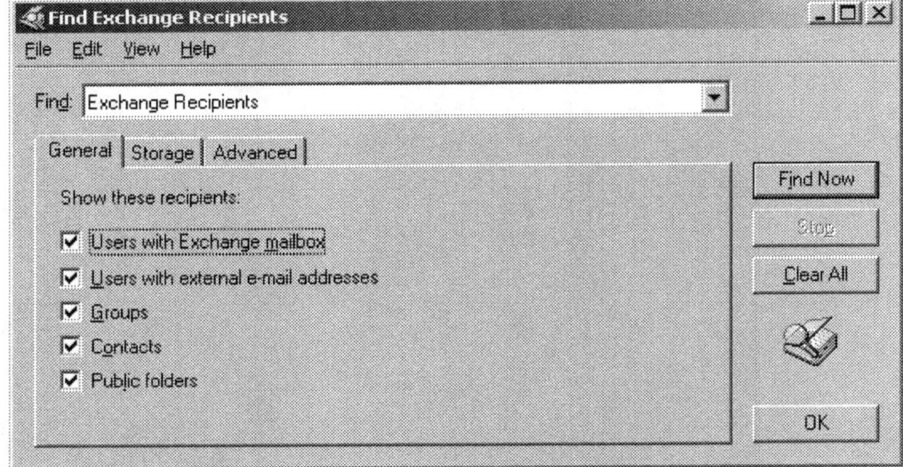

Figure 11.6 Creating a filter rule for the new policy.

A dialog box with the following text will appear: "When a recipient policy filter changes it does not mean that proxy addresses for recipients who may no longer be under the control of the policy will be automatically reevaluated. For these recipients to receive proxies from the new policies to which they belong, use 'Apply this policy now' on the policies that now affect these recipients." Because this is our first new policy, this message is superfluous and can be ignored.

A filter rule has now been created that selects mailbox-enabled objects of type User that have their Department attribute set to the value Marketing. This rule looks like the following code:

```
(&(&(&(& (mailnickname=*) (| (&(objectCategory=person)
(objectClass=user)(|(homeMDB=*)(msExchHomeServerName=*)))
)))(objectCategory=user)(department=Marketing)))
```

It's not necessary for us to understand the syntax of this LDAP filter rule, so let's continue by switching to the E-Mail Addresses tab on the Properties Sheet for our new policy.

On this tab, click New and create a new proxy address of type SMTP. On the SMTP Address Properties Sheet (Figure 11.4) enter the proxy address as @marketing.mtit.com and click OK. Select the checkbox to enable the new proxy address for users in the marketing department and click OK and then Yes to create the new policy and have it applied.

In System Manager, force the policy by right-clicking on it and selecting Apply This Policy Now and then check a few minutes later in ADUC to see if the effect is what you wanted.

NOTE

On the face of it, we have created a secondary address for our marketing users that enables them to send and receive email using SMTP addresses of the form <username>@marketing.mtit.com. Of course, messages addressed like this will never be delivered unless you also configure the DNS name servers to forward mail addressed to the marketing.mtit.com domain to the appropriate Exchange servers. Setting up DNS name servers for your Exchange servers involves creating address (A) records with their IP addresses and mail exchanger (MX) records to identify the SMTP domains serviced by these servers. For example, our first Exchange server Box14 has the IP address 172.16.11.14 in our testbed set-up and would need DNS records similar to the following code within the mtit.com zone on the name server:

```
BOX14          A              172.16.11.14
Marketing      MX      10     BOX14
```

This will result in all mail addressed to either the zone domain (mtit.com) or the marketing subdomain (marketing.mtit.com) to be forwarded to Exchange server Box14 for handling. For further information on configuring DNS name servers for handling SMTP mail, see any good book on DNS.

Modifying a Recipient Policy

Walkthrough

Making changes to an existing recipient policy is easy: just double-click on the policy in System Manager to open its Properties Sheet and then make the changes you want. You can make the following changes to a recipient policy:

- Change the name
- Create, remove, or modify filter rules
- Change the proxy address
- Change which proxy address is the primary one

You can also delete a recipient policy by right-clicking on it in System Manager and selecting Delete.

NOTE

You cannot delete the default recipient policy because it is needed to create default proxy addresses for all recipients in your organization. You can only delete custom recipient policies.

Setting the Priority of Recipient Policies

Walkthrough

If you have more than one recipient policy matching the filter conditions of a specific recipient or group of recipients, you can change the priority of your policies to determine which one is applied. As we mentioned earlier, only one recipient policy is applied to any given recipient, unlike Group Policies in Windows 2000, in which several policies may be applied to an object, the result being a cumulative (overriding) effect.

At this point we only have two recipient policies for our organization, and if we view them in System Manager they look like this:

- Recipient policy for Marketing users (priority = 1)
- Default policy (priority = lowest)

Note that the default policy always has the lowest priority of any policy in your organization. This means that, if a filter condition indicates that both the default policy and a custom policy (such as our Recipient Policy for Marketing Users) match a given recipient, then only the custom policy is applied to that recipient. In other words, our default policy is not applied to mailbox-enabled users in the marketing department.

Because we can't change the priority of our default policy, we can't change it for our single custom policy unless we create another. Create a new policy called Recipient Policy for Users in Vancouver as follows:

- Create a filter rule that selects only mailbox-enabled users where their City attribute is set to the value Vancouver (make sure Jane Smith has this value for the attribute).
- Create a new SMTP proxy address @vancouver.mtit.com and enable this proxy address in the policy.

Figure 11.7 shows our list of recipient policies now in System Manager. Note that our new policy has priority 2 and is beneath our earlier policy in the list but above the default policy.

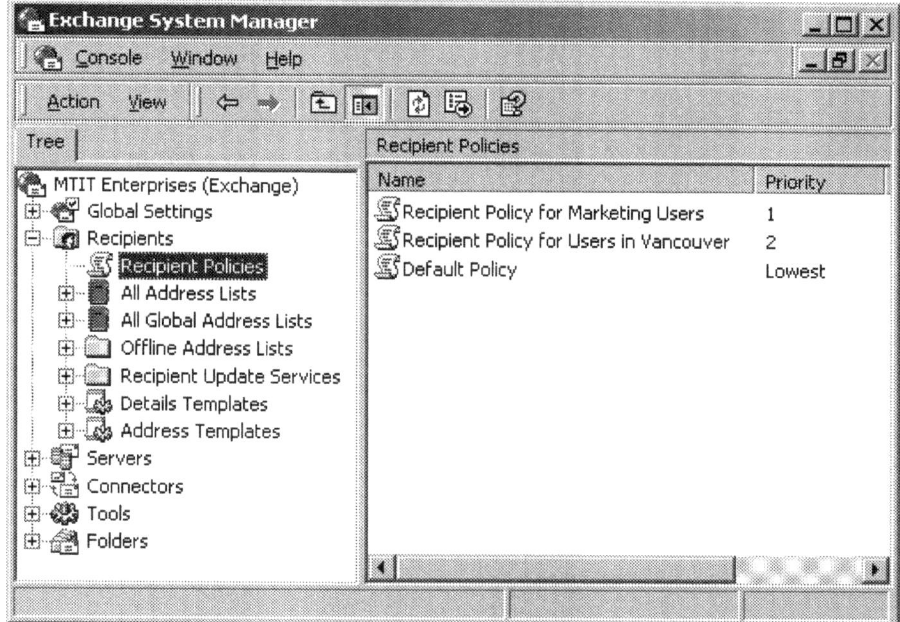

Figure 11.7 Setting the priority of recipient policies for your organization.

Now apply the new policy immediately by right-clicking on it and selecting Apply This Policy Now. What do you expect to occur? Here's the rule for how recipient policies are applied: The policy that is applied to a recipient is the one that has the highest priority with the specified filter conditions that match the recipient.

Obviously policies 1 and 2 match recipient Jane Smith, because she is both a member of the marketing department and works in Vancouver. However, because only one of these policies can be applied to her, it is the one with highest priority that is applied, namely the Recipient Policy for Marketing Users (priority = 1). This means she will have a secondary address, jsmith@marketing.mtit.com, created but not one like jsmith@vancouver.mtit.com.

Let's change the priority of the two custom policies so that Vancouver will be highest. To do this, right-click on Recipient Policy for Users in Vancouver and select All Tasks → Move Up. The order of the two custom policies is reversed, and at the next policy update interval the policies will be reapplied (see the Under the Hood note on how recipient policy updates are scheduled).

UNDER THE HOOD

How Recipient Policy Updates are Scheduled

The way that recipient policies are applied depends on the configuration of the recipient update service *(RUS) for your organization. The RUS is an Exchange service that runs within the context or the System Attendant service.*

To configure the recipient policy update interval, open System Manager and select Recipient Update Services in the Recipients Container. The right-hand pane contains one RUS for your entire enterprise and one for each domain in your forest. Double-click the RUS you want to configure to open its Properties Sheet. By default, the Update Interval is set to Always Run, which means recipient policies are automatically reapplied whenever they are modified (although it may take up to an hour for them to be applied). You can select the following values for the update interval:

Always Run
Run every hour
Run every 2 hours
Run every 4 hours
Never run
Use custom schedule

You probably want to change the update interval from Always Run to some other value if you have a large organization with many recipients.

Forcing Recipient Policy Updates

Walkthrough

You can force recipient policy updates to occur in two ways:

1. To force a particular recipient policy to be applied immediately, right-click on the policy in System Manager and select Apply This Policy Now.

2. To force all recipient policies to be applied immediately (the preferred method when multiple policies exist for your organization), select the Recipient Update Services container in the Recipients container in System Manager. Right-click on the appropriate Recipient Update Service node in the right-hand pane and select Update Now.

Wait a few minutes and check the results. If the policies don't seem to be applied properly (the recipients don't have the expected proxy addresses created for them), try right-clicking the same Recipient Update Service again but this time select Rebuild. This will rebuild the proxy addresses for all recipients in your organization from scratch. This can take a long time if you have many recipients, so rebuild during off hours to avoid mail problems for your users.

Overriding Recipient Policies

Walkthrough

You can override the effect of recipient policies for any recipient by opening the Properties Sheet for that recipient and making any changes you want on the E-Mail Addresses tab. After making your changes, make sure you deselect the checkbox labeled "Automatically update e-mail addresses based on recipient policy" so your changes won't be overridden during the next update interval.

Summary

We've covered a great deal concerning managing recipients up to this point because recipients represent users, and users are what messaging systems are designed to support.

We're going to move on to deeper aspects of Exchange relating to the servers themselves and how they can be managed. We'll begin in Chapter 12 with a look at *administrative groups* and what they are used for.

CHAPTER 12

Administrative Groups

This chapter introduces the concept of administrative groups, a new feature of Exchange 2000 that simplifies the management of Exchange resources in an enterprise-level messaging environment. We'll look at how to create and use Administrative groups, and examine the difference between running Exchange in native versus mixed mode.

There are nine walkthroughs in this chapter:

- Enable support for administrative groups
- Change the operations mode
- Rename the default first administrative group
- Create a new administrative group
- Install an Exchange server into an administrative group
- Add a container to an administrative group
- Move an object between administrative groups
- Copy an object between administrative groups
- Delete an administrative group

Administrative Groups

Administrative groups are a new feature of Exchange 2000 that helps to simplify the administration of a large Exchange organization by overcoming some of the limitations of sites in Exchange 5.5 and previous versions (see the Backgrounder note).

Enterprise-level messaging systems basically involve two different structures or topologies:

- *Logical topology.* This term refers to the fact that your company is structured into different elements such as branch offices at different locations, different departments or business units, and different management groups or divisions. Windows 2000 allows the logical topology of your company to be mirrored through the use of forests, trees, domains, and organizational units.
- *Physical topology.* This term refers to the collection of network elements (LANs and WAN links) that make up an enterprise-level network. LANs consist of network devices (computers, switches, routers, and so on) that are joined together using permanent, high-speed connections. WAN links may be either dedicated (permanent) or dial-up (on demand) and high-speed or low-speed. Windows 2000 lets you mirror the physical topology of your network using sites and site links.

This flexibility provided by Windows 2000 of being able to separate the logical and physical topologies of your network forms the underlying basis of the new administration model of Exchange 2000. Specifically, Exchange lets you define two new types of groups:

- *Administration groups.* These are used to partition the logical topology of your network into different portions for more flexible administration of your Exchange organization. They are called *administrative groups* because they mirror the administrative organization of your company (as locations, departments, divisions, and so on) and network (as trees, domains, and organizational units within your enterprise's forest).
- *Routing groups.* These are used to partition the physical topology of your network into different portions for greater control over message routing throughout your Exchange organization. They are called *routing groups* because they mirror the routing topology of your network, which itself depends on and typically mirrors the different types of network connectivity (LAN or WAN, fast or slow, permanent or dial-up) within your enterprise's network.

NOTE

Although administrative and routing groups are called groups, they are not groups in the same sense of security or distribution groups, which are collections of users. Rather, they are groups in the more general Windows 2000 sense of "collections of objects within Active Directory."

We will look at routing groups in Chapter 21. In this chapter, we'll look at administrative groups to see the power and flexibility they bring to the administration of a large Exchange organization.

BACKGROUNDER

Exchange 5.5 Sites versus Exchange 2000 Administrative Groups

In earlier versions of Exchange, both message routing and administration were closely tied to the concept of a site. An Exchange 5.5 site consisted of a collection of Exchange servers connected together using high-speed, permanent, reliable network connections. Sites formed the boundaries of both the management of the messaging system (logical boundary) and message routing (physical boundary). In other words, you could delegate administration of an Exchange 5.5 site to a person or group of persons, and you could route to or from different sites using connectors and bridgehead servers. For example, you could have different people manage the servers in Vancouver and Chicago, but typically all messages routed in or out of these cities might be managed by a single bridgehead server in each city.

In Exchange 2000, the logical and physical network topologies are distinct and can be defined and managed separately, which means you can define your routing topology separately from your administrative topology. For example, you could establish different routing groups for servers in Vancouver and Chicago to handle routing of mail between them over a slow WAN link but have the servers in both locations belong to the same administrative group to allow you to administer your Exchange organization centrally. We'll look more at the different administration models you can use for Exchange 2000 later in this chapter.

How Administrative Groups Work

A large organization typically creates several administrative groups to divide administration of its messaging system between different groups of people in an IT division. Permissions are assigned to each administrative group to specify the scope and level of access different members of an IT staff will have over the contents of each group. Various Exchange resources are then added to each administrative group, which automatically causes the Exchange permissions assigned to the group to propagate downward to the resources within the group. The kinds of resources you can add to administrative groups are:

- Exchange servers
- Public folder trees
- System policies
- Routing groups

From this discussion we can see that the main advantage of using administrative groups is that it simplifies the management of permissions for Exchange resources. These resources are all objects within Active Directory (as are administrative groups), so Exchange makes use of the permissions-inheritance features of Active Directory to simplify assignment of permissions to Exchange configuration objects. We'll see how to do this in a practical way later in this chapter, and we'll cover Exchange permissions in Chapter 13.

TIP

Administrative groups can also function as logical containers for Exchange 5.5 sites within a mixed Exchange 2000/5.5 messaging environment. We'll look at this later when we talk about upgrading Exchange in Chapter 25.

The Default Administrative Group

When you first install an Exchange 2000 server in a new Exchange deployment (as in our testbed MTIT Enterprises deployment), the following default administrative and routing groups are created:

- A default administrative group called First Administrative Group
- A default routing group called First Routing Group

These two groups are essentially just containers within Active Directory, and you won't normally see them in the Exchange hierarchy within System Manager because in a new Exchange 2000 deployment the first server is configured to run by default in mixed mode in case you need to interoperate with an existing Exchange 5.5 organization during the migration period from the old mail system to Exchange 2000. We'll talk about the mixed-mode operation of Exchange later in this chapter, and we'll see soon how to make the default First Administrative Group visible in System Manager.

When to Create Additional Administrative Groups

The key to using administrative groups is "Don't create any additional ones unless you need to!" In other words, try to get along with the default First Administrative Group unless you need the extra flexibility (and complexity!) that comes with using additional administrative groups.

If you are deploying a new Exchange 2000 messaging system in a small- or medium-sized company with only one geographic location, you probably don't need to create any additional administrative groups or even display the default group in System Manager. All the Exchange servers will belong to a single administrative group and will be managed as a unit by a single person or group of persons in the IT division.

However, if your company is a large-scale enterprise, typically having multiple offices in different states or countries, then creating additional administrative groups is probably a good idea because it allows you to group Exchange servers and other messaging resources together for administration purposes. For example, if you have branch offices in Boston, New York, and Halifax, you might create three administrative groups, once for each location, and place the Exchange servers in each location within their associated administrative group. That way all Exchange servers in Halifax can be managed by IT staff in Halifax, all servers in Boston by staff in Boston, and so on. There are other ways to assign administrative responsibilities depending on the administrative model that your company follows, and we'll discuss several of these models in a moment.

In addition, if you are moving from an existing Exchange 5.5 messaging system to Exchange 2000, and if your existing messaging system has multiple sites, then you will be initially working with several administrative groups in the mixed Exchange 2000/5.5 deployment because changing from Exchange 5.5 to Exchange 2000 causes each Exchange 5.5 site to become Exchange 2000 administrative and routing groups by default. Once migration is complete, you can choose to consolidate all your Exchange 2000 servers into a single administrative group, if your network connectivity supports such an option.

The point is, planning makes perfect. It's a good idea when deploying a new Exchange 2000 messaging system that will span several locations to plan the structure of administrative and routing groups before you begin deployment. Immediately after you've installed your first Exchange 2000 server is the best time to create additional administrative and routing groups. This is especially important if you plan to continue running in mixed mode for a while (to support connectivity with your downlevel Exchange 5.5 messaging system, if you have one) because in mixed mode Exchange servers cannot be moved from one administrative group to another. If you have multiple administrative groups defined for your organization, each time you run Setup to install a new Exchange server you will be prompted on which administrative and routing group the server is to join. If the server is running in mixed mode, then your decision is final unless you switch to native mode.

Administrative Models for Exchange Organizations

Before we actually start creating and using administrative groups in our walkthroughs, let's take a deeper look at planning issues related to deploying them in a large enterprise.

There are basically three different ways that network resources can be managed by the IT division of a large company that spans multiple geographic locations:

- Centralized administration from one location by one person or group of people
- Decentralized (distributed) administration, where each location is managed by a different person or group of people, typically people who are on site
- Some kind of mixture of the two

The overall choice you make for the management model of your IT division will determine how you use administrative groups in your Exchange organization.

Centralized Administration Model

Centralized administration means that one person or group of people runs everything. If your company is located in only one geographic location, then centralized administration is a cost-effective way of managing computing resources. In this case, you will typically only have one administrative group, the default First Administrative Group, and one or more routing groups depending on how you route messages around your campus (assuming you have a multibuilding operation located on a campus or industrial park).

If you have smaller sites within the same city as your main operation, then you may still choose a centralized administration model and have IT staff drive to the other sites when they need to upgrade hardware or perform other hands-on tasks. For example, you might have your headquarters in a skyscraper downtown, your warehouse in an industrial park in the suburbs, and your accounting department in an office across the river. One administrative group will suffice, but you may implement several routing groups to better manage message routing between the different locations.

If you have a large main office in one city and small branch offices in other towns or states, then you might be able to get away with using only one administrative group. When hardware breaks down or needs to be upgraded at a remote branch office, you could fly a member of the IT division to the remote location perform the job. Typically, with small branch offices, it may be more cost effective to fly people in occasionally than hire a full-time administrator on site.

Distributed Administration Model

Distributed administration means decentralized management of resources. In other words, no single person or group is responsible for managing all computing resources. Distributed administration is typically used when the enterprise consists of multiple large- or medium-sized business units that are located in different states, countries, or continents. In this case each location requires its own on-site IT staff, so why not have it manage its own on-site computing resources? Exchange 2000 administration groups allow you to do this easily: simply create an administrative group for each geographic location where your company has a significant business presence (that is, business units that operate relatively independently of corporate headquarters) and assign management of on-site Exchange resources (servers, public folders, system policies, and so on) to the on-site IT staff.

In this scenario, you would still have a central IT division at headquarters, but its responsibilities would be limited to managing Exchange resources at headquarters and to developing standards and guidelines for the rest of the enterprise to follow.

If you migrate an existing multisite Exchange 5.5 messaging system to Exchange 2000, then by default you end up with just this sort of distributed administration model, with one administration group and one routing group automatically created for each of the existing Exchange 5.5 sites.

Mixed Administration Model

Most common in large companies is a mixed administration model that combines aspects of both centralized and distributed administrations of IT resources. What we are describing is decentralized administration overall (each location manages its own resources) with specific centralized administration on top; for example:

- You could create a special administrative group to manage the routing topology of the messaging backbone and delegate access for these resources to qualified members of the divisional staff at headquarters. This is a good idea because the routing topology of the network is the backbone of its operation and needs to be handled only by experts. All other aspects of day-to-day administration of Exchange can be handled by regional administrators at each location.
- You could create another administrative group to manage system policies for the entire Exchange organization to ensure uniformity of standards and operations across all Exchange servers in the enterprise. Alternatively, you could have central IT create and manage some policies and regional IT manage other less critical ones.

Whatever you decide, it's a good idea to plan deployment of administrative and routing groups ahead of time to ensure optimum management and message routing in a large Exchange 2000–based messaging rollout.

Enable Support for Administrative Groups

Walkthrough

It's time to start working hands-on with administrative groups so we can see how they operate. We'll begin by enabling support for administrative (and routing) groups in System Manager. This procedure simply reveals the two default containers created when our first Exchange 2000 server Box14 was installed.

Administrative (and routing) groups are hidden by default in System Manager to simplify the initial task of administering a new Exchange 2000 deployment. To make them visible, start System Manager, right-click on the Root (organization) container in the directory hierarchy or console tree (left-hand pane), and select Properties. On the General tab, select Display Administrative Groups (Figure 12.1). We won't bother displaying routing groups at this juncture because we plan to discuss them in more detail in Chapter 21.

Click OK to close the Properties Sheet and enable support for administrative groups in System Manager. A message box appears with the test, "You will need to exit and restart the Microsoft Exchange System Manager to view the results of these changes." Click OK and exit System Manager.

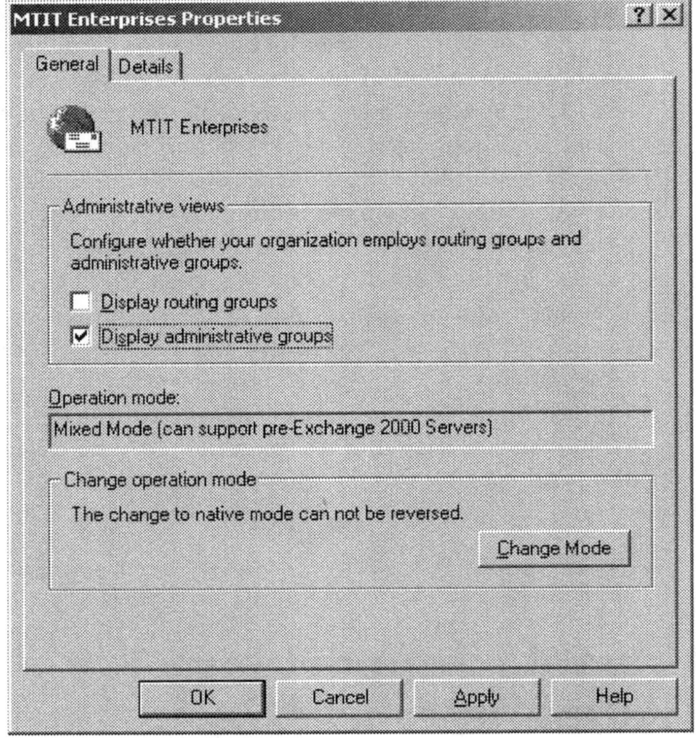

Figure 12.1 Enabling support for administrative groups in System Manager.

Restart System Manager and you can see that the top-level containers in the console tree have changed (Figure 12.2). Specifically, instead of the original six top-level containers (Global Settings, Recipients, Servers, Connectors, Tools, and Folders), you now have only four (Global Settings, Recipients, Tools, and a new container called Administrative Groups). The three missing top-level containers (Servers, Connectors, and Folders) have simply been moved so that they are within the First Administrative Group container, which is within the new Administrative Groups top-level container. Nothing has actually changed in Active Directory—objects are merely displayed differently in System Manager.

Change the Operations Mode

Walkthrough

To use the full power of administrative groups your Exchange servers need to be running in native mode. Exchange 2000 has two operations modes: native and mixed. These modes are global settings and apply to

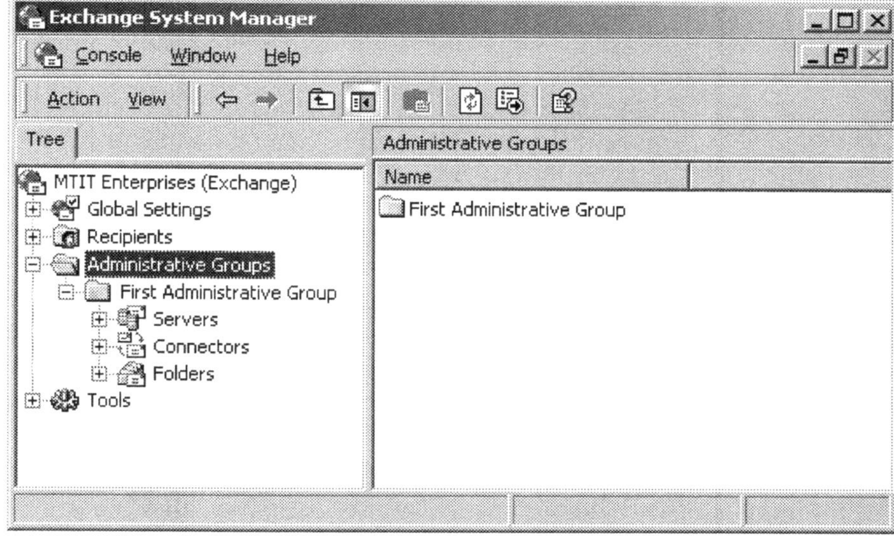

Figure 12.2 The Administrative Groups container in System Manager.

the entire Exchange organization, not to individual servers. Let's take a moment to examine these two modes of operation.

NOTE

The terms native mode *and* mixed mode *in Exchange mean something different than the same terms in Windows 2000. In Windows 2000,* mixed mode *means support for downlevel Windows NT backup domain controllers, and* native mode *means all the domain controllers are running Windows 2000.*

Mixed Mode

When you install your first Exchange 2000 server to deploy a new Exchange organization, this server by default is running in mixed mode. The advantage of mixed mode is its interoperability with downlevel Exchange 5.5 and Exchange 5.0 servers, so you typically leave your Exchange 2000 deployment running in mixed mode until your migration from Exchange 5.5 is complete.

The disadvantage of mixed mode is that it makes administrative groups in Exchange 2000 effectively the same as sites in Exchange 5.5, that is, it enforces a one-to-one mapping between administrative and routing groups. In other words, you cannot create multiple routing groups within an administrative group if you are running in mixed mode—each administrative group can contain only one routing group. Mixed mode therefore forces the logical and physical topologies of the messaging system to be identical.

Another disadvantage of running in mixed mode is that you cannot move mailboxes from servers in one administrative group to servers in another. In other words, maintaining interoperability with downlevel Exchange servers by remaining in mixed mode severely limits the administration options.

Native Mode

Switching the Exchange 2000 organization to native mode provides much more flexibility in configuring and administering your messaging system. Native mode allows you to create multiple routing groups for each administrative group, effectively allowing you to separate the physical and logical topologies of your messaging system and configure them differently for optimum performance and manageability. You can easily move mailboxes between servers in different administrative groups.

The disadvantage of running in native mode is that, if there are any remaining Exchange 5.5 or Exchange 5.0 servers around, your Exchange 2000 servers won't even see them and you will be unable to migrate them. You should only switch from mixed to native mode when you have migrated all your downlevel Exchange servers to Exchange 2000. And you should be aware that the switch from mixed to native mode is an irreversible step.

Changing from Mixed to Native Mode

We want to have the full flexibility of administrative groups in our test-bed deployment of Exchange, so let's switch the operations mode from mixed to native. To do this, right-click on the Root (organization) node at the top of the console tree in System Manager and select Properties. Click the Change Mode button shown in Figure 12.1. A dialog box warns you that this step is irreversible—click Yes to continue and then OK to close the Properties Sheet. No reboot is required to change modes!

Open the Properties Sheet for the Organization node again and note that the Change Mode button is no longer present—once you switch to native mode there's no going back. Otherwise, everything should look the same in System Manager.

Exit and then restart System Manager and restart and open the Organization node properties again. This time note that the checkbox for Display Administrative Groups is disabled, which means that you can no longer hide administrative groups in System Manager. However, you can view or hide routing groups as desired (more on routing groups in Chapter 21).

Rename the Default First Administrative Group

Let's rename our default administrative group, First Administrative Group, to something more descriptive. If our two Exchange servers Box14 and Box15 are located in Vancouver, then we can change the name of the default administrative group to Vancouver.

To do this, right-click on First Administrative Group as shown in Figure 12.2 and select Rename. Type "Vancouver" (without the quotation marks) as the new name and press Enter to establish the new name.

Changing the name of an administrative group changes the Active Directory namespace of all objects within the group.

Create a New Administrative Group

Our testbed deployment currently includes two Exchange servers located in Vancouver, but we have a branch office in Seattle and want to install a third server there. Before installing our third server, we should create a second administrative group, called Seattle, to which this new server will belong (we want to follow a distributed administration model for our Exchange organization).

To create the Seattle administrative group, right-click on the Administrative Groups container shown in Figure 12.2 and select New → Administrative Group. Specify Seattle as the name of the new group and click OK. At this point, our new administrative group is simply an empty container with no configurable properties other than its name (Figure 12.3).

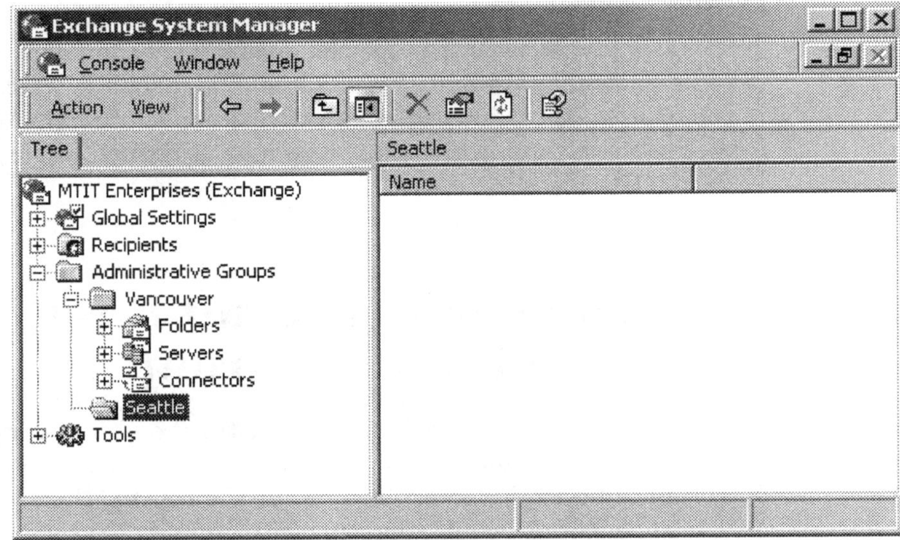

Figure 12.3 The Seattle administrative group.

Install an Exchange Server Into an Administrative Group

We'll now install Exchange on a new machine called Box16 and specify during installation that the server join the existing Seattle administrative group. For simplicity we'll assume both the Vancouver and Seattle offices belong to the same domain mtit.com (this is possible because they are connected by a permanent high-speed T1 link).

We'll perform another network installation of Exchange 2000 for our third Exchange server in the organization MTIT Enterprises. The identity of the system it will be installed on is as follows:

- Computer name: Box16
- Windows 2000 domain: mtit.com
- Role: member server

Log on to the machine using an enterprisewide administrator account such as the default Administrator account in the forest root domain. Make sure you are logged on to the domain and not to the member server using the local Administrator account.

Connect to the network distribution point where the Exchange installation files are located and run `\Setup\I386\Setup.exe`. Walk through the Exchange installation wizard as previously. The only new step to appear will be when you are prompted to specify the administrative group that your new server will belong to (Figure 12.4). This extra step is present only because there are now multiple administrative groups in our Exchange organization. Select Seattle from the drop-down list of administrative groups and continue through the remaining steps of the installation wizard.

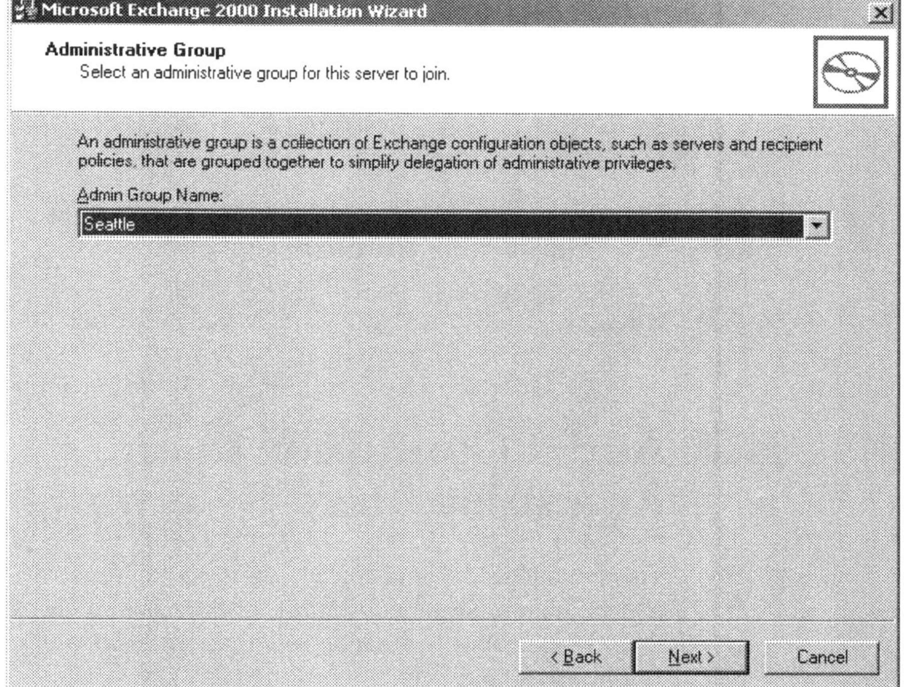

Figure 12.4 Selecting which administrative group a new Exchange server should join.

Once Setup is finished, start System Manager and select the Seattle administrative group in the console tree (left pane). This container, previously empty (Figure 12.3), now contains a Servers container. And within that Servers container, as expected, is Box16, our new Exchange server in Seattle (Figure 12.5).

NOTE

The Vancouver administrative group, which was our default First Administrative Group, has three containers within it: Servers, Connectors, and Folders. The next walkthrough looks at how we can add additional containers to an administrative group.

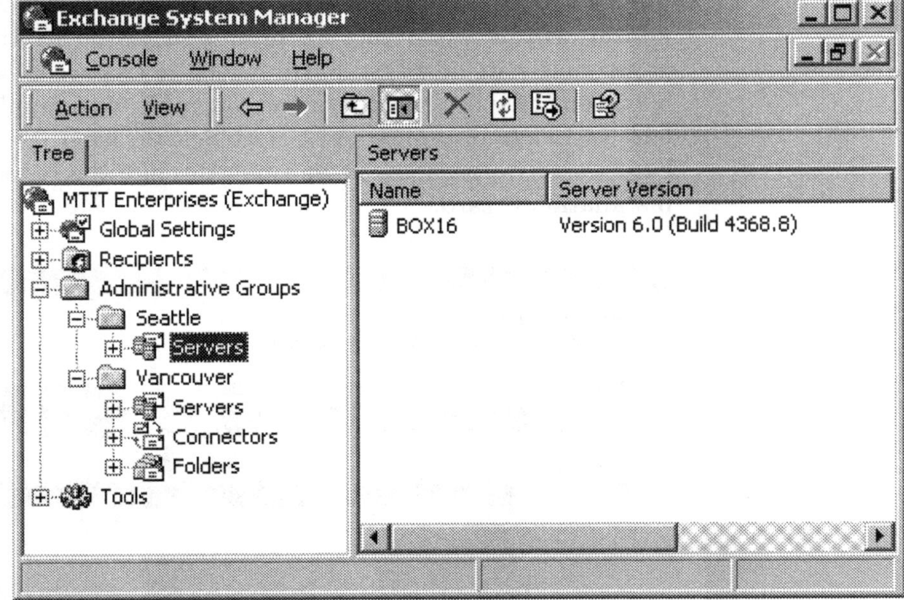

Figure 12.5 Box16 in the Servers container within the Seattle administrative group.

Add a Container to an Administrative Group

You can add additional containers to an administrative group using System Manager. These additional containers may be necessary if you plan to add other objects such as system policies or public-folder trees to the administrative group.

To add a container to an administrative group, right-click on the group in System Manager and select New → <container_type>, where the following types of containers can be created:

- Routing Groups container
- System Policy container
- Public Folders container

Go ahead and create a new Public Folder Container within the Seattle administrative group. A new container called Folders appears within the Seattle administrative group. We'll need this new container in our next walkthrough.

NOTE

Additional types of containers may be added when additional Exchange services such as the Exchange Chat Service have been installed.

Move an Object Between Administrative Groups

Walkthrough

You can move some Exchange configuration objects from one administrative group to another. One restriction is that objects can be moved only from one subcontainer to a similar one in a different administrative group; therefore, if the target administrative group lacks the appropriate container, you will need to create it first (see previous walkthrough for how to do this).

As an example of moving an object, let's move the public-folder tree from the Vancouver to the Seattle administrative group. You can do this two ways:

- Right-click the Public Folders object within the Folders container in the Vancouver administrative group and select Cut from the shortcut menu. Then right-click the Folders container in the Seattle administrative group and select Paste from the shortcut menu.
- Alternatively, select the Folders container in the Vancouver administrative group and then drag the Public Folders object from the right pane to the Folders container in the Seattle administrative group in the console tree. Drag it back to the Vancouver group once you've finished.

Copy an Object Between Administrative Groups

Walkthrough

You can also copy some Exchange objects from one administrative group to another. For example, you could copy a system policy from one group to other groups and then customize the copied policies as needed. The procedure is similar to moving an object except that you use Copy instead of Cut (or hold down the CTRL key while dragging to copy instead of move).

Delete an Administrative Group

Before you delete an administrative group, make sure you have removed all Exchange objects from it. You can do this by either moving objects to different administrative groups or, if they are no longer needed, deleting them. After you have removed all objects from the administrative group, right-click on the group and select Delete to remove it from your Exchange organization.

Summary

In this chapter we looked at how to set up administrative groups in an Exchange organization. Administrative groups can be a powerful way of providing flexibility in administering a large Exchange organization.

Once you have defined your administrative groups and installed your Exchange servers, you then need to learn how to use these administrative groups to manage permissions on Exchange configuration objects. To understand how to do this, we need to understand the Exchange *permissions* model and how it integrates with the Windows 2000 permissions model—and this is the topic of Chapter 13.

CHAPTER 13

Permissions

This chapter covers Exchange permissions and how they can be used to control access to the administration of an Exchange environment. This chapter builds on Chapter 12, which described how to deploy administrative groups but didn't explain how to use these groups to simplify Exchange administration.

There are three walkthroughs in this chapter:

- Delegating control over your entire Exchange organization
- Delegating control over administrative groups
- Delegating recipient creation privileges

Permissions

Understanding permissions is an important aspect of both securing and managing Exchange in an enterprise. We'll start with the general observation that permissions have two basic functions:

- They are used to secure objects by controlling who has access to objects and what level of access users have to those objects. In this sense permissions fulfill a negative criterion of protecting objects against unauthorized access or tampering. In other words, permissions are an aspect of security for the system or network on which the objects reside.
- They are used to grant access to objects so that users, groups, and services can manage those objects with the required level of access. In this sense, permissions fulfill a positive criterion of enabling controlled, distributed management of the system or network.

A simple example will illustrate these points. You can secure a file on an NTFS volume by assigning it NTFS permissions, which automatically deny access to everyone except those to whom access is explicitly granted (either directly or by inheritance). Assigning appropriate NTFS permissions is critical to protect files from unauthorized access. The issue in this case is a negative one, namely the security of the file, which is accomplished by denying access to all but authorized users and groups.

However, you can also grant different NTFS permissions on the file to different users and groups depending on the level of access these people require. In this way, you might grant administrators Full Control of the file so that they can delete it, if necessary, or modify its permissions, assign those who work with the file Modify permission so that they can edit it, and those who simply need access to the information Read permission so that they can read but not alter the file's contents. The issue in this case is a positive one, namely management of the file, which is accomplished by granting access at the appropriate level for different users and groups.

BACKGROUNDER

Windows 2000 Permissions Model

When we talk about permissions and Exchange, we really mean Active Directory (AD) permissions, because Exchange configuration information is stored as objects within AD. Therefore, we need to start with some background on how permissions work in Windows 2000 because Exchange 2000 is built on the foundation of AD and depends on AD for most of its functions.

In Windows 2000 entities such as users, groups, and contacts are objects within AD. These objects are defined by the values of their various attributes. Examples of attributes for a user-type object would be name and telephone number. All user-type objects in AD have the same attributes but are distinguished from one another by having different values.

Access to users, groups, and other objects within AD is determined by controlled permissions. Permissions are authorization to perform operations on objects and may be allowed or denied. Permissions are implemented in Windows 2000 by assigning a security descriptor to each object. A security descriptor is essentially a list of users and groups that can access the object and the level of access (i.e., what permission) they have with regard to the object. A security descriptor is a data structure that contains the following information:

- *Owner SID.* This uniquely identifies the owner of the object within the enterprise. The owner of an object is the security principal who has an intrinsic right to manage the permissions of the object. A security principal is any object that has an account associated with it; the object may be a user, group, computer, or service. A SID (security identifier) is a numeric value that uniquely identifies the object within AD. The name and other attributes of an object may change but its SID never changes.
- *Group SID.* This uniquely identifies the group(s) to which the owner belongs.
- *System Access Control List (SACL).* This specifies how access to the object will be audited by the security subsystem.

- *Discretionary Access Control List (DACL).* This specifies the permissions assigned for the object to different users and groups. The DACL is a data structure containing Access Control Entries (ACEs). Each ACE specifies the permission assigned for the object to a specific user or group, and whether that permission is allowed or denied.

When a security principal (a user, group, computer, or service) wants to access an object within AD, it must first be authenticated. For example, let's say a user wants to access an object within AD to view or modify the values of its attributes by using some tool. When the user logs on to some domain, a domain controller authenticates the user's credentials and grants the user an access token. An access token is a data structure associated with a security principal and contains the following information (we'll use the example of a user account as our security principal):

- *User SID.* This uniquely identifies the user within the enterprise.
- *Group SID.* This uniquely identifies the groups to which the user belongs.
- *User Rights.* This is a list of the privileges that the user has on the local machine.

Once the security principal (that is, user) has an access token, he can try to access objects within AD. To determine whether the user can access the object and the level of access it has, the user's access token is compared with the security descriptor attached to the object. This matching process is done by the Windows 2000 security subsystem, of which AD itself is only a part.

In this matching process, the user SID from the user's access token is compared with each ACE within the DACL of the object's security descriptor (Figure 13.1). First the user SID is compared with each DenyACE in the DACL; if a match is found, then the user is denied access to the object and the matching process stops. If no match is found in the DenyACE, the user SID is compared with each AllowACE in the DACL; if matches are found, the effective (cumulative) permission for the user to access the object is determined and access is granted; if no matches are found for the AllowACEs, then the user is denied access to the object.

What gives the Windows 2000 permissions model its real power is inheritance. Inheritance is the process by which permissions assigned to a parent object are copied to a child object. By default, all permissions assigned to parent objects (such as organizational units and other containers) in AD are copied to all child objects beneath that parent. In other words, you can apply permissions to an entire subtree of objects within the AD hierarchy at a single stroke. You can also choose to override inheritance, if you like, as we will see later. Inheritance simplifies the application of permissions in AD and makes them easier to manage.

This information is probably more than you ever wanted to know about the innards of Windows 2000 (and there's even deeper stuff we haven't covered), but it's important to understand the Windows 2000 permissions model because Exchange 2000 permissions are based on the same underlying mechanism.

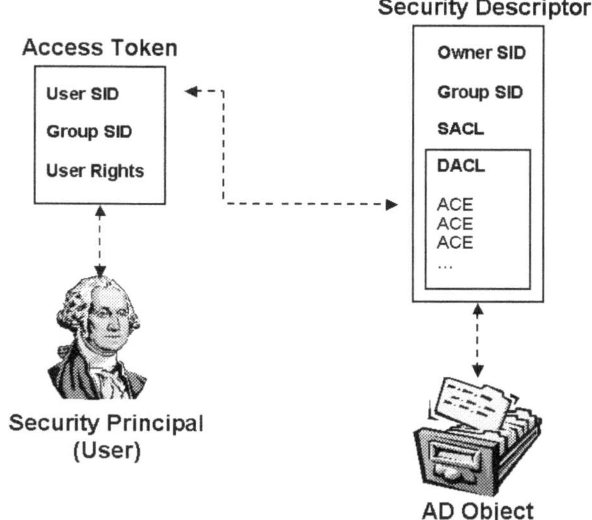

Figure 13.1 How permissions control access to objects in Windows 2000.

Common Active Directory Permissions

Windows 2000 controls access to objects in AD through permissions, and there are several different categories of permissions:

- *Standard permissions.* These permissions generally apply to all (or almost all) classes of objects within AD.
- *Object-specific permissions.* These permissions apply only to objects in certain classes.
- *Extended permissions.* These permissions apply only to objects managed by applications like Exchange, which extend the AD schema when installed.

We won't cover all the possible permissions available for securing AD; instead, Table 13.1 presents a summary of the most common AD permissions that apply to a wide range of different objects (excluding those managed by Exchange, which are covered in the next section). Each of these permissions may be allowed or denied access by a specific security principal for different objects. Some of these permissions are easy to understand, whereas others are a bit esoteric. The table is provided for informational purposes only—we don't want to get sidetracked in too much detail.

TABLE 13.1

Some common Active Directory permissions.

Permission	Description
Add/Remove Self As Member	Permits adding and removing an object as a member
All Extended Writes	Permits all extended writes
All Validated Writes	Permits all types of validated writes
Change Password	Permits changing password for the object
Create All Child Objects	Permits creation of all child objects
Create Object	Permits creating an object of a specific type
Delete	Permits deleting an object
Delete All Child Objects	Permits deletion of all child objects
Delete Object	Permits deleting an object of a specific type
Delete Subtree	Permits deleting an object and its child objects
Extended Write To...	Permits a specific type of extended write
Full Control	Permits reading, writing, deleting, and modifying an object
List Contents	Permits displaying the contents of an object
Modify Owner	Permits changing the ownership of an object
Read All Properties	Permits reading all properties of an object
Read Property	Permits reading a specific property of an object
Receive As	Permits receiving an object
Reset Password	Permits resetting the password for an object
Send As	Permits sending an object
Write All Properties	Permits writing all properties of an object
Write Property	Permits writing a specific property of an object
Validate Write To...	Permits a specific type of validated write

Exchange Server Extended Permissions

Table 13.2 lists the extended permissions available after Exchange 2000 has been installed. Installing Exchange causes the AD schema to be modified to include new classes of objects and new attributes and provides for new permissions that can be applied to these objects. The permissions listed in Table 13.2 are used for controlling administration and usage of Exchange, but not all of these permissions apply to any given Exchange object.

NOTE

The permissions listed in Table 13.2 are related to administering Exchange configuration objects. There are other Exchange permissions available for managing access to Exchange recipients. To see these, select View → Advanced Features in ADUC, and open the Properties Sheet for a mailbox-enabled user. Select the Security tab on this Properties Sheet and scroll through the list of permissions assigned to this recipient object for each security principal listed. In addition to the many common permissions such as Read and Write, you'll find Exchange permissions such as Read Phone and Mail Options.

TABLE 13.2
Extended AD permissions when Exchange 2000 Is installed.

Permission	Description
Add PF To Admin Group	Permits adding a public folder to an administrative group
Administer Information Store	Permits administration of information store
Create Named Properties In The Information Store	Permits creating named properties in information store
Create Public Folder	Permits creating a public folder beneath a top-level public folder
Create Top-Level Public Folder	Permits creating a top-level public folder
Full Store Access	Permits full access to information store
Mail-Enable Public Folder	Permits a public folder to be mail-enabled
Modify Public Folder ACL	Permits the ACL on a public folder to be modified
Modify Public Folder Admin ACL	Permits the Admin ACL on a public folder to be modified
Modify Public Folder Deleted Item Retention	Permits the deleted-item retention period of a public folder to be modified

continued on next page

TABLE 13.2 Extended AD permissions when Exchange 2000 Is installed (continued).

Permission	Description
Modify Public Folder Expiry	Permits the expiration date of a public folder to be modified
Modify Public Folder Quotas	Permits the quota of a public folder to be modified
Modify Public Folder Replica List	Permits the replication list for a public folder to be modified
Open Mail Send Queue	Permits the mail-send queue to be opened
Remove PF From Admin Group	Permits a public folder to be removed
View Information Store Status	Permits the status of information store to be displayed

Managing Permissions

Now that we understand a bit about permissions and how they work in Windows 2000 and Exchange 2000, let's consider how to work with them. There are two ways to view or modify permissions for an object within AD:

- By accessing the Security tab of an object's Properties Sheet in the console used for administering the object.
- By using a wizard such as the Exchange Server Delegation Wizard.

Let's take a look at these two methods and then we'll do some walk-throughs.

Security Tab

The Security tab gives you full control over how you modify the permissions on an object. Figure 13.2 shows the Properties Sheet for Exchange server Box14, with the focus on the Security tab. Note the following:

- The permissions currently displayed are those assigned to the Administrator account for the root domain of the forest. In general, when you view the permissions for an Exchange object, you'll see that these permissions have been assigned to at least the following different security principals:
  - Administrator account in the server's domain
  - Authenticated users' built-in system identity

  - Computer account for the Exchange server itself (in this case, Box14$)
  - Domain Admins group of the forest-root domain
  - Enterprise Admins group for the forest
  - Everyone's built-in system identity
  - Exchange Domain Servers security group
- The permissions currently assigned to the selected security principal are displayed in the lower listbox. If you scroll down this listbox, you'll see standard, object-specific, and Exchange extended types of permissions. A checkbox means the permission is either allowed or denied, depending on which column it is in. A grayed-out checkbox means the permission has be inherited from some parent object in the Exchange hierarchy.
- The checkbox at the bottom of the Security tab allows permissions to propagate from parent objects to the selected object. Clearing this checkbox will disable permissions inheritance for this object and allow you to set all permissions for the object directly.
- The Advanced button opens an Access Control Settings box that gives you even greater control over how you display and modify individual permissions.

NOTE

Never fool around with permissions of AD objects without knowing what you're doing, or you can easily trash your installation. The general rules for modifying permissions, especially advanced ones, are make the minimum changes necessary and only if you know what you're doing.

Exchange Default Permissions

We mentioned some of the security principals that have Exchange permissions assigned to them. When you install Exchange, specific permissions are assigned to these security principals by default to simplify the job of administering Exchange. In particular, the following five built-in security principals (built-in user accounts, groups, and system identities) have specific default permissions assigned to them at the Exchange organization level:

- Administrators group
- Authenticated users' system identity
- Domain Admins group (in the forest-root domain)

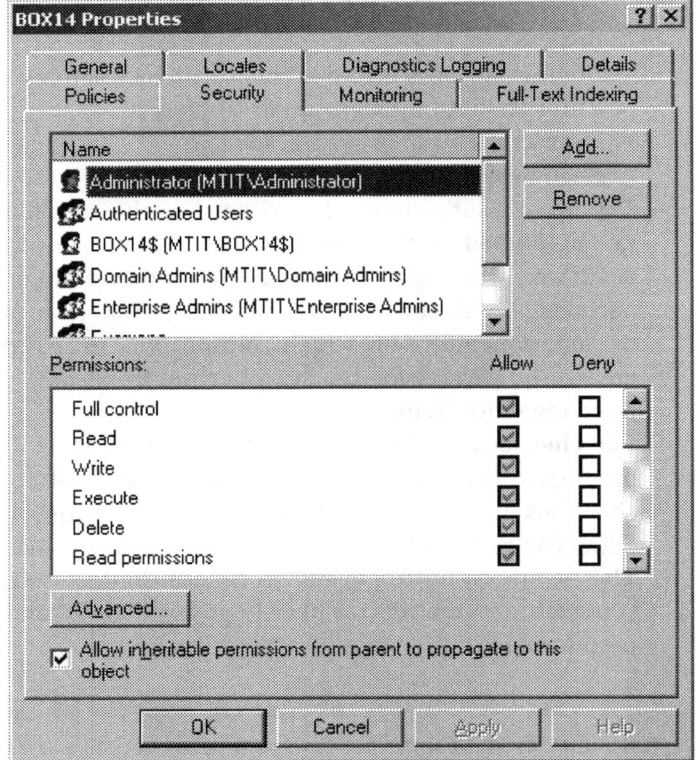

Figure 13.2 The Security tab for Exchange server Box14.

- Enterprise Admins group
- Exchange Domain Servers group

NOTE

By saying that default permissions are assigned to these principals at the organization level, we mean that they are assigned to the Organization container at the top of the Exchange hierarchy within AD. The Organization container is the top of the subtree of objects within AD that contain configuration information for your Exchange organization. In our testbed deployment, this would be the MTIT Enterprises root node in System Manager. By applying these default permissions to the Organization container, they are automatically inherited by all objects further down in the Exchange hierarchy.

Table 13.3 lists the default permissions (both common and Exchange specific) assigned to these different security principals at the Exchange organization level.

TABLE 13.3

Permissions assigned to the prganization container at the top of the Exchange hierarchy in AD.

Permission	Administrators	Authenticated Users	Domain Admins	Enterprise Admins	Exchange Domain Servers
Administer Information Store	✔		✔	✔	
Create All Child Objects	✔		✔	✔	
Create Named Properties in the Information Store	✔		✔	✔	
Create Public Folder	✔		✔	✔	
Create Top-Level Public Folder	✔		✔	✔	
Delete All Child Objects	✔			✔	
Full Control	✔			✔	
Modify Public Folder Admin ACL	✔		✔	✔	
Modify Public Folder Replica List	✔		✔	✔	
Read	✔		✔	✔	✔
Write	✔		✔	✔	
View Information Store Status	✔		✔	✔	

Delegation Wizard

Not all Exchange configuration objects have a Security tab on their Properties Sheets in System Manager. For example, if you right-click on the Organzation (root) node in System Manager and select Properties, only the General and Details tab are available. How do you change the permissions assigned to this object in AD?

NOTE

Some configuration objects in the Exchange hierarchy in System Manager have no Properties Sheet at all! For example, if you right-click on the Administrative Groups container (see Figure 12.2), you'll see that it doesn't have a Properties Sheet. Therefore, permissions cannot be set at the level of this container in the hierarchy.

Permissions for some objects are assigned with the Exchange Administration Delegation Wizard (Figure 13.3) rather than the Security tab because:

- Using a wizard simplifies the process of assigning permissions, especially if these permissions can be assigned according to different predefined administrative roles.
- Using a wizard has less chance of error than manually assigning permissions with the Security tab, which is especially important because permissions are inherited by default, and changing one permission on a container high up in the Exchange hierarchy may have disastrous results if done carelessly.
- Using a wizard hides some of the complicated machinery of specific permissions, and, in most cases, access to this machinery is rarely needed by the typical Exchange administrator.

The Exchange Administration Delegation Wizard is used for modifying permissions for the following Exchange configuration objects:

- The organization (root) node, which is MTIT Enterprises in our testbed deployment.
- Specific administrative groups, such as Vancouver and Seattle in our testbed deployment.

We'll walk through this wizard in a moment but for now let's look at the different Exchange administration roles that can be assigned using this wizard.

TIP

Using the Exchange Administration Delegation Wizard to assign an Exchange administration role to a user doesn't give that user general administrative privileges on the machines running Exchange. If your delegated Exchange administrators to perform actions such as editing the registry on Exchange servers, backing up Exchange servers, or managing the local file system on these machines, you also need to make these users (or the global groups they belong to) members of appropriate built-in groups such as Administrators, Backup Operators, Server Operators, and so on, depending on the level of administrative access you want to give them.

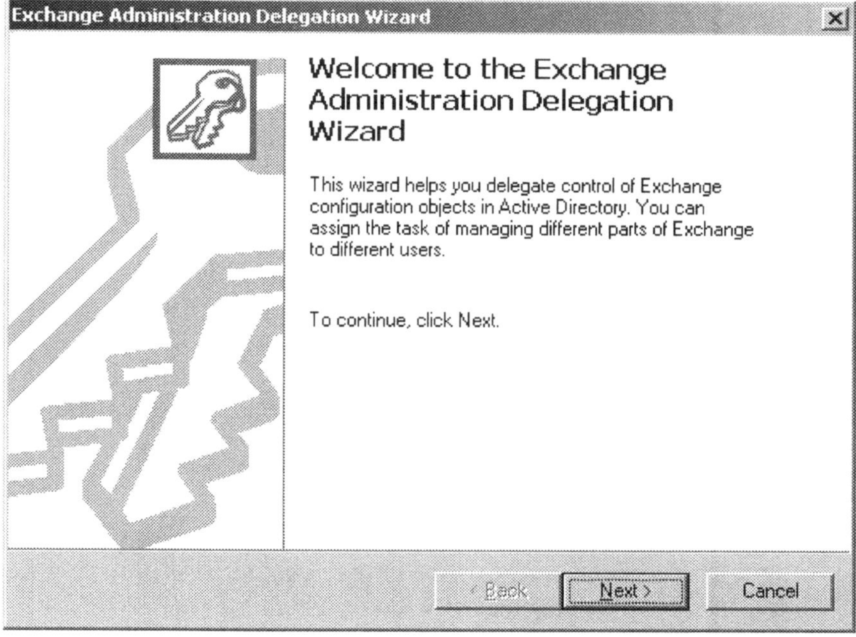

Figure 13.3 The Exchange Administration Delegation Wizard.

Administration Roles

There are three different Exchange administration roles that can be assigned to security principals (users or groups) using the Exchange Administration Delegation Wizard:

- *Exchange Full Administrator.* Users with this role have full control over all aspects of an Exchange organization. Membership in groups having this role should be restricted to those people with the highest level of competency with Exchange.
- *Exchange Administrator.* Users with this role can fully administer any aspect of an Exchange organization but are not permitted to modify the permissions of configuration objects in the Exchange hierarchy. Most Exchange administrators in your enterprise should have this role because it prevents them from what is surely the easiest way of terminally damaging an Exchange organization, namely altering Exchange permissions!

NOTE

Besides not being able to modify permissions, users with Exchange Administrator permissions on the Organization container also cannot run the ForestPrep and DomainPrep utilities and cannot create new mailbox-enabled users unless they are also members of the Account Operators or Administrators built-in groups. Users with Full Exchange Administrator permissions on an administrative group can create or delete the information store for the first virtual server on an Exchange server in the administrative group but cannot do this for the second or higher virtual server unless they also have local Administrator privileges on the machine running Exchange.

- *Exchange View Only Administrator.* Users with this role can view but not modify Exchange configuration settings. Junior support staff should be assigned this role.

TIP

Always assign a role to a group, not to a user. For example, if you assign a certain group the role of Exchange View Only Administrator, you can grant a specific user the role simply by making the user a member of that group, and you can revoke that role for the user by removing the user from the group.

Permissions Strategies

Before we do some walkthroughs with Exchange permissions, let's discuss some strategies for organizing your IT department for the best deployment of Exchange. Microsoft recommends that you organize your Exchange support staff in the three following levels:

- *Enterprise administrators.* These individuals will have the highest level of responsibility for the entire Exchange organization. To assign someone these privileges, make them a member of the Enterprise Admins Global (or universal) security group in ADUC. Because the Enterprise Admins group is a member of the local administrators group on each Exchange server, these administrators will have full control over all aspects of administering each Exchange server throughout the organization.
- *Administrative group administrators.* If you have implemented administrative groups in your enterprise (Chapter 12), what you've

done is essentially partition the management of your Exchange organization into different sections. To take advantage of this, create a global (or universal) security group, calling it something like AdminGroupA or AdminGroupB (unless you can think of something more creative). Then use the Exchange Administration Delegation Wizard to assign the appropriate role (typically Exchange Administrator) to each group for each corresponding administration group in your Exchange organization. Add the appropriate user accounts to each group. We'll do this shortly in our walkthrough.

- *Recipient administrators.* These administrators perform day-to-day tasks involving managing Exchange recipients in your organization. One way of defining this group to use the existing Account Operators built-in groups for each domain and to use the Delegation Wizard to assign the Exchange View Only Administrator role for each administrative group as appropriate. Or you could assign Account Operators this role for the Organization node to allow them to manage recipients throughout the enterprise and not just within specific administrative groups.

UNDER THE HOOD

Built-in Groups in Exchange

We mentioned in Chapter 1 that installing Exchange 2000 creates two new built-in groups in AD: the Exchange Domain Servers and Exchange Enterprise Servers. Actually, several built-in groups and identities are granted some level of Exchange permissions by default when you first install Exchange. The most important ones are:

- Domain Admins. *Members of this Windows 2000 built-in group can manage all aspects of their domain but have less than full control over Exchange servers within their domain. However, because Domain Admins are members of the local administrators group for the domain and because (as we shall see in our first walkthrough) the administrators group has the Exchange Full Control role assigned to it, members of Domain Admins are full Exchange administrators in the domain. The Administrator account in the domain is a member of Domain Admins by default and therefore is also a full Exchange administrator by default for all Exchange servers in the domain.*
- Enterprise Admins. *Members of this Windows 2000 built-in group can manage all aspects of the enterprise. The Enterprise Admins group is a member of the administrators group for each domain in the forest, so*

members of Enterprise Admins have full Exchange administrators throughout the enterprise. The Administrator account in the root domain of the forest is a member of Enterprise Admins by default and therefore is also a full Exchange administrator by default for all Exchange servers in the enterprise.

- Exchange Domain Servers. *All machines running Exchange 2000 in the domain are automatically members of this Exchange 2000 built-in group. You shouldn't modify the membership of this group unless instructed to do so by Microsoft support specialists.*
- Exchange Enterprise Servers. *All Exchange Domain Servers groups in the enterprise are automatically members of this Exchange 2000 built-in group. You shouldn't modify the membership of this group unless instructed to do so by Microsoft support specialists.*
- Everyone. *This built-in special identity is also granted certain Exchange permissions within the Exchange organization, namely permission to create new top-level public folders, public folders beneath an existing top-level public folders, and named properties in the information store.*

Preliminaries to Walkthroughs for this Chapter

Before performing these walkthroughs, make sure you have the following configuration set up on your testbed deployment of Exchange (assuming you are following as we go along):

- The two administrative groups Vancouver and Seattle (Chapter 12).
- A new organizational unit (OU) called IT in the mtit.com domain. This OU will contain members of your IT department (you should create a half dozen or so new users within this OU as well).
- Five new global (or universal) groups created in your IT OU:
  - ExFullAdmins
  - VancouverExAdmins
  - SeattleExAdmins
  - RecipientAdmins
  - ExSupportGroup

Each of these global groups should have as members at least one of IT users.

Delegating Control Over Your Entire Exchange Organization

Walkthrough

We'll use the Exchange Administration Delegation Wizard to assign the Exchange Full Administrator role to the ExFullAdmins global group for our entire Exchange organization, MTIT Enterprises.

Start by opening System Manager and right-clicking on the Organization (root) node in the console tree (this node is called MTIT Enterprises in our testbed deployment). Select Delete Control from the shortcut menu to open the Exchange Administration Delegation Wizard welcome screen (see Figure 13.3).

The first screen of the wizard lets you select which security principals (users and groups) you want to delegate control. The group MTIT\Administrators (the administrators group in the MTIT domain) should be the only group currently displayed and should have the Exchange Full Administrator role assigned to it.

Click Add to open the Delegate Control dialog box. Click Browse to display a list of security principals in AD, select the ExFullAdmins global group you created earlier, and click OK to return to the Delegate Control box. Use the drop-down listbox to select the role Exchange Full Administrator for this global group (Figure 13.4). Click OK to assign the role.

Delegate Control
Group (recommended) or User:
MTIT\ExFullAdmins
Browse...
Role:
Exchange Full Administrator
Role description
The selected group or user can fully administer Exchange system information and modify permissions.
OK
Cancel

Figure 13.4 *Assigning the Exchange Full Administrator role to the ExFullAdmins global group.*

Repeat these steps to assign the Exchange View Only Administrator role to the ExSupportGroup global group. The Users or Groups page of the wizard should now look like Figure 13.5. Click Next and then Finish to close the wizard and delegate the roles. Wait a few moments while the modified permissions are inherited down the entire Exchange configuration subtree of objects within AD.

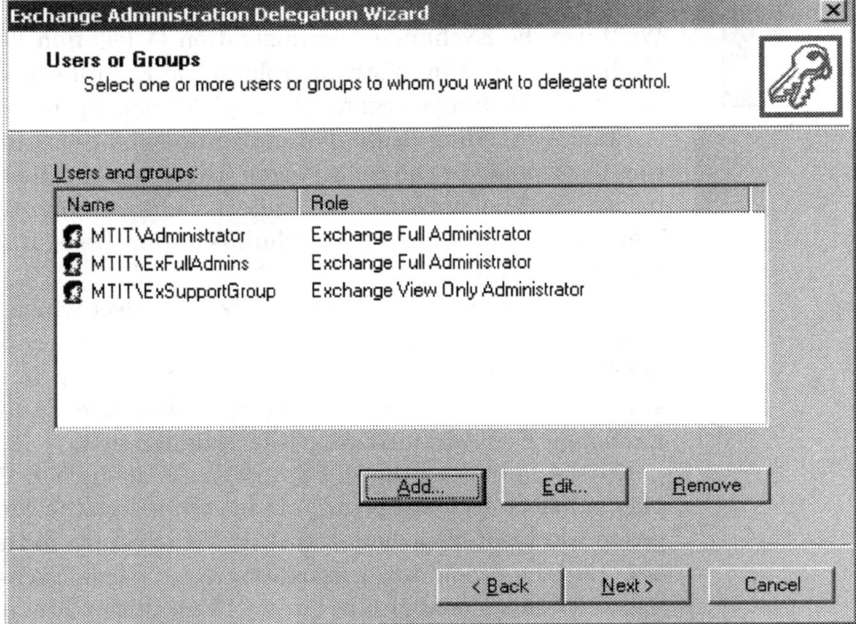

Figure 13.5 Delegating various roles to different groups for administering the entire Exchange organization.

Now test your permissions assignment. Log off and then log on as a user who is a member of the ExFullAdmins global group (in my setup, the user is George Franklin or gfranklin@mtit.com). Open System Manager, open the Properties Sheet for object Box14 within the Servers container for Vancouver, and select the checkbox to enable message tracking on the General tab. Click Apply and, if there's no error message, you've successfully modified a property of Box14. Clear the checkbox and click Apply again to restore the system to its previous state.

To tell if we truly have the Exchange Full Administrator role for this user, we need to test whether the user can modify permissions for Exchange objects. Switch to the Security tab of the Box14 Properties Sheet, select the ExFullAdmins group from the Name listbox, and change the Modify Public Folder Replica List permission from the inherited Allow to explicitly Deny and click Apply. A warning box appears saying "Caution! Deny entries take priority over Allow entries, which can cause unintended effects due to group memberships. Do you want to continue?" Click Yes and the permission is applied. George does in fact have the Exchange Full Administrator role because he can both modify Exchange configuration settings and change permissions on Exchange objects in AD. Change the permission back the way it was previously by clearing the Deny checkbox you previously selected and close the Box14 Properties Sheet.

Now log off and then log on as a user who is a member of the ExSupportGroup global group (my user is Sharon Lee or slee@mtit.com). Sharon should be able to view Exchange configuration information but not change it. Open System Manager and try to make the same changes you did for George. When you try to apply your changes you should receive a dialog box saying "Access denied."

The wizard works as expected. Log off and then on again as the default administrator account to perform the next walkthrough.

TIP

In a smaller Exchange organization, you don't need to create a special global group and assign it the Exchange Full Administrator role. Instead, you can use the built-in global groups Domain Admins and Enterprise Admins, which are members of the local administrators group and therefore have the full Exchange administrator permissions assigned to that group. However, you may find it cleaner to work with your own set of groups rather than the built-in ones.

Delegating Control Over Administrative Groups

Walkthrough

Next we'll use the Exchange Administration Delegation Wizard to delegate Exchange administrative permissions to different groups of users for different administrative groups in our organization. In particular, we will:

- Assign the Exchange Administrator role to the VancouverExAdmins global group for the Vancouver administrative group.
- Assign the Exchange Administrator role to the SeattleExAdmins global group for the Seattle administrative group.

Open System Manager and right-click on the Vancouver node within the Administrative Groups container. Select Delete Control to start the wizard. Note that the permissions previously assigned to the Organization container have been inherited by the Vancouver container.

Click Add and browse to select the VancouverExAdmins group and assign this group the Exchange Administrator role in the Delegate Control dialog box (see Figure 13.4). Your wizard screen should now look like Figure 13.6. Finish the wizard.

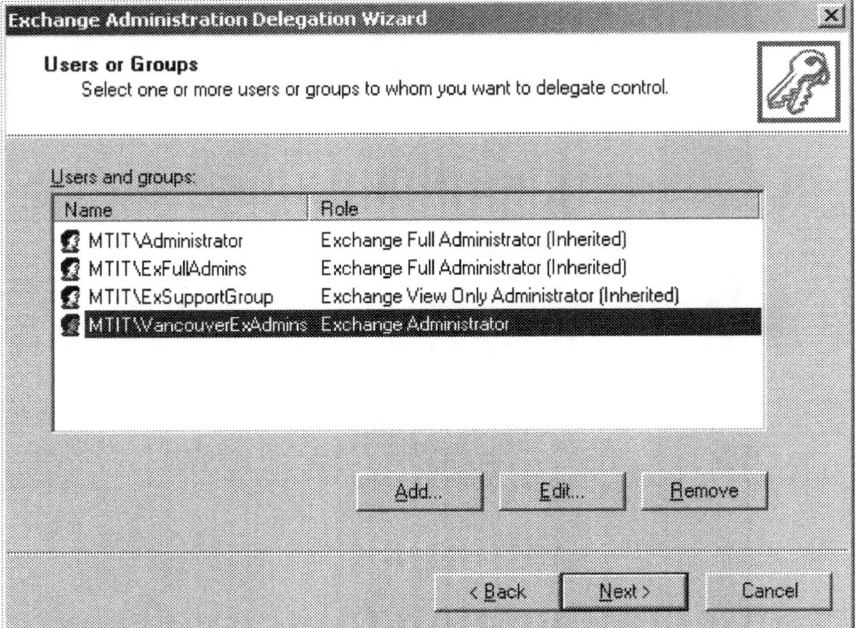

Figure 13.6 Assigning the Exchange Administrator role to the VancouverExAdmin global group for the Vancouver administrative group.

Now repeat these steps, only this time assign the Exchange Administrator role to the SeattleExAdmins global group for the Seattle administrative group.

Once you've completed these steps, test your permissions assignment by logging off and then logging on as a user that belongs to the VancouverExAdmins global group (in my case this is Hannah Parker or hparker@mtit.com). You should find that Hannah can edit Exchange configuration settings for Box14 in Vancouver but cannot edit the configuration of Box16 in Seattle, nor can she modify permissions settings on the Security tab in either administrative group or the Exchange Administration Delegation Wizard. Test a user in the SeattleExAdmins group the same way.

Now we can see what administrative groups, which we covered in Chapter 12, are really for!

Delegating Recipient Creation Privileges

Walkthrough

To create a mailbox, a user needs to be able to create a user in AD. Members of the Account Operators group are supposed to have this privilege by default, so let's test this.

Log on as Administrator, start ADUC, and create a new user called Jason Heart (jheart@mtit.com) in the IT organizational unit. Make Jason a member of the Accounting Operators built-in group.

Now log off and then log on as jheart@mtit.com and see if Jason can use ADUC to create a second user, Susan Olivetti (solivetti@mtit.com). The New Object User wizard lets Jason create the new user but not an associated mailbox for Susan (Figure 13.7). Therefore, members of Account Operators can create new users but cannot mailbox- or mail-enable these users.

Figure 13.7 Members of the Account Operators group cannot mail-enable users by default.

Log off and then on as Administrator and use the Exchange Administration Delegation Wizard to delegate the Exchange View Only Administrator role to the Account Operators built-in group for the Organization node in System Manager. Log off and then on as Jason, start

ADUC, right-click on Susan Olivetti in the IT organizational unit, and select Exchange Tasks to run the Exchange Task Wizard and create a mailbox for Susan. Also try creating another new mailbox-enabled user from scratch. We've now enabled members of the Account Operators group to create and manage Exchange recipients using ADUC.

Log off and then on as Administrator, start System Manager, run the Exchange Administration Delegation Wizard for the Organization node, and delegate the exchange View Only Administrator role to the RecipientAdmins global group you created earlier. Log off and then on as a user who belongs to the RecipientAdmins group (mine is named Randy Jamieson or rjamieson@mtit.com) and see whether he can use ADUC to create a mailbox-enabled user. It won't work—Randy doesn't even have the New option on his shortcut menu in ADUC!

Log on as Administrator and try adding the RecipientAdmins group to the Account operators group. Log on as Randy and try to create a mailbox-enabled user. This time it works! This second method is more flexible than the first one, especially in a larger enterprise.

Summary

In this chapter we've looked at how to use Exchange extended permissions and the Exchange Administration Delegation Wizard to grant different Exchange administration roles to different users and groups. We've also tied this in with administrative groups, covered in Chapter 12, and seen how we can delegate Exchange administration roles to different users using these administration groups.

In Chapter 14, we'll begin our consideration of Exchange data storage architecture by looking at the concept of *storage groups*.

CHAPTER 14

Storage Groups

In this and the next few chapters, we consider how to manage the Exchange information store and its various components. We begin by looking at storage groups, a feature new to this version of Exchange that provides greater flexibility in how the information store is managed.

There are six walkthroughs in this chapter:

- Creating a new storage group
- Renaming a storage group
- Deleting a storage group
- Moving transaction log files
- Enabling or disabling circular logging
- Zeroing out deleted database pages

Storage Groups

Storage groups are new to Exchange 2000 and provide a more flexible model of administering message and data storage than previous versions of Exchange. A storage group is a logical grouping of data stores that can be managed as a single administrative entity. To understand this concept more clearly, we need to explain the terminology used to describe the different storage components of Exchange.

Storage Terminology

The broadest storage entity in Exchange is the information store. Each Exchange server has its own (and only one) information store, which is used to store messages, attachments, and documents posted to public folders (Figure 14.1).

The information store contains one or more storage groups, up to a maximum of 15 user-defined storage groups per information store (that is, per Exchange server). Each storage group can contain zero or to a maximum of six *data stores* per storage group, which means that a single Exchange 2000 server can contain up to $6 \times 15 = 90$ separate data stores. There are two different types of data stores that a storage group can contain:

- *Mailbox store.* This type of data store contains messages and attachments. Mailbox stores contain the mailboxes for mailbox-enabled users in the organization.

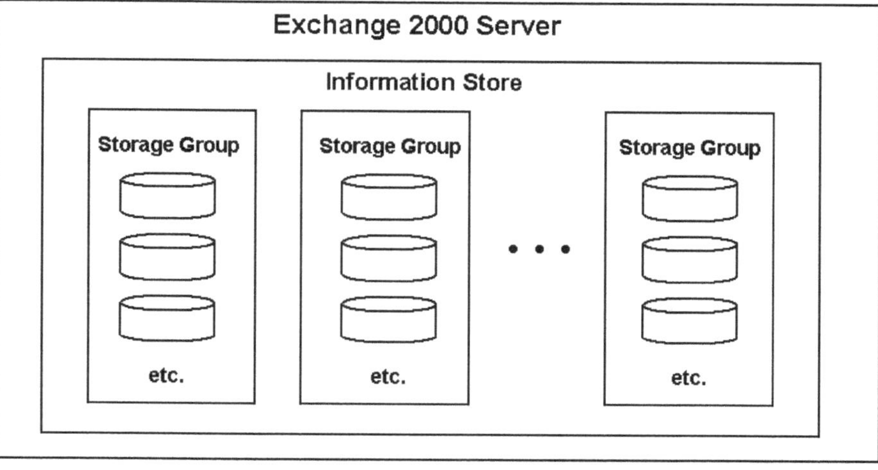

Figure 14.1 The Exchange 2000 information store consists of up to 15 storage groups, each of which contains up to six data stores.

- *Public-folder store.* This type of data store contains public folders and their contents (documents and files of various types).

NOTE

The Exchange 2000 information store is very different from the information store of previous versions. In Exchange 5.5, each server could have only one mailbox store or one public-folder store.

Active Directory versus Information Store

Before we proceed, we should mention that Exchange 2000 actually stores information in two separate places:

- *Active Directory.* Exchange stores information about recipients and its system configuration information in Active Directory. This makes this information available anywhere in the enterprise and allows an entire Exchange organization to be managed from a single administrative console.
- *Information store.* Each Exchange server has an information store that contains the messages and attachments that users send and receive and the documents and files that are posted to public folders in the organization.

Let's make this even clearer: the telephone number of a user is a property of that user and is therefore stored in Active Directory on multiple domain controllers throughout the enterprise, whereas an email message received by that user is stored in the information store on the single Exchange server where the user's mailbox is located.

Both of these storage mechanisms involve databases: Active Directory stores directory information on domain controllers in a database called NTDS.DIT, whereas the information store keeps its data in either .edb databases for rich-text information or .stm databases for streaming Internet (MIME) content. We'll talk more about Exchange databases later in this chapter.

NOTE

The information store is also a service running on the Exchange server (see Chapter 1 for a list of Exchange services). This service is associated with the process STORE.EXE that is located in the folder

```
\Program Files\Exchange\bin
```

Advantages of Storage Groups

Storage groups provide a great deal of flexibility in how Exchange handles data, as messages and their attachments or as documents posted to public folders. There are several advantages to storage groups:

- Each storage group can be backed up and restored separately, which means faster back-up and restoration of user data. Partitioning the information store into storage groups is more time efficient than using a single, large, monolithic information store, as in previous versions of Exchange, because the larger store takes longer to back up or restore from tape.
- A really large store can take so long to restore that it becomes unmanageable, which means there are practical limits to how many users could be hosted on an Exchange 5.5 system. With Exchange 2000, however, by partitioning the information store into storage groups with multiple data stores, scalability is increased so that a virtually unlimited number of users can be hosted in the organization.
- Users' mailboxes can be segregated in different storage groups to keep them separate from each other. Each department in a company might have a different storage group or a different mailbox store within a storage group.

- Each storage group can be configured differently depending on the requirements. For example, mailbox stores containing mailboxes for users with critically important data can be placed in storage groups with circular logging disabled so that data can be restored quickly in an emergency. Public-folder stores containing USENET newsfeeds and other low-priority data can be placed in storage groups with circular logging enabled to reduce their disk space requirements as their loss in an emergency is not critical.
- Storage groups also facilitate hosting of multiple companies on a single Exchange server because each company can have its own storage group, thereby separating the data for each company.

We'll see how to implement some of these scenarios later in this chapter.

Storage Group Architecture

UNDER THE HOOD

Let's look deeper into the architecture of how storage groups work. As we said earlier, Exchange uses databases to store data written to the information store. Each storage group can contain multiple databases depending on how many data stores the storage group contains. The difference between a data store and a database is that a data store is a logical unit of storage, whereas a database consists of a set of physical files. We'll look deeper into this in a moment.

Transaction Logs

Exchange uses transactions to manage data written to its databases. A transaction is basically a single write to a database. Each transaction that occurs is also written to a log file called a *transaction log*. In effect, the transaction log keeps a record of all writes made to the database. If a transaction is successful, it is committed to the database; if a transaction fails for any reason, the transaction log is used to roll the transaction back to return the database to its original state before the transaction. In other words, transaction logs provide fault tolerance for Exchange databases: if problems such as database corruption occur, the transaction log can be "played through" to reconstruct the database to the state it should be in.

Each storage group has a single set of transaction logs regardless of the number of data stores or databases it contains. For example, a storage group might contain three mailbox stores and one public-folder store, but all transactions written to the databases representing these stores is recorded in a single set of transaction logs.

Table 14.1 lists the different files associated with the transaction logs for a given storage group. All of these files are exactly 5 MB by default, whether or not they contain useful data. In a default Exchange installation with a single storage group, these log files are located in the MDBDATA folder, which is found in `\Program Files\Exchsrvr\MDBDATA`.

TABLE 14.1

Transaction log files for a given storage group.

File	Description
Enn.LOG	Primary transaction log for storage group nn; for the first storage group this would be E00.LOG
Ennxxxxxx.LOG	Secondary transaction logs for storage group nn, where xxxxxx runs sequentially starting from 000000; these files may be numerous if circular logging is disabled on the Exchange server
RES1.LOG and RES2.LOG	Reserved log that acts as a buffer to allow Exchange to continue writing transactions when the disk has run out of space

Storage groups also have associated system files that support their operation. Table 14.2 lists the system files associated with a given storage group. Note that additional files may be present on a server under certain conditions. For example, a template transaction log file EDBTMP.LOG is temporarily present when you initiate the process of creating a new storage group.

TABLE 14.2

Additional system files for a given storage group,

File	Description
Enn.CHK	Checks file for storage group nn; for the first storage group, this would be E00.CHK. Checks files containing recovered file fragments
TMP.EDB	A temporary workspace file used for processing transactions

Database Files

Whereas Exchange transaction logs are defined at the storage-group level, Exchange databases are defined further down at the data-store level.

Each data store has a set of two database files associated with it. The names of the database files are different depending on whether the data store is a mailbox store or a public-folder store, but each data store, regardless of type, always has one database file of each of the following types associated with it:

- *EDB database.* This is a rich-text database file that can store message headers, message text, and standard attachments (static documents such as Word files or bitmap images).
- *STM database.* This is a streaming content file that can contain audio, video, and other media formatted in Multipurpose Internet Mail Extension (MIME) data. SMT databases can store multimedia content in their native format instead of converting them to some other format, which enhances the performance of Exchange when handling this content.

NOTE

EDB database files are based on the same Extensible Storage Engine (ESE) database technology used in both Active Directory and in Exchange 5.5. ESE is based on the earlier Microsoft JET database engine. STM database files are written sequentially, which is more in keeping with the kind of data they store, namely data from Internet clients using protocols such as HTTP, SMTP, POP3, or IMAP4 (if a MAPI client like Outlook requests data from an SMT database, Exchange converts the data to an attachment).

Table 14.3 shows the names of the database files associated with both mailbox stores and public-folder stores in the default First Storage Group. If you create additional data stores in this group, the names of these files are the same as the names given to the new data stores. For example, if you create a mailbox store called SALES, then by default its database files will be named SALES.EDB and SALES.STM.

TABLE 14.3 Exchange database files.

Data-store type	EDB database	STM database
Mailbox store	PRIV1.EDB	PRIV1.STM
Public-folder store	PUB1.EDB	PUB1.STM

First Storage Group

We just mentioned something called the First Storage Group. When you install Exchange, this storage group is created by default and contains two default data stores. Figure 14.2 shows the First Storage Group for Exchange server Box14, which is located in the Vancouver administrative group in our testbed deployment.

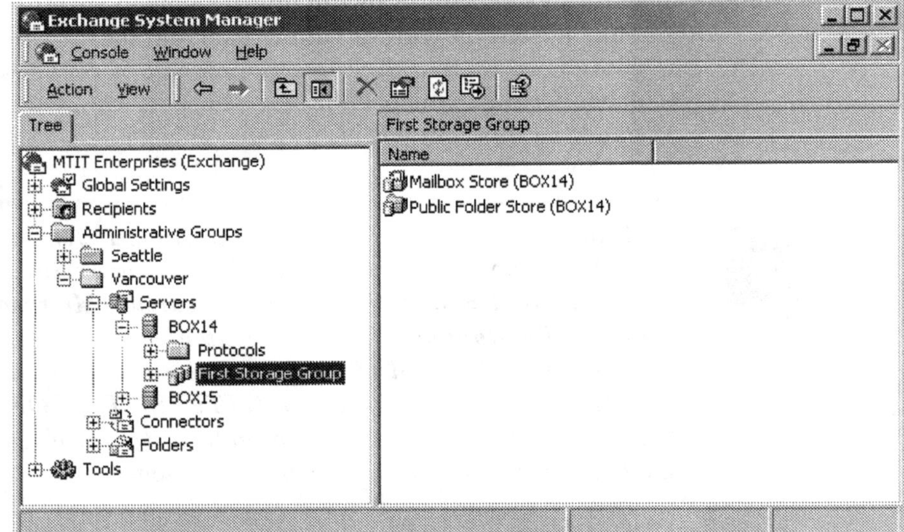

Figure 14.2 The default First Storage Group for Exchange server Box14 in the Vancouver administrative group.

The First Storage Group for Exchange server Box14 contains two data stores by default: mailbox store (Box14) and public-folder store (Box14).

You can rename this storage group if you like (and the data stores too) but you should be aware of one consequence. The storage group as a data storage entity resides on the Exchange server, but its properties also exist as an object in Active Directory for management purposes. Renaming any parent object in Active Directory means you are modifying the namespace for all child objects under it.

Therefore, if you rename a storage group, then corresponding objects representing the data stores, mailboxes, and public folders within this storage group are also renamed in Active Directory, and then these changes must be replicated to other domain controllers throughout the domain, and a wave of network traffic is generated. Therefore, renaming storage groups (or other Exchange configuration objects) is best done during off hours.

Temporary Storage Group

We said that the information store on an Exchange server can contain up to 15 storage groups and that each storage group can contain up to six data stores. Actually that's not quite true: Exchange supports up to 16 storage groups, but you are only allowed to create 15. The 16th storage group is reserved for use during database-recovery operations.

Similarly, Exchange actually supports up to 16 × 6 = 96 data stores, but in practice you can only create 15 × 6 = 90. The six possible data stores of the 16th storage group are reserved for recovery operations.

Single-Instance Message Storage

Exchange uses single-instance message storage at the database level. Single-instance storage means only a single copy of a message is stored even when the message is sent to multiple recipients.

Single-instance message storage saves valuable space in the Exchange information store. For example, say you send a 100-kB message to 200 recipients in your organization. Without single-instance storage, a copy of the message would be stored in each of the 200 mailboxes associated with these users, which altogether uses up 200 × 100 kB = 20 MB of disk space in the information store. With single-instance storage, however, the message only uses up 1 × 100 kB = 100 kB of disk space—a significant saving!

Single-instance message storage was supported in Exchange 5.5 but is implemented somewhat differently in Exchange 2000 because of its new data-storage architecture. In Exchange 2000, single-instance storage is implemented on a per-database basis, which means that, when you send a message to multiple recipients, one copy of the message is stored on each database where message recipients reside.

For example, say the sales, support, and management departments each have their mailboxes stored in different mailbox stores called

SalesMBS, SupportMBS, and ManagementMBS. A user in management sends a single message addressed to 50 recipients in sales and 25 in support, so that two copies of this message will be stored, one in the SalesMBS.EDB database and one in the SupportMBS.EDB database.

In addition, if the SalesMBS and SupportMBS mailbox stores are located in two different storage groups, then the message is also written to two different sets of transaction logs.

TIP

The moral of the story is obvious: group mailboxes together in mailbox stores and storage groups to take best advantage of single-instance message storage. If a group of users frequently sends mass mail to each other, they should be in the same mailbox store; if not, then users should at least be in the same storage group, if possible, to conserve disk space.

Administering Storage Groups

Let's look at some of the administrative tasks you can perform on storage groups, and then we'll perform walkthroughs of some of these tasks. Managing storage groups involves performing the following tasks:

- Configuring circular logging
- Locating transaction logs
- Zeroing out deleted database pages

Configuring Circular Logging

When Exchange writes data to the information store it also writes a copy of the transaction to the transaction log files for the appropriate storage group. Writing to transaction logs can occur in one of two ways:

- *Circular logging.* When circular logging is enabled for the storage group, transactions are written to the transaction log until the log becomes full, after which the oldest transactions are overwritten. With circular logging, there is only one transaction log for the storage group, which uses up 5 MB of space (regardless of whether or not it is full).
- *Sequential logging.* When circular logging is disabled, transactions are written until the log becomes full, after which another log file is

started. With sequential logging, there will be as many transaction log files as necessary to keep record of the transactions written to the Exchange databases. Each transaction log takes up 5 MB of space, so if you have 20 logs, you'll need 100 MB of disk space to contain them.

NOTE

Fortunately, the number of transaction logs doesn't grow indefinitely under sequential logging, for once a normal (full) backup of the storage group is performed, the transaction logs are no longer needed and are purged except for the first one, which is simply zeroed out. If you don't do regular backups, however, the logs will continue to multiply until you run out of disk space.

The advantage of enabling circular logging is that it requires much less disk space than sequential logging. The disadvantages are enormous. If circular logging is enabled and the Exchange server crashes and loses disk integrity, you can only restore the information store to the point of the last full back-up because, when circular logging is enabled, Exchange will not support incremental or differential backups (because these backup modes require complete sets of transaction logs). As a result, you would have to perform full backups every day (time consuming). Even then, chances are the transaction log would become full and overwrite, so that some message data would be lost if a crash occurred middle of the day.

The moral of the story? *Always leave circular logging disabled on your storage groups.* What if you run low on disk space? Buy more disks—they're cheap nowadays. Circular logging is a holdover from days when disks were expensive, and it should have been eliminated entirely from the product.

Locating Transaction Logs

Exchange lets you relocate the files associated with transaction logs to a different drive, if desired. This may be necessary if a disk is becoming full and new disks are added to the server.

We'll look at how to do this in our walkthroughs, and we'll talk more about recommended disk configurations for Exchange in a moment. Choosing the proper disk configuration is an extremely important issue with regard to the performance of Exchange.

Zeroing Out Deleted Database Pages

If your Exchange server runs in a high-security environment, you may want to configure storage groups to zero out deleted database pages. The way Exchange databases work is to read and write data in units called *pages*. If the database needs more space to write data, it does so by creating new pages and then writing to them. Instead of creating new pages, however, you can configure Exchange to reuse existing pages where data is no longer stored by zeroing out (writing zeros to) these pages to prepare them to receive new writes. As a result, when users delete messages or documents from the information store, it really is deleted (that is, replaced by zeros)!

The down side is that enabling this feature adds a performance hit on the Exchange server, so it should only be used when absolutely necessary. We'll learn how to do this in a later walkthrough.

Implementing Storage Groups

Before we move to our walkthroughs, let's discuss different strategies for implementing storage groups in Exchange. The main questions to discuss are:

- When should you create and use more than one storage group?
- When should you create and use more than one mailbox and public-folder store?
- What arrangement of disks provides optimum performance and reliability for Exchange transaction and database files?

Using Multiple Storage Groups

The key point about information stores is that they are managed as a single unit (in fact, each storage group is managed as a separate server process). You configure circular logging and locate transaction logs at the storage-group level, and these are the primary considerations determining the number of storage groups you should use.

Generally speaking, try to use only one storage group (the default First Storage Group), if possible (to keep administration simple). Create multiple data stores within this storage group, if necessary; once you reach six data stores, then you may want to consider creating a second storage group.

However, if your organization consists of two different types of data, namely data that is critically important such as users' messages and data that is relatively benign such as USENET newsgroups hosted in public folders, then you may want to disable circular logging for the critical data and enable circular logging for the less important data. In this case you could create two storage groups:

- *CriticalSG.* This storage group would contain all mailbox stores and any public-folder stores containing working documents posted by users. Circular logging should be disabled for this storage group because losing any of this data could mean losing business dollars. Make sure the disk containing the transaction logs for this storage group has lots of free space.
- *DiscardableSG.* This storage group would contain all public-folder stores used to host USENET newsgroup postings. Enable circular logging for this storage group to conserve disk space (USENET newsgroups contain tens of thousands of postings per day) because losing this data in a crash is not critical.

There is a resource cost associated with creating new storage groups on an Exchange server. You need a minimum of about 50 MB of free disk space to create a new storage group. This breaks down to 11 MB for the storage-group system files and transaction-log files, 5 MB for a mailbox store created within the group, 8 MB for a public-folder store created within the group, and the rest for temporary storage of template files and the like while the storage group is being created (temporary files are removed once the group has been created).

If you plan to host multiple companies on a single Exchange server, then use a separate storage group for each company to keep each company's files completely separate. This simplifies backup and restore as well as management and provides better security.

Using multiple storage groups also allows you to stagger backup schedules to take best advantage of your backup systems.

TIP

Keep in mind that you can restore multiple storage groups simultaneously if you have sufficient free (unused) storage groups for temporary storage. If you have 12 storage groups, for instance, you can do a parallel restore of up to four groups at the same time because the maximum number of groups permitted is 16.

Using Multiple Data Stores per Storage Group

The main consideration with implementing multiple data stores is to keep each data store down to a small enough size so that it can be backed up or restored in a reasonable amount of time. It's much easier to back up and restore five 20-MB data stores than one 100-MB store, and the down time has less effect when a smaller store crashes.

The other issue in designing data-store topology within your storage groups is to arrange mailbox stores to take best advantage of the single-instance message storage feature of Exchange. If members of the marketing department frequently send mass mailings to each other but rarely to outside groups, consider placing all mailboxes for users in this department in the same mailbox store. However, too many small data stores could add up to extra overhead for administrators. Basically, you need to find the right balance between usability and manageability.

Be aware that there is also a resource cost when using multiple data stores. Exchange allocates about 10 MB of RAM for each data store you create and mount, and this memory requirement increases as the size of the store increases. Make sure your Exchange server has sufficient RAM to support the number of data stores you want to host before creating them.

Typical Disk Configuration

Exchange 5.5 used to have an administrative tool called Performance Optimizer that could analyze your server's hardware and file system configuration and make recommendations about where to locate database files and transaction logs and other stuff. Performance Optimizer is not included with Exchange 2000, however, so you need to plan your disk subsystem carefully on the Exchange 2000 servers to ensure optimum performance, reliability, and recoverability.

TABLE 14.4

A typical disk subsystem for an Exchange 2000 Server.

Logical drive	Function
C:	Boot/system drive (mirrored)
D:	Paging file
E:	Transaction logs for first storage group (mirror set)
F:	Transaction logs for second storage group (mirror set)
G:	Database files for both storage groups (RAID5)

Table 14.4 shows a typical disk subsystem for an Exchange 2000 server that is configured with two storage groups. Let's look at why this configuration works and why it's designed the way it is:

- The boot/system drive C: is mirrored to protect the operating system files from disk failure (two hard disks required).
- The paging file is placed on a separate physical drive for better performance (one hard disk required).
- The transaction logs are on their own separate drives. These drives are mirrored to protect the logs in case of disk failure because transaction logs are critical in recovering data stores when a disaster occurs (two sets of logs, both mirrored, means four hard disks are required).
- The Exchange database files for the data stores in both storage groups are stored on the same drive, but this drive is RAID5 (stripe set with parity) to protect the data. Hardware RAID is the best solution in this case if you can afford it (separate disk system), and it should be configured as a single SCSI channel. For even better performance in a transaction-intensive messaging environment, consider the use of RAID6 or RAID10 technologies.

TIP

Whatever you do, if you have two or more storage groups, never place their transaction log files on the same physical drive or performance will be terrible! Writing transaction logs is a very disk-intensive process and needs its own separate physical drive (with its own controller) for each set of logs.

From this setup, with its liberal use of fault-tolerant disk technologies (disk mirroring and hardware RAID), we can see that our Exchange data is well protected against operating-system crashes and data loss. If you have a smaller organization, you may be able to manage with a simpler configuration, but you need to answer the following questions: How important is the messaging data to the health of my company? What would happen if I lost a few days (or even a few hours) of this data? How much money would I lose in this case? After answering these questions honestly and carefully, determine how much this disk configuration would cost for your Exchange server and make your decision!

NOTE

Logical drives where transaction logs are located must be formatted using NTFS, but it's a good practice to use NTFS for all the drives on an Exchange server due to the added security and recoverability they provide.

Preliminaries to Walkthroughs for This Chapter

We're finally ready to create and configure new storage groups on our testbed Exchange server Box14. But before we do this, if you have some free (unused) space on your disks, create several new partitions using Disk Management in the Computer Management console and format these partitions into logical drives using NTFS. My system has logical drives C: through H:, with D: as the CD drive.

Creating a New Storage Group

Walkthrough

Open System Manager on Box14 and find the server container named Box14 (this is found within the Servers container for the Vancouver administrative group). Right-click on Box14 and select New → Storage Group to open a Property Sheet called Second Storage Group Properties (Figure 14.3).

Let's name our new storage group DiscardableSG as we plan to use it for hosting unimportant public-folder data such as USENET newsgroups. Type in this name and note that Exchange automatically enters default paths for the transaction logs and system files associated with the new storage group. The path chosen by default for both types of files in this case is C:\Program Files\Exchsrvr\DiscardableSG.

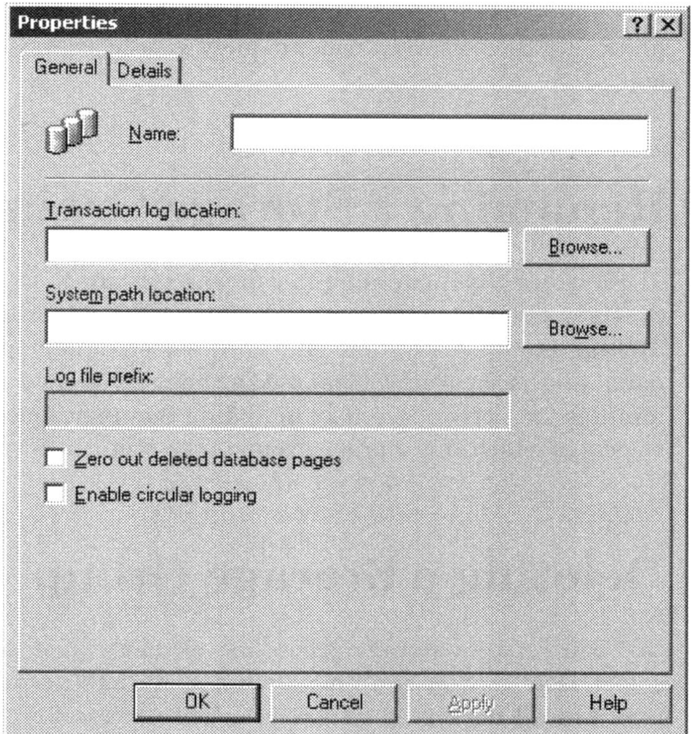

Figure 14.3 Creating a new storage group.

This is not the best path because the transaction logs for both storage groups (the existing default group and the new group we are creating) will be located on the same C: drive, so let's change these two paths. Click the first Browse button to open a select drive box, choose H: drive, and click OK to locate the transaction logs on the root of H: drive. Because this is our only purpose for drive H:, we may as well store the files in the root of the drive, but you have the alternative to create a new folder on any drive you select and locate the files in the folder. Click the other Browse button and locate the system files in the same folder (this is an OK setup unless you want to put them on a separate drive from the transaction logs—if you have enough drives!).

Click OK to close the Properties Sheet, which is now titled DiscardableSG Properties. Your storage group has been created. If you check in Windows Explorer, H: drive is still empty at this point. The next logical step would be to create a mailbox store or public-folder store within the group, but we'll leave this until Chapter 15.

If you look in System Manager, you'll see two storage groups now under the Box14 server node, namely First Storage Group and DiscardableSG.

Renaming a Storage Group

The next step is renaming First Storage Group as CriticalSG to be more consistent with what we did earlier in this chapter. Right-click First Storage Group in System Manager, select Rename, and type the new name and press Enter. That's it, although you may want to wait a few minutes for Active Directory to update the namespace for the subtree of objects of which this storage group is the root.

Deleting a Storage Group

You can delete a storage group just as easily: just right-click on it and select Delete. You can only delete a storage group if you have first removed all data stores from it, which means first moving mailboxes and public-folder trees in these stores to other stores. We'll discuss this in more detail in Chapter 15. For now, don't delete anything!

Moving Transaction Log Files

The transaction log files for our original storage group (now called CriticalSG) is still on the C: drive, which is not a good location because operating system files are located there. Let's move these files to the G: drive by right-clicking on CriticalSG in System Manager and selecting Properties to open the Properties Sheet for this storage group (Figure 14.4).

Note the log file prefix (E00) for the transaction logs associated with this storage group. As discussed earlier, this prefix means that the transaction logs for this group will have names like E00.LOG, E00000001.LOG, E00000002.LOG, and so on. What do you think the log file prefix will be for the other storage group?

Click each Browse button and move the transaction logs and system files for the CriticalSG to the G: drive. Click OK to close the Property

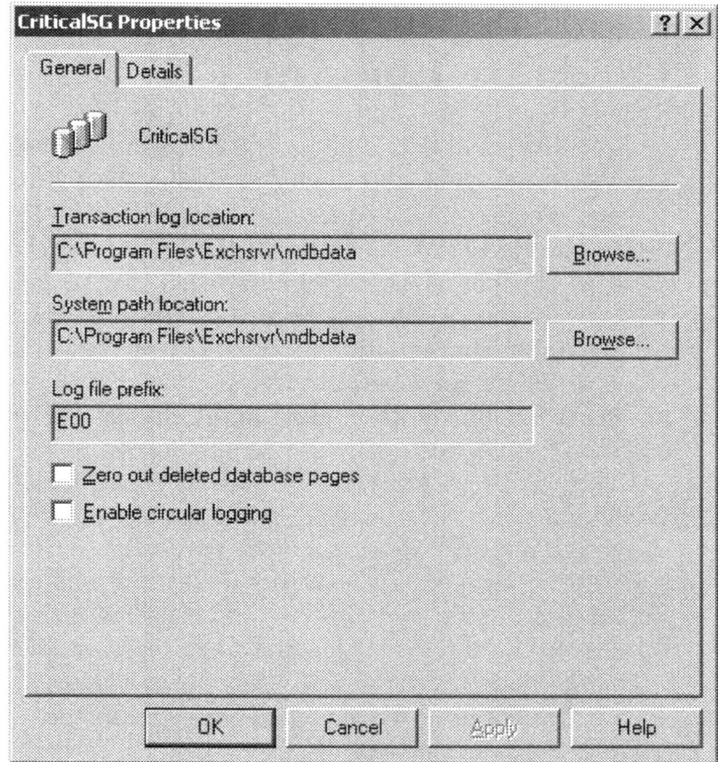

Figure 14.4 Moving the transaction logs for the CriticalSG storage group.

Sheet and begin the move process. A message box will appear: "To perform the request operation all the stores associated with this storage group must be temporarily dismounted, which will make them inaccessible to any user, do you wish to continue?" Fortunately, it's 3 A.M. and no one is using the mail system so it's OK to click Yes to initiate the process. Be aware that Exchange does not notify users that this step is being taken, so you should inform them ahead of time and preferably disconnect the server from the network during the actual move process.

Click Yes to see the stores dismounted, moved to the G: drive, and remounted. You can test whether the action was successful by using Outlook client to send and receive mail after the move is complete. If you check the \Exchsrvr\mdbdata directory after the move, you'll see that the database files for the mailbox store (PRIV1.EDB) and public folder store (PUB1.EDB) are still there, but the transaction log files and associated system files are now in the root of G: drive.

Enabling or Disabling Circular Logging

Walkthrough

Let's enable circular logging for the DiscardableSG storage group to conserve disk space (circular logging is automatically disabled for each new storage group created). Open the DiscardableSG Properties Sheet and select the checkbox to enable circular logging and click OK. A warning message appears: "With the circular logging option enabled databases in this storage group can only be restored to the time of the last backup. Additionally, incremental or differential backups will no longer be allowed. This change will not take effect until you stop and restart the Microsoft Exchange Information Store service. Are you sure you want to continue?" Click Yes.

Open the Services console from the Administrative Tools program group and select the Microsoft Exchange Information Store service from the list. Right-click on this service and select Restart to stop and then start the service. Note that this will also stop and start dependent services such as POP3 and IMAP4, which is fine. Click Yes to restart the services to enable circular logging on the DiscardableSG storage group.

If you check the H: drive in Windows Explorer, you won't see any transaction log files. We have to create a data store in the storage group before the transaction logs are created, which we'll discuss in Chapter 15.

Zeroing Out Deleted Database Pages

Walkthrough

Our final administrative task concerning storage groups is to configure zeroing out of deleted database pages to enhance security. Open the CriticalSG Properties Sheet and select the checkbox to enable this feature. Actually, because we don't really need the extra security offered by this feature in our testbed environment, disable it.

Summary

In this chapter we've learned how to create and configure storage groups, which provide flexibility in administering the Exchange information store. Having created new storage groups, we now need to create *data stores* (mailbox and public-folder stores) within these groups to give them functionality. This is the topic of Chapter 15 and succeeding chapters.

CHAPTER 15

Mailbox Stores

In this chapter we continue our examination of the new data storage architecture of Exchange 2000 by looking at mailbox stores and how to create and manage them.

There are seven walkthroughs in this chapter:

- Creating a new mailbox store
- Renaming a mailbox store
- Deleting a mailbox store
- Viewing mailbox store logon information
- Mounting and dismounting a mailbox store
- Configuring storage limits for a mailbox store
- Configuring a deleted-item retention period for a mailbox store

Mailbox Stores

In Chapter 14, we looked at the new data-storage architecture of Exchange 2000. This new architecture involves a hierarchy of Active Directory objects:

- *Information store*. This is the top of the storage hierarchy. Each Exchange server has one and only one information store.
- *Storage groups*. These are logical containers for organizing data storage according to function, department, location, and so on. The information store can contain one or more storage groups.
- *Data stores*. These are the logical containers that correspond to the actual databases that store Exchange messages, attachments, and documents. Each data store has two database files associated with it, one for rich-text content (.edb) and one for streaming MIME content (.stm).
- *Mailbox and public-folder stores*. These are the two different types of data stores you can create and manage. We'll look at mailbox stores in this chapter and public folder stores in the next.

Mailboxes

Mailbox stores contain the mailboxes associated with the mailbox-enabled users in your organization. A *mailbox* is the place associated with a user within an information store on an Exchange server to which inbound messages addressed to the user are delivered. A mailbox can contain messages and their attachments.

There is a one-to-one correspondence between mailboxes and mailbox-enabled user accounts in Exchange 2000: each mailbox-enabled user can have one and only one mailbox, and each mailbox belongs to one and only one user account.

When we talk about mailboxes (or any data-storage element of Exchange 2000), we are really talking about two different things that reside in two different locations.

- A mailbox is represented by an *Active Directory (AD) object*, meaning that there is an object in AD corresponding to each mailbox-enabled user in the organization. This object contains the properties of the mailbox and is replicated to all domain controllers in the domain.
- A mailbox as a data-storage element is a *collection of database files within the information store* on a specific Exchange server in the organization. When we use the term *mailbox*, we are usually referring to this rather than the associated AD object.

NOTE

There are some administrative tasks you can perform on individual mailboxes within mailbox stores. These tasks include granting permissions for other users to access a mailbox, deleting a mailbox-enabled user, recovering a mailbox, and purging (permanently deleting) a mailbox. These tasks are covered in Chapter 16.

Default Mailbox Store

When Exchange 2000 is installed, a default mailbox store is created within the default First Storage Group on that server. You can use this default mailbox store exclusively or create additional mailbox stores, if you need them. Figure 14.2 shows the default mailbox store for Exchange server Box14 in our testbed deployment. This default store is called Mailbox Store (Box14).

NOTE

You should be careful about renaming or deleting the default mailbox store on your server because the System Attendant mailbox resides in this mailbox store, and renaming or deleting this store can cause problems for this service when communicating with other Exchange servers in your organization. Also, if you dismount the default mailbox store on the server, you may be unable to move mailboxes from other servers to your server.

Advantages of Using Multiple Mailbox Stores

The ability to create multiple mailbox stores in Exchange 2000 is a definite benefit over previous versions of Exchange where this was not possible. Multiple mailbox stores increase the scalability of Exchange for large organizations because it is easier and faster to back up and restore a small mailbox store than a large one. With previous versions of Exchange, the number of users that could be supported for a single Exchange server was limited by the size of the private information store. If the private information store was too large, it became impractical to back up and restore it. By using multiple, smaller mailbox stores instead of a single, large, private information store, Exchange 2000 servers can support a virtually unlimited number of users, provided sufficient disk space, memory, and processing power are available.

Performance can be significantly improved with the use of multiple rather than single mailbox stores. The best way to do this would be to place each mailbox store on a different physical drive with its own controller.

If you create multiple mailbox stores in your storage groups on your Exchange servers, you can mount and dismount these stores separately for maintenance and recovery purposes. For example, let's say you had three mailbox stores named MarketingMS, SupportMS, and ManagementMS within your First Storage Group. If your ManagementMS store became corrupt, you could dismount only that store, perform a recovery from tape or some other maintenance action on the store, and remount the store. Dismounting one store has no effect on the operation of the other stores on the server, which allows you to perform selective maintenance and recovery actions on specific stores while the rest of your Exchange users are unaffected.

Another advantage of using multiple mailbox stores is that you can configure the properties of each store differently. The properties of a mailbox store include the storage limits, deleted-item retention period, content indexing, permissions, and other settings. For example, you could enable full-text indexing on one mailbox store where valuable messages are kept and often need to be found and disable it on another store where messages are of less importance.

If you have multiple mailbox stores, you can also apply different mailbox-store policies to each mailbox store. Mailbox-store policies are one type of Exchange system policy and are discussed further in Chapter 20.

You also might want to create different mailbox stores for different purposes. For example, if you have a number of general-purpose mailboxes such as sales@mtit.com, support@mtit.com, and info@mtit.com within your organization, you could create a mailbox store to host all of these general mailboxes to keep them separate from user-specific mailboxes.

Implementation Tips

Here are some additional tips on how you might implement multiple mailbox stores in Exchange 2000:

- If your organization is small to medium sized, you may be able to use only one mailbox store (the default mailbox store) and save on the extra administrative overhead of managing multiple mailbox stores. In a large enterprise, however, multiple data stores are essential for scalability and easy maintenance and disaster recovery.
- You might want to create separate mailbox stores for different organizational units in your domain. AD users are usually organized within a domain into organizational units (OUs) according to criteria such as department, division, team function, and location.
- Content indexing allows for fast searches of information stored in mailboxes and public folders. Content indexing can be configured in either standard (properties only) or full-text (properties and contents) mode. Full-text indexing is a very CPU-intensive process, so you might want to segregate your mailboxes into those that need full-text indexing and those that don't, and locate these mailboxes in two different data stores. Content indexing is discussed further in Chapter 19.
- Very important people (VIPs) like the boss may consider their mail to be extremely valuable and important that it always be accessible. In this case, you could create a separate mailbox store that contains a single mailbox, namely the boss's mailbox. This will allow fastest recovery of the information in the event of a disaster, but be aware of the disadvantages of hosting stores containing single mailboxes:
    - They require extra hardware resources (typically 10 MB RAM per mailbox store is needed).

- They add extra administrative work (more mailbox stores to manage).

TIP

Don't forget to organize your mailbox stores to take best advantage of single-instance messaging, something we discussed in the previous chapter. If all users in the organization need to frequently send mass mailings to all other users in the organization, you might be best served with a single mailbox store. However, the size of the organization (number of recipients) is also a determining factor.

Administering Mailbox Stores

There are a number of administrative tasks you can perform on mailbox stores:

- *Creating mailbox stores.* As we discussed in the previous chapter, you can create from zero to six different data stores within a single storage group, or 6 − n mailbox stores when you have n public-folder stores defined within the group. Remember also that you can have up to 15 different storage groups on a single Exchange server, which means the maximum number of mailbox stores on each server is $15 \times 6 = 90$.
- *Renaming mailbox stores.* Mailbox stores can be given friendly names so that you can remember what types of mailboxes they contain. Before you implement Exchange 2000 in your enterprise, decide on a naming system for your administrative groups, storage groups, and mailbox stores and stick with this system for the sake of consistency. You'll be glad later that you did.
- *Deleting mailbox stores.* Mailbox stores may be deleted when they are no longer required. You can only delete a mailbox store if it's empty, so you must move any mailboxes in the store to other mailbox stores before deleting the original store. We'll look at moving mailboxes later on in Chapter 16.
- *Viewing mailbox-store logons and other information.* You can use System Manager to display the names of users currently logged on to a given mailbox store, the size of mailboxes in the store, and the state of content indexing for the store.
- *Dismount a mailbox store for maintenance or recovery purposes.* You can dismount a mailbox store to perform maintenance on it or recover

its contents from backup media and then remount the store once maintenance is complete. Other mailbox stores are unaffected during this process. You can also configure the maintenance interval for the store.

- *Configuring storage limits and deleted-item retention periods for a mailbox store.* These settings can be configured when you create or modify the store.

Preliminaries to Walkthroughs for this Chapter

Before we perform the walkthroughs for this chapter, let's review the configuration of our testbed Exchange deployment:

- *Administrative groups.* We have two administrative groups in our Exchange organization MTIT Enterprises:
  - *Vancouver.* There are two Exchange servers in this administrative group, namely Box14 and Box15.
  - *Seattle.* There is one Exchange server in this administrative group, namely Box16.
- *Storage groups.* The storage groups for each of our three Exchange servers are configured as follows:
  - *Box14.* There are two storage groups for this server:
    - *CriticalSG.* This was originally named First Storage Group. This storage group is located on the G: drive and contains the two default data stores for the server, namely the default mailbox store and the default public-folder store. Circular logging is disabled for this storage group.
    - *DiscardableSG.* This storage group is located on the H: drive and contains no data stores as yet (we'll create some in a moment). Circular logging is enabled for this storage group.
  - *Box15.* This server has only the default First Storage Group and its two default data stores, the default mailbox store and the default public folder store.
  - *Box16.* This server also has only the default First Storage Group and its two default data stores, the default mailbox store and the default public-folder store.

Creating a New Mailbox Store

Walkthrough

Let's create two new mailbox stores in the storage group DiscardableSG on the Exchange server Box14 in the Vancouver administrative group. We'll create separate mailbox stores for the accounting and research departments and name these two mailbox stores AccountingMS and ManagementMS, respectively.

Open System Manager and expand the nodes in the console tree as follows: Organization (root) → Administrative Groups → Vancouver → Servers → Box14 → DiscardableSG. Right-click on the DiscardableSG storage group and select New → Mailbox Store to open an empty Properties sheet for the new mailbox store (Figure 15.1). Type "AccountingMS" (without quotation marks) as the name of the new store.

NOTE

We originally created the DiscardableSG storage group for storing unimportant content such as USENET newsgroup postings. Why are we using it here to host departmental mailboxes? We'll leave Dilbert to comment on that!

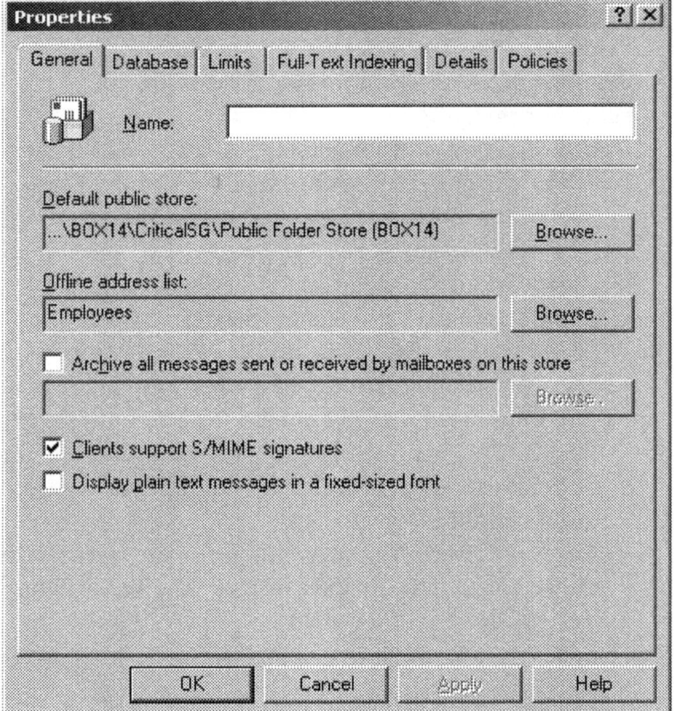

Figure 15.1
Creating a new mailbox store.

There are a number of settings that can be configured using the General tab at this point:

- You can specify a public-folder store to be associated with this new mailbox store. Each mailbox store must be associated with a public store, or users whose mailboxes are hosted in the mailbox store may be unable to access the default public-folder tree. If you click the Browse button, you'll see the various public stores that are available (one for each Exchange server in the organization). Public-folder trees are covered in Chapter 17.

NOTE

You should generally select one of the default public-folder stores that contain the All Public Folders tree as the public-folder store associated with a mailbox store. If you associate a public-folder store containing a different public-folder tree with your mailbox store, the users who have mailboxes in your store will be unable to access the public-folder store with a MAPI client like Microsoft Outlook.

- You can associate a specific offline address list with the new mailbox store. Offline address lists enable users to browse the Exchange organization for recipient addresses while disconnected from the network and were discussed in an earlier chapter.
- You can enable archiving of all messages sent or received by mailboxes or distribution lists hosted on this mailbox store. Archived messages are stored in the mailbox you select here. This can be the mailbox of an ordinary user, but you should create a new mailbox-enabled user whose mailbox will be used to hold all archived messages. This is a useful feature if your company requires that you keep a copy of all messages sent and received by the Exchange servers, but make sure the server hosting this mailbox has sufficient disk space and processing power to handle the extra load.
- There are other options for configuring support for S/MIME signatures and displaying plain-text messages using a fixed font (Courier) for older email clients.

Let's leave the settings on the General tab at their default values for now and switch to the Database tab (Figure 15.2). Note the names of the two database files created for this store (AccountingMS.edb and AccountingMS.stm). These names are automatically generated from the

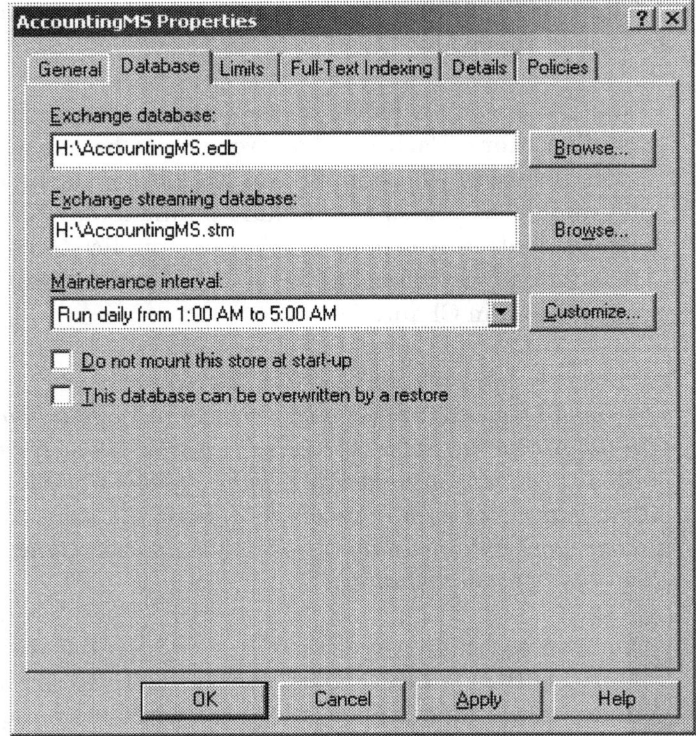

Figure 15.2
The Database tab for a mailbox store.

name of the mailbox store itself but can be changed, if desired (although there's no real reason for changing the default names).

By default, a new store is configured to be mounted as soon as it is created. Mounting a store makes it available for users who have mailboxes on the store. When a store is dismounted, users cannot access their mailboxes on the store.

TIP

About the only time you might want to prevent mailbox stores from automatically being mounted during startup is when you are restoring the Exchange server from a complete server crash, in which case you might want to restore all the stores before mounting any of them.

Selecting the bottom checkbox will allow the contents of the store to be overwritten when you perform a restore from backup media. This results in all messages since the last backup being lost, so it's best to leave this box deselected unless the store is corrupted beyond repair or you can get by without this data.

The maintenance schedule indicates the time of day when Exchange automatically runs various maintenance routines against the store. These routines clear extra space in the store by removing items marked for deletion, defragment the store to improve performance, and so on. Select the best time associated with low user activity to perform these maintenance routines or specify a custom schedule if required.

We'll leave the remaining settings at their default values and just mention their functions here:

- *Limits tab.* Used to configure storage limits and deleted-item retention period, which is covered in another walkthrough.
- *Full-text indexing tab.* Used to configure content indexing, which is discussed in Chapter 19.
- *Details tab.* Lets you add a brief administrative note to describe the purpose of this mailbox store.
- *Policy tab.* Displays system policies configured for this mailbox store. System policies are covered in Chapter 20.

Apart from specifying the name of the new mailbox store, leave all the other default settings and click OK to create the new mailbox store. A dialog box will soon appear asking if you want to mount the new store. Click Yes to mount the store (this changes the icon for the store by removing the red star that indicated a dismounted store). Exchange will take a minute to create the database and other files associated with the new store.

Before we go further, let's take a look at the database and other files associated with our new mailbox. Open Windows Explorer and display the contents of the H: drive (Figure 15.3). Note that we've selected Tools → Folder Options → View → clear the checkbox "Hide file extensions for known file types" in Windows Explorer. You can clearly see the two AccountingMS database files (AccountingMS.edb and AccountingMS.stm) associated with the AccountingMS mailbox store and the various system files and transaction log files associated with the storage group DiscardableSG. See the previous chapter for an explanation of the functions of these various files.

Once this is complete, go ahead and create a second mailbox store named ManagementMS within the same storage group. Once this is complete, the two new mailbox stores should be displayed in System Manager (Figure 15.4). Check the H: drive again in Windows Explorer and you should see two new files in the database files for the ManagementMS mailbox store. Although the storage group has two mailbox stores, it has only has one set of transaction logs.

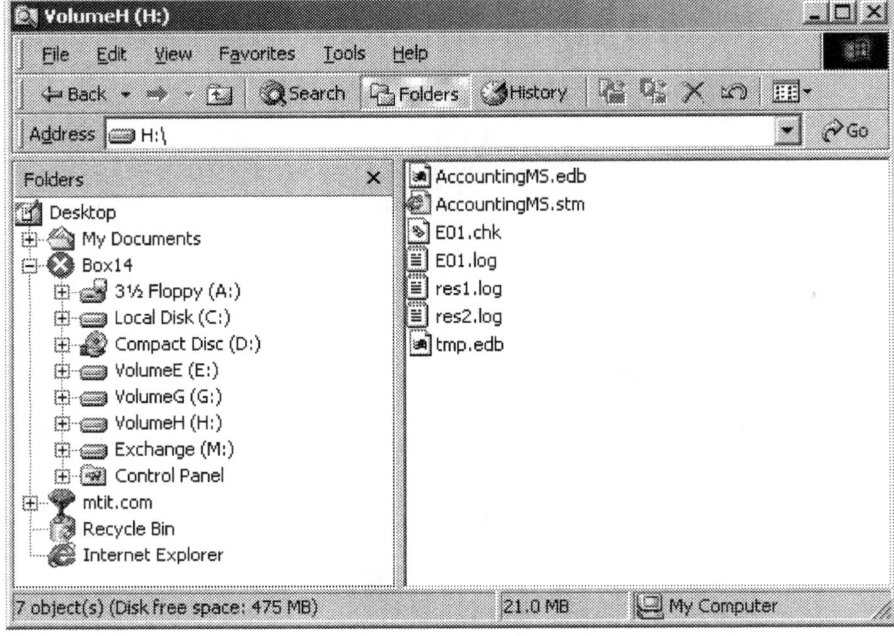

Figure 15.3 Database and other files associated with mailbox store AccountingMS within storage group DiscardableSG.

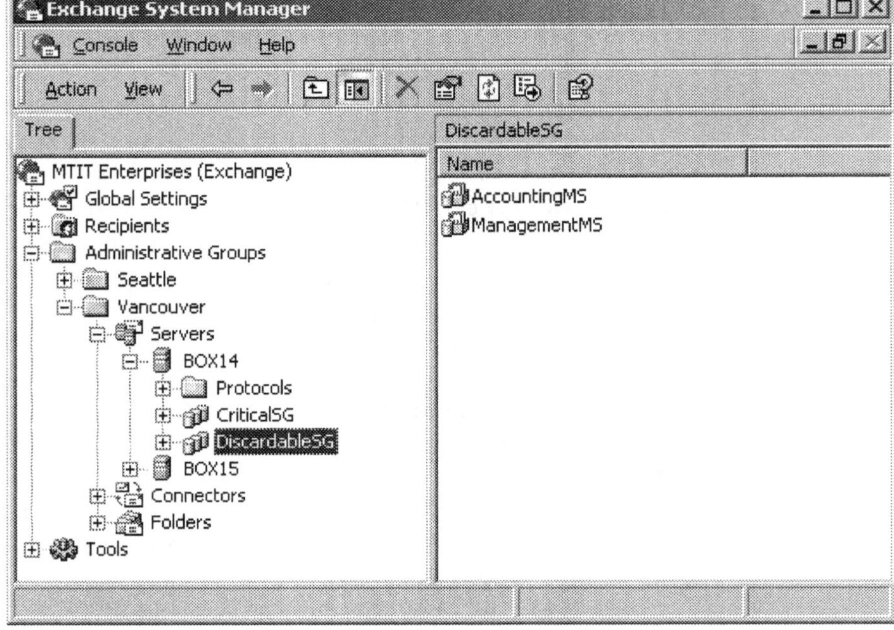

Figure 15.4 Two new mailbox stores within the DiscardableSG storage group.

Renaming a Mailbox Store

You can rename a mailbox store by right-clicking on the store and selecting Rename from the shortcut menu. Similar to storage groups discussed in the previous chapter, renaming a mailbox store results in modification of the AD namespace for all objects contained in the store.

Go ahead and rename the ManagementMS mailbox store ExecutiveMS. What do you think happens to the names of the two database files associated with the store? Check it out with Windows Explorer.

Deleting a Mailbox Store

As you might expect, you can only delete a mailbox store if it is empty. If your mailbox store currently contains mailboxes, you need to either permanently delete (purge) these mailboxes or move them to a different store before you can delete the original store. Purging and moving mailboxes is discussed in Chapter 16.

Viewing Mailbox Store Logon Information

A mailbox store is a container object in System Manager. If you expand the node for a mailbox store in the console tree (left pane), you'll see three child nodes beneath it:

- *Logons*. Selecting this node in the console tree displays information about user and system accounts that are currently logged on to the mailbox store. This is discussed further below.
- *Mailboxes*. Selecting this node displays information about the various mailboxes within the store. We'll return to this subject in Chapter 16.
- *Full-text indexing*. Selecting this node displays information about the current status of content indexing for the store. We'll cover this subject in Chapter 19.

Let's take a closer look at the Logons node for a mailbox store. Select the Logons node under the AccountingMS store in System Manager

(Figure 15.5). The following information is displayed about current logons to the store:

- The name of the user (in this case, two system accounts)
- The Windows 2000 account associated with the user (here the SYSTEM built-in special identity)
- The time when the account last logged on to the store
- The time when the account last accessed the store
- The version of the client (for local Exchange services, either SMTP or OLEDB is displayed)

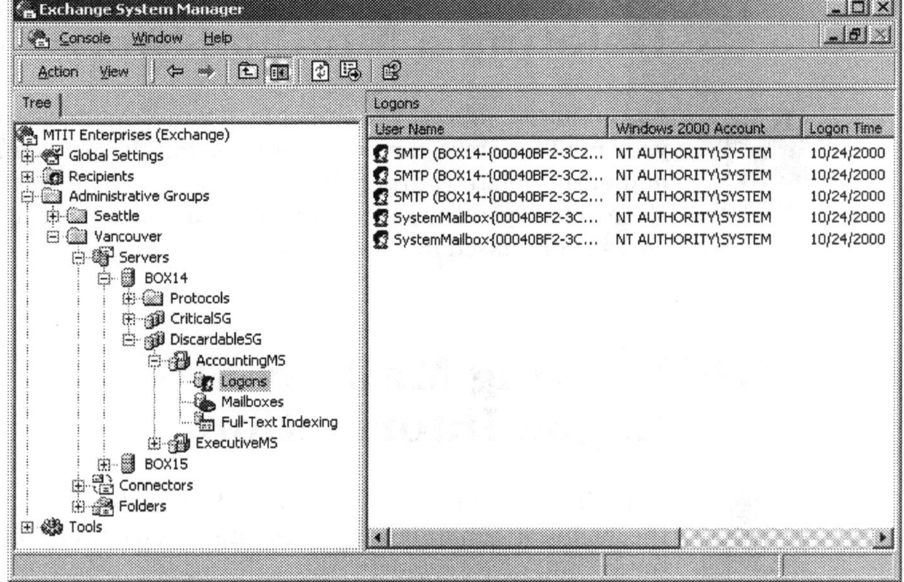

Figure 15.5 Viewing mailbox store logons.

There's lots more information you can display by selecting View → Choose Columns from the toolbar of System Manager. Most of this information is used for high-level troubleshooting. A few of the more useful ones include:

- *Full mailbox directory name*. The distinguished name (DN) of the mailbox that the account is accessing within the store.
- *Host address*. The IP address of the client accessing the store. If on the local machine, the logged-on service is listed instead.
- *Messaging ops*. The number of messaging operations (opening, closing, and deleting messages) that have been performed in the last 60 seconds on the mailbox store by all users logged onto the store.

- *Open messages*. The total number of messages in the store that are currently opened.

Let's now create a new mailbox-enabled user whose mailbox will be within the ExecutiveMS mailbox store within the DiscardableSG storage group on Box14. Start Active Directory Users and Computers and create a new OU called Executive Users within the mtit.com domain. Create a new user within this OU and give the user the name Dean Moriarty (dmoriarty@mtit.com). In the screen that prompts you to create an Exchange mailbox for the new user, select Box14 in the Vancouver administrative group as the server that will host the user's mailbox. Then select the ExecutiveMS mailbox store within the DiscardableSG storage group as the specific location for the new mailbox (Figure 15.6).

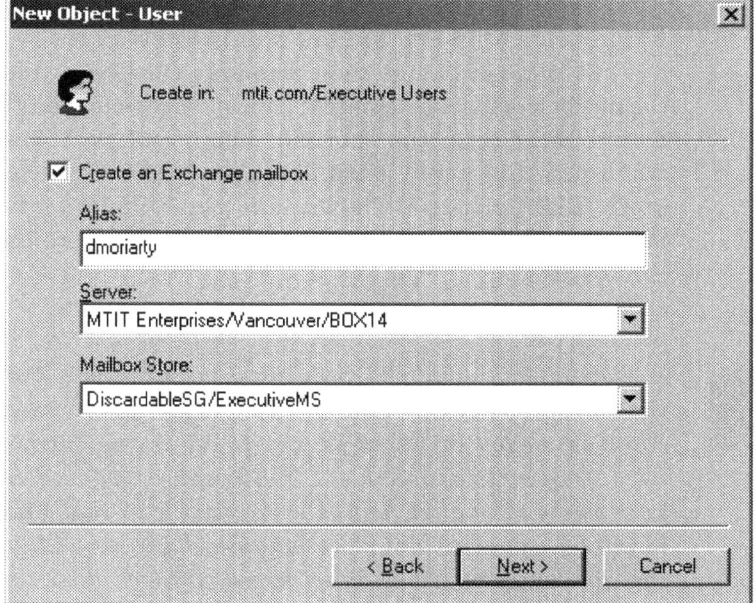

Figure 15.6 Creating a mailbox-enabled user whose mailbox is located within the ExecutiveMS mailbox store within the DiscardableSG storage group of Box14.

Now go to a client machine and log on as dmoriarty@mtit.com. Start Outlook and connect to the user's mailbox. Then return to Box14 and view the Logons node for the ExecutiveMS mailbox store in System Manager. You may need to close System Manager and open it again (Action → Refresh may not make the user visible). You will typically see several logon instances for each user logged onto the store.

Mounting and Dismounting a Mailbox Store

Walkthrough

To repair or perform maintenance on a mailbox store, you need to dismount it. A mounted store is available for users to access; a dismounted store is inaccessible to users. To find out if a mailbox store is mounted or dismounted, examine the icon for the store in System Manager. If the icon has a small, red, down-pointing arrow beside it, it is dismounted; otherwise, it's mounted.

TIP

In real life you would notify users before dismounting a store containing their mailboxes to prevent them from losing work.

Let's dismount and then remount the ExecutiveMS mailbox store (formerly the ManagementMS store). Right-click on the store, select Dismount Store from the shortcut menu, and click Yes to proceed. A red down-pointing arrow should appear beside the icon representing the store. Right-click on it again and select Mount Store to remount the store. A message box should confirm that the store has been successfully remounted.

TIP

A dismounted store may indicate a problem with the store, such as corruption in one of the database files associated with the store. Check the Application log in Event Viewer to see if any entries can shed light on why the store is dismounted. In general you should restore the corrupted portions of Exchange from backup media in this situation; do not try to manually remount the store because doing so will create new database files for the store, resulting in permanent loss of the data in the store.

NOTE

If users were currently logged on to the store when you dismounted it, they won't be able to access it again after remounting unless they restart their mail client. You might want to try this out with your testbed setup of Exchange.

Configuring Storage Limits for a Mailbox Store

Walkthrough

We skipped over the Limits tab of the mailbox store Properties Sheet when we created our new mailbox stores, so let's look at this tab now (Figure 15.7). The top set of settings on the Limits tab is used to control how much storage space each user has for his mailbox within the store. The settings you can enable and specify here are:

Figure 15.7 Specifying mailbox storage limits for a mailbox store.

ExecutiveMS Properties

Details | Policies | Security

General | Database | Limits | Full-Text Indexing

Storage limits

Issue warning at (KB):

Prohibit send at (KB):

Prohibit send and receive at (KB):

Warning message interval:

Run daily at Midnight

Customize...

Deletion settings

Keep deleted items for (days): 0

Keep deleted mailboxes for (days): 30

Do not permanently delete mailboxes and items until the store has been backed up

OK | Cancel | Apply | Help

- *Issue warning at (KB)*. If enabled, a warning message is issued to the user who exceeds this limit. The message tells the user to clean out her mailbox.
- *Prohibit send at (KB)*. If enabled, a user who reaches this limit is prevented from sending any new messages until his mailbox is emptied.
- *Prohibit send and receive at (KB)*. Things get really serious if the user reaches this limit: the user can neither send nor receive messages.

Incoming mail is lost until the user cleans out his mailbox, so this limit should be enabled only under extraordinary circumstances (extremely negligent users).

- *Warning message interval*. This specifies when these warning messages are sent to users who have violated their mailbox limits. The default is midnight, but other times can be selected or a custom schedule can be specified.

For some extra practice, you should enable these limits, specify various values, and then test them using Outlook on your client machine.

Configuring Deleted-item Retention Period for a Mailbox Store

Walkthrough

Our final walkthrough involves configuring deleted-item retention for a mailbox store. Users sometimes delete messages they wish they hadn't deleted and then empty their Deleted Items folder in Microsoft Outlook to permanently delete the message. Deleted-item retention provides a way of recovering such "permanently" deleted items in this kind of situation. The deleted-item retention period is the time interval during which items deleted from user mailboxes can still be recovered by them in an emergency. Once this period has elapsed, the message is gone forever.

To configure deleted-item retention for the ExecutiveMS mailbox store, open the Properties Sheet for the store and switch to the Limits tab (Figure 15.7). The settings to configure are:

- *Keep deleted items for (days)*. Use this setting to specify how long deleted items will be kept before permanently removing them from the store. The default is 0 day, but a typical value might be 7 or 14 days to allow the users sufficient time to discover their mistake. The longer you keep deleted messages, the more space is used for the mailbox store. The maximum retention period is 24,855 days, and a setting of zero means deleted items are permanently removed immediately from the information store.
- *Keep deleted mailboxes for (days)*. If you accidentally delete a mailbox (say for a user who has left the company), then you can still recover it up to the time interval specified in this setting. It's usually a good

idea to leave this interval to the default value of 30 days. The maximum retention period is 24,855 days, and a setting of zero means that deleted mailboxes are unrecoverable as they are immediately and permanently removed.

- *Do not permanently delete mailboxes and items until the store is backed up*. This setting keeps all deleted items and deleted mailboxes until the information store has been backed up and then deletes them. If you back up the store daily then this setting is best left unchecked.

TIP

To recover a deleted item in Outlook 2000, log on as the user who deleted the item, select the Deleted Items folder in the Outlook bar, and then select Tools → Recover Deleted Items From. Select the items you wish to recover and click Recover Selected Items.

Summary

In this chapter we've examined the data-storage architecture of Exchange 2000 by learning how to create and manage mailbox stores. Because mailbox stores contain mailboxes, this is the logical topic for Chapter 16.

CHAPTER 16

Mailboxes

This chapter deals with managing mailboxes and complements Chapter 15, which dealt with mailbox stores. It focuses on the various tasks involving mailboxes that an administrator needs to perform.

There are eight walkthroughs in this chapter:

- Viewing mailbox information
- Moving a mailbox between mailbox stores
- Moving a mailbox between storage groups
- Moving a mailbox between exchange servers
- Disassociating a mailbox from its owner
- Recovering a deleted mailbox
- Purging a mailbox
- Granting permissions to access another user's mailbox

Managing Mailboxes

In Chapter 3, we learned that, when Exchange 2000 is installed on a Windows 2000 network and you try to create a new user in Active Directory Users and Computers (ADUC), a mailbox is automatically created by default for the user as well. Such a user is called a mailbox-enabled user. Exchange 2000 thus allows you to manage user accounts and their mailboxes as a single unit with the same administrative tool, which is different from previous versions of Exchange where mailboxes and user accounts were managed separately using different tools.

There's more to managing mailboxes than just creating them, however. Mailboxes are located in mailbox stores, which are found in storage groups within the information store on Exchange servers. Exchange lets you perform various administrative tasks on these mailboxes including:

- Displaying the current disk space used by a mailbox, the number of messages stored in it, and other information.
- Moving mailboxes between different mailbox stores or storage groups.
- Removing the association between a mailbox and its owner and reassigning the mailbox to a different user.
- Recovering a mailbox that has been deleted or permanently deleting the mailbox.
- Assigning permissions to a mailbox to allow users other than the mailbox owner access to its contents.

In the rest of this chapter, we'll perform some walkthroughs to illustrate these tasks and how to perform them. Management of mailboxes is an important day-to-day task for Exchange administrators and knowledge of these tasks is essential.

Preliminaries to Walkthroughs for this Chapter

Before we start the walkthroughs for this chapter, log on to a client computer (for example, Dean Moriarty or dmoriarty@mtit.com), start Outlook 2000, and send several messages to yourself, leave these messages in your Inbox, and leave Outlook running on the machine. We'll need to use Dean as our test user for the walkthroughs.

Remember that Dean's mailbox is currently located in the ExecutiveMS mailbox store within the DiscardableSG storage group on server Box14 within the Vancouver administrative group of our testbed Exchange organization MTIT Enterprises. See the Preliminaries section of the previous chapter for more on the current configuration of our Exchange organization.

Viewing Mailbox Information

Walkthrough

We can display all kinds of useful information about users' mailboxes using System Manager. This information can be helpful in troubleshooting problems, assessing user habits and disk-space needs, planning additional resource deployments, and so on.

Let's take a look. Start System Manager and select the Mailboxes node under the ExecutiveMS mailbox store in the console tree. The details pane displays information about the mailboxes located in that mailbox store (Figure 16.1).

SMTP and System Mailboxes

UNDER THE HOOD

Figure 16.1 shows two mailboxes in addition to Dean Moriarty's mailbox: the SMTP mailbox and the System mailbox. These two mailboxes are special mailboxes used internally by Exchange and have the following functions:

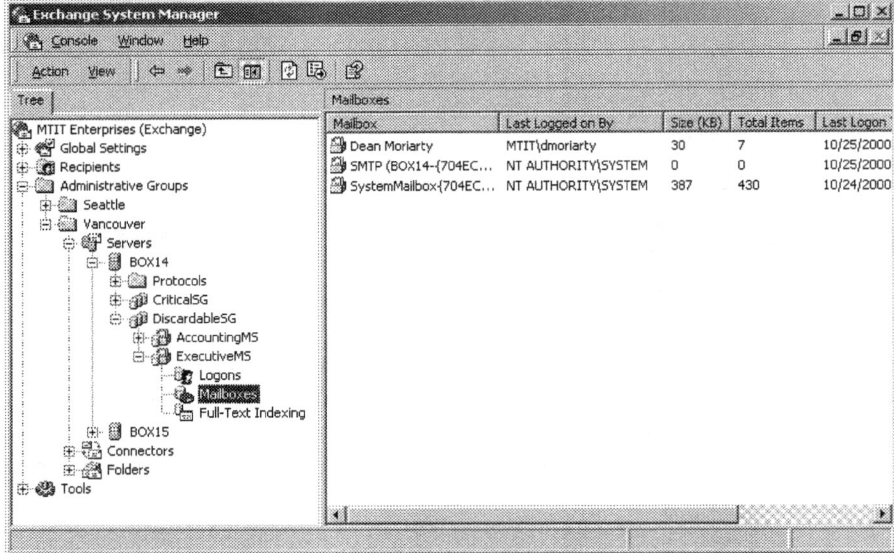

Figure 16.1
Mailboxes within the ExecutiveMS mailbox store in the DiscardableSG storage group on server Box14.

- SMTP mailbox. *This mailbox is used as a placeholder (temporary storage location) for messages. If you are a recipient on the local Exchange server and send a message to another recipient on either the local server or a remote server, the message is first placed in the SMTP mailbox, which resides within the mailbox store where the sender's mailbox resides. It is then either moved to the target recipient's mailbox within the information store on the local server or passed to the message transfer agent (MTA) if the target recipient is on a different Exchange server. The actual name of this SMTP mailbox is SMTP <servername>-<GUID>, where <servername> is the name of the local Exchange server and <GUID> is the globally unique identifier for the mailbox within Active Directory.*
- System mailbox. *This mailbox is used internally by Exchange to control its various services. Its actual name is SystemMailbox-<GUID> and it is possible to log on to the System Mailbox and view the messages within it. The procedure for doing this is described in Knowledge Base article Q253784 on Microsoft TechNet. Microsoft recommends you do not do log on unless instructed to under the supervision of Microsoft Product Support Services (PSS).*

Each mailbox store in Exchange has its own SMTP and System mailboxes to keep track of things. If you check the default Mailbox Store (or whatever you've renamed this store) on each Exchange server, you'll also find a mailbox for the System Attendant, an Exchange service that manages various housekeeping functions on the Exchange server.

By default, a number of columns of information are displayed for each mailbox. For example, Dean Moriarty's mailbox occupies 30 KB of space within the mailbox store and has seven items (messages and attachments) within it. We can also see when Dean last logged on and off to the store. You can add additional columns to the details pane using View → Choose Columns from the toolbar. Table 16.1 shows the most useful fields that can be displayed and what they mean. The first six fields are displayed by default.

TABLE 16.1

Fields displayed by the mailbox node for a mailbox store.

Field	Description
Name	Name of mailbox
Last Logged On By	Windows 2000 user account or built-in system identity that last logged on to the mailbox store to access the mailbox
Size (KB)	Amount of space currently occupied by the mailbox in kilobytes
Total Items	Total number of messages and attachments in the mailbox
Last Logon Time	Time when the last logon to the mailbox store occurred
Last Logoff Time	Time when the last logoff from mailbox store occurred
Deleted Items	Number of items that have been deleted from the Deleted Items folder of the mailbox (these items may be recoverable depending on how the deleted-item retention period has been configured for the store)
Full Mailbox Directory Name	The distinguished name (DN) of the object representing the mailbox in Active Directory
Storage Limits	Currently configured storage limits for the mailbox store where the mailbox resides (No Checking means no limits have been configured)

NOTE

If you check it out, you'll find that the full mailbox directory name (DN) of the object representing Dean Moriarty's mailbox in Active Directory is:

```
/O-MTIT ENTERPRISES/OU=FIRST ADMINISTRATIVE GROUP
   /CN=RECIPIENTS/CN=DMORIARTY
```

This is a relative DN because its address starts at the organizational level for Exchange.

Moving a Mailbox Between Mailbox Stores

Walkthrough

Go to the client machine and close Outlook but stay logged on as Dean Moriarty. Now we're going to move Dean's mailbox from the ExecutiveMS mailbox store to the AccountingMS mailbox store within the same DiscardableSG storage group on Box14. It would be nice if you could do this using System Manager but we have to use Active Directory Users and Computers (ADUC) instead.

Start ADUC and find Dean Moriarty's user account, which is within the Executive Users OU in the mtit.com domain. Double-click on Dean's account to open its Properties Sheet and switch to the Exchange General tab. Note the mailbox store where Dean's mailbox currently resides, displayed here as: Box14\DiscardableSG\ExecutiveMS.

Close the Properties Sheet by clicking Cancel. Now right-click on user Dean Moriarty in the details pane and select Exchange Tasks from the shortcut menu (don't select Move because this simply moves the user object to a different OU but doesn't have any effect on the location of the associated mailbox). The Exchange Task Wizard appears. Click Next and select Move Mailbox. Click Next and select the AccountingMS mailbox store on Box14 as the target store for the move operation (Figure 16.2). Click Next and a status bar indicates the progress of the move operation.

After a short time the wizard is complete. Click Finish and check the Exchange General tab for Dean to make sure the mailbox store location is correct. Check the Mailboxes node under ExecutiveMS in System Manager (press F5 to refresh the view) and Dean's mailbox should disappear. Check the Mailboxes node under AccountingMS and the mailbox should now be listed there. Go to the client machine and start Outlook and verify that Dean can still connect to his mailbox and send test messages to himself.

Moving a Mailbox Between Storage Groups

Walkthrough

Moving mailboxes between different storage groups is just as simple as moving them between different mailbox stores within the same storage group. Follow the procedure outlined in the previous walkthrough and move Dean's mailbox from the AccountingMS mailbox store in the Dis-

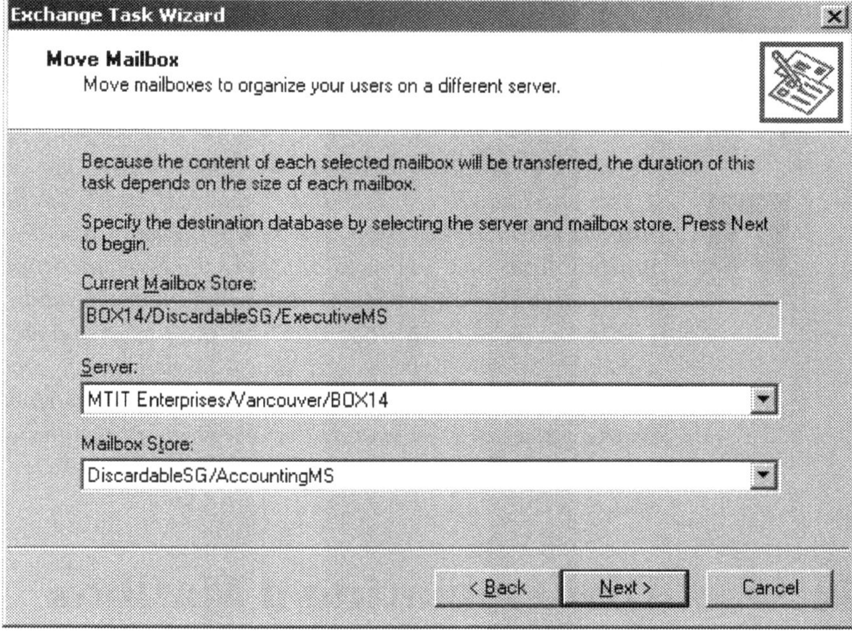

Figure 16.2 Moving Dean's mailbox from the ExecutiveMS mailbox store to the AccountingMS mailbox store within the same DiscardableSG storage group on server Box14.

cardableSG storage group on Box14 to the default Mailbox Store in the CriticalSG storage group on the same Exchange server. Check that the move has worked by using ADUC and System Manager, and see if Dean can still access his mailbox using Outlook (be sure to shut down and restart Outlook first).

Moving a Mailbox Between Exchange Servers

Walkthrough

You can also easily move mailboxes between different Exchange servers. The procedure is the same as in the previous walkthroughs and works even if the servers are in different administrative groups. Try moving Dean's mailbox from the default Mailbox Store in the CriticalSG storage group on Box14 in the Vancouver administrative group to the default Mailbox Store in the First Storage Group on Box16 in the Seattle administrative group. No problem! Check it out using ADUC, System Manager, and Outlook.

NOTE

You can only move mailboxes between servers in different administrative groups if your Exchange organization is running in native, not mixed, mode.

TIP

If you can't move a mailbox between different Exchange servers, verify that the default Mailbox Store on the target server is mounted. To move a mailbox from one server to another, the System Attendant service on the initiating server must be able to connect to the System Attendant Mailbox within the default Mailbox Store on the target server. If the default Mailbox Store on the target server is not mounted, try rebooting the server. If this fails to mount the store, you may have to perform disaster recovery on the store and recover the store from tape media because trying to mount the store manually could result in loss of data in the store.

Disassociating a Mailbox from its Owner

Walkthrough

You can disassociate a mailbox from its owner user account. This action marks the mailbox for deletion, but the mailbox isn't permanently deleted until the deleted-item recover period has expired (if configured for the server).

Let's test this out. First check the Limits tab on the Properties Sheet for the default Mailbox Store on Box16 in System Manager and verify that the Keep Deleted Mailboxes setting has its default value of 30 days. Now switch to ADUC and right-click on user Dean Moriarty and select Exchange Tasks to start the Exchange Tasks Wizard. Select Delete Mailbox from the list of available tasks and complete the wizard. Open the Properties Sheet for the user in ADUC and verify that all Exchange tabs are now gone—the user is no longer mailbox-enabled.

Switch to System Manager and refresh the view by pressing F5. Select the Mailboxes node under the default Mailbox Store container in the First Storage Group of server Box16 in Seattle. Dean's mailbox should still be visible but with a red X beside it, indicating that it is marked for deletion (Figure 16.3).

It may take from 15 minutes to 1 hour for this change in the mailbox icon to be displayed. Alternatively, you can run the Mailbox Cleanup Agent on the mailbox store that contains the mailbox to display the change immediately (Figure 16.3). Using System Manager, right-click on the Mailboxes node beneath the default Mailbox Store in the First Storage Group on Box16 in Seattle. Select Run Cleanup Agent from the shortcut menu. A short time later the red X should appear beside Dean's mailbox. This means the mailbox is orphaned—that is, no longer associated with any specific object in Active Directory. Test this by restarting Outlook on the client computer while logged on as Dean. You should receive a message saying "Outlook is unable to open your default email folders. The attempt to log on to the Exchange server has failed." Close Outlook on your client machine but leave Dean logged in.

We'll reconnect the mailbox to Dean's user account in the next walkthrough.

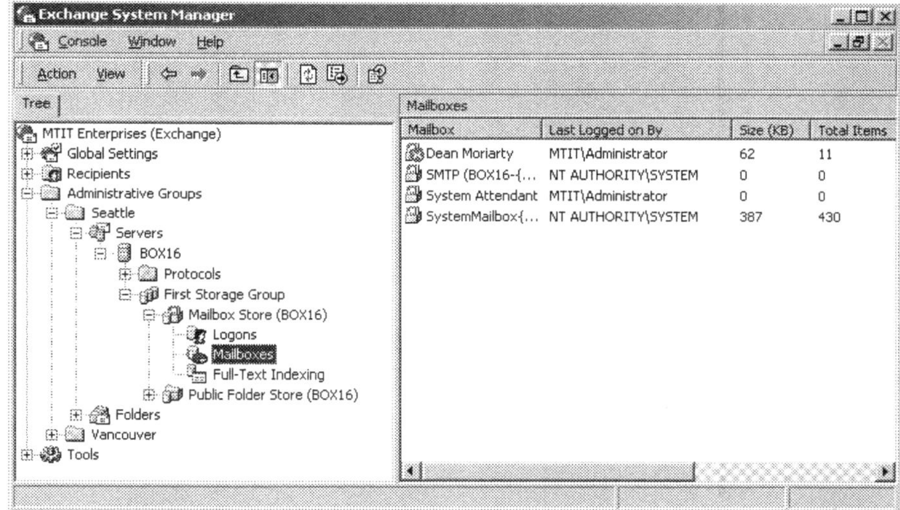

Figure 16.3 The mailbox that belonged to Dean Moriarty is orphaned and marked for deletion.

Recovering a Deleted Mailbox

Walkthrough

Let's reconnect the mailbox we orphaned in the previous walkthrough to Dean Moriarty's user account. Find what was formerly Deans' mailbox in System Manager (Figure 16.3). Right-click on the orphaned mailbox and select Reconnect from the shortcut menu. Select Dean's user account in the dialog box (Figure 16.4) and click OK. The red X then disappears from the mailbox.

Test the reconnection by checking the Property Sheet for the mailbox in ADUC—the Exchange tabs should be visible again. Test if Dean can now access his mailbox using Outlook.

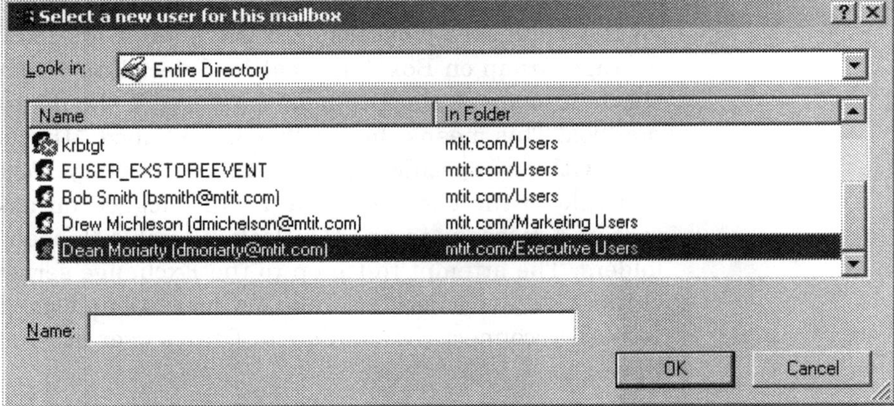

Figure 16.4 Recovering a deleted mailbox.

You may have to delete and create the default Outlook profile on your client machine to get Outlook to recognize the reattached mailbox. Right-click on the Outlook icon on your desktop and select Properties. Select Exchange Server and click Remove. Then click Add, select Exchange server, and specify mailbox dmoriarty on server Box16. Click Check Names; if this works, then Outlook has found the reconnected mailbox.

TIP

This process is typically used to remove a mailbox from an existing user (such as an employee leaving the company) and assigning the mailbox to a new user who isn't mail-enabled (such as the employee's replacement worker). You can't assign an orphaned mailbox to a user who already has a mailbox because Exchange recipients can have only one mailbox.

Purging a Mailbox

Walkthrough

Purging a mailbox means deleting it permanently from both the mailbox store and from Active Directory. In the above walkthroughs, right-click on any mailbox that has been disassociated from a user account (that is, a mailbox that has a red X beside it in System Manager) and select Purge to delete it.

Don't delete Dean's mailbox just yet.

Granting Permissions to Access Another User's Mailbox

Walkthrough

We'll finish this chapter with a brief look at granting other users access to a mailbox by assigning permissions to the mailbox. We talked about permissions generally in Chapter 13. In this chapter, we'll look at a couple of specific examples of using permissions to manage Exchange mailboxes.

Let's say you want to grant a manager the right to access a worker's mailbox. (Warning! Make sure your company has a policy in place with regard to this type of access and be aware of any legal or privacy issues that might be involved!) For example, let's say that user Jane Smith is the manager of Dean Moriarty. We want to grant Jane access to Dean's mailbox. To do this, log on to the Exchange server as an Exchange Full Administrator (we'll use the default Administrator account in the domain) and start ADUC. Select View → Advanced Features from the toolbar. Open the Properties Sheet for user Dean Moriarty and switch to the Exchange Advanced tab that is now visible. Click the Mailbox Rights button to open the Permissions for Dean Moriarty page (Figure 16.5).

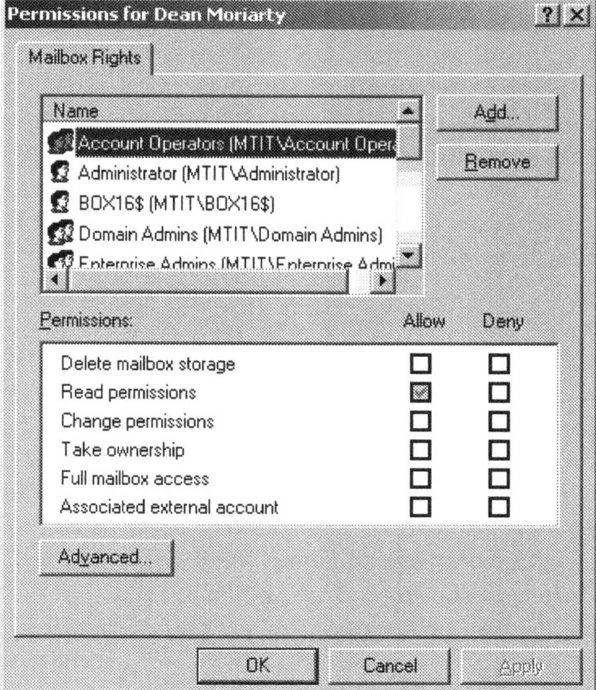

Figure 16.5 *Assigning permissions to allow another user access to Dean's mailbox.*

Click Add and select user Jane Smith in the directory and click OK to return to the Permissions page. Select Jane Smith in the Name listbox of the Permissions page and click Allow next to Full Mailbox Access. Click OK to close the page and assign the permissions and then click OK again to close the Properties Sheet for Dean. Jane has now been assigned full access to Dean's mailbox.

Now let's test this using Outlook. Log off your client machine and log on again as Jane Smith (jsmith@mtit.com) and start Outlook to connect to Jane's mailbox. Make sure that the folder list is displayed in Outlook (select View → Folder List to toggle it on). Right-click on Outlook Today at the top of Jane's folder list and select Open Other Folder → Other User's Folder from the shortcut menu. An Open Other User's Folder dialog box appears (Figure 16.6).

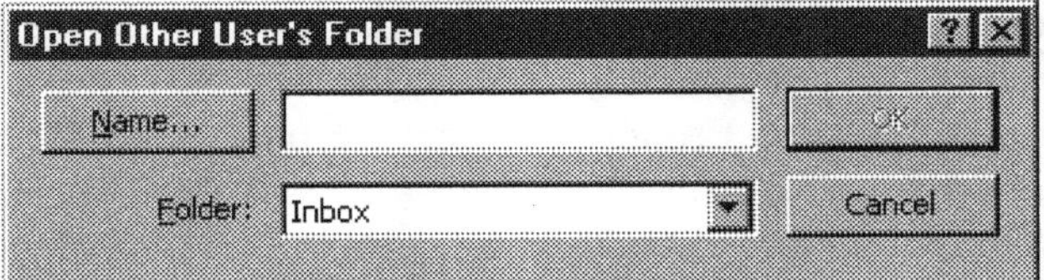

Figure 16.6 Opening another user's folder in Outlook.

Click the Name button, select Dean Moriarty from the Global Address List displayed, and click OK (the image in Figure 16.6 is displayed). Dean's name is now underlined in the box, which means that Outlook has found Dean's mailbox on the Exchange server and has permission to access its contents. Select the folder you want to access in Dean's mailbox (we'll choose Inbox) and click OK to close the dialog box. A new Outlook window now opens, displaying the contents of Dean's Inbox to user Jane Smith, as desired (Figure 16.7).

TIP

One more tip regarding Exchange permissions. By default, even an Exchange Full Administrator does not have the permission to log onto any mailbox within a given mailbox store. You can grant an administrator this right, however, which can be useful in some troubleshooting scenarios. Using System Manager, open the Properties Sheet for the mailbox store to which you want to grant this right. Select the Security tab and select the user or group to whom you want to grant the ability to log onto any mailbox in the store. Scroll down the list of permissions and explicitly Allow the user or may want to test this as an additional exercise.

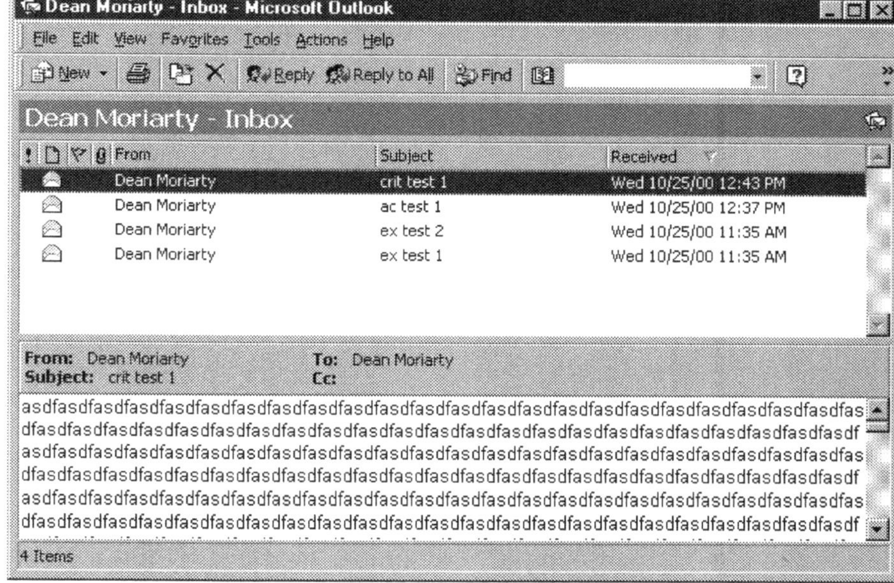

Figure 16.7 *Jane Smith can successfully access Dean Moriarty's Inbox.*

Summary

In Chapters 15 and 16, we've looked at mailbox stores and the mailboxes they contain. But mailbox stores are only one type of data store that Exchange supports. The other type is the public-folder store, the topic of Chapter 17.

CHAPTER 17

Public-folder Stores and Trees

This chapter covers public-folder stores and how to create and manage them. Public-folder stores are used to host public folders, a tool that enables users to collaborate on projects by sharing messages and documents with each other. Because there is a direct correspondence between public-folder stores and public folder trees in Exchange 2000 and you cannot create a public-folder store without assigning it to a public-folder tree, we also cover public-folder trees.

There are five walkthroughs in this chapter:

- Creating a new public-folder tree
- Creating a new public-folder store
- Displaying public-folder logons and other information
- Assigning permissions for creating new public-folders in public-folder trees
- Assigning a default public-folder store to a mailbox store

Public-folder Stores

In Chapter 16, we discussed the data-storage architecture for Exchange 2000 and found that there are two types of data stores: mailbox stores for hosting users' mailboxes and public-folder stores for hosting public folders and the messages and documents they can contain. This chapter deals with public-folder stores. To understand public-folder stores, we need to make sure we first understand public-folder terminology in Exchange 2000.

Public Folder Terminology

A *public folder* contains items from multiple users in an Exchange organization. Public folders can contain messages, attachments, documents (such as Word or Excel files), Web pages, binary files (such as image, music, or video files), executable files, zipped files, and just about anything else. Users generally put items in public folders to make them "public," that is, to make them available for other users to read, edit, copy, and so on. Public folders can have *permissions* set on them so that only selected groups can access the folder contents and perform only specified actions. We'll look more at the uses of public folders in Chapter 18.

Public folders are grouped together into treelike structures called *public-folder trees*. A public-folder tree is a hierarchical structure of public folders that can be administered as a unit. Another name for public-folder tree is *top-level hierarchy* (TLH) but that is an older term not generally used with the current version of Exchange. Exchange 2000 includes a default public-folder tree, discussed further below, but you can also create new public folder trees for reasons we'll soon discuss.

Public folder trees may actually exist in several locations:

- As a hierarchy of objects in Active Directory (AD) and as such are found on all domain controllers in the forest to make them available throughout the enterprise. AD contains the attributes and properties of each public-folder tree in the organization but not the actual contents (messages and files) within the public folders of that tree.
- Within a public-folder store on one or more Exchange servers throughout the organization. The actual contents (messages and files) within the public folders of the tree reside here, within public-folder stores, which are explained next.

NOTE

Actually, a public-folder tree when it is first created exists only in AD until you assign it to a particular public-folder store, where its contents will initially reside.

A *public-folder store* is a type of data store that can contain one and only one public-folder tree. Exchange servers may have from zero to six public-folder stores per storage group, depending on how many mailbox stores there are within the storage group. We've talked about storage groups several times, so we won't go into the details here.

An important difference between mailboxes (which are located within mailbox stores) and public folders (located within public-folder stores) is that, whereas a user's mailbox resides on one and only one Exchange server in the organization, public folders and their contents can be replicated to multiple Exchange servers to provide fault tolerance, load balancing, and easy access for users distributed throughout the enterprise. A *replica* is a copy of a public folder and its contents stored in a public-folder store on some Exchange server. All replicas are equal—there is no master replica for a public folder. Public-folder replication can be managed in different ways, as we'll see in Chapter 18.

Default Public-folder Tree

The *default public-folder tree* is created by default when you install your first Exchange 2000 server in your organization. This tree corresponds to the single public-folder tree that existed in previous versions of Exchange, and its name as displayed in System Manager is simply *Public Folders*. When you view this tree in Outlook, however, it has the name *All Public Folders*, which can be a bit confusing.

You can create additional public-folder trees for your organization if you like. These additional trees are called alternate (or custom) public-folder trees. There are advantages and disadvantages to adding trees, as explained below.

Default Public-folder Store

For clients to access public folders within the default public-folder tree, this default tree must be hosted somewhere. When you install your first Exchange server, two data stores are automatically created within the First Storage Group in the information store on that server. These two data stores are the default mailbox store and the *default public-folder store*. The default public-folder store hosts the default public-folder tree so clients can immediately access this tree.

You can create additional public-folder stores on your Exchange servers, but each public-folder store can host one and only one public-folder tree, and each store on the same server must be assigned a different public-folder tree to host. There are advantages and disadvantages to adding stores, which we will discuss below.

NOTE

Each Exchange server has a default First Storage Group on it, and this storage group always contains two data stores, a default mailbox store and a default public-folder store. The default public store on each server always has the default public-folder tree assigned to it and you cannot change this assignment. Having such a default public-folder store on every Exchange server in your organization enables users whose mailboxes are hosted on a specific Exchange server to easily access public folders within the default public-folder tree. If you like, you can remove the default public-folder store on a server (for example, to make your server a dedicated mailbox server), but you cannot delete the default public-folder tree from your Exchange organization because doing so would prevent messaging application programming interface clients like Outlook from accessing any public folders.

Implementing Public-folder Trees

Because public-folder trees are an organized structure containing a hierarchy of public folders that your users will access, it's important to plan this hierarchy carefully to ensure good performance and facilitate easy access by users. The most important planning issue to consider is whether you will deploy one or many public-folder trees in your organization.

Advantages of Using Multiple Public-folder Trees

Having multiple public-folder trees can be a good idea for an organization that needs them. One of the main advantages is that, when public-folder trees grow to large (too deep a hierarchy, too many subfolders, or too much content), they become unwieldy to manage and replicate. Therefore you can partition your public-folder data in a large enterprise by planning multiple public-folder trees from the start to make public-folder administration more flexible and assign different administrators the job of managing different public-folder trees.

Another reason to use multiple trees might be security. You could choose to use the default public-folder tree for internal company use to share documents and facilitate collaboration between workers and then create an alternate public-folder tree for hosting content for external users only or to allow employees to collaborate with external users. By keeping the two trees separate, you can configure their replication and security differently to keep your data safe and provide best performance.

A third possibility is an enterprise with relatively independent branch offices at several locations: you could create a separate public-folder tree for each location and let local Exchange administrators manage these trees separately. Each tree would host content important only to that location. The default public-folder tree could be reserved for information of companywide importance and made available at all locations as well.

Another advantage of using multiple public-folder trees concerns replication. Because the default public-folder tree is found on every Exchange server on which the default public-store resides and this tree is always replicated, there is a replication cost in terms of additional network traffic. By using additional, alternate public-folder trees, some of this replication can be reduced by hosting alternate trees on servers whose users require access to them. Overall network traffic can thus be reduced by properly deploying multiple trees.

Having multiple public folder trees also enables you to configure them differently with regard to folder replication. This added flexibility can be beneficial in an environment where some types of user data are more important than other types. Important data can be located in public-folder trees that are replicated for fault tolerance and load balancing.

Disadvantages of Using Multiple Public-folder Trees

Using multiple public-folder trees sounds like a great idea, but there are other considerations for planning your Exchange deployment. The main consideration is the issue of client support for different public-folder trees, which is different for default and alternate public-folder trees:

- The default public-folder tree can be accessed by clients using the following protocols:
  - Microsoft's Messaging Application Programming Interface (MAPI) protocol
  - Internet Message Access Protocol version 4 (IMAPv4)
  - Network News Transport Protocol (NNTP)
  - Hypertext Transfer Protocol (HTTP)
- Alternate (custom) public-folder trees can be accessed only by clients using these protocols:
  - Network News Transport Protocol (NNTP)
  - Hypertext Transfer Protocol (HTTP)

The important point here is that Outlook 2000, the recommended client for Microsoft Exchange, is a MAPI client. Users who have Outlook 2000 therefore can access the default public-folder tree (as All Public Folders) but not the alternate trees you create! So if Outlook is going to be the primary messaging and collaboration client for your users, you probably need to stay within the bounds of having only one public-folder tree, namely the default public-folder tree.

Alternative public-folder trees cannot be accessed using MAPI but can be accessed several other ways:

- Web browsers that support Web Distributed Authoring and Versioning (WebDAV) like Microsoft Internet Explorer 5.0 and higher can access both default and alternative public-folder trees using HTTP. WebDav even allows Web browsers to create and manage public folders and their content remotely over the Internet. Microsoft Office 2000 also supports WebDAV.
- Installable File System (IFS), a new feature of Windows 2000, allows applications to access default and alternate public-folder trees, in the same way that applications access network shares.

We'll look more at how public folders can be accessed in Chapter 18. For now, the important point is the difference in protocol support between the default and alternate public-folder trees in Exchange 2000.

Managing Public-folder Trees

There are a number of administrative tasks that can be performed on public-folder trees:

- Creating, renaming, copying, moving, and deleting public-folder trees
- Assigning a public-folder tree to a public-folder store
- Assigning permissions to control access to public-folder tress

We'll look at many of these tasks in the walkthroughs later in this chapter.

Implementing Public-folder Stores

Creating additional public-folder trees means creating additional public-folder stores because each public-folder store must have a public-folder tree assigned to it. Because the default public store is automatically associated with the default public-folder tree, this association cannot be changed. Implementing additional stores has advantages and disadvantages, some of which are similar to those for implementing multiple mailbox stores. Planning implementation of public-folder stores is essential for successful deployment of Exchange public folders in any organization.

NOTE

An additional point is that each mailbox store in an Exchange organization must be assigned a public-folder store. The assigned public-folder store contains the public-folder tree to which mailboxes in the associated mailbox store will have access. The best practice is to make sure that the public-folder store assigned to each mailbox store is a default public store. In this way, all MAPI clients will be able to access the default public-folder tree in the organization. The public-folder store associated with a mailbox store does not have to be on the same Exchange server as the mailbox store.

Advantages of Using Multiple Public-folder Stores

There are several good reasons to create additional public-folder stores. Some of these concern implementing additional public-folder trees, so that advantages associated with these trees also apply to additional stores.

The ability to mount and dismount individual stores (whether mailbox or public-folder stores) independently of one another provides another advantage of implementing multiple public-folder stores. If a particular store requires maintenance or needs to be restored from backup, it can be dismounted, repaired or recovered, and remounted, all without interrupting users' access to other public-folder stores in the enterprise.

Performance can be enhanced by using multiple stores as well. Each store can be placed on a different drive with its own controller for maximum performance.

Having multiple public-folder stores allows you to use several smaller stores rather than one large default store and allows for faster backups and restores, which can be critical in the case of an emergency. It also provides greater scalability for large companies, where one large default public-folder store simply becomes too big to manage effectively.

Having separate public-folder stores also provides the additional security of being able to isolate data between different groups, departments, companies, or business units. This is especially useful in an application service provider (ASP) environment where Exchange 2000 is being used to host messaging and collaboration services for many independent companies.

Having separate stores also enables you to configure them differently with regard to settings such as storage limits, deleted-item retention period, content indexing, and system policies.

In addition, although replication for the default public-folder tree always occurs, replication between alternate trees, which are hosted in additional public-folder stores you create, can be managed and controlled to a greater degree.

Disadvantages of Using Multiple Public-folder Stores

The main disadvantage of implementing multiple public-folder stores is the same as that for implementing multiple public-folder trees: more limited client access. In addition, there may be administrative overhead associated with managing multiple stores rather than one.

Managing Public-folder Stores

Whatever your decision regarding the implementation of public-folder stores in your organization, you should know and be familiar with basic administrative tasks involving these stores:

- Creating, configuring, renaming, and deleting public-folder stores
- Configuring storage limits, age limits, and deleted-item retention time
- Viewing public-folder store logon information, replication status, and full-text indexing status
- Mounting and dismounting public-folder stores to perform maintenance or restore from backup media

Many of these tasks are covered in the walkthroughs in this chapter and some are covered in later chapters.

TIP

Deciding where to place public-folder stores, mailbox stores, connectors, and other Exchange components can be an important decision, especially in a large enterprise where many Exchange servers will be involved. In a small company with only a few Exchange servers, each server may contain both a mailbox and public-folder store (or several of each). In a large enterprise, however, Exchange components might perform best if they are put on different Exchange servers. For example, you might have dedicated mailbox servers, public-folder servers, connector servers, front-end protocol servers, and so on.

Preliminaries to Walkthroughs in this Chapter

Our testbed deployment of three Exchange servers (Box14 and Box15 in the Vancouver administrative group and Box16 in the Seattle administrative group) currently has only one public-folder tree, namely the default public-folder tree. There currently are three public-folder stores:

- The default-public folder store in the CriticalSG storage group on Box14
- The default-public folder store in the First Storage Group on Box15
- The default-public folder store in the First Storage Group on Box16

Note that Box14 has two storage groups, CriticalSG and DiscardableSG. DiscardableSG currently has two mailbox stores (AccountingMS and ExecutiveMS) but no public-folder stores.

Creating a New Public-folder Tree

Walkthrough

We'll begin by creating a new public-folder tree, a necessary preliminary for creating a new public-folder store. We'll call this new tree ProjectFolders because it will contain public folders used for collaboration by employees on different projects that your company is working on.

We should note at this point that we have two different administrative groups, Vancouver and Seattle, in our Exchange organization, which is important because public-folder trees are stored in special Folders containers within administrative groups. To see this, expand the node for each administrative group to display the containers immediately beneath them (Figure 17.1). Each administrative group has a Folders container under it, and the Folders container in Vancouver contains the default public-folder tree (called Public Folders in System Manager) but the Folders container in Seattle is empty.

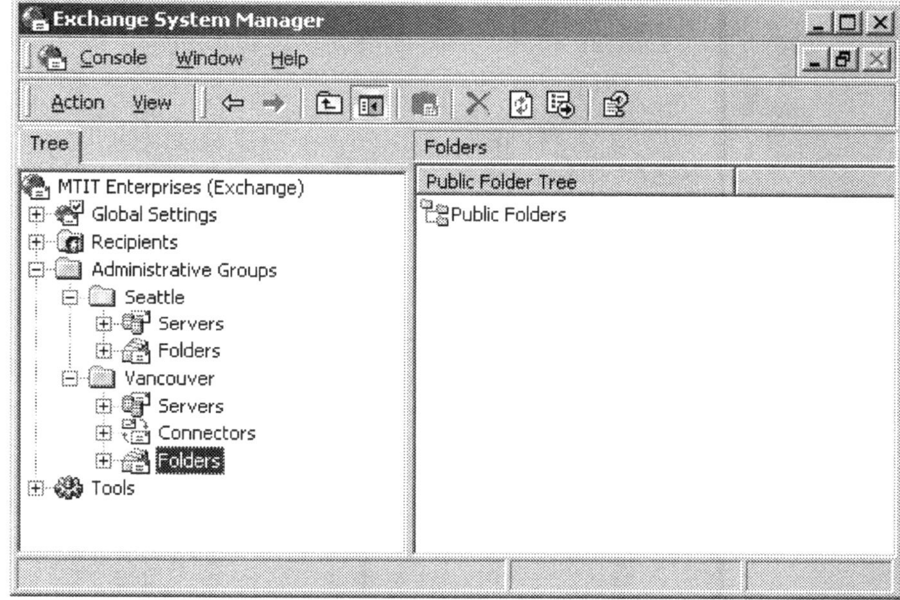

Figure 17.1 The Folders containers in the Vancouver and Seattle administrative groups.

NOTE

In Chapter 12, when we first created the Seattle administrative group, the container representing that group had no objects within it. Then, when we installed Exchange server Box16, we assigned it to this administrative group and this created a Servers container within it. Then we manually created a Folders container within the Servers container to host future public-folder trees. We then moved the public-folder tree from Vancouver's Folders container to Seattle's and then moved it back. So we've already worked with public-folder trees, even though you may not have known exactly what they were at that point! Incidentally, that walk-through illustrated that you can move (or copy) public-folder trees between different storage groups in different administrative groups (when your Exchange organization is running in native mode).

The point is, before you create a new public-folder tree within an administrative group, you must make sure that there is a Folders container within that group to contain the new tree. If there isn't a Folders container, right-click on the administrative group and select New →

Public Folders Container to create one. Note that the First Administrative Group (or whatever name you've given it) in your Exchange organization already has a Folders container by default.

NOTE

You can create only one Folders container in each administrative group; once you've created that container, the shortcut menu option for creating them disappears. However, each Folders container can contain multiple public-folder trees, if desired. The reason for placing public-folder trees in different administrative groups is to be able to delegate administrative control over them to different Exchange administrators in your organization.

We'll create our ProjectFolders public-folder tree in the Folders container of the Seattle administrative group so that our Seattle administrator can manage it. Right-click on the Folders container in Seattle and select New → Public Folder Tree. Type the name ProjectFolders for the new tree (Figure 17.2). At this point, our new tree has no association with any public store, and there is no place on this properties page to create such an association (you create the association later from the store, not from the tree). Click OK to create the new tree. The tree should now be visible in System Manager within the Folders container in Seattle. Our next step is to create a new public-folder store to host this tree.

NOTE

You can administer a specific replica of a public-folder tree by right-clicking the public-folder tree and selecting Connect To from the shortcut menu. This may be necessary if you want to set permissions on the tree or create public folders in the tree but cannot access one or more replicas of the tree because of network conditions.

TIP

Don't include any spaces in the name of your public-folder trees because you may want some users to be able to access the tree using a Web browser, and URLs cannot have spaces in them. If you must use a name with spaces for your public-folder tree, users will have to insert a special escape code, `%20`, *wherever a space should be in the URL. This is messy and confusing to most users and should be avoided.*

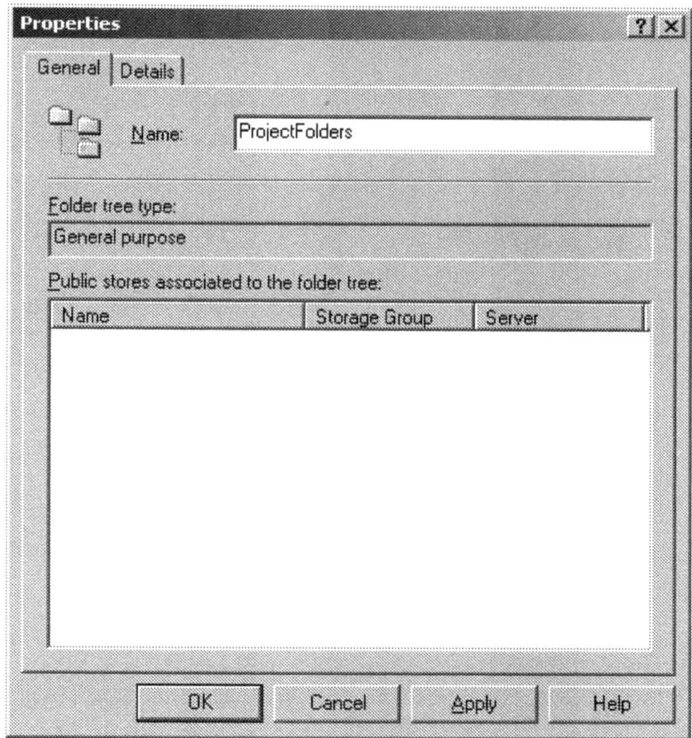

Figure 17.2 Creating a new public-folder tree.

Creating a New Public-folder Store

Let's now create a new public-folder store and assign our ProjectFolders tree to the store. We'll create our new store in the First Storage Group on Box16 in Seattle and we'll call it ProjectsPS.

Right-click on the First Storage Group on Box16 and select New → Public Store from the shortcut menu. A blank Properties Sheet should appear for the new public-folder store. Type the name ProjectsPS in the Name textbox on the General tab (Figure 17.3).

If a dialog box saying "All the public folder trees already have an associated public folder store on this server. You need to create a new public folder tree before creating this new public store" instead of the Properties Sheet shown in Figure 17.3, then the new public-folder store can't be created because there are no unassigned public-folder trees available to

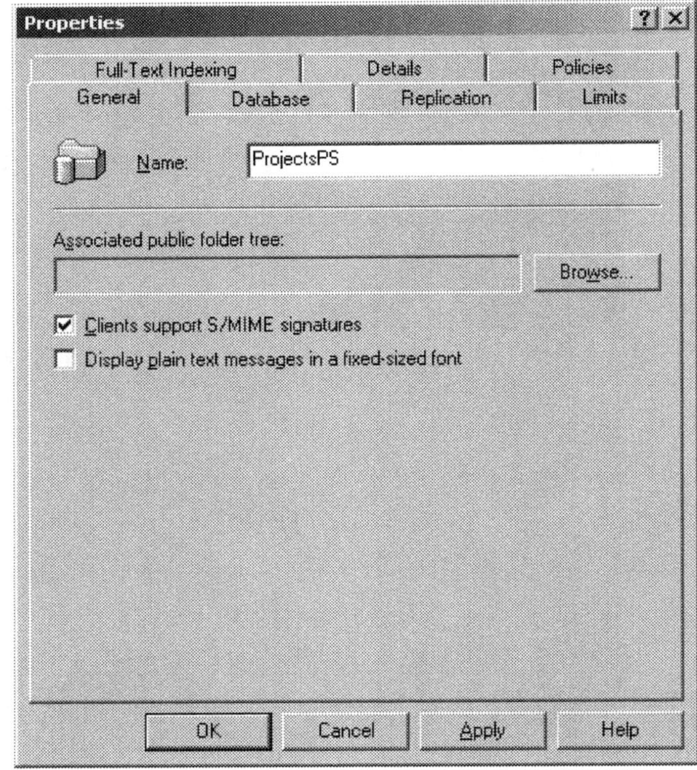

Figure 17.3 Creating a new public-folder store called ProjectsPS to host the ProjectFolders public-folder tree created earlier.

associate with the new store. You must create a new public-folder tree before you can create a new public-folder store to host it.

Our next step is to associate our new store with the ProjectFolders tree we created earlier. Click the Browse button to display a list of available (unassigned) public-folder trees in the organization (Figure 17.4). The only available tree should be ProjectFolders, so select that tree and click OK to assign it to the new store. The General tab shown in Figure 17.3 should display the name of the assigned public-folder tree.

Click OK to create the new store or further configure the store using the other tabs on the Properties Sheet. Many of these configuration settings are similar to those used for mailbox stores (Chapter 15), so we'll just summarize them here and focus only on those new to public-folder stores. The configuration tabs for public-folder stores include:

- *Database tab.* This is used to specify the name of the two database files (.edb and .stm files) associated with the new store and can also

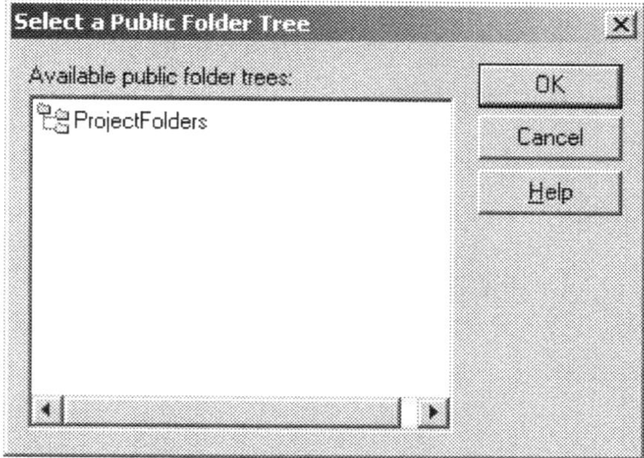

Figure 17.4 *Assigning an available public-folder tree to a new public-folder store.*

be used to specify the location of these files. These considerations are similar to those of mailbox stores.

- *Replication tab.* This is something new and specifies parameters for when and how replication of the contents of this store will occur. We'll cover public-folder replication in Chapter 18.
- *Limits tab.* Like mailbox stores, you can configure various storage limits and the deleted-item retention time for messages, documents, and files in the store. The only new parameter is Age Limits, which specifies the number of days that a new item will remain in the store before it is deleted from the store. By default, this setting is disabled for the store.

TIP

Setting appropriate storage limits is probably even more important on public-folder stores than on mailbox stores because users tend to post huge amounts of information to public stores without any consideration for how much disk space they might be using!

TIP

Items deleted accidentally from public folders whose store has a non-zero deleted-item retention period configured can be recovered using Outlook in the same way as messages deleted from mailboxes are recovered (Chapter 16).

TIP

Enabling and specifying an age limit for a store can be tricky. You wouldn't want users to post important documents to the store only to find them mysteriously purged after a certain period. Age limits should only be configured on stores where data is of low importance but where postings are frequent or large. This will help the store from growing too large and running out of disk space.

- *Full-text indexing tab*. This is used to configure content indexing and is discussed in Chapter 19.
- *Details tab*. This is used to add an administrative note (a note to yourself concerning the store).
- *Policies tab*. This displays system policies configured for this public-folder store. System policies are covered in Chapter 20.

Let's finish the process and create the new store. Click OK to close the Properties Sheet and follow the prompts to create and mount the new store. Figure 17.5 shows the new ProjectPS store within the First Storage Group on Box16 in Seattle. Now that you've created a new public-folder tree and assigned it to a new public-folder store, you can create public folders within this tree and post messages and documents to the folders (Chapter 18).

NOTE

Exchange 2000 requires at least one default public-folder store for each administrative group. When you install the first Exchange server in a new administrative group, this store is created on the server.

NOTE

There is a one-to-one correspondence between new public-folder trees and new public-folder stores. Each public-folder store must have one and only one public-folder tree assigned to it; when you assign a public-folder tree to one store, it becomes unavailable for assignment to other stores. You cannot split a single public folder tree across multiple public-folder stores.

NOTE

You can rename, delete, mount, and dismount public-folder stores in the same way as with mailbox stores. As expected, you cannot delete a public-folder tree unless you first move or delete all public folders in the tree, and you cannot delete public folders unless you first move or delete the messages and files they contain. Be aware that, unlike deleted mailboxes, deleted public-folder trees cannot be "undeleted" except by restoring from backup media.

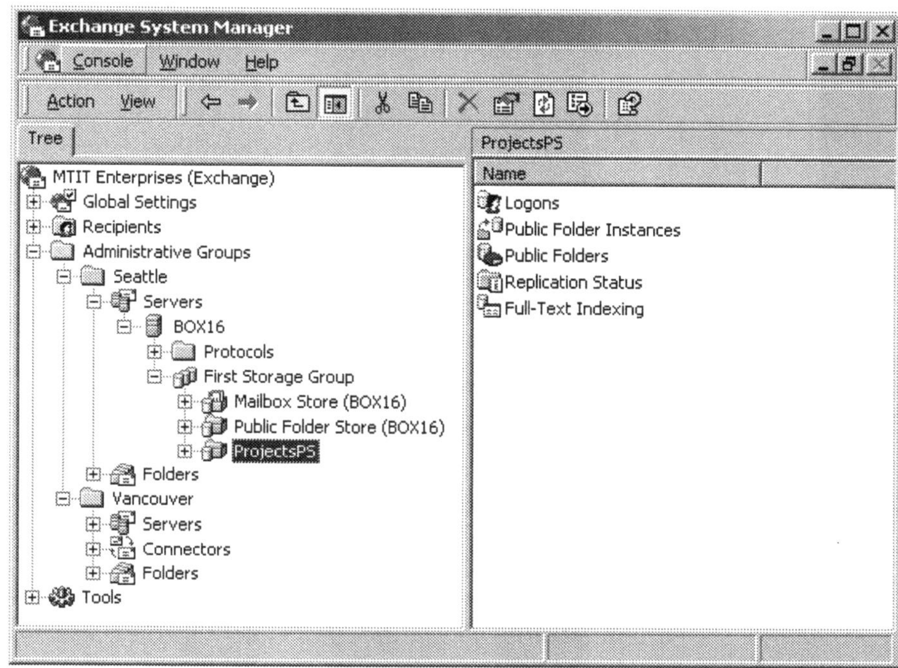

Figure 17.5 The new ProjectsPS public-folder store.

Displaying Public-folder Logons and Other Information

Walkthrough

Figure 17.5 shows five nodes beneath the new public-folder store node (ProjectPS) we just created. These five nodes allow you to display information concerning the store:

- *Logons*. Selecting this node in the console tree displays details about which users are currently logged on to the public-folder tree hosted by the store. The information displayed is similar to that for the Logons node for a mailbox store. By selecting View → Choose Columns, you can display additional columns of information about the store, including the number of open folders, open messages, and open attachments.
- *Public-folder instances*. This displays all public folders within the tree. The Details pane displays the name of each public folder, the current size of the folder in kilobytes, and other information. You also use this node to add new replicas of a public folder, as we will see in Chapter 18.
- *Public folders*. This displays additional information including the number of items within each public folder, the date of creation of the

folder, the time the folder was last accessed, and so on. By selecting View → Choose Columns, you can also display the disk space occupied by deleted items in the folder and other information.

- *Replication status*. This node shows the replication status of each folder, if replication has been configured for the tree (replication is configured by default for the default public-folder tree). We'll talk more about replication in Chapter 18.
- *Full-text indexing*. This displays the progress of content indexing for each folder.

UNDER THE HOOD

System Folders

Figure 17.6 displays the details of the Public Folders node for the default Public Folders Store in the First Storage Group on Box16. The public folders currently displayed are system folders, which are hidden public folders. System folders are automatically created in each public-folder store you create. Some stores like the default Public Folder Store in the First Storage Group on the first Exchange server installed in a given administrative group may have more of these system folders than other public-folder stores in your organization. You generally shouldn't delete or modify these system folders.

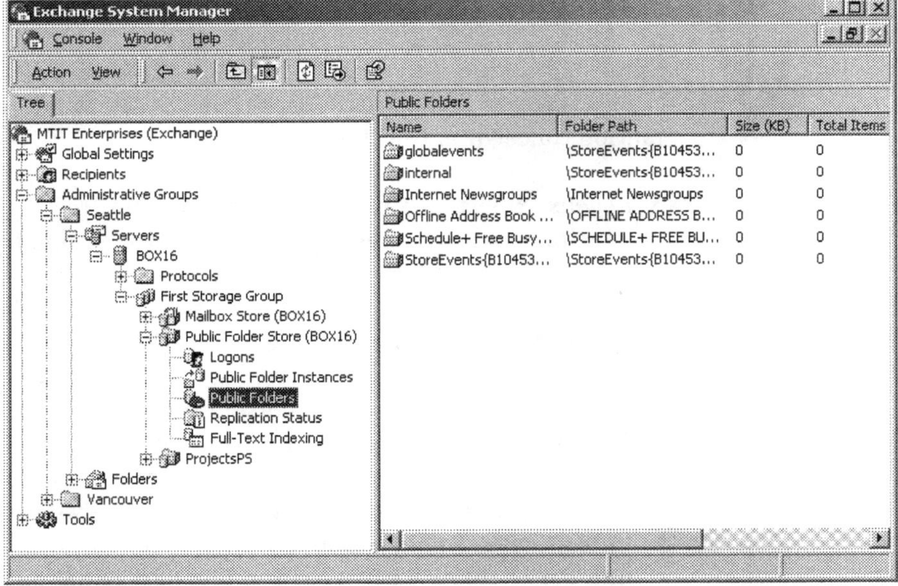

Figure 17.6
System folders in the default public folder store on the first Exchange server in the Seattle administrative group.

Assigning Permissions for Creating New Public Folders in Public-folder Trees

Walkthrough

The default permissions for creating new public folders in a public-folder tree are pretty broad—any user can create new folders in the tree. You may want to modify this default setting as follows:

1. Find the public-folder tree whose permissions you want to modify in System Manager. Public-folder trees are located within the Folders container of each administrative group. We'll select the ProjectFolders tree we created earlier.
2. Right-click the public-folder tree and select Properties and switch to the Security tab (Figure 17.7).

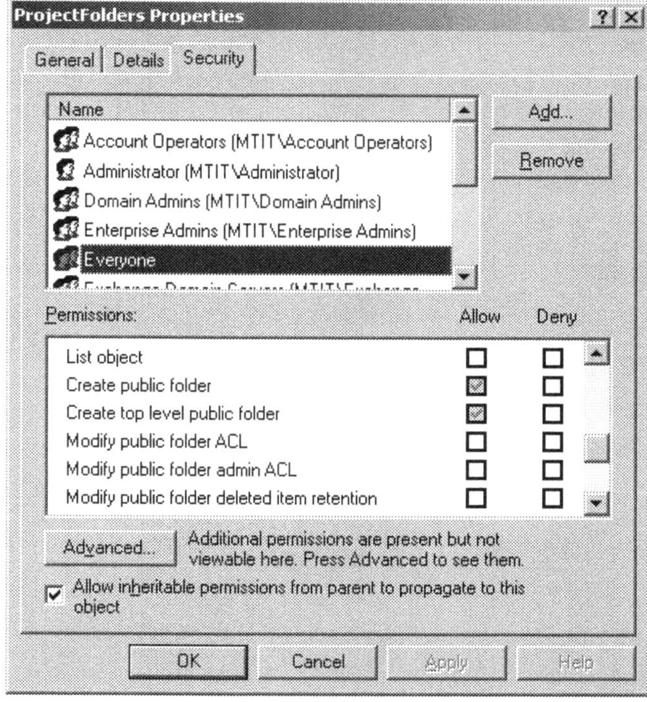

Figure 17.7 *Assigning permissions for creating new public folders in public-folder trees.*

3. Click Add and select the user or group you want to grant the ability to create and manage new public folders in this tree.

4. Make sure you allow at least the following permissions for the selected user or group:
   - Create public folders
   - Create top-level public folders
   - Create named properties in the Information Store
5. Select the Everyone built-in special identity and Deny the above permissions.
6. Click OK.

Assigning a Default Public-folder Store to a Mailbox Store

Each mailbox store needs to have a public-folder store assigned to it. This must be a default public-folder store that enables users whose mailboxes are hosted in the mailbox store to access the default public-folder tree for the organization. To view the public store assigned to a given mailbox store, open the Properties Sheet for the mailbox store and examine the General tab (see Figure 15.1). If you click Browse, you can select any default Public Folder Store on any of the Exchange servers in your organization that has a public-folder store in its information store, but you cannot select an alternate public-folder store to associate with a mailbox store.

Summary

Now that we're familiar with how to create and manage public-folder stores and public-folder trees, it's time to consider how to create and manage public folders and their replicas, the topic of Chapter 18.

CHAPTER 18

Public Folders and Replicas

In the previous chapter we discussed public-folder stores and trees and how to create and manage them. This chapter discusses how to create public folders and replicate them across your organization.

There are nineteen walkthroughs in this chapter:

- Creating a public folder using System Manager
- Creating a public folder using a MAPI client
- Creating a public folder using a Web browser
- Creating a public folder using an IMAP4 client
- Accessing a public folder using a MAPI client
- Accessing a public folder using an IMAP client
- Accessing alternate public-folder trees using a Web browser
- Accessing a public folder using a network share
- Configuring replication settings for a public-folder store
- Replicating public folders
- Viewing replication status
- Verifying public-folder replication
- Adding and removing public-folder replicas
- Configuring age limits for replicas
- Copying and moving public folders
- Propagating public-folder settings
- Modifying email addresses for public folders
- Configuring administrative and directory permissions for managing public folders
- Configuring client permissions for controlling access to public folders

Public Folders

In Chapter 17, we looked at how to create new public-folder trees and configure the existing default tree, which is called Public Folders in System Manager and All Public Folders in Microsoft Outlook. But we haven't actually created any public folders in these trees, and that's what we'll do in this chapter. After that, we'll look at how to access these public folders and configure replications of public folders within our organization.

Public-folder Replication

We covered public-folder terminology in the previous chapter, but we didn't talk much about public-folder replication. The real power of public folders in Exchange is the ability replicate the content of different folders across different Exchange servers in an enterprise.

A *replica* is a copy of the contents of a public folder. Replicas reside in public-folder stores on Exchange servers throughout an organization. By default, when you create a new public folder, only one replica exists—the replica you created. You often want to create additional replicas of folders for the following reasons:

- *Fault tolerance*. If the same data is stored on several servers, one server can go down but the data remain available to those users who can access the remaining servers.
- *Load balancing*. Having all users access public folders on one server puts a terrific load on that server. It makes more sense to replicate frequently accessed public folders to at least one server in each location, site, or administrative group. Clients such as Outlook will then automatically try to access the closest replica before trying elsewhere. In a scenario where there are multiple sites connected by slow WAN links, placing replicas at each site prevents the WAN links from getting clogged with traffic generated by users accessing public-folder replicas at different sites.

NOTE

There is no master replica of a public folder. Once you have created a second replica of a folder, both replicas are equal.

The ability of replicating public-folder content makes public folders (and public-folder trees and stores) more complex to administer than mailboxes and mailbox stores. However, the effort is well worth it because implementing public folders in an enterprise is a powerful tool that enables users to collaborate on projects, create collections of documents, create FAQs, hold discussions on important issues, and so on.

TIP

If you plan to allow anonymous users from outside the organization access to some public folders (for example, over the Internet using a Web browser), you probably want to host your public folders on dedicated public-folder servers that don't contain employee mailboxes. This is a good way of isolating and thus protecting your mailboxes from public folders.

Creating and Accessing Public Folders

With previous versions of Exchange, you could create public folders only with a client such as Outlook. Exchange 2000 provides a number of methods using:

- Exchange System Manager
- MAPI clients such as Microsoft Outlook
- IMAP4 clients such as Microsoft Outlook Express
- Web browsers such as Internet Explorer that support WebDAV

MAPI, IMAP4, and WebDAV

MAPI *stands for messaging application programming interface and refers to the proprietary application programming interface developed by Microsoft. Microsoft Outlook is an example of a messaging client that uses MAPI to communicate with Exchange (that is, when it is configured in Corporate or Workgroup mode).*

IMAP4 *stands for Internet Message Access Protocol 4 and is a standard Internet protocol for messaging clients to access their mailboxes on mail servers. IMAP4 is more powerful than its predecessor, POP3, because it supports selective downloading, searching messages on the server, and access to public folders. IMAP4 is supported by many Internet mail clients such as Microsoft Outlook Express and Microsoft Outlook when it is configured in Internet Only mode.*

WebDAV *stands for Web-based Distributed Authoring and Versioning and is a draft Internet standard that extends the HTTP 1.1 protocol by enabling Web browser clients to move, copy, delete, and otherwise manage documents using HTTP. WebDAV is supported by Microsoft Internet Explorer 5.0 and higher and by Microsoft Office 2000.*

Creating a Public Folder Using System Manager

We'll start by using System Manager to create a top-level public folder called Accounts in the default Public Folders tree. Log on to Box14 as Administrator and start System Manager. Right-click on the Public

Folders node within the Folders container in the Vancouver administrative group and select New → Public Folder from the shortcut menu. A blank Properties Sheet appears for the new public folder (Figure 18.1). Type Accounts in the Name field and enter a brief description, if desired, in the Description field. For now, we'll leave the remaining folder default settings and just click OK to create the new public folder.

TIP

It's best give public folders names without embedded spaces because the name you give the folder is used in the email address for the folder, and some clients may have problems using addresses with embedded spaces in them.

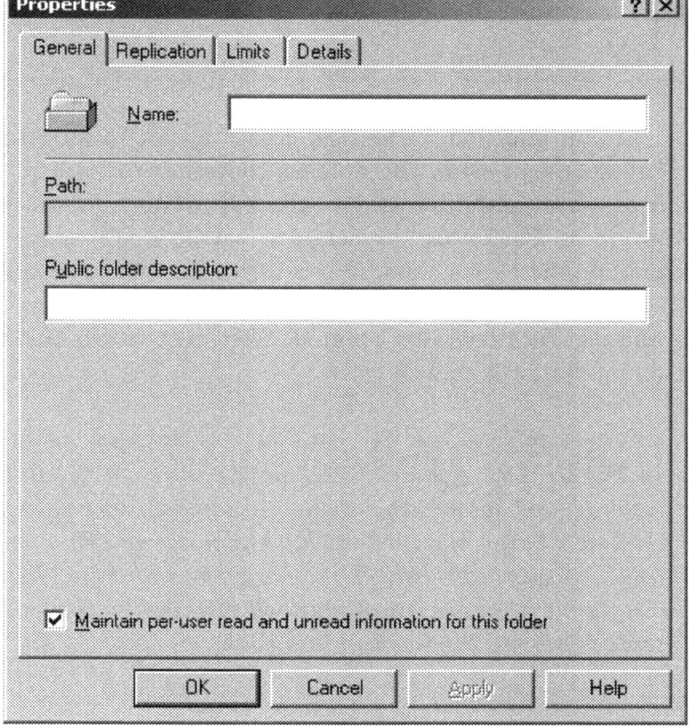

Figure 18.1 Creating a new top-level public folder using Exchange System Manager.

The Public Folders container in Vancouver should now display the Accounts public folder that you just created (Figure 18.2). If you double-click on the new folder, you can display properties such as the storage limits and replication settings for the folder. We'll cover other configurations of these properties later in this chapter.

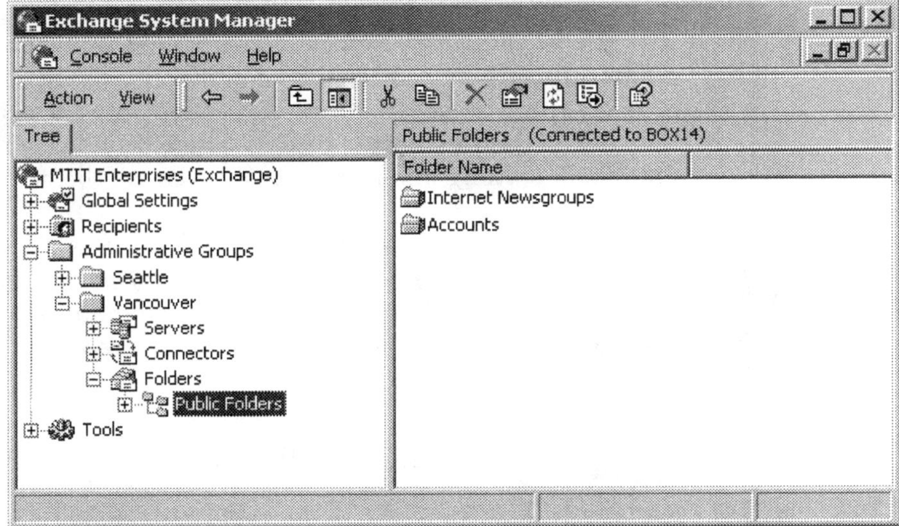

Figure 18.2 The Accounts public folder within the default Public Folders tree.

As an additional exercise, create a new (alternate) public-folder tree called Inventory in the Folders container in Vancouver and then create a new public-folder store called NewStore in the CriticalSG storage group on Box14 and associate it with the Inventory tree. Now create a new public folder called Parts in the Inventory tree using System Manager. We've now created two new public folders, one in the default tree and one in a tree just created. We'll test which clients can access these folders later in this chapter.

NOTE

In Figure 18.2 you can also see another public folder called Internet Newsgroups, which was created in the default Public Folders tree during the installation of your first Exchange server. This top-level folder can be used to replicate USENET newsgroups and can be accessed by NNTP clients such as Microsoft Outlook Express or Outlook Newsreader. This topic is beyond the scope of this book.

Creating a Public Folder Using a MAPI Client

Walkthrough

Now let's use Outlook to create some public folders. Log on to a client machine as user Jane Smith, a member of the marketing department and an ordinary user, not an administrator. Start Outlook and make sure the Folder List is displayed (if not, then select View → Folder List to display it). Right-click on All Public Folders under Public Folders in the Folder List and select New Folder. This opens a Create New Folder dialog box. Type Records as the name of the new public folder you will create, leave the Folder Contains listbox set to Mail Items to enable you to post messages to the folder, and select All Public Folders to make your new folder a top-level folder (Figure 18.3). Click OK to create the new folder and verify that it appears under All Public Folders in the Folder List in Outlook.

Let's create another public folder called "2000" beneath the Records folder we just created. Right-click on Records in the Folder List and select New Folder to open the Create New Folder box again. Enter "2000" as the name of the new folder and select Records as the top-level folder in which to create this new folder. Click OK and verify in both Outlook on the client machine and in System Manager on Box14 that your new folders have been created. We'll post test messages to them in a moment.

Figure 18.3 Creating a new top-level public folder using a MAPI client like Outlook.

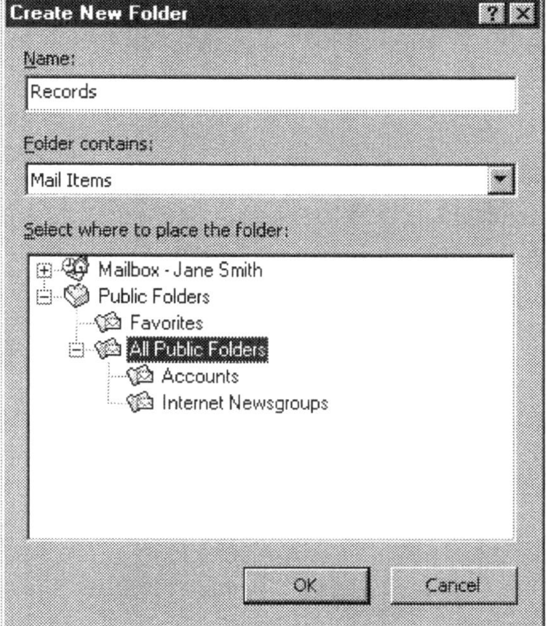

One last thing: while logged on to the client as Jane Smith, try creating a new public folder under the Accounts top-level folder created earlier by Administrator using System Manager. You can't—the option New Folder on the shortcut menu is unavailable (or it may generate an error message saying that you have insufficient rights to create the new folder). Because Administrator created the Accounts top-level folder, Administrator is the owner and has permission to create new subfolder within the folder. Later in this chapter, we'll learn how to grant the permissions required to complete this task.

NOTE

Once a user has created a new top-level public folder using Outlook, an administrator can use System Manager to further configure the folder's properties such as storage limits and replication settings. By default, all users are allowed to create new top-level folders, a right you may want to restrict. See Chapter 17 for more information.

NOTE

Outlook cannot access the Inventory public-folder tree you created at the end of the previous walkthrough. MAPI clients such as Outlook can access only the default Public Folders tree, called All Public Folders in Outlook. Later in this chapter, we'll see how to configure Exchange so that the WebDAV-enabled Web browser Internet Explorer can be used to access alternate public-folder trees.

Creating a Public Folder Using a Web Browser

Walkthrough

Next we'll create a new public folder using a WebDAV-compliant browser such as Internet Explorer. While still logged on as Jane Smith on the client machine, close Outlook and start Internet Explorer. Once the browser is open, type in the following URL: http://box14/public. This will connect to Box14 using Outlook Web Access (OWA) and display the default Public Folders tree. Right-click on the Records top-level folder and select New Folder from the shortcut menu that appears. Create a new public folder called "2001" under Records—the process is remarkably similar to using the actual Outlook client in the previous walkthrough. The finished result is shown in Figure 18.4.

Here are some additional notes on accessing public folders using Internet Explorer:

- To go directly to the Records public folder, use URL `http://box14/public/records`.
- To display Jane's mailbox folders and public folders, use URL `http://box14/exchange`.

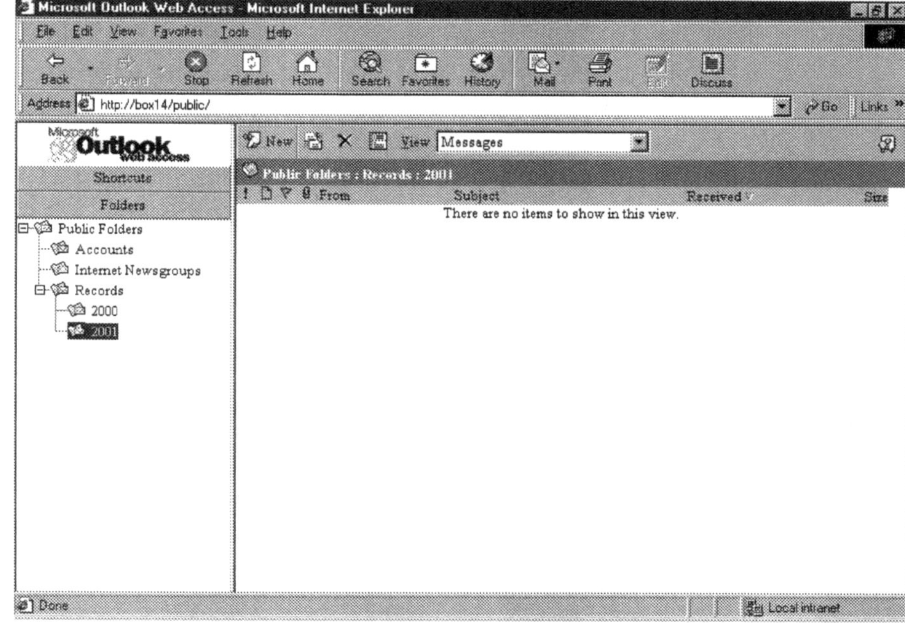

Figure 18.4 Creating a new top-level public folder using a WebDav-compliant Web browser such as Internet Explorer.

- If you have DNS properly configured on the client server, you could use URL http://box14.mtit.com/public.

Creating a Public Folder Using an IMAP4 Client

Walkthrough

Let's create a new public folder using IMAP4 client Outlook Express. Log on to a client machine as a different user such as Fred Jones and start Outlook Express. If this is your first time starting the program on this machine, you will be prompted to create an account. Configure the account settings as follows:

- Display name: Fred Jones
- Email address: fjones@mtit.com
- Incoming mail server type: IMAP
- Incoming mail server name: box14.mtit.com
- Outgoing mail server name: box14.mtit.com
- Account name: fjones
- Password: (whatever you chose when you created the user)

When you finish the New Account Wizard, Outlook Express will start and you will be prompted to select which IMAP folders you want to display. Double-click on Public Folders and all folders under it and click OK.

Now right-click on the Public Folders node in the Folders pane and select New Folder from the shortcut menu. Enter Projects as the name of the new top-level public folder and make sure it is visible under the Public Folders node. After you create the new top-level folder, Outlook Express should appear similar to the view shown in Figure 18.5.

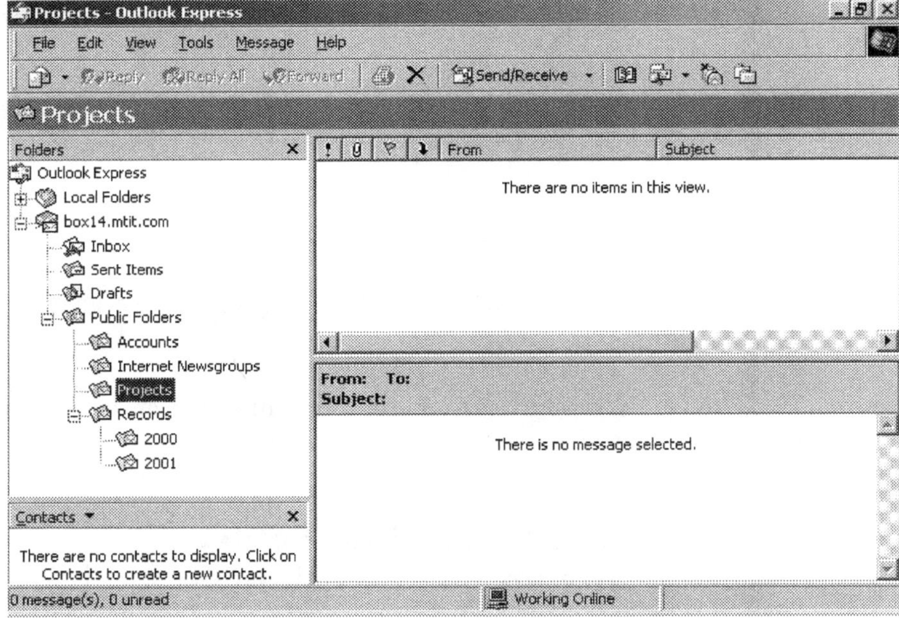

Figure 18.5 Creating a new public folder using IMAP client Outlook Express.

Accessing a Public Folder Using a MAPI Client

Walkthrough

Posting items to public folders with a MAPI client like Outlook is straightforward, and anyone who has worked with Outlook before is probably familiar with this. As a test, log on to a client machine as Jane Smith (jsmith@mtit.com), select the Accounts public folder in the Folder List, click New, type a message, and click Post to publish the item to the folder. Do the same with the other public folders in the default Public Folders tree.

Accessing a Public Folder Using an IMAP Client

Accessing public folders using IMAP clients such as Outlook Express (or Outlook when it is configured for Corporate or Workgroup mode) is just as easy. Log on to another client as Fred Jones (fjones@mtit.com), start Outlook Express (the program should be configured properly because Fred has used it), and see if you can read the items Jane posted to the various public folders.

Post a new item to the Accounts public folder by selecting the folder and clicking the New Mail button on the toolbar to open a New Message box. We'll send a one-off message to the folder by typing the email address of the folder directly into the To textbox. The email address for the folder should be accounts@mtit.com. Type a subject and message body and click Send. The message should appear immediately in the folder.

If the posted item does not appear when the Accounts folder is selected in Outlook Express, the public folder may not be mail-enabled. Go to Box14, start System Manager, right-click on the Accounts folder, and select Properties. If the folder is mail-enabled, then it will have the Exchange General, Exchange Advanced, and E-mail Addresses tabs visible. If it is not mail-enabled, then close the Properties Sheet, right-click on the folder, and select All Tasks → Mail Enable from the shortcut menu. Folders only need to be mail-enabled if you are going to access them using IMAP clients, because MAPI clients can access public folders directly.

Accessing a Public Folder Using a Web Browser

From the client machine where Jane Smith is currently logged on, close Outlook and open Internet Explorer. Enter the URL `http://box14/public`. (OWA) will open and you should be able to read the various messages that have been posted to the public folders. Post a new message to one of the folders—the procedure is almost identical to using Outlook. Before we go on, let's look under the hood of Exchange to learn more about how public folders work.

NOTE

WebDAV-enabled HTTP clients like Internet Explorer can post messages to public folders regardless of whether they have been mail-enabled, just like MAPI clients.

Accessing Alternate Public-Folder Trees Using a Web Browser

Walkthrough

How does entering the URL http://box14/public provide a Web client with access to the default Public Folders tree on Box14? It all has to do with M: drive, which Exchange 2000 uses to store public folders and other data that need to be shared by Exchange. If you open Windows Explorer on Box14 and expand My Computer, you'll see a logical drive labeled Exchange (M:) listed. This M: drive is where the Installable File System (IFS) is installed on your Exchange server.

BACKGROUNDER

IFS

IFS is a new storage technology in Exchange 2000 running on Windows 2000 that allows items contained in mailboxes and public folders to be exposed to the file system as file shares. IFS enables WebDAV-enabled clients like Internet Explorer 5.0 and Office 2000 to access the information store on Exchange servers. When you examine the contents of the M: drive in Windows Explorer, the items displayed in the various mailbox and public folders are actually located within the mailbox and public folder stores on the server. IFS merely exposes them to the file system as items on the M: drive. Because of this ability for Web-based clients like Internet Explorer 5.0 and Office 2000 to access the Exchange 2000 information store using HTTP/WebDAV, this store is generally referred to by the name Web Store.

The only folder on the M: drive should be one representing the DNS domain your server resides in, in this case mtit.com (there may be additional folders if multiple domains are hosted by your server). Under this domain folder you will find several other folders (Figure 18.6):

- *Public folders*. This is the root folder of the default public-folder tree. Under it you'll find individual folders for each public folder, and within these folders are the items posted to these public folders.

- *Inventory*. We created a new public-folder tree earlier in this chapter, and the root of this tree is this folder.
- *MBX*. This is the root of all the mailboxes on this server.

Figure 18.6 Logical drive M: on Exchange server Box14.

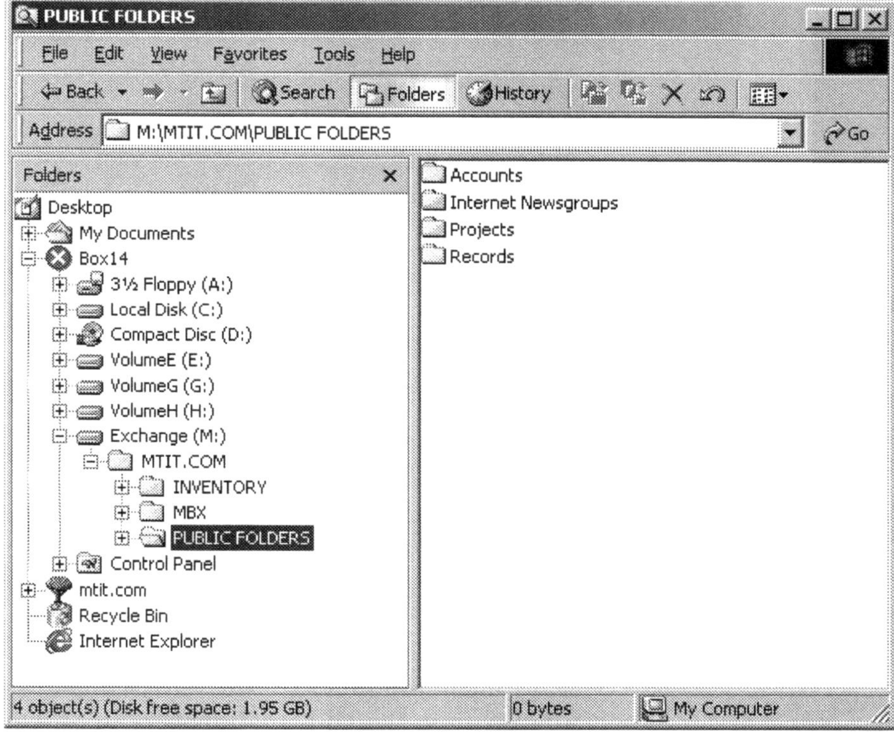

Let's take a closer look at the folder named Public Folders, which is the root of the default public-folder tree on Box14. Right-click on Public Folders, select Properties to open the folder's Properties Sheet, and select the Web Sharing tab (Figure 18.7).

To understand these settings, we first need to understand that Internet Information Services (IIS) is the underlying protocol engine on Exchange 2000. IIS provides support for SMTP, POP3, IMAP4, and HTTP protocols by using virtual servers. A *virtual server* is an instance of a server that has all the properties of a real server. You can configure multiple virtual servers on a single physical machine using IIS, but Exchange uses the existing default virtual server. When you try to access the URL http://box14 using Internet Explorer, you end up opening the home page of the Default HTTP virtual server (Default Web Site) hosted on IIS on Box14.

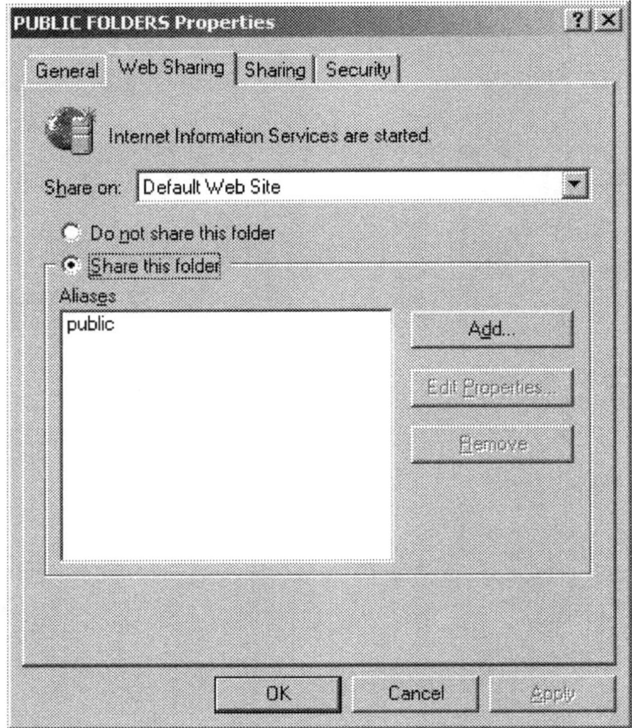

Figure 18.7 Web Sharing settings for the Public Folders folder on Box14.

Each virtual server can have multiple virtual directories in it (which are typically displayed in an Under Construction page). A *virtual directory* is a folder from the URL that appears to be a subfolder of the root folder of the virtual server but is actually mapped to a different folder on the machine (or on a remote machine).

In Figure 18.7, we can see that the default public-folder tree is shared on the Default virtual server (Default Web Site), and the alias (virtual directory) of the Public Folders folder is simply "public." These two elements together allow us to access the default public-folder tree with OWA by opening URL:

```
http://box14   +  /public   =   http://box14/public
```

which we verified previously.

What about accessing your personal mailbox using OWA? Open the Properties Sheet for the MBX folder under mtit.com on the M: drive and select the Web Sharing tab. Note that this folder tree is also shared on the Default virtual server (Default Web Site) but with the alias "exchange." Therefore, to access our personal mailbox on Box14, we open URL:

```
http://box14    +  /exchange   =   http://box14/exchange
```

as shown in Chapter 3.

We now know how to access an alternate public-folder tree like the Inventory tree we created earlier in this chapter. This tree can't be accessed by MAPI clients such as Outlook, but we can access it using OWA by configuring Web Sharing for this tree. Several steps are involved:

1. Find the HTTP container under the Protocols container under Box14 in System Manager. The only virtual server you should see in this HTTP container is the default Exchange Virtual Server.
2. Right-click on the Exchange Virtual Server and select New → Virtual Directory from the shortcut menu. This opens a Properties Sheet for the new virtual directory (Figure 18.8).

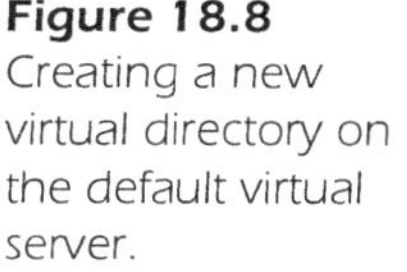

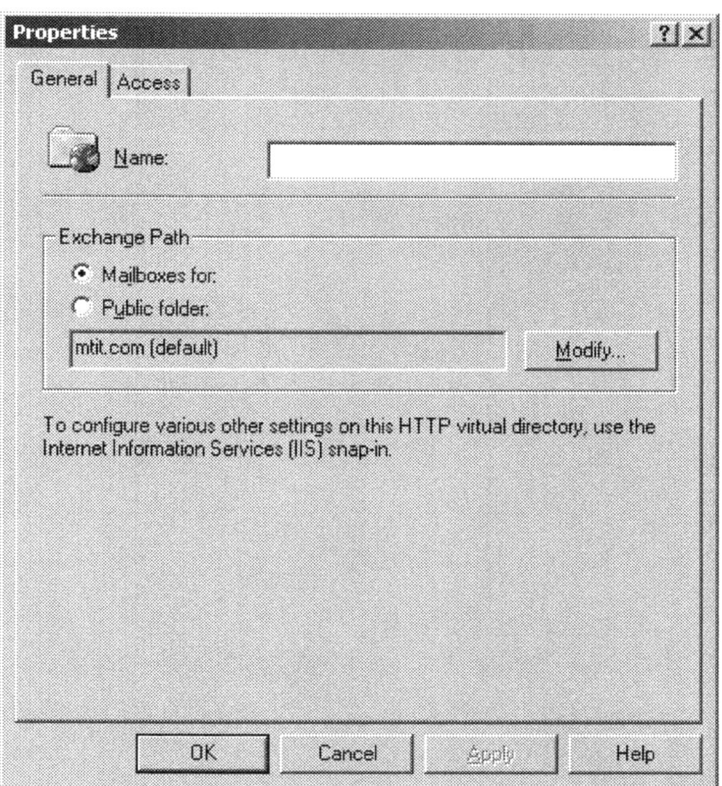

Figure 18.8 Creating a new virtual directory on the default virtual server.

3. Type "inv" (without the quotes) as the name (or alias) for the new virtual directory.
4. Under Exchange Path, select Public Folder, click Modify, and choose the Inventory public-folder tree as the one you will associate with this new virtual directory.
5. Switch to the Access tab and view the permissions for this virtual directory. Leave them at their default settings for now.
6. Click OK to create the new virtual directory.

Let's check if the virtual directory has been created properly. Switch to Windows Explorer and right-click on the Inventory folder under mtit.com on the M: drive to open the Inventory folder's Properties Sheet. Switch to the Web Sharing tab and note that the folder now has a virtual directory with the alias "inv" associated with it.

Now let's test our procedures to determine whether we can access the Inventory public-folder tree using OWA. Start Internet Explorer and open URL `http://box14/inv`; everything should be fine (Figure 18.9)!

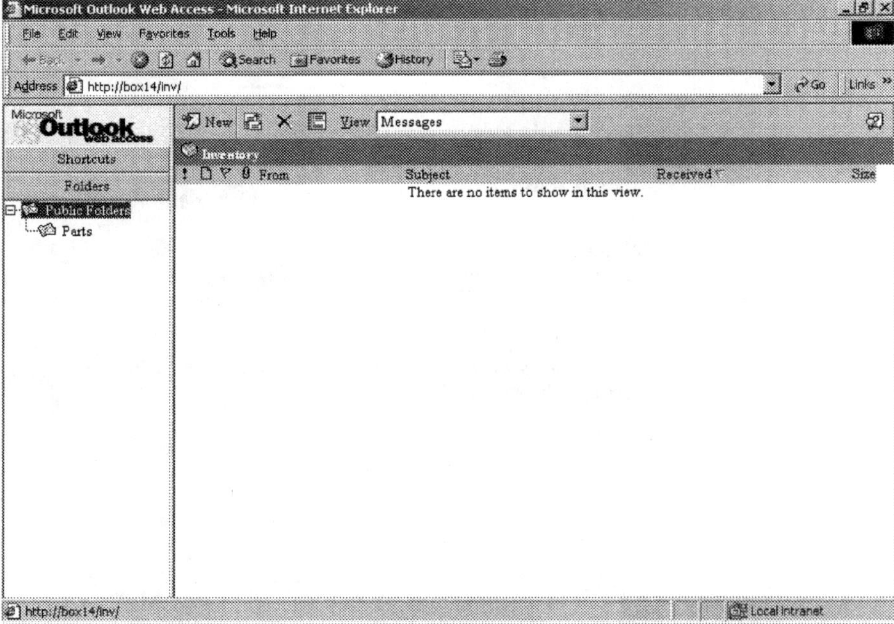

Figure 18.9 Accessing an alternate public-folder tree using OWA.

TIP

When naming virtual directories, do not use embedded spaces. We'll talk more about virtual servers later on in this book, but for a fuller treatment of virtual directories and virtual servers, see Administering IIS5 *by Mitch Tulloch and Patrick Santry (McGraw-Hill / Osborne).*

Accessing a Public Folder Using a Network Share

Walkthrough

You can also access public folders as network shares using the IFS feature of Windows 2000. IFS is installed by default on logical drive M:, which is created when Exchange 2000 is installed on a server, but the folders on this drive are not shared by default (be careful to distinguish between sharing and Web sharing here). You can share a folder like Public Folders by opening its Properties Sheet in Windows Explorer, selecting the Sharing tab, choosing Share This Folder, and specifying a suitable share name such as PUB. By default, Everyone has full share permissions when you create a new share. If the Public Folders folder on the M: drive on Box14 is shared with share name PUB, then users can access the public folders in this tree with Start → Run → \\BOX14\PUB → OK in the usual way.

NOTE

Do not share the MBX folder on the M: drive unless you fully understand the security issues involved. You may be giving all users access to each others' mailboxes!

Managing Public Folders

Once public folders are set up, they should be managed carefully to ensure that problems don't occur. Some of the administrative tasks you need to be able to perform include:

- Setting up public-folder replication
- Configuring storage limits
- Copying and moving public folders
- Propagating public-folder settings
- Modifying email addresses

- Assigning administrative and client permissions

Let's look at some of these tasks now.

Configuring Replication Settings for a Public-folder Store

Walkthrough

In the previous chapter we mentioned that you can configure replication settings at the public-folder store level. The settings you configure at this level apply by default to all public folders in a given store.

Let's configure replication settings for the default public-folder store on BOX14. Start System Manager and expand the console tree as follows: Vancouver administrative group → Servers → Box14 → CriticalSG storage group → Public Folder Store (Box14). Right-click this default public-folder store and select Properties and then switch to the Replication tab (Figure 18.10).

Figure 18.10 Replication properties of the default public-folder store on Box14.

The settings here govern how public folders in the store are replicated. The important settings here are:

- *Replication interval*. This setting determines how often replication occurs. By default, it is set to Always Run, meaning that replication occurs whenever changes are made to the store, but other possible settings include:
  - Run every hour
  - Run every 2 hours
  - Run every 4 hours
  - Never run
  - Use custom schedule

  We'll leave this setting at Always Run because it's easier to test replication this way.
- *Replication interval for always (minutes)*. If you choose Always Run as your replication interval, then a value of 15 minutes should suffice.
- *Replication message size limit (kilobytes)*. The default size limit for replication messages is 300 KB, but you can change it to suit the latency and speed of your network connection, especially when slower WAN links are involved.
- *Restore defaults*. If you make changes to the Limits settings on this tab, clicking this button will restore the settings to their original values of 15 minutes and 300 KB.

Now that we've configured replication settings for the default public store on Box14, we can configure replication at the individual folder level, which we'll do next.

Replicating Public Folders

Walkthrough

We'll start by replicating the contents of the Accounts public folder in the default public-folder tree to the default public store on server Box16 in the Seattle administrative group. Before starting, try the following simple exercise.

Go to Box16 in Seattle and start Internet Explorer. Then try to open the following URL using OWA: http://box16/public/accounts. The contents of the Accounting folder are displayed in the browser, but the Address bar indicates that these contents have been retrieved from URL http://box14/public/accounts instead of Box16, as desired! This occurred because OWA tried to access the contents of the Accounting public folder from the default public-folder store on Box16 but didn't find anything there, so OWA then tried to contact another server on which the default public store resides and ended up accessing this store on Box14, where we previously created our public folders and posted messages to them. This makes sense: if a client can't access a folder on one Exchange server, it should automatically contact other servers until it either finds what it's looking for or gives up.

NOTE

There is another method to verify that the folders have not been replicated to Seattle. In the console tree of System Manager, select the Public Folders node under Public Folder Store (Box14) in the CriticalSG storage group on Box14 in Vancouver. In addition to other system folders, you should see the public folders we created earlier in the Details (right side) pane of the console, namely Accounts, Projects, Records, 2000, and 2001. Now select the Public Folders node under the Public Folder Store (Box16) in the First Storage Group on Box16 in Seattle. The folders we created are missing—because they haven't been replicated to Box16 yet!

However, it makes sense to replicate the contents of public folders from Box14 in Vancouver to Box16 in Seattle. Otherwise, users in Seattle who try to access public folders will use valuable bandwidth on the slower WAN link between the two locations. Let's perform this replication now.

On Box14 start System Manager and navigate to the default Public Folders tree within the Folders container in the Vancouver administrative group. Right-click on Public Folders and select Properties (Figure 18.11). Observe from the General tab that the default Public Folders tree (also called the MAPI tree) is associated with the default Public Folder Stores on each of our three servers (Box14 and Box15 in Vancouver and Box16 in Seattle). This doesn't mean that the contents of the public folders in the default tree are replicated to each store, however; it just means that a client can try connecting to any of these stores to access the contents of public folders in the default tree. Click OK to close this Properties Sheet.

Go to the Accounts public folder, which is beneath the Public Folders container in Vancouver, and open the Properties Sheet for this public folder. Switch to the Replication tab on this Accounts Properties Sheet (Figure 18.12). According to this tab, a replica of the Accounts folder currently resides only in the default Public Folder Store (Box14) in the CriticalSG storage group on server Box14 in Vancouver.

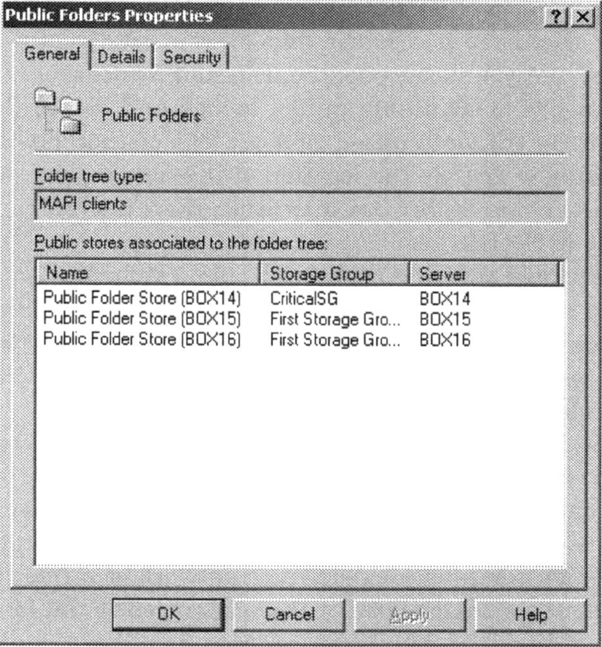

Figure 18.11 Viewing public-folder stores associated with the default public-folder tree.

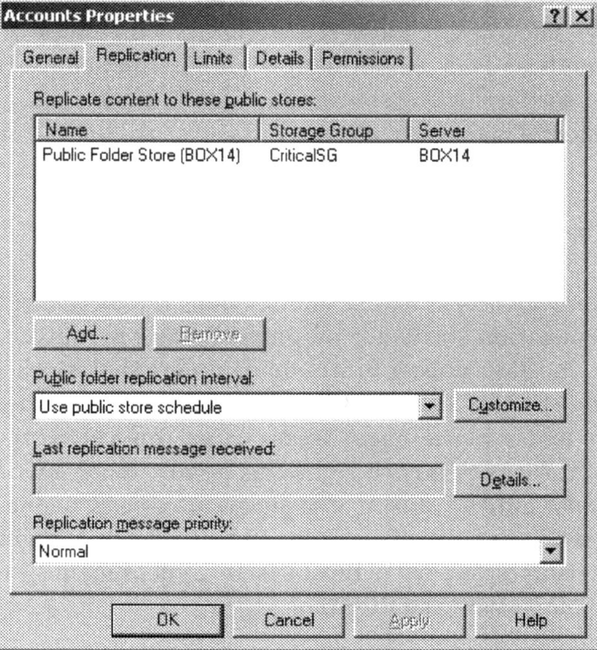

Figure 18.12 Configuring replication of the Accounts public folder.

We want to create a second replica of the Accounts folder in Seattle so users there can access the folder's contents locally instead of over the slower WAN link between Seattle and Vancouver. So click Add to display a list of available public stores and select Box16 from the list (Box15 is the only other choice). The listbox on the Replication tab should now display the location of the new replica, which is the default Public Folder Store (Box16) within the First Storage Group on server Box16 in Seattle.

Next note that the replication interval for the Accounts folder is currently set to Use Public Store Schedule, so the value we configured in our previous walkthrough (the global replication setting for all folders in the store) will be used here (it was Always Run). If you like, you can override the store setting here on a per-folder basis.

The Details button can be used to view recent replication statistics (try this later because we haven't replicated the folder yet), and the replication message priority can be used to specify the urgency of retransmission of replication messages when replication has been interrupted for some reason (such as a network or server problem).

Before we create the new replica, switch to the Limits tab to view the storage limits, deleted-item retention settings, and age limits for the folder. These can be left at those values set globally for the store or they can be overridden here on a per-folder basis, as desired.

Now click OK to close the Accounts Properties Sheet and create the new replica. This should happen almost immediately because the replication setting for our store is Always Run, but let's give it a few minutes to replicate before we test it.

Viewing Replication Status

Walkthrough

We can view the status of public-folder replication several ways. To view the replication status for all public folders in a given public-folder store, select the Replication Status node under that store in System Manager (Figure 18.13). The Details pane then displays the public folders and public-folder hierarchies (trees) being replicated, the last time replication data was returned from the server (received time), the number of replicas, and the status of replication of each folder or tree. The status field can take on the values listed in Table 18.1. Figure 18.13 shows that the Accounts folder on Box14 is In Sync, meaning that replication has been completed with Box16.

TIP

You can also verify that replication has occurred by selecting the Public Folders node under the Public Folder Store (Box16) in the First Storage Group on Box16 and pressing F5 to refresh. The Accounts folder should now be listed as one of the public-folder replicas on Box16.

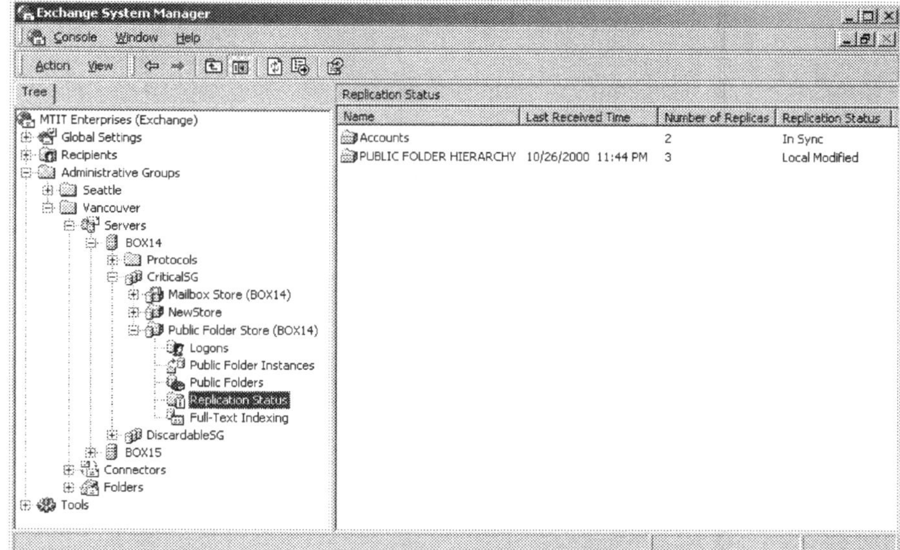

Figure 18.13 Viewing the status of public-folder replication for a given store.

TABLE 18.1 Possible values for replication status for public-folder replication.

Value	Description
In Sync	The replicas are the same on the local and remote servers
Local Modified	The replica has changed on the local server
Remote Modified	The replica has changed on the remote server
Both Modified	The replica has changed on the local and remote servers

Another way of viewing the status of replication for a specific public folder is to open the Properties Sheet for the folder in System Manager. For example, select the Accounts node under Public Folders under Folders in Vancouver and open its Properties Sheet. Switch to the Replication tab (Figure 18.12) and click the Details button to open a Replication Status dialog box, which provides additional information about the replication of this particular public folder.

Verifying Public-folder Replication

Walkthrough

Let's test whether the Accounts folder replicated to Box16 the old-fashioned way: go to Box16, start Internet Explorer, and open URL http://box16/public/accounts. This time the contents of the Accounts folder should be displayed and the Address bar of Internet Explorer should display the URL we entered instead of being redirected to the default public store on Box14 to find the desired folder.

The next walkthrough is another way to test replication.

Adding and Removing Public-folder Replicas

Walkthrough

In a previous walkthrough (Replicating Public Folders), we added a new replica of the Accounts public folder to the default public-folder store on server Box16 in the Seattle administrative group by modifying the Replication tab properties of the Accounts public folder on Box14 in Vancouver.

There's a simpler way of adding replicas in Exchange. Say we want to replicate the Projects folder from Box14 to Box16. Open System Manager and navigate to the Public Folder Instances node under Public Folder Store (Box16) under the First Storage Group on Box16 in Seattle. The Details pane should display the Accounts replica and other system folders. Now right-click on Public Folder Instances and select All Tasks → Add Replica to open the Public Store dialog box (Figure 18.14). Expand the tree to select the Projects folder and click OK to create a replica of Projects on Box16. After a few minutes, verify that the new replica has been added by using the methods described previously.

We can remove a replica of a public folder from a public-folder store just as easily as we added it. However, make sure all replicas of the folder are fully In Sync before removing any of them.

Configuring Age Limits for Replicas

Walkthrough

Once you've created new replicas of folders, you can configure these replicas on an individual basis. To see this, select the Public Folder Instances node under Public Folder Store (Box14) in the CriticalSG storage group on Box14. In the Details pane, the name, current size, folder path, and other information are displayed for each replica hosted within the public-folder store. Right-click on a replica such as Accounts and select either:

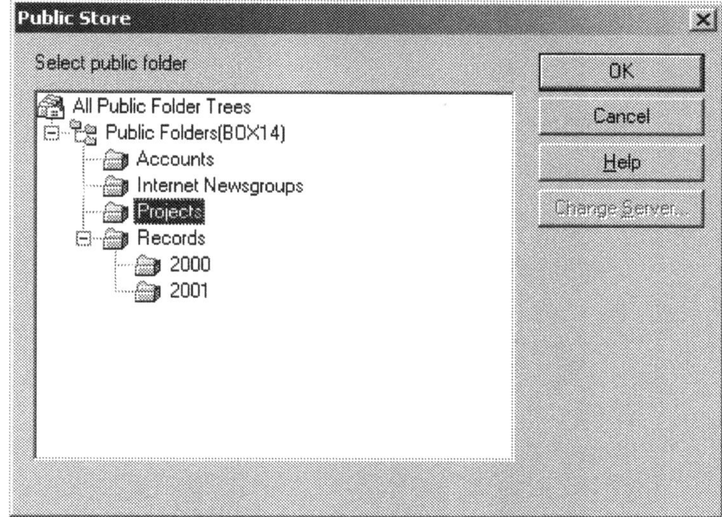

Figure 18.14 *Adding a new replica.*

- *Folder Properties.* This opens the Properties Sheet for the public folder and allows you to specify settings that apply to all replicas of the folder.
- *Replica Properties.* This opens a Properties Sheet for the selected replica only and allows you to configure an age limit for that replica (Figure 18.15).

By specifying an age limit for the replica, you specify that the replica should be deleted from its public store after a given number of days if no updates to the folder have occurred during that interval. By default no age limit is configured for replicas, so they can remain indefinitely on the servers. If the replica contains data of low importance, you may want to configure an age limit for it.

Copying and Moving Public Folders

Walkthrough

You can copy or move public folders in Exchange, but only within the same public-folder tree. For example, let's move the Accounts public folder so that it becomes a subfolder of the Records folder. Open System Manager and navigate to the default Public Folders tree under the Folders container in Vancouver. Right-click on the Accounts folder and select Cut and then right-click on Records and select Paste. Expand the Records node to verify the move. Note that this changes the URL that

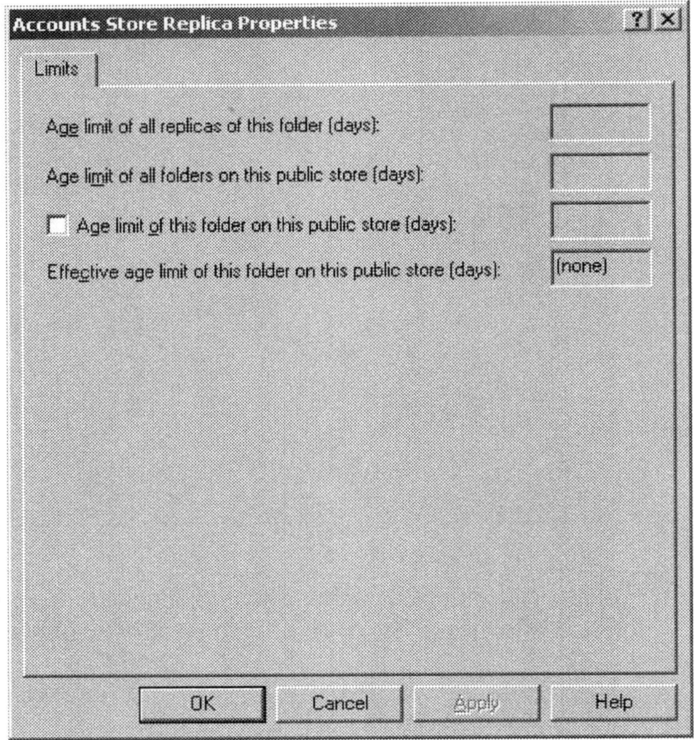

Figure 18.15 Configuring age limits for a replica.

OWA users will use to access the Accounts folder—try accessing the folder now, using the new URL http://box14/public/records/accounts.

TIP

You can also drag and drop public folders to move them around the tree. You can also rename public folders, if desired, but warn users before you start doing this!

Propagating Public-folder Settings

Walkthrough

If you modify the settings for a public folder that contains subfolders, the settings on these subfolders are not automatically inherited from the parent. To force subfolders to inherit settings from a parent folder, right-click the parent folder in System Manager and select Propagate Settings from the shortcut menu.

To verify the change, right-click on the Records folder under Public Folders in the Folders container in Vancouver and select Properties.

Switch to the Limits tab, clear the User Public Store Defaults checkbox under Age Limits, and specify an age limit of 3 days for replicas. Click OK. Now open the Properties Sheet for the subfolder named "2000" under Records. Verify that the Limits tab still has the Use Public Store Defaults checkbox selected. Close the Properties Sheet. Now right-click on the Records folder and select All Tasks → Propagate Settings (this task is only available if there are subfolders beneath the current folder). A dialog box called Propagate Folder Settings appears, asking you to specify which settings to propagate to the subfolders of this folder (Figure 18.16). Select the Age Limits checkbox and click OK. Now open the Properties Sheet of each subfolder under Records and verify that the setting was propagated as desired.

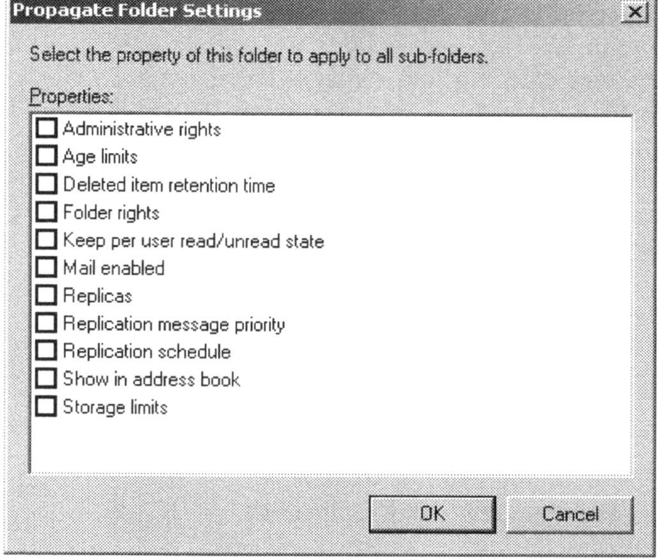

Figure 18.16 Selecting folder settings to propagate to subfolders.

Modifying Email Addresses for Public Folders

Walkthrough

For public folders that have been mail-enabled, you can view and modify the following settings using various tabs on the folder's Properties Sheet:

- *Exchange General tab.* This displays the name of the public-folder tree where the folder resides, the alias for the folder (used in generating email addresses for the folder), delivery restrictions for messages sent or received from the folder, and other delivery options. We covered this material in Chapter 3 on mailbox-enabled users.

- *E-mail Addresses tab*. This tab displays the email addresses that have been generated for the folder by Exchange. You can add or remove addresses as described in Chapter 3 for mail-enabled users.
- *Exchange Advanced tab*. This tab lets you specify a simple display name, hide the public folder from Exchange address lists, and view or modify custom attributes for the folder.

Configuring Administrative and Directory Permissions for Managing Public Folders

Walkthrough

By default, only administrators can modify public-folder settings and configure client permissions to control access to public folders, but you can also delegate this ability to other users and groups, if desired. To do this, open the Properties Sheet for the Projects public folder in System Manager and switch to the Permissions tab (Figure 18.17). Click the Administrative Rights button to specify which users and groups should be allowed to administer the settings for the folder. The permissions you can allow or deny here are self-explanatory and include:

- Control access
- Modify public-folder ACL
- Modify public-folder admin ACL
- Modify public-folder deleted-item retention
- Modify public-folder expiry
- Modify public-folder quotas
- Modify public-folder replica list
- Administer information store
- View information-store status

By default, administrators are given all of these individual permissions for every public folder.

NOTE

You can also grant permissions on the objects in Active Directory that are associated with each public folder in your organization. Click the Directory Rights button to specify which users and groups should be allowed to administer the directory object associated with the folder. For more information on Exchange permissions, see Chapter 13.

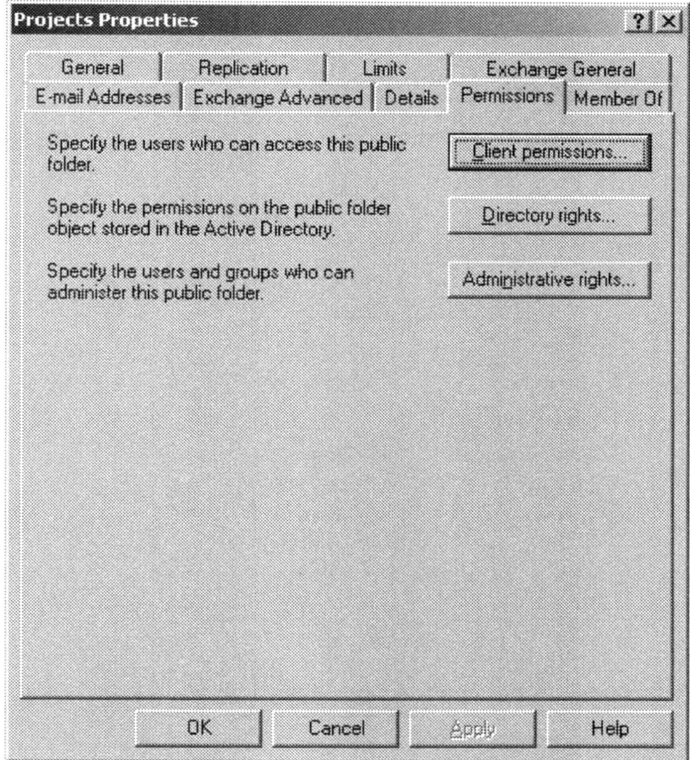

Figure 18.17 Setting permissions for public folders.

Configuring Client Permissions for Controlling Access to Public Folders

Walkthrough

We can control which users and groups can access different public folders and the level of access they have. This is called setting client permissions for the folder. The default setting is that all authenticated users can access a folder, read existing items in it, post new items to it, and edit or delete the items that they themselves have posted to the folder. Anonymous users connecting to public folders over the Internet also have many of these permissions, as we'll see below.

Let's look at the default client permissions configured for the Projects folder. Open the Properties Sheet for the folder, switch to the Permissions tab, and click the Client Permissions button. This opens a Client Permissions box for the folder (Figure 18.18).

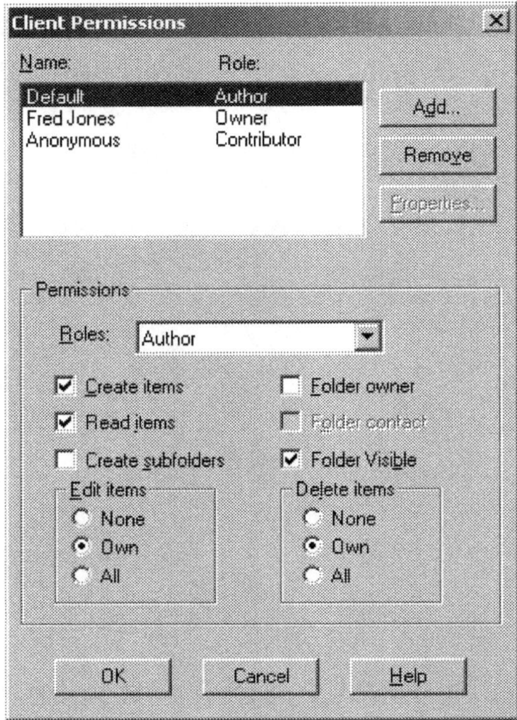

Figure 18.18
Client permissions for a public folder.

By default, there are three security principles with permissions configured for the folder:

- *Default*. This represents any authenticated user who accesses the folder. Authenticated users are assigned the Author role over the folder.
- *Owner* (here Fred Jones). This is the user who owns the folder (the user who created the folder). The owner is assigned the Owner role over the folder.
- *Anonymous*. This represents anonymous users who access the folder, for example, users who access the folder over the Internet using a Web browser. Anonymous is assigned the Contributor role over the folder.

Table 18.2 summarizes the different roles that can be assigned to users and groups over a public folder.

TABLE 18.2

Client permission roles for public folders.

Role	Description
None	User has no access to the folder, but the folder is visible in the folder list on the client (unless the folder has been hidden by the administrator)
Contributor	User can create new items in the folder but cannot read existing ones or view the contents of the folder
Reviewer	User can read existing items in the folder and view the folder's contents but cannot create new items or modify existing ones
Nonediting Author	User can create new items and read existing ones in the folder but cannot modify any items (even ones they create); however, users can delete their own posted items
Author	User can create new items and edit them, view existing items but not edit them, and delete his or her own posted items
Publishing Author	Like the Author role except that the user can also create new subfolders within the folder
Editor	Like the Author role except that the user can also edit or delete other people's posted items
Publishing Editor	Like the Publishing Author role except that the user can also edit or delete other people's posted items
Owner	User can do anything with the folder except delete the folder itself

Try assigning different roles to different users and testing their ability to access the Projects public folder. This is what we call "unstructured play" in the Ed-biz!

Summary

In Chapters 17 and 18, we've covered how to administer and use public folders, public-folder trees, public-folder replication, and public-folder stores. Before that, we covered mailbox stores and mailboxes. However, we're not quite through working with the storage technologies of Exchange, and in the next chapter we'll look at a feature that provides a powerful way to search for content within mailboxes and public folders, namely *content indexing*.

CHAPTER 19

Content Indexing

This chapter deals with another feature of Exchange's data-storage system: indexing of contents of mailboxes and public folders. This chapter covers how to configure and manage content indexing on Exchange servers throughout an enterprise.

There are seven walkthroughs in this chapter:

- Specifying indexing priority for a server
- Creating a full-text index
- Populating a new index
- Viewing indexing statistics
- Scheduling indexing
- Rebuilding a corrupt index
- Other indexing tasks

Content Indexing

Users often need to find specific messages in the mailboxes, which can take time if their mailboxes contain many messages. The same need arises when users need to locate specific postings in public folders containing thousands of postings. When users of earlier versions of Exchange searched for messages within such folders, they had to search through every item in the folder to find the desired items. As a result, searching scaled poorly and search times increased with the size of the information store.

Exchange 2000 speeds up the search process by creating indexes for messages in mailboxes and items in public folders. Then, when a user uses the Find feature of Microsoft Outlook, the search query is issued against the appropriate index instead of the items themselves, which generates results more promptly than without indices.

Two Types of Indexing

Exchange supports two different kinds of indexing using the Microsoft Search Service:

- *Standard indexing.* By default, Exchange implements standard indexing, a process that automatically builds an index of key fields of messages and postings. Key fields indexed for messages in mailboxes include Subject, To, Cc, and other fields; those indexed for postings in public folders include Subject and From fields. When an user uses the standard Find function in Outlook to find a message with a specific subject or addressed to a specific recipient, the query is issued against the standard index instead of searching one by one through each message in the folder. Standard indexing does not support searching for information within attachments to messages.

- *Full-text indexing*. An optional feature that must be specifically enabled on a data store (mailbox store or public-folder store) is full-text indexing. This creates an index of all searchable text for mailboxes or public folders within the store, allowing users to use the Advanced Find feature of Outlook to search for specific words or text strings within message headers, message bodies, and even attached documents of supported types. If an Outlook user tried to search for a text string within messages without having full-text indexing enabled, then mailbox messages would be searched one by one for the string, a process that could take a long time if the mailbox contains many messages.

NOTE

Full-text indexing also supports searching for values of custom attributes and document properties. For example, you could find all documents in a public folder written by the same person or by persons in the same department.

How Indexing Works

UNDER THE HOOD

Understanding how indexing works is important to manage this process effectively, especially for full-text indexing, the focus of this section.

Full-text indexes are built and maintained by the Microsoft Search service mssearch.exe. This service is started by default and configured for automatic startup after reboot. However, full-text indexes are not created by default (we'll soon see how to create an index).

Full-text indexing is established on a per-store basis on Exchange servers. You can create a full-text index for one mailbox or public store and leave other stores configured for standard indexing only. When you configure a store for full-text indexing, Exchange starts crawling through the store one folder at a time, indexing each document in the folder, and building a master index. Once this process is complete, any query issued against the index returns all messages in which the text string is found.

As new messages are added to mailboxes or new postings to public folders, the information store informs the Search service that changes have occurred. The new items are then indexed and the master index is updated immediately or on a scheduled basis, depending on how indexing for the store is configured. If indexes are updated on a scheduled basis such as once a day, then the results of queries issued against an index will not include items posted that day. In other words, scheduling updates for indexes causes these indexes to be out of sync with the items they contain.

It might seem better to configure indexes to update immediately whenever contents of the store changes, but, because indexing is a resource-intensive activity for the system (high CPU and disk usage), this is generally not a good idea except on specific stores where timeliness of results from queries is of high importance.

Probably the most important consideration for successfully implementing full-text indexing in Exchange is planning for sufficient disk-space requirements. Specifically, an index typically occupies approximately 20 percent of the disk space occupied by the collection of files being indexed. Thus, if a data store contains 100 MB of messages and attachments, an additional 20 MB of free disk space is required before full-text indexing can be enabled. Furthermore, adding additional messages to the store causes the index to grow incrementally.

TIP

The process of building the initial index for a given store is likewise a resource-intensive activity and may take many hours for stores containing large amounts of data. Therefore, you should generally create new indexes only at times of low user activity such as late at night or on weekends.

The Microsoft Search service indexes not only standard email messages and postings to public folders but also files attached to messages and documents published in public folders. However, full-text indexing is supported only for specific file types such as:

- ASCII text files (*.txt)
- Web pages (*.htm, *.html, and *.asp)
- Microsoft Word documents (*.doc)
- Microsoft Excel documents (*.xls)
- Microsoft PowerPoint documents (*.ppt)
- Embedded MIME messages (*.eml)

NOTE

File types are identified to the Microsoft Search service by their file extensions. Full-text indexing is not supported for binary files such as executable or image files. If the service encounters a file type not supported for indexing, the service skips the file and logs an error to the Application Log at the end of the indexing process that indicates how many documents could not be indexed. The names of specific files not indexed can be found in gather files (.gthr), which are written to the directory:*

```
\Exchsrvr\ExchangeServer_<servername>\GatherLogs
```

How Full-Text Searches Work

UNDER THE HOOD

When the Advanced Find feature of Microsoft Outlook is used to perform a search, the query is first passed to a query processor that determines whether to pass the query to the native Exchange 2000 search mechanism or to Microsoft Search. For example, if the query contains specific words to be found in the subject or body portion of messages, the query processor uses Microsoft Search to query the full-text index for this information. If the query includes specific recipients to search for in the To field of messages, the query processor uses the native search mechanism of Exchange. If a query contains a combination of these, the full-text index is queried first to find all messages with instances of the specified word in the subject or body portion of messages, and then filters this information for specific To recipients.

There are a few things to be aware of when full-text searches are performed:

- Full-text searching in Exchange is word, not character, based. If you search for instances of "spring," Microsoft Search will return all messages containing this word but not messages containing "springtime" or "Springer." However, if full-text indexing is not enabled on a data store, then MAPI clients like Outlook use slow character-based matching when searching the store.
- If the word being searched for appears in the attachment to a message that has multiple attachments, the result set of the query specifies the message only, not which attachment contains the word.
- Full-text searching can be performed only by MAPI and IMAP clients. POP3 clients or HTTP/WebDAV clients like OWA cannot make use of

this feature and can only perform slow message-by-message character-based searches.
- Full-text searching functions only on messages stored on the server, not on messages stored on the client in .pst files.

TIP

When performing a backup of Exchange Server, do not back up any indexes on the machine. Then, if you ever perform a restore, force a rebuild of the index or let it rebuild automatically because a backed-up index easily gets out of sync with the contents of data stores on the machine and can return erroneous results when queried by Outlook users. If the index becomes out of sync or corrupt as evidenced by errors in the result sets returned by client queries, rebuild the index to correct the situation. How to do this is described later in this chapter.

Managing Indexing

Once you've taken account of the CPU and disk-space requirements for implementing full-text indexing on a server and have enabled indexing for one or more data stores by creating indexes for them, there are other administrative tasks you need to be able to understand and perform:

- Configuring indexing priority for the server
- Monitoring indexing statistics to ensure proper functioning of the Microsoft Search service
- Scheduling indexing updates and rebuilds to best use idle system resources
- Manually rebuilding indexes when they become corrupt
- Relocating index files when disk space is running out
- Deleting an index when it is corrupt or no longer needed

We'll look at these various tasks now in our walkthroughs for this chapter.

Specifying Indexing Priority for a Server

Before actually creating your first index on an Exchange server, it's a good idea to specify an indexing priority for your server. This means telling the server how much system resources (specifically CPU and RAM) the server can use for the indexing process. This setting is configured on a per-server basis and has four possible values:

- *Minimum*. This setting has the smallest impact on total system performance and interferes least with other services running on the server, but selecting this value means that indexes take a long time to build and update. The result can be that indexes may never be fully up to date in busy messaging environments and users' search queries may not generate all the results expected.
- *Low*. This is the default setting and has a minimal impact on system resources but generally builds and updates indexes at a satisfactory speed.
- *High*. This has greater impact on system resources and can have some effect on other services running on the machine. If there is sufficient CPU power and RAM, then it should be acceptable in all but the busiest messaging environments.
- *Maximum*. This causes indexing to have a higher priority than other services and can cause poor performance if there are insufficient system resources. However, indexes are built and updated the fastest using this setting and therefore are always up to date on the server.

To configure indexing priority for an Exchange server, open System Manager and right-click on the node representing the server (we'll use Box14 in Vancouver) to open its Properties Sheet. Switch to the Full-Text Indexing tab on this sheet and select the priority desired (Figure 19.1). This setting applies to all indexes created on the server.

Creating a Full-text Index

Once indexing priority is configured, we can enable full-text indexing for any data store (mailbox store or public folder) on the server. Full-text indexing is enabled by creating an index for a store. We'll create a full-

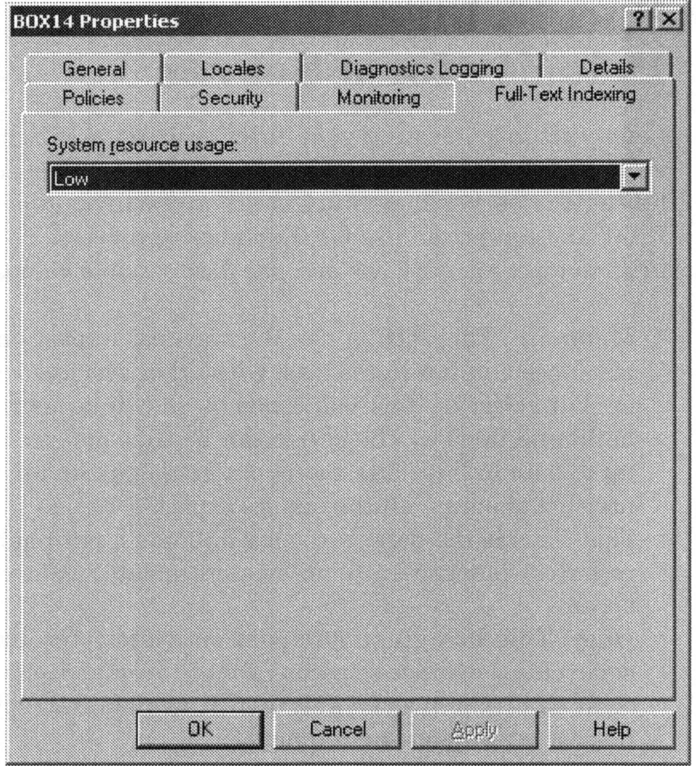

Figure 19.1 Specifying indexing priority for server Box14.

text index for the default mailbox store in the CriticalSG storage group on server Box14 in Vancouver in our testbed setup.

Open System Manager, right-click on Mailbox Store (Box14), and select Create Full-Text Index from the shortcut menu. A dialog box appears with the default path to where the index files will be created (Figure 19.2). This default path is:

```
\Exchsrvr\ExchangeServer_<servername>\Projects
```

You can accept the default location or specify a different one, as desired, but make sure you have sufficient disk space for the index including projected size growth.

Now click OK to create the index. In System Manager immediately select the Full-Text Indexing node beneath Mailbox Store (Box14) in the console tree and continue with the walkthrough.

As we shall see shortly, the Full-Text Indexing node under a mailbox or public folder store in System Manager is used to display the current

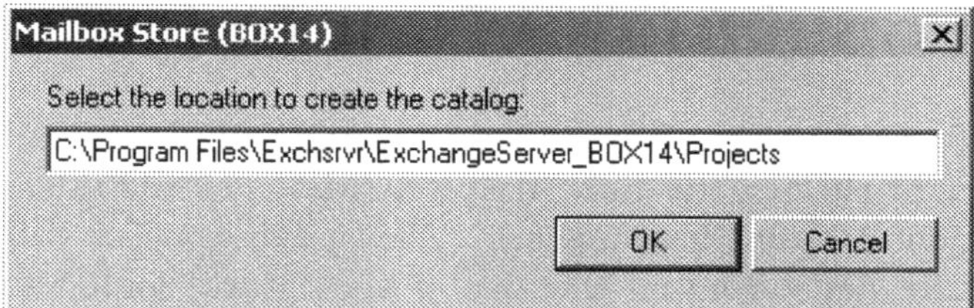

Figure 19.2
Specifying a location for the index files

state and statistics of the index associated with that store. Immediately after finishing the previous walkthrough, this node displays the information shown in Figure 19.3. We'll soon explain the various fields here.

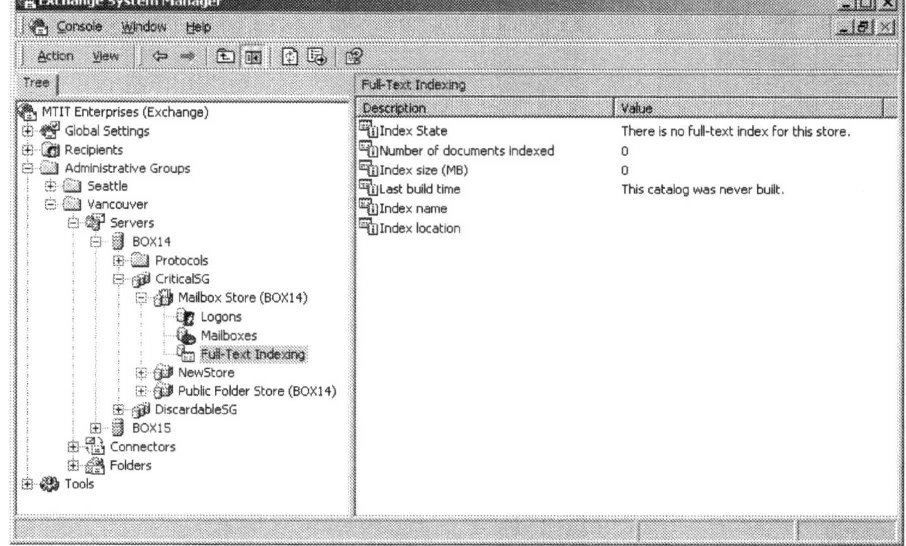

Figure 19.3
State of the index immediately after selecting Create Full-Text Index for Mailbox Store (Box14).

The steps we have performed have created the necessary directories and files for the index but have not actually built the index. That is, the index needs to be populated with information concerning the various messages and attachments stored in its associated mailbox store. By default, Exchange does not populate a new index; you have to do this manually, which is the topic of the next walkthrough.

NOTE

If you use Windows Explorer to browse to the index location specified in Figure 19.2, you'll see a whole tree of directories with various files where there were none before.

Populating a New Index

Walkthrough

To populate the new index we just created for Mailbox Store (Box14), right-click on the store in System Manager and select Start Full Population. A dialog box appears: "The update process will start immediately and, depending on the size of your store, could take time and server resources. Do you want to continue?" Click Yes. Then select the Full-Text Indexing node beneath the store to watch the statistics change in the Details pane and move immediately to the next walkthrough.

TIP

Instead of manually performing the initial build, you can schedule it to occur automatically. See the walkthrough on Scheduling Indexing.

Viewing Indexing Statistics

Walkthrough

While viewing the statistics for the indexing process in System Manager, you can press F5 anytime to immediately refresh the view. Figure 19.4 shows the indexing statistics for Mailbox Store (Box14) shortly after the process has begun.

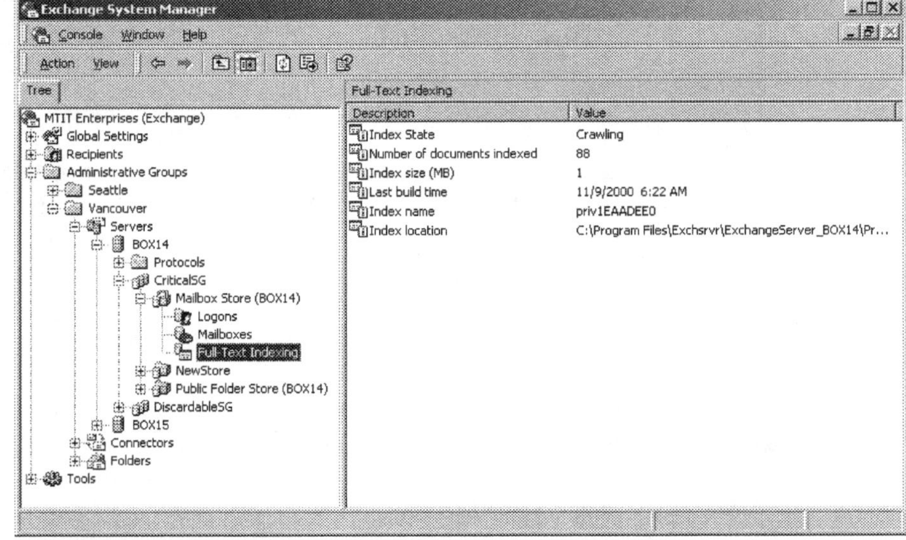

Figure 19.4 Indexing statistics for the index associated with Mailbox Store (Box14).

There are six different information records displayed in the Details pane when the Full-Text Indexing node for a data store is selected in the console tree. These fields are defined as follows:

- *Index state.* This field indicates the state of the indexing process for the store and can take on one of the following values:
- *Crawling.* The index is being populated, as displayed in Figure 19.4.
- *Idle.* Indexing is not occurring (that is, the index is up to date).
- *Paused.* Indexing has been paused by an administrator to perform maintenance or some other action.
- *Number of documents indexed.* This figure includes both messages and attachments.
- *Index size* (megabytes). The total disk space occupied by the index.
- *Last build time.* The last date and time at which the index was built. Before you create the index, this field says "There is no full-text index for this store"; after you create the index but before you manually populate it, the field says "This catalog was never built."
- *Index name.* The name assigned to the index by Exchange and the name assigned to the subdirectory under the indexing location (see Figure 19.2) where the index files for this data store are located.
- *Index location.* The path previously specified to the index files.

NOTE

The state of the index a few moments after initiating full population should be "crawling." After a few minutes (or hours, if you have a lot of messages in the store), pressing F5 should make the "idle" state appear. If new messages are constantly being added to the store (or old ones deleted), the index may always be in a "crawling" and never in an "idle" state.

Scheduling Indexing

Walkthrough

Once you create a new index, you need to schedule how it will be updated and rebuilt. *Updating* an index means incrementally populating it with information about changes to the associated data store. *Rebuilding* an index means recreating the index from scratch. You simply schedule the times for these processes to occur, sit back, and let Exchange handle everything else.

Let's look at the scheduling options for our new index. In System Manager, right-click on Mailbox Store (Box14), select Properties, and then switch to the Full-Text Indexing tab (Figure 19.5).

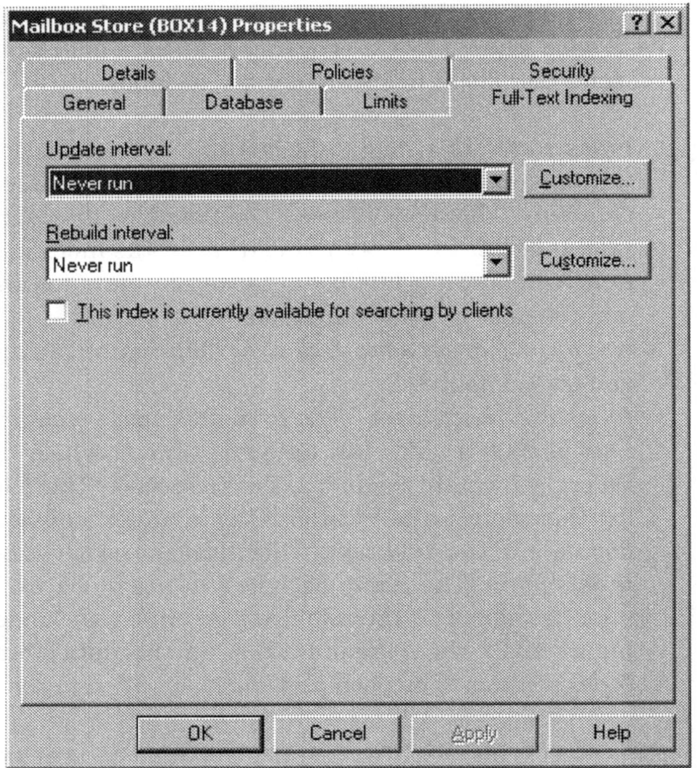

Figure 19.5
Scheduling indexing.

There are two intervals you can schedule on this tab:

- *Update interval*. This specifies the times at which incremental population of the index should take place. Updating the index regularly is necessary to prevent its information from becoming out of date and leading to incomplete result sets from search queries initiated by clients. The options for Update interval are:
  - Never run (the default setting)
  - Run daily at <time>, where <time> can be 10:00 P.M., 1:00 A.M., or 3:00 A.M.
  - Run every hour
  - Always run
  - Use custom schedule

  The default setting is Never Run, which means indexing must be administered manually. Switching it to Always Run will cause the index to be always up to date but will increase server load in heavy messaging environments, make sure your server has sufficient system resources to support this option before selecting it. Specifying a time of day will cause the index to be updated daily, and searches performed will not return messages posted on that day in the result set. You also can specify a custom schedule such as every 3 hours by selecting Use Custom Schedule.

- *Rebuild interval*. This specifies the days and times a full population (recreation from scratch) of the index will occur. Rebuilds work by purging and re-indexing the index information for each message in the store one message at a time rather than purging the entire index and re-creating it. However, the index will not be accessible to clients during the rebuild process. These settings are:
  - Never run (the default setting)
  - Run Friday at midnight
  - Run Saturday at midnight
  - Run Sunday at midnight
  - Use custom schedule

TIP

Rebuilding an index is a resource-intensive process and should always be scheduled for periods of low user activity.

Another option on this tab is the checkbox "This index is currently available for searching by clients". Make sure this checkbox is selected to enable Outlook users to query the index.

NOTE

Rebuilding an index from time to time is a necessary occurrence because updating an index adds new information but does not remove information regarding messages or attachments that have been deleted from the store. Indexes should be rebuilt once a week to ensure efficient use of disk space.

Rebuilding a Corrupt Index

Walkthrough

Indexes may become corrupt and manifest corruption in different ways:

- The number of documents indexed as displayed in the indexing statistics in System Manager seems wrong.

- Outlook clients who perform searches against the index obtain result sets that leave out messages that are expected to be included, or strange results are returned by search queries.
- Outlook clients performing search queries complain that these searches take an inordinate amount of time, indicating that searches are being performed in character-based Exchange native mode instead of the full-text indexing mode supported by Microsoft Search.
- Events written in the Application Log of Event Viewer indicate problems with the index.

To fix a corrupt index you need to manually rebuild it using the following steps:

1. Take the index off-line by opening the Properties Sheet for its associated mailbox or public store, switching to the Full-Text Indexing tab (Figure 19.5), and clearing the checkbox labeled "This index is currently available for searching by clients". Click OK.
2. Right-click on the mailbox or public store again and select Start Full Population to start the rebuild. Then view the statistics for the indexing process and wait until the state changes from "crawling" to "idle," indicating that the rebuild is complete.
3. Open the Properties Sheet again for the store, switch to the Full-Text Indexing tab, and reselect the checkbox cleared earlier.

TIP

Rebuilds can take a long time for indexes associated with large stores. If you need to, you can pause the rebuild to perform other actions on Exchange and then resume the rebuild. To do this, right-click on the mailbox or public store and select Pause Population (do not use Services to pause the Microsoft Search service), perform your administrative tasks, and then right-click the store again and select Resume Population. You can also stop the indexing process by selecting Stop Population and Start Population, but this should not be done when performing a rebuild because you will have to reinitiate the build process. The Pause and Stop options are only available when the indexing state is in "crawl," not in "idle."

Other Indexing Tasks

There are a few other administrative tasks you can perform on full-text indexes.

- *Manually update an index.* If you have your index scheduled to update once a day but users urgently require an up-to-date index (for example, because a large collection of new company policy documents has just been added to the associated public folder), then you can right-click on the store in System Manager and select Start Incremental Population to force an immediate update to the index without changing its update schedule.
- *Moving index files.* If you are running out of disk space, you can move the index files to a different location. This is performed by using the following hack: disable client access to the index, stop population of the index if it is occurring, change the update and rebuild schedules for the index to Never Run, delete the index, and then re-create a new index for the store from scratch in the new location.
- *Deleting an index.* If you no longer require full-text indexing for a given store (or determine that the server has insufficient system resources to effectively support it at present), you can permanently delete an index by disabling client access to the index, stopping population if it is occurring, changing the update and rebuild schedules to Never Run, right-clicking on the store in System Manager, and selecting Delete Full-Text Index. This removes the catalog file for the index from the location you previously specified.

Summary

In this chapter we continued the discussion of managing Exchange data stores by covering the creation and administration of full-text indexes. In the next chapter, we look at a powerful method for managing Exchange configuration settings by implementing Exchange *System Policies*.

CHAPTER 20

System Policies

In addition to managing individual mailbox and public-folder stores and their associated Exchange servers directly, Exchange 2000 supports a powerful feature called *system policies* that lets you make configuration changes to multiple mailbox stores, public-folder stores, and Exchange servers at the same time and enforce these changes. This chapter deals with this topic of system policies and looks at the different kinds of policies and how they are created, applied, and managed.

There are six different walkthroughs in this chapter:

- Creating a server policy
- Creating a mailbox-store policy
- Creating a public-store policy
- Adding items to a policy
- Applying a policy
- Modifying a policy

System Policies

Managing individual mailbox and public-folder stores on different Exchange servers can be a headache when there are many stores on many servers. Sometimes you want to make the same configuration change on all data stores on a group of servers or on all public-folder stores throughout the organization—Exchange system policies provide a way of doing this.

A system policy is a set of configuration settings that can be applied to servers, mailbox stores, and public-folder stores. Unlike recipient policies that are client-side policies and applied to mail-enabled objects, system policies are server-side policies and are used for managing servers and data stores. By using system policies, administrators can make changes to the configuration settings of multiple servers and data stores simultaneously across an organization. This is a significant improvement from earlier versions of Exchange where the only choice was to change configuration settings on a single server or on all servers within a given site. There was no way of making such changes to arbitrary groups of servers or across an entire multisite organization.

NOTE

Don't confuse Exchange system policies with group policies in Windows 2000. They are two different things and they work differently, as we shall soon see. Also, the term system policy *meant something entirely different under the earlier Windows NT platform from what it does with the present version of Exchange.*

Advantages of Using System Policies

Policy-based management adds flexibility and power to the management of Exchange servers and data stores. Consider, for example, the management of public-folder replication throughout your organization. You could manage this feature three different ways:

- *By configuring replication settings on individual public folders using their Properties Sheets*. This would be tedious in a large organization with many public folders. Exchange only provides this level of specificity to allow administrators the option of configuring some folders differently from others, if needed.
- *By configuring replication settings on individual public folder stores using their Properties Sheets*. Configuring replication on a store-by-store basis is obviously much less work than doing it by individual folder, but it can still be a chore if you have multiple stores in different storage groups on your server. If a particular folder within a store requires different replication settings, you can configure the folder properties separately to override the store properties.
- *By configuring replication settings on a selected group of public stores using system policies*. Administrators can use one system policy to define and then apply replication settings for all public stores on a server. This simplifies the task of administering replication settings and reduces the overhead of public-folder management. Furthermore, if replication settings for all the selected stores need to be modified afterward, it can be accomplished in one step by modifying and reapplying the policy. Multiple policies can also be created to manage different groups of stores differently.

Types of System Policies

As you might have guessed from this discussion, there are three different types of system policies in Exchange:

- *Server policies*. These are policies applied to one or more Exchange servers to manage settings such as message tracking and logging functions.
- *Mailbox-store policies*. These are policies applied to one or more mailbox stores to manage settings such as storage limits, deleted-item retention settings, and other store-related settings.
- *Public-store policies*. These are policies applied to one or more public-folder stores to manage settings such as storage limits, replication, and other store-related settings.

We'll look at each of these types of policies in more detail in a moment and at how to create, implement, and manage them.

Implementing System Policies

Implementing system policies is somewhat different from implementing recipient policies. A recipient policy is applied by the Recipient Update Service (RUS), an Exchange service that runs in the background. System policies have to be specifically applied to take effect. The process involves three steps:

1. Create the new system policy.
2. Apply the policy to specified Exchange servers or data stores.
3. Enforce the policy to make it take effect.

We'll look at each of these steps in more detail soon.

Policy Conflicts

You can create and use multiple system policies for Exchange, but it works differently from group policies in Windows 2000. When you have multiple group policies applied to the same object, the effect is cumulative. With system policies, however, no two policies applied to the same object can govern the same settings.

This means that you can have multiple system policies applied to a given server or data store, but each policy must configure different settings for that server or store. For example, you can configure one policy to set storage limits on a mailbox store and another policy to configure full-text indexing for the same store, but you cannot have two policies for the same store that both configure storage limits for the store. Exchange will inform you if you are creating conflicting policies and will prevent you from doing so if you proceed.

What if you create a policy to configure storage limits for all mailbox stores on a group of Exchange servers and then try to override this policy for a particular mailbox store by creating a policy only for that store? You'll be notified of the conflict and asked for another, nonconflicting policy.

Server Policies

Let's examine server policies in more detail and how to create them. Server policies are the simplest kind of system policy because they have few possible settings relating to message tracking and logging. Once these settings are applied to a group of Exchange servers, you cannot override them on the Properties Sheets for the individual servers because the settings have been disabled.

Creating a Server Policy

Walkthrough

We'll now create a new server policy in the System Policies container in the Vancouver administrative group of our testbed MTIT Enterprises organization. If there is no System Policies beneath the Vancouver node in System Manager, begin by right-clicking on Vancouver and selecting New → System Policy Container. Now right-click on System Policies under Vancouver and select New → Server Policy to open the New Policy dialog box (Figure 20.1). The New Policy box lists the various property pages that can be included for the new policy. When you create a server policy, there is only one property page to select: General.

Select the checkbox for General and click OK. This opens up a blank Properties sheet for the new policy. The sheet has three tabs:

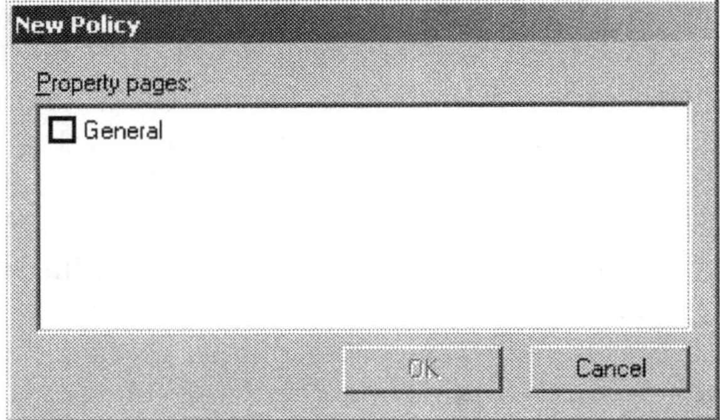

Figure 20.1 Creating a new server policy.

- *General*. Every policy has this tab, and it's simply used to assign a name to the new policy. Use something descriptive here so you'll know what your policy is about (I'll use something dull like "Test Policy #1" because I'm not very creative!).
- *General (Policy)*. Any tab that has "(Policy)" in its name contains settings that the policy will apply. More on this in a moment.
- *Details*. Add an administrative note to help you remember what the policy is about if the name you gave it on the General tab is insufficient.

Let's look in detail at the General (Policy) tab, where the actual policy settings reside (Figure 20.2). There are only a couple of system policy settings we can configure at the server level:

- *Enable subject logging and display*. This causes the subject field to be logged for any messages processed by the servers to which the policy is applied. Message tracking must also be enabled for this to work.
- *Enable message tracking*. This turns on message tracking for all messages processed by the servers to which the policy is applied.
- *Remove log files*. This purges log files older than the number of days specified, which can be between 1 and 99 days.

TIP

Don't enable message tracking unless you are troubleshooting message delivery problems because message tracking adds an additional hit on the server and can affect performance.

TIP

It's a good idea to purge old log files because they can eat up disk space quickly on an Exchange server.

Figure 20.2
Configuring a new server policy.

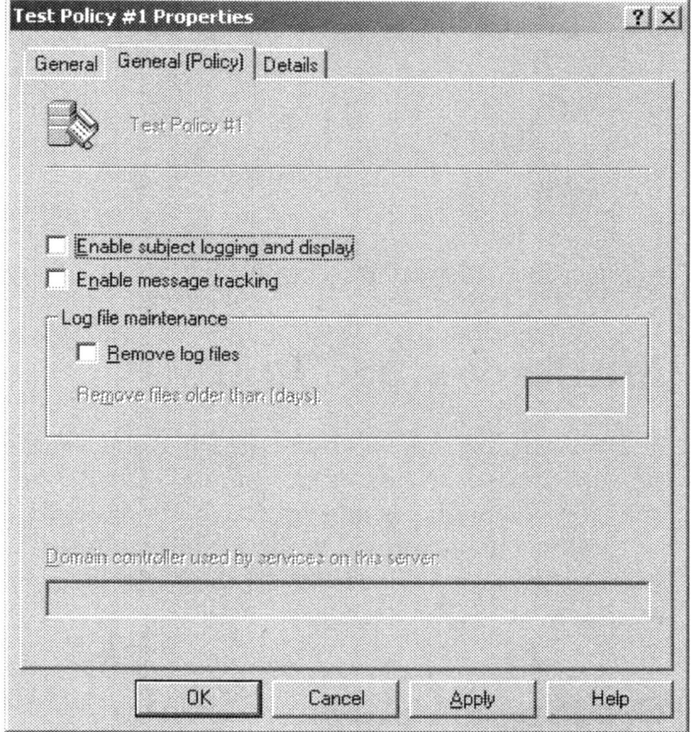

Select all three checkboxes and specify that files older than 10 days will be removed and then click OK to create the new policy. The new policy will now be displayed beneath the System Policies node in the Vancouver administrative group in System Manager (Figure 20.3). At this point, we would next add servers to the policy and then apply the policy, but we'll do that later in this chapter. For now, let's discuss the other types, namely mailbox-store and public-store policies.

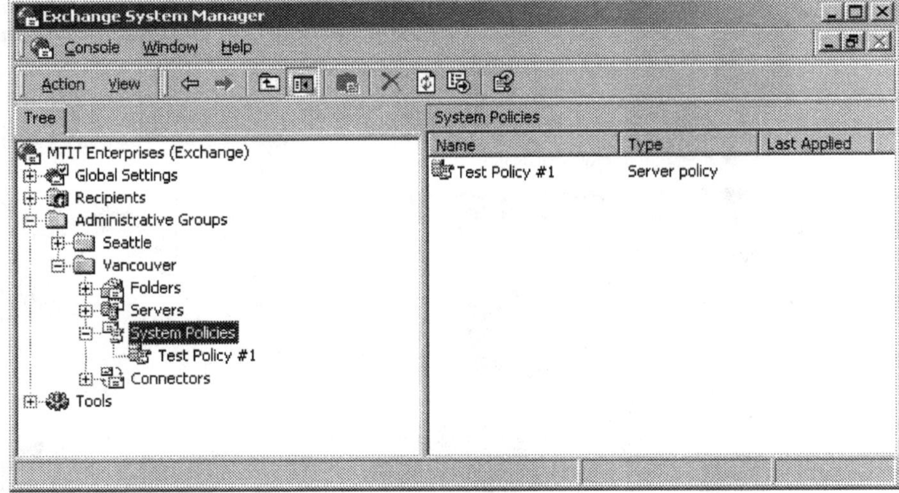

Figure 20.3 The new system policy in the System Policies container in Vancouver.

Mailbox-store Policies

Mailbox-store policies offer more configurable settings than server policies and let you specify storage limits deleted-item retention settings, and store maintenance settings for groups of mailbox stores. Once these settings are applied to a group of mailbox stores, you cannot override them on the Properties Sheets for the individual stores because the settings here have been disabled.

Creating a Mailbox-store Policy

We'll create a mailbox store policy in the same System Policies container we created for the Vancouver administrative group. Right-click on the System Policies container and select New → Mailbox Store Policy to open the New Policy dialog box (Figure 20.4). We can choose up to four different tabs for this new policy, namely General, Database, Limits, and Full-Text Indexing. Any tabs you don't select here won't appear on the Properties Sheet for the new policy.

Select all the checkboxes in the New Policy dialog box and click OK. A blank Properties Sheet with six tabs appears for the new policy. In addition to the General and Details tabs discussed previously, these four tabs have the following configurable settings:

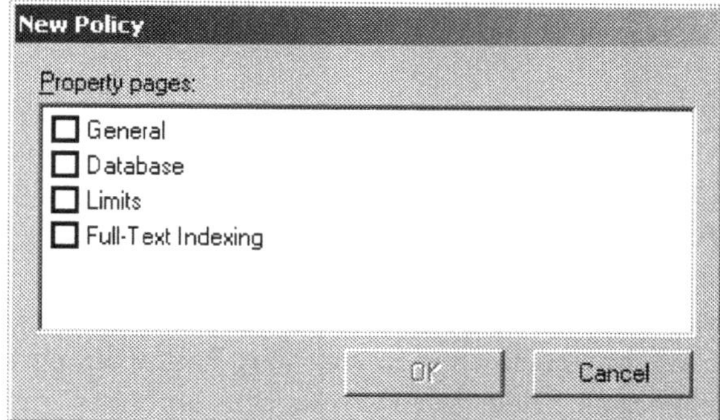

Figure 20.4 Creating a new mailbox-store policy.

- *General (Policy) tab*. This tab is used for configuring settings of general importance for mailbox stores including the default public store and offline address list associated with mailbox stores, whether messages should be archived, and so on. These settings are the same as those on the General tab of the Properties Sheet for any mailbox store (Chapter 15).
- *Database (Policy) tab*. This tab is used for configuring the maintenance interval for mailbox stores (Chapter 15).
- Limits (Policy) tab. This tab is used for configuring storage limits and deleted-item retention settings for mailbox stores (Chapter 15).
- *Full-Text Indexing (Policy) tab*. This tab is used for configuring update and rebuild intervals for full-text indexing for mailbox stores (Chapter 19).

Insert the new policy name "Test MBS Policy" on the General tab, specify a storage limit to issue a warning at 3000 KB, and then click OK to create the new mailbox-store policy. We'll see later how to add mailbox stores to the policy.

Public-store Policy

Public-store policies offer configurable settings similar to those of mailbox-store settings, with the addition of a fifth tab for configuring replication settings. Once these settings are applied to a group of public-folder stores, you cannot override them on the Properties Sheets for the individual stores because the settings have been disabled.

Creating a Public-store Policy

Walkthrough

Let's create a public-store policy in the same System Policies container we used for Vancouver. Right-click on the System Policies container and select New → Public Store Policy to open the New Policy dialog box. There are up to five different tabs for this new policy, namely General, Database, Replication, Limits, and Full-Text Indexing. Any tabs you don't select here won't appear on the Properties Sheet for the new policy.

Select all the checkboxes in the New Policy dialog box and click OK. A blank Properties Sheet with seven tabs appears for the new policy. In addition to the General and Details tabs, these five tabs have configurable settings similar or identical to those on the Properties Sheets for the individual public-folder stores (Chapter 17). Specify a name like "Test PFS Policy" for the new policy on the General tab and click OK to create the new public-store policy.

NOTE

The icons for server policies and mailbox- and public-store policies look different in System Manager.

Implementing System Policies

Having created our new system policies, we need to implement them. Implementing a policy means specifying which servers or stores the policy affects and then applying the policy to make it take effect. The remaining walkthroughs touch on several ways of implementing system policies.

Adding Items to a Policy

Walkthrough

Let's start by renaming our server policy from "Tests Policy #1" to "Test SRV Policy," which is a bit more descriptive. Right-click on the policy in System Manager and select Rename.

Now add server Box14 in Vancouver to the server policy. Adding a server to a server policy means specifying that the server will be controlled (affected) by this policy (by default, a newly created system policy doesn't control any servers or data stores).

Right-click on Test SRV Policy and select Add Server to open a dialog box with the unwieldy name of "Select the items to place under the control of this policy" (Figure 20.5). Select Box14 in the top listbox, click Add, and then click OK to bring server Box14 under the control of the policy. A message box asks you to confirm your decision.

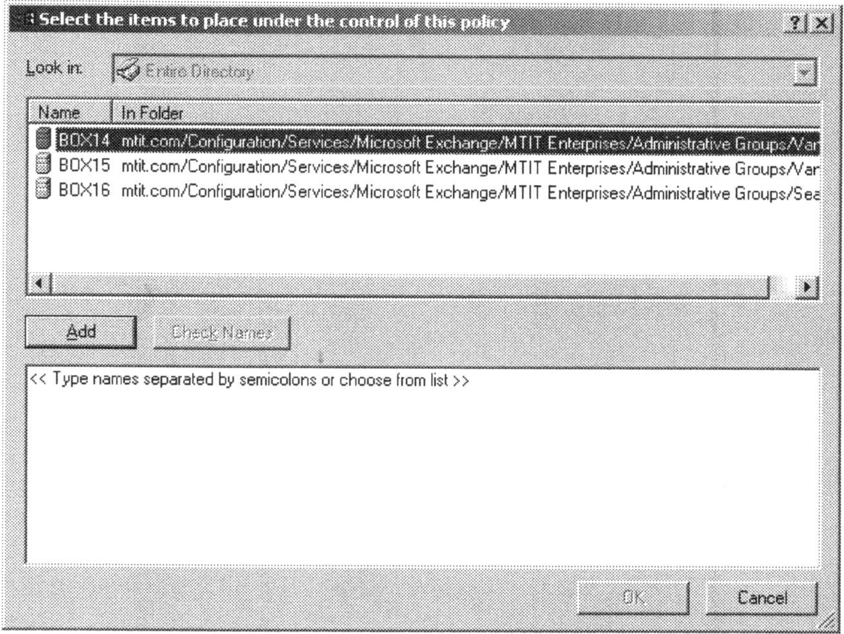

Figure 20.5 Specifying the servers that a server policy will control.

NOTE

Figure 20.5 shows that, even though our server policy belongs to the Vancouver administrative group, we can use this policy to control Exchange servers throughout our organization because Box16 belongs to a different administrative group, Seattle. Creating system policies in one administrative group versus another determines who gets to manage this policy.

The immediate result of adding Box14 to Test SRV Policy is that a node labeled Box14 appears in the Details pane when we select the policy in the tree pane of System Manager (Figure 20.6). This Box14 node actually lets us access the same Box Properties Sheets that we would normally access by using the Box14 node under the Servers container in Vancouver.

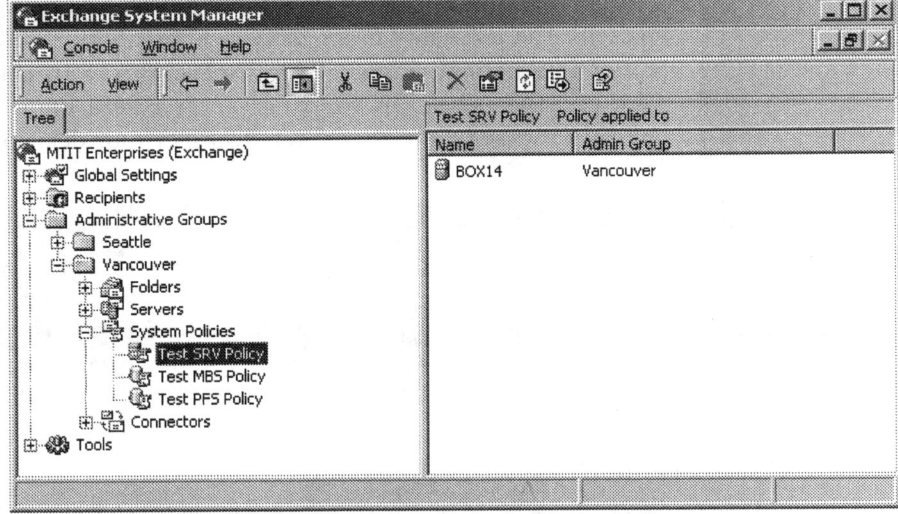

Figure 20.6 Exchange server BOX14 is under the control of server policy Test SRV Policy.

We've added a server to our server policy, but we haven't actually applied the policy. First, let's experiment with our mailbox-store policy Test MBS Policy. Right-click this mailbox-store policy and select Add Mailbox Store. A dialog box similar to the one shown in Figure 20.5 appears, listing all mailbox stores on all servers in our organization. Select several different mailbox stores on different servers from each administrative group (I've selected the ExecutiveMS and AccoutingMS stores in the DiscardableSG on server Box14 in Vancouver and the default Mailbox Store in the First Storage Group on server Box16 in Seattle) and bring them under the control of the policy. Then select the Test MBS Policy in the tree pane and examine the fields displayed in the Details pane for each store controlled by the policy.

Applying a Policy

Walkthrough

Creating a new policy and adding items (servers or stores) to it is not enough—you still need to apply the policy before it can take effect. We'll begin by applying our Test SRV Policy so that it will take control of the settings of server Box14. Right-click on the server policy Test SRV Policy and select Apply Now. That's it.

Now let's examine the Properties Sheet for Box14 to see the effect of applying the server policy. You can open the Box14 Properties Sheet two ways:

- By using the Box14 node under the Servers container in the Vancouver administrative group.
- By using the Box14 node under the Test SRV Policy node under the System Policies container in the Vancouver administrative group.

Either way, open the Box14 Properties Sheet and check the General tab. Notice that the options to enable subject logging and message tracking are unavailable (Figure 20.7) because the policy now controls these settings for Box14 and you cannot override them using the Properties Sheet for the server. Switch to the Policies tab, where you'll see that the Test SRV Policy is the only policy currently controlling the server. More on this tab in a moment.

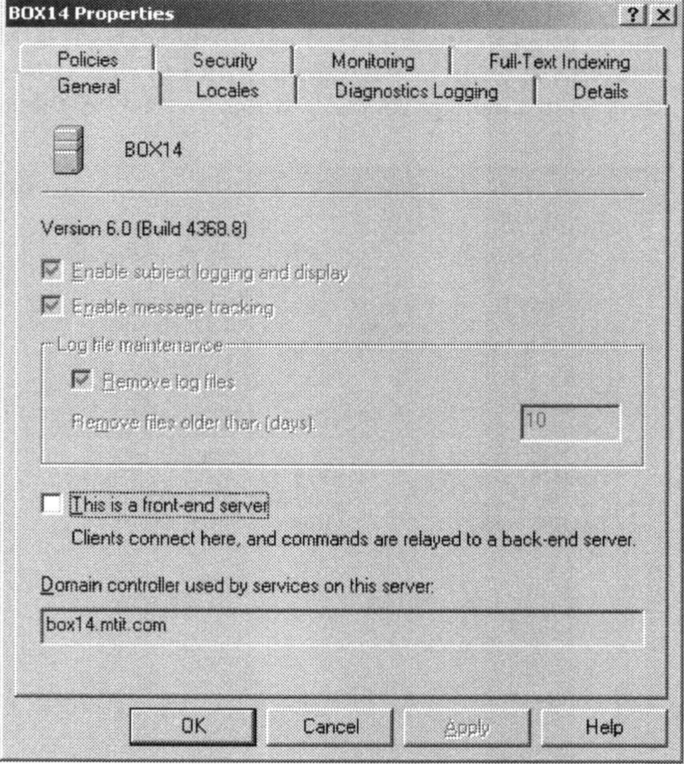

Figure 20.7 You cannot override the server policy settings for Box14.

TIP

You don't have to apply a policy manually to make it take effect. You can wait until the configured maintenance cycle comes round for the selected server or information store and the policy will be applied automatically.

We can also manually apply our mailbox-store policy Test MBS Policy. Right-click on this policy and select Apply Now. Open the Properties Sheet for one of the mailbox stores controlled by this policy. All settings on the General, Database, Limits, and Full-Text Indexing tabs should be unavailable (ghosted out). In addition, the Storage Limit tab should show Issue Warning at 3000 KB as we defined in our policy settings. This may seem a bit strange at first: Why are all the settings on the four tabs unavailable when we only specified one setting (Issue Warning on the Storage Limits tab) when we created the policy? When we created the policy, we selected all four available tabs for the policy, and the policy therefore controls all settings on these tabs even though we used the default settings. We'll see how to change the tabs controlled by our policy in another walkthrough.

Switch to the Policies tab to view which mailbox-store policies affect the selected mailbox store (Figure 20.8). The Test MBS Policy appears four times, once for each Properties tab that it controls. It is evident that system policies control settings on a tab-by-tab basis.

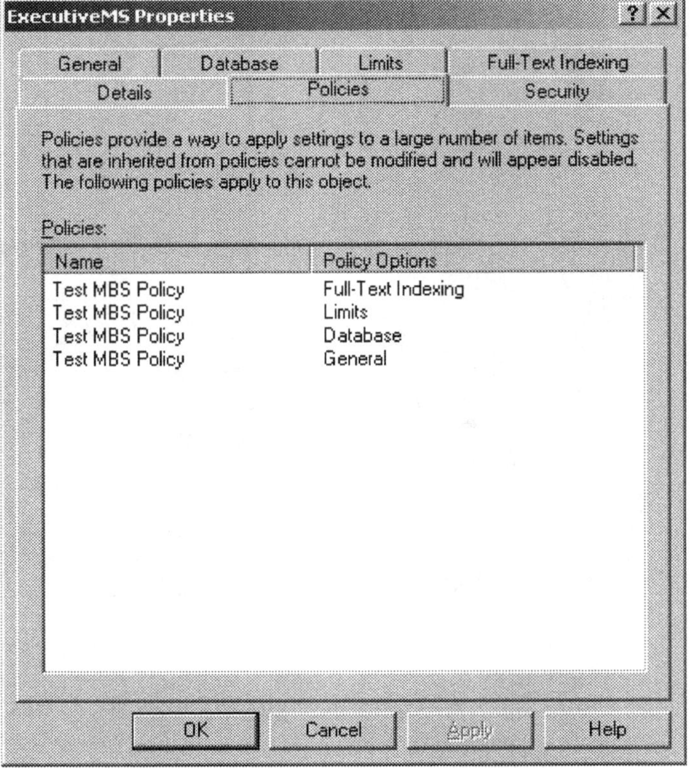

Figure 20.8 Policies controlling the ExecutiveMS mailbox store.

As an experiment, let's try to create a conflicting system policy and see what happens. Right-click on the System Policies container in Vancouver and select New → Mailbox Store Policy. Select the Database option only from the New Policy dialog box (Figure 20.4) and click OK. Give your policy a name (I chose "Test of Conflicting Policy") and change the Maintenance Interval setting on the Database (Policy) tab of the new policy to something different. Click OK to create the new policy.

No conflict so far—that's because we created the new mailbox-store policy but haven't configured it to actually control any mailbox stores. Right-click on the new policy, select Add Mailbox Store, and try to add the ExecutiveMS store to the policy. A message box should appear, similar to the one shown in Figure 20.9.

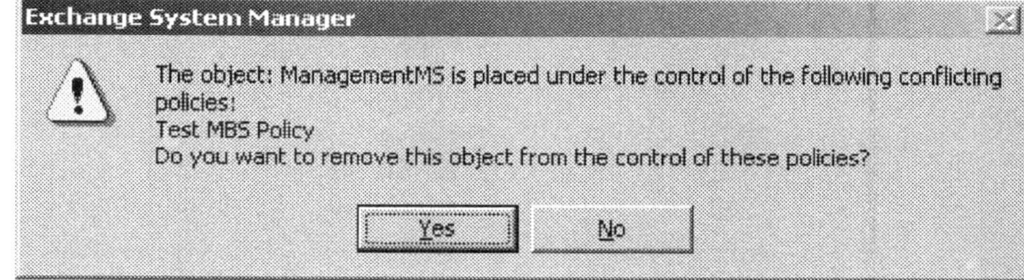

Figure 20.9
Policy conflict.

NOTE

Why does the message shown in Figure 20.9 mention ManagementMS instead of ExecutiveMS? Although the mailbox store is named ExecutiveMS in System Manager, the .edb and .stm database files for the databases associated with this store were named ManagmenetMS in an earlier walkthrough.

If we click No in response to the message box shown in Figure 20.9, then our new policy will not be applied to the ExecutiveMS mailbox store and things will be unchanged. If we click Yes, the previous Test MBS Policy, which until now has been controlling the settings of the store, will be removed from controlling the store, but only with respect to the Database tab settings, and the new policy will control the Database tab settings for the store.

Click Yes to see this. ExecutiveMS appears under both the Test MBS Policy and Test of Conflicting Policy nodes. Open the Properties Sheet for the ExecutiveMS node under the Test of Conflicting Policy node. Switch to the Policies tab and note that the only policy which controls this store is the new one (Test of Conflicting Policy). Switch to the Storage Limits tab. Note that the Issue Warning is set to 3,000 KB as before, and the remaining settings are now configurable and no longer ghosted. Why is the Issue Warning set to 3,000 KB if the Test MBS Policy no longer controls this store? Test MBS Policy specified this value, and removing the store from its control doesn't change the store's settings; it only makes the settings available for modification.

Modifying a Policy

Walkthrough

There are several ways to modify system policies and how they take effect:

- Right-click a system policy in System Manager and select Properties. This opens up the Properties Sheet for the policy, allowing you to change the values of the settings that the policy will enforce. Once you've made these changes, don't forget that you need to reapply the policy before the changes take effect on the servers or stores controlled by the policy. Exchange makes this easier by prompting you to apply the settings immediately to all items associated with the policy when you click OK to close the Properties Sheet for the policy. If the settings don't take effect properly, try applying the policy manually afterward.
- If you want to increase or decrease the scope of a policy by adding or removing property pages, right-click on the policy and select Change Property Pages. This opens the New Policy dialog box (Figures 20.1 and 20.4), which allows you to change the policy by adding or deleting property pages. When you remove a property page from the policy and reapply it, the settings for this page for the items under the control of the policy remain as they were previously established by the policy. You must manually reapply a policy to make the changes take effect.
- If you want to remove a server or store from the control of a policy, select the policy in the tree pane of System Manager, right-click on the server or store in the Details pane, and select Remove From Policy. The settings of the server or store remain unchanged but become available for direct modification using their Properties Sheets.
- You can also copy policies from one administrative group to another or move them by using cut and paste or by dragging. Remember that system policies must always reside in the System Policies container within an administrative group.
- You can delete a policy if it is no longer needed.

You might want to disable a policy instead of deleting it. Deleting is a permanent action that cannot be reversed, whereas disabling lets you use the policy again if you change your mind. To disable a policy, simply remove all items (servers or stores) from under its control.

Summary

In the last few chapters we've looked at how to manage the Exchange data-storage structure of storage groups, data stores, mailboxes, and public folders. We've seen how to do this directly and how to do it using system policies. In Chapter 21, we'll look at how to administer routing groups and connectors in a large Exchange organization distributed across different geographic locations.

CHAPTER 21

Routing Groups

In this chapter we examine routing groups in Exchange 2000. We also look under the hood of Exchange to understand how message routing and delivery take place under different circumstances and learn how to manage message routing in a large Exchange organization using routing groups.

There are eight walkthroughs in this chapter:

- Enabling routing groups
- Creating a routing group container
- Creating a new routing group
- Renaming a routing group
- Moving servers between routing groups
- Designating routing group masters
- Connecting routing groups
- Deleting a routing group

Routing Groups

So far in this book we've considered a relatively limited deployment of Exchange with only a few servers in only two locations connected by a high-speed permanent connection. What if we want to deploy Exchange in a large enterprise that spans many geographic locations that are connected with different kinds of WAN links, some high bandwidth and some low, some permanent and some dial-on-demand? The solution is to make use of routing groups, a feature of Exchange 2000 that in some ways mirrors the functionality of sites in previous versions of Exchange.

To understand routing groups, let's backtrack for a moment and consider the role of sites in Exchange 5.5.

Sites in Exchange 5.5

If your company spanned multiple geographic locations and you were using earlier versions of Exchange, you had to create multiple sites within your Exchange organization. A *site* is a grouping of Exchange servers that is based on specific network connectivity requirements: all servers in the same site must be connected by permanent high-speed network links that support synchronous *remote procedure call* (RPC) connections. Typically, this connection required dedicated LAN connections of 10 Mbps or higher, but dedicated WAN connections with a minimum of 56 kbps (or preferably 128 kbps) of available bandwidth could also be used to connect servers in a site. In other words, if the WAN links were permanent and had sufficient bandwidth, then a site could span multiple geographic locations.

In earlier versions of Exchange, messages were routed between sites by different kinds of *connectors*. The collection of all sites in an organization together with the various connectors joining these sites formed the *messaging topology* of the Exchange organization.

In addition to being routing boundaries, sites in earlier versions of Exchange were administrative boundaries because all servers at the same site would be managed by an administrator in that location. An administrator who managed servers at one site typically would not necessarily be able to manage servers at a different site.

Routing versus Administrative Groups

In Exchange 2000, the idea of sites has been transformed into two separate kinds of organizational entities: administrative groups and routing groups. We covered administrative groups in previous chapters, but we mention them because of their connection with the concept of sites in earlier versions of Exchange.

In this new version of Exchange, the administrative and routing aspects of sites have been separated. Previously, all servers in a given site would route messages and be managed as a unit; now you can group the servers you want to manage together into administrative groups and servers you want to route messages into routing groups.

A *routing group* is a collection of Exchange 2000 servers that are connected by a reliable, permanent network connection—either a LAN connection or a dedicated WAN link. In contrast, an *administrative group* is a collection of servers that can be managed as a unit.

NOTE

In other words, administrative groups mirror the logical organization of your company, whereas routing groups mirror its physical organization.

Separating the routing and administrative functions of sites provides increased flexibility in how Exchange 2000 can be deployed in large-scale enterprises because administrative and routing groups are managed separately. Two servers can be in the same administrative group yet be in different routing groups, or they could be in the same routing group but in different administrative groups, and so on. In other words, routing and administrative groups can be defined separately, keeping the management topology of an organization distinct from its messaging topology. There are advantages and disadvantages to doing this, as we'll see in a moment.

UNDER THE HOOD

Exchange 2000 and SMTP

The network connection between servers in a routing group needs to be permanent and reliable, but it doesn't have to be high bandwidth as connections within an Exchange 5.5 site needed to be. In contrast to Exchange 5.5, where RPCs were used to deliver messages between different servers within the same site, Exchange 2000 now uses SMTP as its underlying message transport, and SMTP can operate even when bandwidth is so limited that RPC communications become unreliable.

NOTE

If you had to choose which Exchange 2000 feature (routing or administrative groups) is closest to the Exchange 5.5 feature of sites, you would have to choose routing groups. The primary function of sites was to control message routing through an Exchange 5.5 organization. It just so happened that sites formed administrative as well as routing boundaries.

Default Routing Group

When you install your first Exchange 2000 server, it automatically creates a default routing group. Any additional servers you install, regardless of what administrative group they belong to, automatically join this default routing group.

If possible, you may want to get by with using only this default routing group and not creating any new ones. Adding new routing groups to an organization creates an additional level of complexity to its management, primarily because connectors must be installed and configured to establish messaging flow between different routing groups. No connectors are required if there is only the default routing group. Therefore, if your organization consisted of a few Exchange servers at a single location, then you wouldn't need more than one routing group.

NOTE

If your Exchange 2000 organization is configured to run in mixed mode (the default), then you can't create additional routing groups. All Exchange 2000 servers automatically belong to the default routing group in this case. Remember that mixed mode allows Exchange 2000 servers to interoperate with downlevel Exchange 5.5 servers.

Also, when Exchange is running in mixed mode, you can create administrative groups in addition to the default one; however, each administrative group has its own unique default routing group associated with it.

If Exchange is running in native mode, routing groups and administrative groups can be configured separately in any fashion desired.

When to Use Multiple Routing Groups

The scenarios where you probably want to create additional routing groups include:

- Your enterprise spans multiple geographic locations and reliable, permanent network connections do *not* exist between these locations, for example, a company with a headquarters in one location and several smaller branch offices with dial-on-demand connections. These connections are nonpermanent and may require that messages be routed according to a specified schedule. Another example is when the network connection between two locations is unreliable, possibly due to the connection being saturated with regard to bandwidth.
- Your enterprise spans multiple geographic locations and you need to have explicit control over how messages are routed between those locations. The connections between the locations may be permanent but slower, requiring careful management of bandwidth consumption by Exchange messaging be managed carefully to avoid starving other services. Alternatively, connections between different locations are unreliable or need to be scheduled.
- You want to have greater control over the replication of public folders between different locations where your company has a business presence. Implementing multiple routing groups enables you to do this.
- You need to be able to monitor message flow regularly within your organization. Implementing routing groups and then enabling message tracking when needed could be a way of meeting these requirements.

- You need to schedule message delivery between locations because of WAN link costs, link unreliability, or some other reason.

NOTE

We said previously that in mixed mode we were confined to using only the default routing group. Another way of saying this is that, to create and take advantage of additional routing groups, you need to be running your Exchange organization in native mode.

Managing Routing Groups

Managing routing groups adds additional complexity to an Exchange 2000 organization and involves proficiency in a number of administrative tasks including:

- Creating and configuring routing groups
- Moving servers between different routing groups
- Establishing messaging connectivity between different routing groups
- Designating a routing group master in each routing group

Before we look at how to perform these various administrative tasks, let's take a look under the hood of Exchange to understand how message routing takes place under different circumstances.

NOTE

Just a few more notes concerning membership in routing groups: all servers within a given routing group must be linked by reliable, permanent connections, must be able to communicate directly with each other using the SMTP protocol, and must belong to the same Windows 2000 forest. In addition, to join a routing group, a server must be able to contact the routing group master for the routing group.

Message Routing in Exchange 2000

UNDER THE HOOD

Before we start working with routing groups, let's step back and view the big picture of how messages travel around an Exchange organization and beyond. We'll begin by introducing some terminology and then move on to some different routing scenarios.

Message Routing Concepts

There are basically two different types of message flow in Exchange that we need to consider:

- *Message flow*. This is the movement of messaging information within an Exchange server and involves an interplay between Exchange and Windows 2000 with elements such as Active Directory, the Web Store, and IIS with its SMTP, POP3, IMAP4, NNTP, and HTTP protocols. It also includes the queuing of messages by an Exchange server in preparation for delivery. We'll look at message flow in more detail in Chapter 23 on virtual servers.
- *Message routing*. This is the movement of messaging information between Exchange servers in an organization, and between an Exchange organization and other external messaging systems such as the Internet's SMTP messaging system, public X.400 messaging systems, third-party systems like Lotus Notes and GroupWise, and so on. Message routing involves routing groups, connectors, gateways, link state tables, and other elements of Exchange. We're focusing on message routing in this chapter.

The basic terminology needed to understand Exchange message routing includes the following concepts and elements:

- *Routing groups*. As we discussed previously, routing groups are the fundamental building blocks of an Exchange organization's messaging topology. Routing groups parallel the physical connectivity of an enterprise's network, and all Exchange servers within a routing group must be connected by permanent, reliable network connections such as LAN connections or dedicated WAN links.
- *Routing group master*. One Exchange server in each routing group must be designated as the routing group master (or master server) for that group (the remaining servers are called member servers—not to be confused with Windows 2000 servers that are not domain controllers). The job of the routing group master is to compile and distribute link state information to the other servers in the group. The routing group master by default is the first Exchange server installed in a given routing group, but this can be reconfigured, as we will see in our walkthroughs.

TIP

Routing group masters or routing masters are also known as routing information daemon (RID) masters. In a mixed mode environment where Exchange 2000 and Exchange 5.5 servers are in the same routing group or site, the RID master can be an Exchange 2000 or an Exchange 5.5 server. There are considerations, however—see Knowledge Base article Q254809 on Microsoft TechNet for more information.

- *Link state table.* Each Exchange server maintains an in-memory database called the link state table that contains information about which routes are currently available in the organization for routing messages. When a server needs to route a message to another server in the organization (or to a different messaging system), it consults the link state table to determine the best way of doing so. Entries for each link (messaging path between servers) in the link state table are either up or down. If a link goes down, the routing group master checks the link every 60 seconds until the link is reestablished. Once the link is up again, the routing group master notifies the other servers in its routing group so that they can route messages using the link, if required.

NOTE

All Exchange servers in the same routing group exchange their routing information using the Exchange 2000 Server Routing Service (RESVC), which uses TCP port 691.

- *Connector.* For messages to travel between different routing groups, a connector must be installed between these groups. Connectors are covered in Chapter 22.
- *Gateway.* This is a term for a connector that is used to establish messaging connectivity between an Exchange organization and a foreign (external) messaging system like the Internet or a third-party messaging system like Lotus Notes or GroupWise.
- *Bridgehead server.* This is the specific server in a routing group that funnels all messages sent from servers in the group using a specific connector. A bridgehead server can be thought of as a point of entry or exit for a routing group through which all messaging traffic flows. But remember that bridgehead servers are defined on a per-connector basis, so if you have multiple connectors in a routing group, then there may be multiple bridgehead servers as well.

NOTE

Exchange uses the target recipient's email address to determine where to route a given message. By default, Exchange creates two types of email addresses for every mail-enabled recipient, SMTP and X.400. The SMTP address is used by default for message routing and the SMTP protocol is used as the underlying message transport mechanism. We'll look at this in more detail in Chapter 23.

NOTE

It is important to monitor the health of the routing group master for each routing group. If the master server becomes unavailable for some reason, the member servers in that routing group will have stale routing information in their link state table until the master becomes available again. If a link goes down, the member servers will not be aware of this and messages delivered using this link will not reach their destinations. The overall result is degraded messaging performance until the master can be brought online again.

How Message Routing Works

There are four basic scenarios by which a message can be routed between sender and receiver using Exchange:

- *Recipient is on the same Exchange server.* If both the sender and recipient have their mailboxes on the same Exchange server, message routing is simple: the message is passed from the sender to the information store, whence it is retrieved by the recipient.
- *Recipient is in the same routing group.* If the sender and recipient have their mailboxes on different Exchange servers but both servers reside in the same routing group, the routing process looks like this: the message is passed from the sender to the local information store, which forwards the message using the SMTP messaging protocol to the information store of the recipient's server. Note that all servers within a given routing group can forward messages directly to each other in a single link or hop. That is, within a routing group message transfer is point to point. Another way to phrase this would be to say that Exchange servers within a given routing group have full-mesh messaging connectivity with each other.

NOTE

However, if you are running your Exchange 2000 organization in mixed mode and one of the servers involved in delivery is a downlevel Exchange 5.5 server, then RPCs are used for transferring messages between servers within the same routing group because in mixed mode the functionality of Exchange 2000 routing groups must match that of Exchange 5.5 sites.

- *Recipient is in a different routing group*. If the sender and recipient are in different routing groups, the sender's server consults its link state table to identify the best route for delivery of the message. The server then forwards the message to the appropriate bridgehead server within the local routing group. The bridgehead server then uses a connector to forward the message to the nearest routing group along the messaging path selected. If the recipient's server is several messaging hops away from the sender, the message is forwarded from bridgehead server to bridgehead server until it reaches its destination.

NOTE

In a well-connected enterprise, there may be multiple network paths between two locations. This is often done for redundancy in case one path goes down. In an enterprise deployment of Exchange 2000, there may likewise be multiple routes between different routing groups. Each of these routes has an associated cost, and, by using the link state table and calculating the cost of different routes, Exchange can select the best route along which to forward the message to its recipient. Note that each bridgehead server along the way in a multihop route does an independent check of the link state table to determine if it should still route the message to the next bridgehead server along the selected route or choose a different route (for instance, one bridgehead server may know of a link ahead that is down but the originating server may not be aware of this fact if it has stale link state information).

Also, if two potential routes have the same cost, Exchange selects one of them at random along which to forward the message, providing a simple form of load balancing for messaging.

- *Recipient is outside the Exchange organization*. If the recipient belongs to an external messaging system, delivery is similar to the previous scenario except that at some point along the messaging path a connector or gateway will forward the message to the external mail system.

NOTE

We're obviously leaving out some of the details of the message routing and delivery process here so we can see the big picture. For example, when you try to send a message to a recipient using your mail client, Exchange begins by looking up the message recipient in Active Directory to determine whether the recipient is in the same routing group as the sender, is in a different routing group, or is outside the Exchange organization. Once the destination address has been resolved, Exchange attempts delivery of the message as described above.

Preliminaries to Walkthroughs in this Chapter

Before we perform our walkthroughs for this chapter, let's briefly review the configuration of our testbed deployment MTIT Enterprises. We have two administrative groups, Vancouver and Seattle. Exchange servers Box14 and Box15 are in Vancouver and Box16 is in Seattle. Our organization is running in Exchange native mode but routing groups have not been enabled.

Create two new mailbox-enabled users in your organization with the following properties:

- vanuser@mtit.com has its mailbox on Box14 in Vancouver (any mailbox store)
- seauser@mtit.com has its mailbox on Box16 in Seattle (any mailbox store)

We'll use these two users to test messaging connectivity as follows: log on as Administrator to the console of both Box14 in Vancouver and Box16 in Seattle. On Box14 open the URL http://localhost/exchange/vanuser and enter the credentials for vanuser to access this user's mailbox using Outlook Web Access (OWA). Similarly, on Box16 open the URL http://localhost/exchange/seauser and enter the credentials for seauser to access this users mailbox using OWA. Now have seauser on Box16 use OWA to send a one-off test message addressed to vanuser@mtit.com. Move to Box14 and click the Refresh button on the browser and you should see the test message sent from Box16.

This exercise simply confirms that right now we have messaging connectivity between the two Exchange servers, which currently both belong to the same default routing group. We'll repeat this test later in this chapter.

Enabling Routing Groups

Before we can create a new routing group, we must enable routing groups for our Exchange organization. To enable support for routing groups, right-click on the organization (root) node in System Manager and select Properties to open the Properties Sheet for our Exchange organization (Figure 21.1).

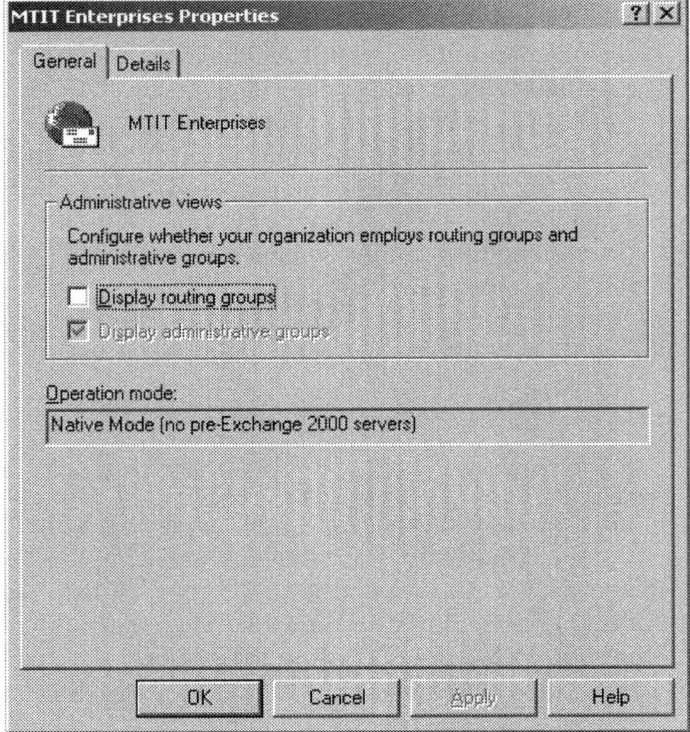

Figure 21.1 Enabling routing groups for an Exchange organization.

Figure 21.1 shows that routing groups are currently not displayed in our testbed organization. Select the checkbox labeled Display Routing Groups and click OK to enable routing groups for our organization.

TIP

We cannot disable the display of administrative groups for our testbed organization because we have switched our Exchange servers from mixed mode to native mode, and this change cannot be undone.

Let's look at the results of our action. Expand the two containers for the Vancouver and Seattle administrative groups in System Manager to display their top-level subcontainers (Figure 21.2). Notice that there is now a Routing Groups container within the Vancouver administrative group, and this Routing Groups container contains the default routing group (called First Routing Group) for that administrative group.

Figure 21.2 Displaying the default routing group for Vancouver.

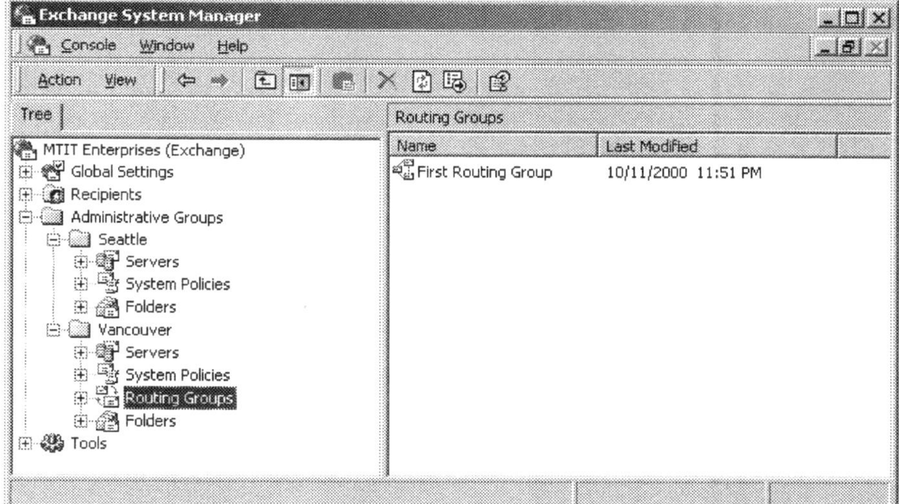

Creating a Routing Group Container

Walkthrough

In the previous walkthrough you may have noted that the Seattle administrative group has no Routing Groups container under it in System Manager (Figure 21.2). The reason is we created the Seattle admin group after we had already switched our organization from mixed to native mode—if we had created the Seattle admin group before changing mode, then it would now have a Routing Groups container under it, which itself contained the First Routing Group for Seattle.

Before we create a new routing group in Seattle, we need to create a Routing Groups container in Seattle to hold the new routing group. To do this right-click on the Seattle node in System Manager and select New → Routing Groups Container.

TIP

If the option for creating a new Routing Group container is unavailable, you are running in mixed mode, where all administrative groups have only the default routing group.

Creating a New Routing Group

Walkthrough

Let's now create a new routing group in the Seattle administrative group. Right-click on the Routing Groups container under Seattle and select New → Routing Group from the shortcut menu. Type the name SeattleRG as the name of the new routing group and click OK to create the routing group. The result is displayed in Figure 21.3.

Note that our new routing group does not contain any Exchange servers. To verify this, expand the SeattleRG container in the tree pane of System Manager to display the Connectors and Members containers beneath it. Then select the Members container in the tree pane and note that the details pane is empty.

NOTE

The Connectors container under a particular routing group contains any connectors installed for that group, and the Members container contains a list of Exchange servers in that routing group.

Renaming a Routing Group

Walkthrough

Let's rename the First Routing Group in Vancouver as follows. Select the Routing Groups container under Vancouver in the tree pane of System Manager, then right-click on First Routing Group in the details pane, and select Rename. Type the new name, VancouverRG, for the routing group.

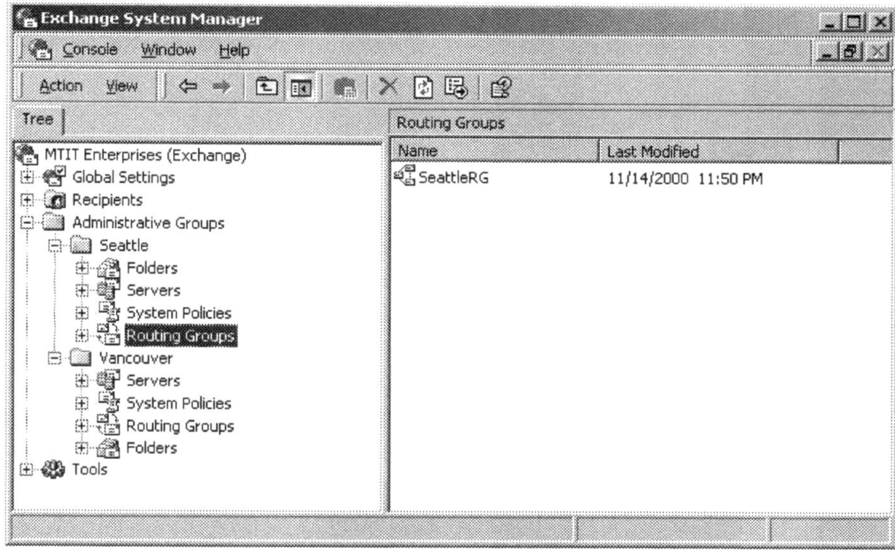

Figure 21.3
Creating a new routing group in Seattle.

Moving Servers Between Routing Groups

We'll try moving an Exchange server from one routing group to another. Expand the VancouverRG container in the console tree to display the Connectors and Members folders under it. Select Members in the tree pane and you'll see three servers listed in the details pane:

- Box14 as server type master
- Box15 as server type member
- Box16 as server type member

We'll expand on the difference between master and member shortly. For now just note that all three of our Exchange servers are currently in the VancouverRG routing group. However, server Box16 actually belongs to the Seattle administrative group, so let's try moving it to the SeattleRG routing group.

To move the server from the VancouverRG routing group to the SeattleRG routing group, simply drag it from one members container to another (or you can use Cut and Paste from the shortcut menu). The move should be successful, and after some disk activity server Box16 now belongs to the SeattleRG routing group. Note that its server type property has changed from member to master as well.

NOTE

There are restrictions on how you can move Exchange servers between routing groups. Specifically, you can move servers between routing groups that belong to the same administrative group, but you cannot move servers between routing groups that belong to different administrative groups. The reason we could move Box16 is that it already belonged to the Seattle administrative group and could therefore be moved to the SeattleRG routing group. Once moved there, you cannot move it back to the VancouverRG routing group because that routing group is in a different administrative group. Furthermore, you can only move servers between routing groups if your Exchange organization is configured to run in native mode operation.

TIP

Normally you specify which routing group an Exchange server will belong to when you install Exchange on the new server. The main reason for moving servers between different routing groups afterward is to group them together according to network connectivity. All Exchange servers that have permanent, high-speed connectivity with each other should generally be placed in the same routing group. However, because Exchange servers can only be moved between routing groups that are in the same administrative group, you are limited in how you can rearrange the Exchange servers in an enterprise, so it's best to plan the topology of routing groups well before you start deploying Exchange in your enterprise.

Designating Routing Group Masters

Walkthrough

Each routing groups has a single Exchange server designated as routing group master (or simply Master in System Manager when the Members container for the server's routing group is selected in the console tree). Each Exchange server in a routing group is either a master or a member, and there can be only one master per routing group.

The routing group master is usually the first Exchange server installed in the specified routing group. If you have more than one server in a routing group, you can change which one is designated as master by right-clicking any server currently displayed as member and selecting Set As Master from the shortcut menu. Try switching the routing group master role for the VancouverRG routing group from Box14 to Box15 as a test.

Connecting Routing Groups

Walkthrough

Our system is organized so that the Vancouver administrative group contains the VancouverRG routing group, which contains only Exchange server Box16, and the Seattle administrative group contains the SeattleRG routing group, which contains the two servers Box14 and Box15.

We previously used OWA to test that we had messaging connectivity between servers Box14 and Box16, but that was when they belonged to the same routing group. Box16 now belongs to a different routing group, the SeattleRG routing group, and so let's test once more whether we can still send messages between these two servers.

Go to Box16 and start OWA to connect to the mailbox for seauser@mtit.com. Compose a one-off test message addressed to vanuser@mtit.com and try to send it. Now go to Box14 and start OWA to connect to the mailbox for vanuser@mtit.com. This time the message from seauser should not be present in vanuser's inbox because the two servers we are testing are in different routing groups and there is no connector configured to provide messaging connectivity between them. In fact, if you return to Box16 and click the Refresh button on the browser, you should see a nondelivery report indicating that the test message could not be delivered to its intended recipient (Figure 21.4).

We'll leave the installation and configuration of connectors until the next chapter. For now, just note that a connector is required to route messages between servers in different routing groups.

TIP

If you find that you can send a test message from Box16 to Box14, it's because the move of the server from one routing group to the other has not yet taken place (although it seems to have done so in System Manager). If this is the case, just reboot Box16 and repeat the exercise and it should work.

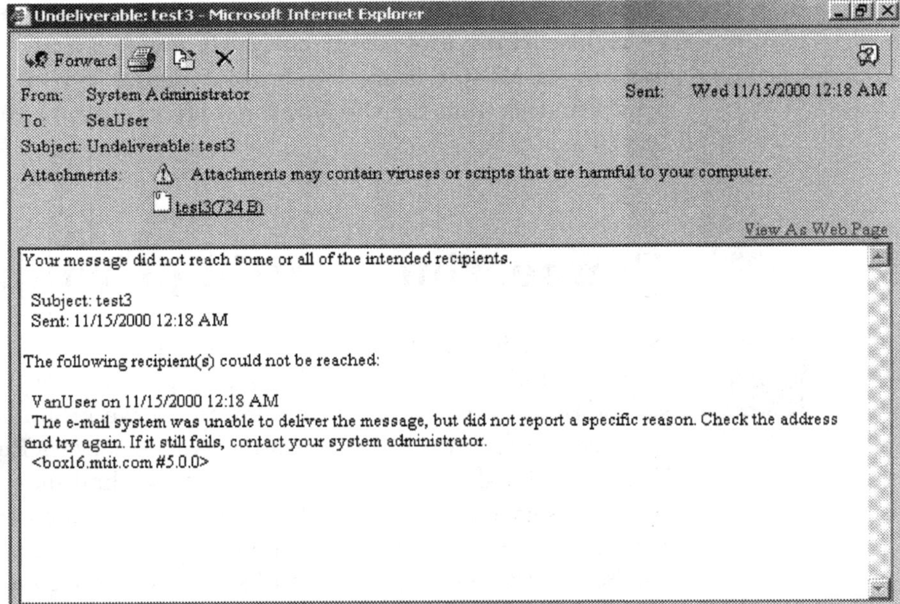

Figure 21.4 No messaging connectivity exists between servers in different routing groups if no connectors have been installed to link them.

Deleting a Routing Group

Walkthrough

You can delete a routing group if it is no longer needed in your Exchange organization (for example, if a branch office consolidates with headquarters and relocates). Before you can delete a routing group, you must move its servers to a different routing group in the same administrative group. Don't delete any of the routing groups because we'll need them for the next chapter.

Summary

In this chapter we've looked at routing groups and how to create and manage them. Message routing in an Exchange organization depends on the topology of routing groups created. However, creating routing groups is not enough—you also have to connect them together using connectors to enable messages to flow between them. Installing and configuring connectors is the topic Chapter 22.

CHAPTER 22

Connectors

We saw in the last chapter that Exchange servers belonging to different routing groups cannot route messages between them unless connectors are installed to establish such messaging connectivity. In this chapter, we'll examine the different kinds of Exchange connectors, how they work, their advantages and disadvantages, and walk through implementing several of them.

There are seven walkthroughs in this chapter:

- Installing routing-group connectors
- Testing routing-group connectors
- Configuring common settings for connectors
- Configuring routing-group connectors
- Removing routing-group connectors
- Installing SMTP connectors
- Configuring SMTP connectors

Connectors

In a small Exchange deployment, only one routing group may be required; all servers would belong to that group and exchange messages directly using SMTP. In larger Exchange deployments, multiple routing groups may be required, especially when the company has many different locations, when network connectivity between these locations is not permanent or reliable, or when message routing between locations needs to be controlled or scheduled.

Whenever you have more than one routing group, you need to install connectors to establish messaging connectivity between them. A *connector* is an Exchange component that enables messages to flow between two routing groups or between an Exchange organization and a foreign, downlevel, or third-party messaging system.

Basic Connectors

Exchange provides different kinds of connectors for different uses. These connectors can be classified in several ways, but the most obvious way is whether they can be used for establishing messaging connectivity between different routing groups.

There are three types of connectors that can be used to connect routing groups together (these basic connectors are sometimes called *routing connectors* because their job is to route messages between routing groups). Some of these connectors have other uses, for example, establishing messaging connectivity with the Internet or foreign messaging systems or with downlevel Exchange 5.5 sites and servers. These three types of connectors are:

- *Routing-group connectors.* These can be used to connect two routing groups together, or to connect an Exchange 2000 routing group to a downlevel Exchange 5.5 site. They cannot be used to connect to an external messaging system. The main uses for this type of connector are joining routing groups and establishing downlevel connectivity with downlevel Exchange 5.5 sites during a migration from Exchange 5.5 to Exchange 2000.
- *SMTP connectors.* These can be used to connect two routing groups together, an Exchange 2000 routing group to a downlevel Exchange 5.5 site, or an Exchange organization to the Internet's system of SMTP messaging hosts. However, SMTP connectors are used mainly for establishing messaging connectivity between an Exchange organization and the Internet. They are rarely used for connecting routing groups together and are sometimes used during a migration from Exchange 5.5 to 2000 when the downlevel Exchange 5.5 messaging system used the Internet Mail Service (IMS) for intersite communications.
- *X400 connectors.* These can be used to connect two routing groups together, an Exchange 2000 routing group to a downlevel Exchange 5.5 site, or an Exchange organization to a foreign X400 messaging system. However, X400 connectors are used mainly for establishing messaging connectivity with a foreign X400 messaging system. They are used for connecting routing groups together only in unusual circumstances and occasionally during a migration from Exchange 5.5 to 2000 when the downlevel Exchange 5.5 messaging system used them for intersite communications.

There is a close correspondence among the three basic Exchange 2000 connectors and the connectors of earlier versions of Exchange. Table 22.1 shows how these Exchange 2000 connectors correspond to those for Exchange 5.5.

TABLE 22.1 Comparison of Exchange 2000 and Exchange 5.5 connectors.

Exchange 2000 Connector	Exchange 5.5 Connector	Comparison
Routing-group connector	Site connector	Similar use and functionality; in mixed-mode environments, the routing-group connector functions like the site connector and uses remote procedure calls to communicate with downlevel Exchange 5.5 sites
SMTP connector	IMS	Similar use and functionality but SMTP connector includes more features
X400 connector	X400 connector	Similar use and functionality

UNDER THE HOOD

Classifying Connectors According to Messaging Architecture

The three connectors compared in Table 22.1 differ in their underlying architectures. In particular, the routing-group connector and the SMTP connector use SMTP by default as their underlying message transport mechanism and bypass the Message Transport Agent (MTA) entirely (the MTA handled all message transfer in previous versions of Exchange). These two connectors can be further differentiated by the fact that the SMTP connector can use only SMTP as its transport mechanism, whereas the routing-group connector can switch to using remote procedure calls (RPCs) and the MTA instead of SMTP when providing connectivity between an Exchange 2000 routing group and a downlevel Exchange 5.5 site.

In contrast, the X400 connector always uses the MTA for its message transport mechanism and operates similarly to X400 connectors in Exchange 5.5. See my book, Administering Exchange Server *(McGraw-Hill), for a detailed look at X400 concepts and terminology and the X400 MTA.*

Other Connectors

Exchange also includes a number of other connectors that can be used to establish messaging connectivity with external or downlevel messaging systems but not to connect routing groups together. These connectors (which are sometimes called *gateway connectors* because their function is to provide a messaging gateway between an Exchange organization and external mail systems) are listed here, but their implementation is beyond the scope of this book.

- *Lotus Notes connector*. This enables messaging connectivity between Exchange and Lotus Notes messaging systems and directory synchronization between Active Directory and Notes.
- *Lotus cc:Mail connector*. This enables messaging connectivity between Exchange and Lotus cc:Mail messaging systems and directory synchronization between Active Directory and cc:Mail.
- *Microsoft Mail connector*. This enables messaging connectivity between Exchange and legacy MS Mail 3.2 and higher messaging systems. In addition, directory synchronization between Active Directory and MS Mail is supported through the use of Microsoft Mail dirsync protocols and sharing of free/busy information through the Schedule+ Free/Busy Connector.
- *Novell GroupWise connector*. This enables messaging connectivity between Exchange and Novell GroupWise messaging systems and directory synchronization between Active Directory and GroupWise.

NOTE

Exchange 2000 no longer includes the PROFS and SNADS connectors that enabled messaging connectivity with legacy IBM mainframe messaging systems. If you still require connectivity with these systems, you must run Exchange 2000 in mixed mode to include a downlevel Exchange 5.5 site running the PROFS/SNADS connector in your organization.

NOTE

What happened to the dynamic remote access service (RAS) connector? This connector was included in Exchange 5.5 to provide dial-on-demand messaging connectivity using the Windows NT RAS, but there is no dynamic RAS connector in Exchange 2000. If you require dial-on-demand messaging connectivity between two Exchange sites or between Exchange and the Internet, use the SMTP connector and configure the Windows 2000 Routing and Remote Access component to enable dial-up access for your Exchange servers.

NOTE

The Active Directory connector is a special connector that enables the replication of information between Active Directory and the directory database of downlevel Exchange 5.5 messaging systems. We'll talk about this more in Chapter 25.

Routing-group Connectors

We'll start our in-depth look at connectors by considering the routing-group connector, which is the easiest one to configure. You can use the routing-group connector to establish messaging connectivity between:

- *Two routing groups.* If Exchange is running in native mode, you can create multiple routing groups to manage message routing efficiently, especially when your enterprise spans several geographic locations.
- *A routing group and a downlevel Exchange 5.5 site.* To support messaging connectivity with downlevel Exchange 5.5 sites, Exchange 2000 must be running in mixed mode.

NOTE

Both routing groups must be in the same Exchange organization—routing-group connectors cannot be used to connect many Exchange 2000 organizations together.

Advantages of Using Routing-group Connectors

The main advantage of using routing-group connectors is their simplicity: as long as you have a reliable, permanent network connection between two routing groups, you can join them together using routing-group connectors. They require little configuration and thus are easy to manage.

On the down side, their very simplicity in configuration means increased complexity under the hood. In particular, they perform poorly over unreliable network connections (such as network connections whose bandwidth is nearly saturated) and have few manual tuning functions (they are essentially self-tuning). Nevertheless, in most circumstances, a large multilocation enterprise will probably need this type of connector for joining routing groups together.

Routing-group connectors provide configuration settings that allow you to manage only the following aspects of messaging between routing groups:

- Message routing schedule
- Message priority
- Message size limits

How Routing-group Connectors Work

Routing-group connectors are very similar to the site connectors in Exchange 5.5. They are easy to configure and, when Exchange 2000 is running in mixed mode, routing-group connectors behave just as site connectors do, in particular by using RPCs instead of SMTP as their underlying messaging transport mechanism and by consulting the Exchange 5.5 GWART routing tables to determine the best route to send a message.

When Exchange 2000 is running in native mode, however, routing-group connectors use SMTP as their messaging transport and consult the Exchange 2000 link state table for determining the best route to send a message.

When connecting two routing groups together using the routing-group connector, you should designate a bridgehead server at each end of the connector. A *bridgehead server* functions as the endpoint for a routing-group connector. When a server in one routing group wants to send a message to a server in another routing group, the first server forwards the message directly to the bridgehead server in its own routing group, which funnels the message directly to the bridgehead server in the remote routing group, which forwards the message directly to the target server in the remote group.

There are several ways in which bridgehead servers can be configured when establishing messaging connectivity between two routing groups using the routing-group connector:

- *No bridgehead server (not recommended).* In this case, all servers in both routing groups act as bridgehead servers; there is no funneling of messages through designated bridgehead servers. This scenario is not recommended. It is usually best to configure specific Exchange servers to function in the role of bridgehead servers and allocate them sufficient system resources to handle the increased load they incur from this designation.
- *One bridgehead server (typical).* In this case, all messages enter and leave the routing group using the bridgehead server, which must have sufficient system resources to function in this role (typically a bridgehead server will not host mailboxes or public folders in a large enterprise but will be used for dedicated message routing services). Using a designated bridgehead server also gives administrators greater control over message routing, supports message tracking, and has other advantages.

- *Multiple bridgehead servers (recommended).* If messaging connectivity between two routing groups is critically important, install multiple connectors in each site and designate multiple servers as bridgehead servers for load balancing and fault tolerance.

NOTE

You designate specific bridgehead servers in each routing group when using the routing-group connector. These can be connected one to one or one to many.

Installing Routing-group Connectors

Walkthrough

Let's now turn to our testbed Exchange organization and install a routing-group connector to establish messaging connectivity between Exchange server Box14, which is in the VancouverRG routing group, and Box16, which is in the SeattleRG routing group that we created in the previous chapter. In each case, we'll designate the local server as the bridgehead server for that routing group.

NOTE

You actually have to install two routing-group connectors, one on Box14 and the other on Box16, to establish messaging connectivity between the two routing groups. However, Exchange includes functionality that allows you to automatically create and configure the second connector when you install the first.

Log on to Box14 in the VancouverRG routing group and start System Manager. Navigate through the console tree as follows: Organization (root) node → Administrative Groups → Vancouver → Routing Groups → VancouverRG → Connectors. Right-click on the Connectors container and select New → Routing Group Connector from the shortcut menu. A blank Properties Sheet for the new connector appears (Figure 22.1).

We'll configure the basic settings needed to make our connector operational, including specifying our bridgehead servers:

- Type "Vancouver-Seattle RGC" (without the quotes) as the name of the new connector.
- Select SeattleRG from the dropdown listbox as the target routing group for the connector.

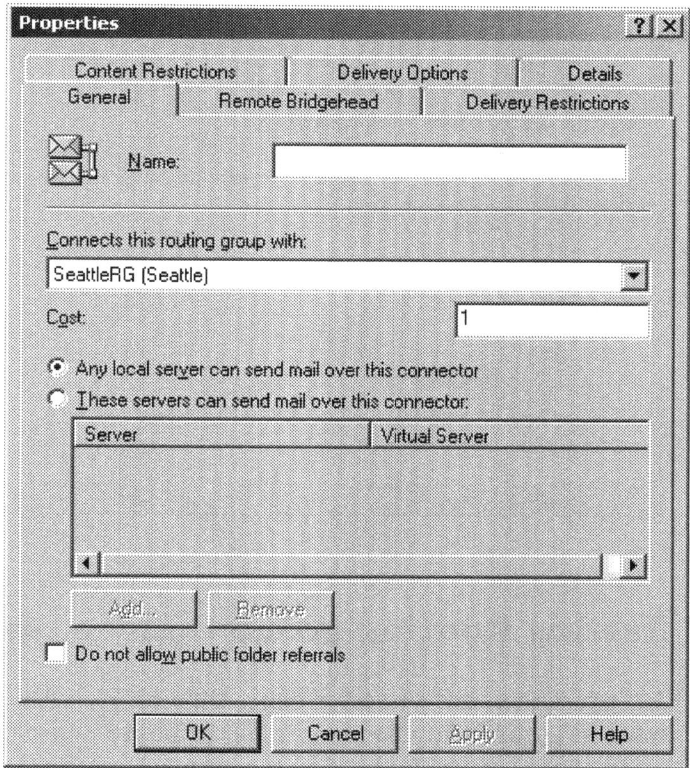

Figure 22.1 *Installing a new routing-group connector.*

- Specify a local bridgehead server by selecting "These servers can send mail over this connector," clicking Add, and selecting the default SMTP virtual server on Box14 (more on virtual servers in Chapter 23).
- Switch to the Remote Bridgehead tab, click Add, and select the default virtual server on Box16 in the SeattleRG as the remote bridgehead server.

Click OK to install the new connector. A dialog box appears asking you if you want to create the routing-group connector in the remote routing group—click Yes to complete the installation of both ends of the connector. Our new routing-group connector should be visible in the Connectors container under VancouverRG and SeattleRG in System Manager (Figure 22.2).

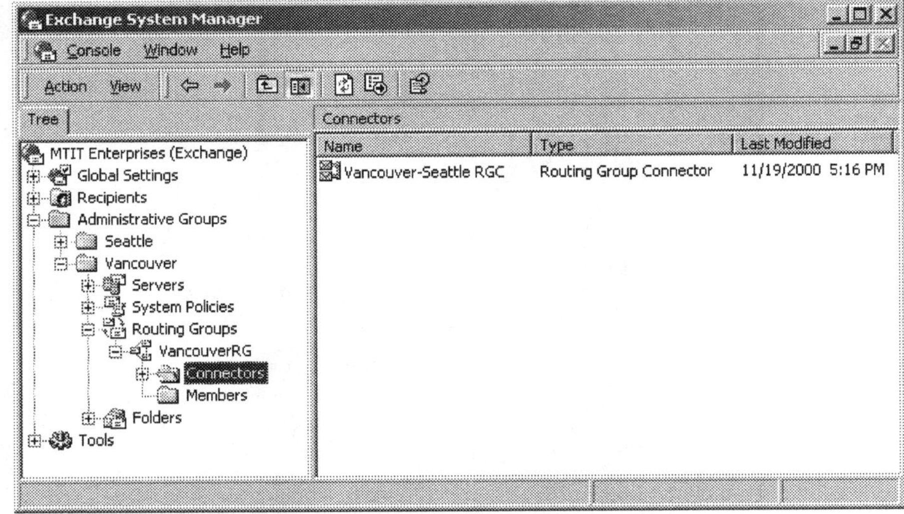

Figure 22.2 The new routing-group connector between the VancouverRG and SeattleRG routing groups.

Testing Routing-group Connectors

Walkthrough

Let's test the new connector using Outlook Web Access (OWA) with the method outlined in Chapter 21. Go to Box16, start OWA, and open the mailbox for seauser@mtit.com, a user whose mailbox is located on Box16 in Seattle, by opening the URL http://localhost/exchange/seauser.

Enter the credentials for seauser to log on to the mailbox. Now create a new one-off test message addressed to vanuser@mtit.com, a user whose mailbox is located on Box14 in Vancouver. Send the message. When we tried this in Chapter 21, our test message bounced because we had no connector configured between the two routing groups. Click Refresh on the browser, and there should be no NDR at this point.

Now move to Box14 in Vancouver and open the mailbox for vanuser@mtit.com by opening the URL http://localhost/exchange/vanuser.

Enter the credentials for vanuser to log on to the mailbox. The one-off message from seauser should be present in the inbox, indicating that the new routing-group connector works as expected. Reply to the message to make sure it works both ways.

Configuring Common Settings for Connectors

Walkthrough

All Exchange 2000 routing connectors have a number of settings that can be configured. There are two types:

- *Common settings*. These settings are common to all routing connectors including routing-group connectors, SMTP connectors, and X400 connectors.
- *Specific settings*. These settings are specific for each type of connector.

Let's look at the various common settings for connectors by using our new routing-group connector as an example. Select the Connectors container under VancouverRG, right-click on the Vancouver-Seattle RGC in the details pane, and select Properties to open the connector's Properties Sheet. The common settings for all routing connectors include:

- *Designating local bridgehead servers (General tab)*. This setting specifies the local bridgehead server (the server in the local routing group through which the connector routes messages to other routing groups). See the General tab of Figure 22.1 in the routing-group connector as an example.

TIP

The routing-group connector and SMTP connector support multiple local bridgehead servers for load-balancing and fault-tolerance features, whereas the X400 connector allows only one local bridgehead server. To load balance X400 messaging, you need to install many X400 connectors.

NOTE

All three routing connectors let you designate local bridgehead servers, but only the routing-group connector and X400 connector make use of remote bridgehead servers. SMTP connectors use smart hosts or RNS MX records for locating remote mail servers. Furthermore, whereas the routing-group connector allows you to designate multiple remote bridgehead servers, the X400 connector lets you specify only a single remote bridgehead server.

- *Designating routing cost (General tab)*. The cost setting is an important one and is used to control the way messages are routed between different routing groups in a large organization. If you have multiple connectors with different assigned cost values that are linking the same routing groups together, message delivery is first attempted using the connector with the lowest cost (if this fails, then the connector with the next lowest cost is tried, and so on). In this fashion, using multiple connectors with different cost values provides a way of configuring redundancy in messaging connections between routing groups. In contrast, if multiple connectors having the same cost values are used to link routing groups together, messaging is load balanced over the connectors. The default cost value is 1 and the maximum value is 100 (Figure 22.1).

- *Allowing public-folder referrals (General tab).* Allowing public-folder referrals lets users located on servers in the remote routing group to access public folders hosted on servers in the local routing group. This setting is enabled by default, but you may want to disable it because configuring public-folder replication between routing groups is a more efficient method in that it allows users in the remote routing group to access replicas of public folders locally.
- *Delivery Restrictions tab.* This tab is used to specify recipients that the connector will accept or reject (Figure 22.3). Accepted messages will be routed by the connector, and rejected messages will be returned to the sender with an NDR. By default, there are no delivery restrictions configured for the connector. Click either Add button to select mail-enabled recipients from Active Directory that you want to have the connector accept or reject messages from.
- Content Restrictions tab. This tab is used to specify what types of messages are accepted for routing by the connector (Figure 22.4) according to the following criteria:
  - Message priority (high, medium, or low)
  - Message type (system or nonsystem)
  - Message size (specifies limit in kilobytes)

By default, no content restrictions are configured for a new connector.

Configuring Routing-group Connectors

Walkthrough

The only settings specific to the routing-group connector are those on the Delivery Options tab (Figure 22.5). These settings allow you to specify a schedule for when the connector will attempt delivery of outbound messages queued for delivery.

The first setting on this tab lets you schedule specific times:

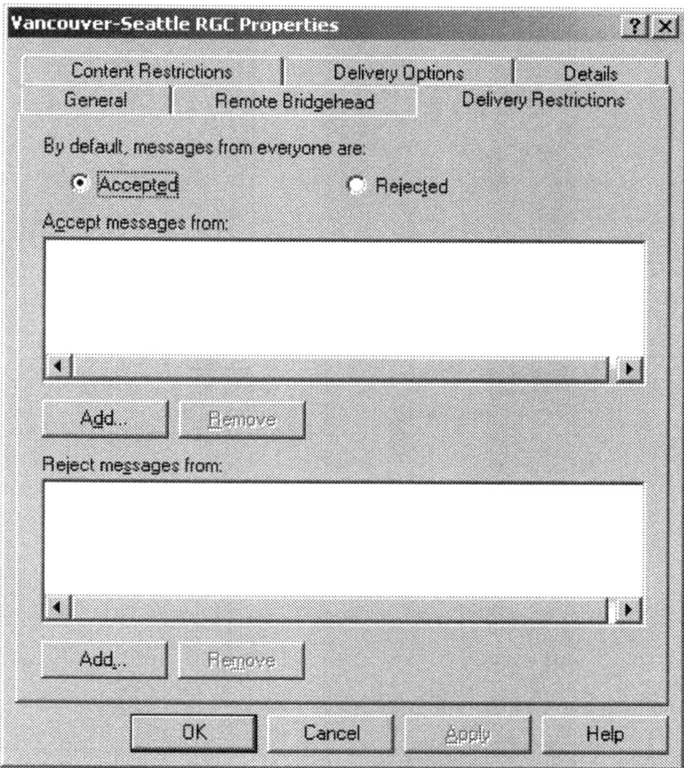

Figure 22.3 Configuring delivery restrictions for a connector.

- Always run (default)
- Run daily at 11:00 PM
- Run daily at midnight
- Run daily at 1:00 AM
- Run daily at 2:00 AM
- Run every hour
- Run every 2 hours
- Run every 4 hours
- Never run
- Use custom schedule

Some of the many scenarios where you might use these different settings are:

- *Always run*. You might use this setting when the network connection between routing groups is permanent and reliable and message delivery is a high priority for your enterprise.

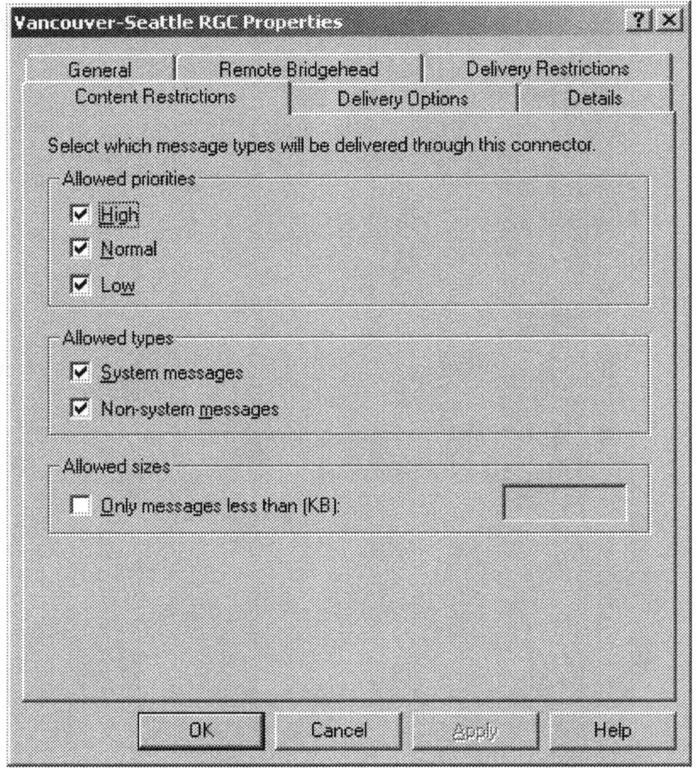

Figure 22.4 Configuring content restrictions for a connector.

- *Run every 2 hours.* You might use this setting if message delivery is not such a high priority.
- *Run daily at 2:00* AM. You might use this setting if the connector primarily replicates public-folder information that is updated infrequently.
- *Never run.* This setting disables the connector, which you might do if you planned maintenance on your server.

The other setting on this tab lets you configure a separate schedule for routing of large messages. For example, if your available bandwidth is limited then you might configure messages larger than 1,000 KB to be routed by the connector at midnight when normal message traffic is low. The possible settings are the same as those described above.

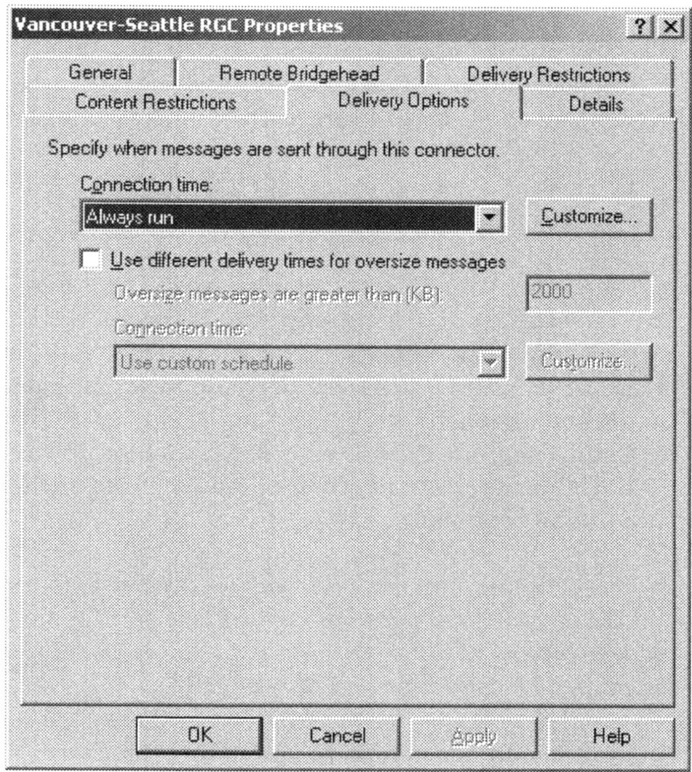

Figure 22.5 Configuring delivery options for a routing-group connector.

Removing Routing-group Connectors

Before removing a routing-group connector, you should disable it by setting the Connection Time property on the Delivery Options tab to Never Run. Then simply right-click on the connector in System Manager and select Delete from the shortcut menu.

SMTP Connectors

The second type of routing connector is the SMTP connector. Like the routing-group connector, it uses SMTP as its underlying message transport mechanism. However, the SMTP connector has additional features that enable it to be used in more scenarios. These additional features include:

- Authentication of connections
- Encryption of message traffic
- Support for ESTMP extensions
- Routing using smart hosts or DNS mail exchange (MX) records

Because of their complexity (and flexibility), SMTP connectors can be used in the following scenarios:

- Connecting two different routing groups together
- Connecting a routing group with a downlevel Exchange 5.5 site on which IMS is installed
- Connecting two different Exchange organizations (two different forests) together
- Connecting an Exchange organization to the Internet's system of SMTP hosts, including non-Microsoft hosts such as UNIX machines running Sendmail

NOTE

Whereas routing-group connectors use SMTP or RPC for transport, depending on whether the organization is running in native or mixed mode, SMTP connectors use only SMTP.

Let's install and configure an SMTP connector between our two routing groups. Along the way, we'll introduce various concepts and terminology relating to these connectors.

Installing SMTP Connectors

Walkthrough

Open System Manager on Box14 and navigate in the console tree to the Connectors container beneath the VancouverRG routing group (Figure 22.2). Right-click on Connectors and select New → SMTP Connector to open a blank Properties Sheet for the new connector (Figure 22.6).

On the General tab, type the name "Vancouver-Seattle SMTP" as the name for your new connector. Then click Add and specify the default SMTP virtual server on the local machine (Box14) as the connector's local bridgehead server.

While on the General tab, you need to decide whether your SMTP connector will route messages using DNS MX records or a smart host:

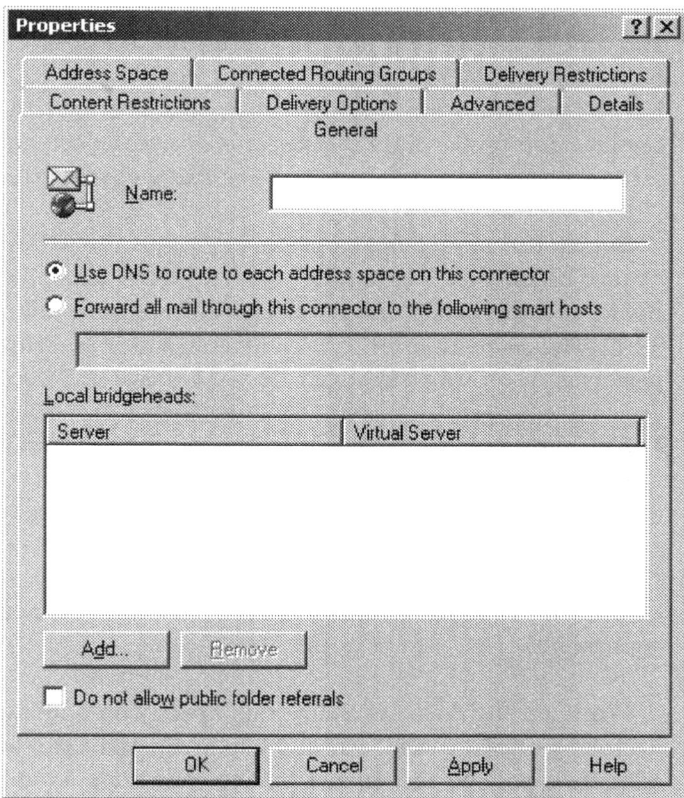

Figure 22.6 Installing a new SMTP connector.

- A *smart host* is an SMTP mail server (Exchange or otherwise) to which the connector forwards all messages that it receives for routing. The smart host then determines how to route the messages further. You can specify the smart host with a name like smart.mtit.com or as an IP address enclosed in square brackets, for example, [172.16.11.22]. If you select the IP option, the connector forwards all messages to the smart host regardless of their addresses.
- DNS *mail exchanger* (MX) records are special resource records in the DNS database that point to one or more SMTP servers in a non-Exchange mail system like the Internet. If you select this option, the connector does a DNS lookup on the domain portion of the SMTP email address for each message routed through it.

TIP

You can also specify a smart host on the Delivery tab of the Properties Sheet for an SMTP virtual server (see Chapter 23 for information on Exchange virtual servers). However, whatever setting you specify on the General tab of the SMTP connector overrides the setting for the SMTP virtual server configured as the local bridgehead server.

Select the smart host option and type the IP address of Box16 in square brackets, for example, [172.16.11.16]. Then switch to the Address Space tab to specify the connector's scope and address spaces (Figure 22.7). The scope of an SMTP connector specifies what role the connector performs in routing messages. There are two possible settings:

- *Entire organization.* Select this setting if you plan to use the connector to establish messaging connectivity between two different Exchange organizations (Windows 2000 forests) or between on Exchange organization and the Internet's SMTP mail system.
- *Routing group.* Select this setting if you plan to use the connector to join two routing groups together (choose this setting for our walk-through).

While on the Address Space tab, specify an address space for the connector by clicking Add. An address space indicates what types of email addresses will be recognized by the connector as valid for routing purposes. When the connector receives a message, it compares the address to which the message is targeted with each address space listed here; if a match is found, the message is routed to its destination. By default, when you try to add a new address space, one type of SMTP will be created, but you can also specify a different address type for the address space if necessary.

Select SMTP as the type of address space and click OK. This opens the Internet Address Space Properties Sheet where you specify the details of the address space (Figure 22.8). By default, the suggested address space is indicated as an asterisk, which represents a wildcard and means that this connector can be used to route messages to any SMTP domain. This is fine if you plan to use the connector to link your organization with the Internet's collection of (mainly) Sendmail hosts. But if you want to restrict the connector to routing messages only within a particular SMTP domain such as mtit.com, you can specify the address space as mtit.com. Accept the default (asterisk) address space by clicking OK.

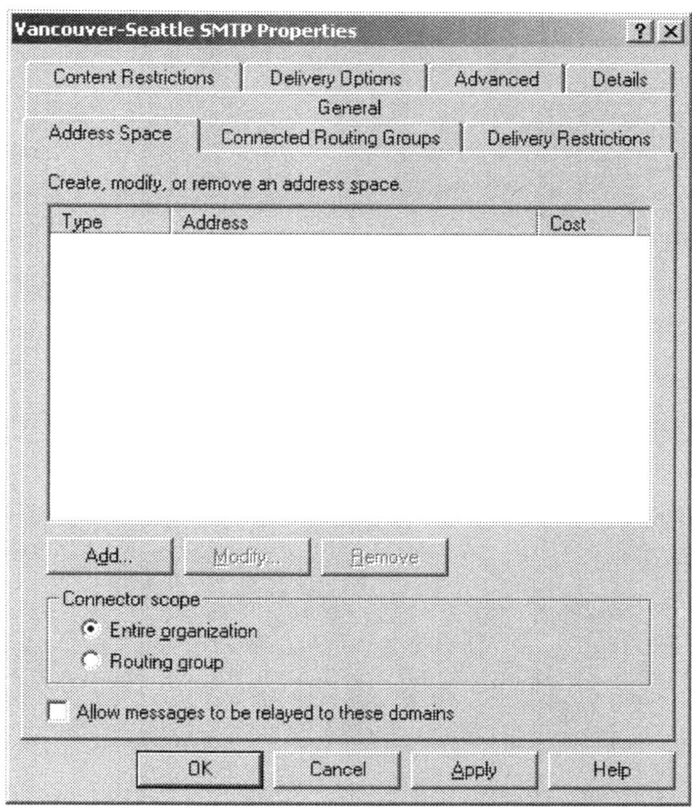

Figure 22.7 Specifying connector scope and address space.

NOTE

You can also specify a cost for your address space. Costs range from 1 to 100, and a lower cost indicates higher priority for routing through the connector. Like the routing-group connector, you can use such costs to add fault tolerance and load balancing to an organization with multiple SMTP connectors.

While on the Address Space tab, you can select "Allow message to be relayed by these domains" if you want to allow the connector to be used to relay messages to domains in the remote routing group. This setting should generally not be enabled if the connector is used to route messages to the Internet because it leaves your server open to propagate "unsolicited commercial email," in other words "spam." Leave it unselected.

Because we're using this SMTP connector to link together the VancouverRG and SeattleRG routing groups, switch to the Connected Routing Groups tab. Click Add to display a list of remote routing groups in

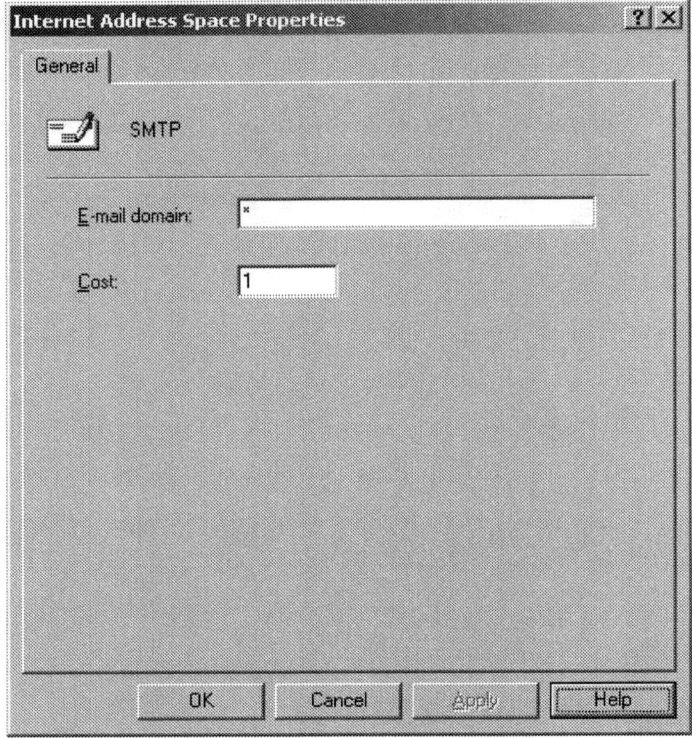

Figure 22.8
An address space for an SMTP connector used to route email to the Internet.

your organization, select the SeattleRG routing group within the Seattle administrative group (displayed here as Seattle/SeattleRG), and switch to the Routing Address tab to view the address space that will be created (Figure 22.9). This address space indicates that the connector can forward messages addressed to any recipient in the organization but not to external recipients belonging to domains other than mtit.com.

Those are the main options to configure when creating the connector. We'll look at the remaining ones in the next walkthrough. Click OK twice to create the new SMTP connector.

NOTE

Installing an SMTP connector in the local routing group to link with a remote routing group is only half the job—you also need to create a similar connector in the remote routing group. Go ahead and complete this process by installing a similar SMTP connector in the SeattleRG routing group to link with the VancouverRG routing group and then test messaging connectivity between these groups (make sure you have disabled the routing-group connectors in both groups if you have not already done so).

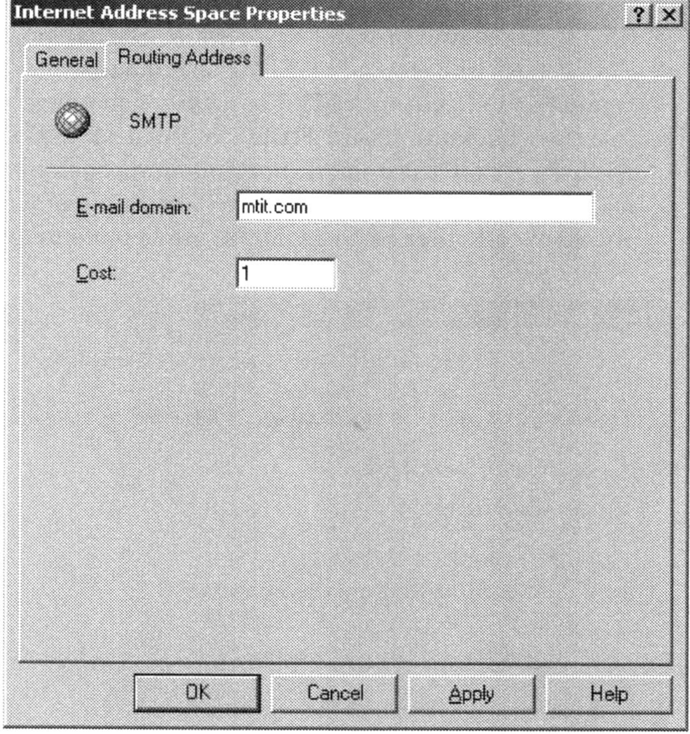

Figure 22.9 Address space for an SMTP connector used to route messages between two routing groups in the mtit.com forest.

Configuring SMTP Connectors

Further configuration of the SMTP connector can be done by opening its Properties Sheet in System Manager. We've already covered the Delivery Restrictions and Content Restrictions tabs common to all routing connectors in a previous walkthrough, so let's look at what's new here:

- *Delivery Options tab*. This tab lets you specify the times when the connector should route messages and is similar to the Delivery Options tab for the routing-group connector except for the additional option "Queue mail for remote triggered delivery," which lets you queue messages for delivery on a per-user basis instead of scheduling the connector for operation. Forwarding of queued messages for the user is then triggered using TURN/ATRN commands when the user logs on and starts the SMTP mail client (if this option is supported).
- *Advanced tab*. This tab is used mainly to specify whether the remote SMTP host supports ESMTP or SMTP (Figure 22.10). ESMTP stands

for extensions to SMTP and adds additional features to the original SMTP messaging protocol. By default, Exchange assumes the remote SMTP host understands ESTMP commands and so sends an EHLO command to begin an SMTP session for message transfer. By selecting the checkbox "Send HELO instead of EHLO," you are telling Exchange that the remote host understands only basic SMTP commands and not ESTMP extended commands. When you select this checkbox, all other settings on the tab become unavailable.

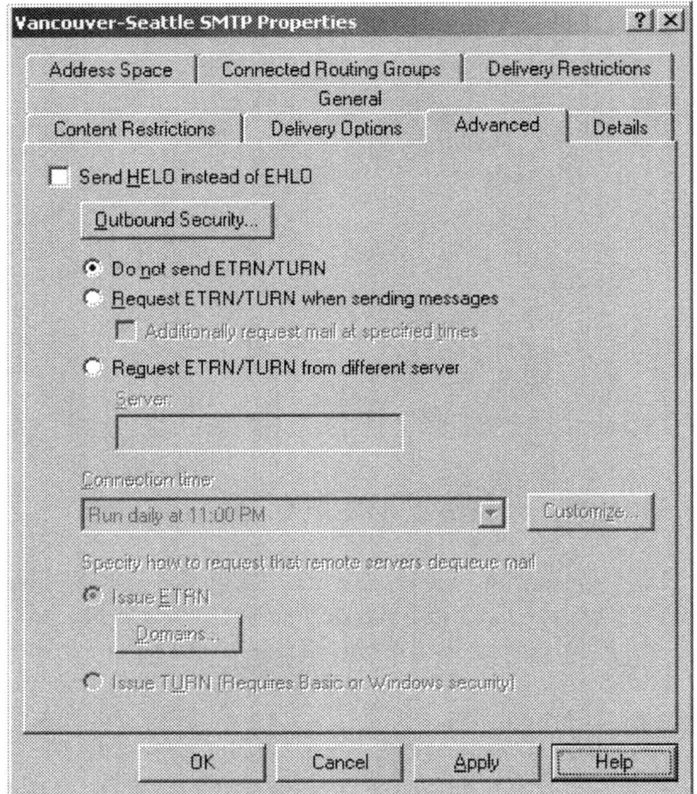

Figure 22.10 Advanced tab for SMTP connector.

If the remote (non-Exchange) messaging system is an older one, it may not support ESTMP. If your connector performs poorly or not at all, try selecting the checkbox.

- *Outbound Security (from Advanced tab).* The Outbound Security dialog box is used to configure authentication for the SMTP connector

(Figure 22.11). By default, SMTP connectors are configured to use Anonymous Access, meaning that they do not authenticate the connection with the remote SMTP host or domain. If you want to have your connector authenticate the connection, you can choose one of these authentication methods:

- *Basic authentication*. This method of authentication transmits credentials as clear text and is supported by virtually all types of SMTP hosts including UNIX Sendmail hosts. Click Modify and enter the name and password of the computer account of the remote host.
- *Integrated Windows Authentication*. This method of authentication is the preferred method when the remote SMTP host belongs to a Microsoft Windows domain.
- *TLS Encryption*. Select this checkbox to enable Transport Layer Security (TLS) authentication with either Basic or Integrated authentication selected. TLS is a variant of SSL.

Figure 22.11 Configuring outbound security for an SMTP connector.

X400 Connectors

We'll close this chapter by briefly considering the X400 connector. X400 connectors are used primarily for connecting with foreign X400 messaging systems, which are, to most intents and purposes, a dying breed.

BACKGROUNDER

X400 Connectors in Exchange 5.5

Enterprises that have implemented Exchange 5.5 sometimes use X400 connectors instead of site connectors for linking remote sites together to establish messaging connectivity. One reason for doing this is that the X400 connector performs somewhat better under low available bandwidth conditions than the site connector, primarily because attachments for X400 messages are more efficiently coded than those for SMTP. Another reason is that the site connector cannot be scheduled for operation, whereas the X400 connector can. Further, the X400 MTA recovers more gracefully from disconnections resulting from network problems than other connectors do, but this is not a major reason for using this connector in Exchange 2000.

When an Exchange 5.5 organization is migrated to Exchange 2000, site connectors become routing-group connectors and X400 connectors remain essentially as they are. Because routing-group connectors can be scheduled for operation in contrast to site connectors, there's not much reason to keep X400 connectors once you have completed the migration and they can usually be replaced with routing-group or SMTP connectors. The only possible reason for maintaining them is if bandwidth between routing groups is low; in that case, an SMTP connector will probably perform even better. Studies have indicated that the SMTP connector can perform more than 300% better than the X400 connector except in situations where available network bandwidth falls below 9.6 Kbp or the latency of WAN links is high. The real solution is to upgrade your WAN hardware and services to a faster, more reliable connection than to try to manage the situation by configuring X400 connectors!

Installing and configuring X400 connectors is a complicated task. For a start, there are two different kinds of X400 connectors, depending on the underlying network transport:

- *TCP X400 connector*. This type uses TCP/IP as its underlying network transport and is the most common type of X400 connector.
- *X25 X400 connector*. This type uses X25 as its underlying transport and is provided only for legacy use because X25 public-data networks are a dying breed.

Before you install an X400 connector, you must install and configure a corresponding X400 transport stack that matches the type used by the connector. Multiple X400 connectors can then make use of each stack for transporting messages. You also need to configure the X400 MTA which is configured using the X400 container's Properties Sheet under the Protocols container for each Exchange server in System Manager.

All this work just to save a few bytes of bandwidth! The X400 connector is really included with Exchange 2000 for legacy reasons and will probably vanish with the next release of Exchange, so we won't consider it further.

NOTE

If you're interested you can find a full explanation of X400 concepts and terminology in my earlier book, Administering Exchange Server *(McGraw-Hill). Much of what applies to the X400 connector for Exchange 5.5 applies also to that in Exchange 2000, except that the new version no longer supports the legacy TP4 network protocol.*

Summary

In Chapters 21 and 22, we looked at routing groups and how to establish messaging connectivity between them using different connectors. In Chapter 23, we'll focus on the concept of the virtual server and discuss its importance in Exchange 2000.

CHAPTER 23

Virtual Servers

This chapter deals with the concept of virtual servers and how they are implemented in Exchange. We'll see how to create and configure virtual servers and perform various administrative tasks regarding them, with an emphasis on SMTP virtual servers. We'll also examine the front-end and back-end architecture supported by Exchange and how this can benefit large enterprises that require scalable, reliable messaging services.

There are eight walkthroughs in this chapter:

- Starting, stopping, and pausing virtual servers
- Specifying a unique identity for a virtual server
- Controlling inbound connections for virtual servers
- Creating a new virtual server
- Display current sessions for a virtual server
- Terminating current sessions for a virtual server
- Configuring the default SMTP virtual server
- Configuring a front-end server

Virtual Servers

A virtual server is a service that appears to clients as a physically separate server. In other words, one physical (real) server can host multiple virtual servers. Each virtual server has its own set of settings that can be configured, and each server can be managed separately. For example, you could stop one virtual server and leave the other virtual servers on the same machine running.

Types of Virtual Servers

Exchange supports five different types of virtual servers: SMTP, POP3, IMAP4, NNTP, and HTTP. In other words, a single machine running Exchange could host one SMTP virtual server, three HTTP virtual servers, two POP3 virtual servers, and so on, but this is seldom necessary.

Exchange and Internet Protocols

Exchange supports five major Internet protocols that run on the application layer of the TCP/IP protocol suite:

Simple Mail Transport Protocol (SMTP). *This is the native protocol used for submission and transport of mail throughout an Exchange organization. Clients such as Outlook Express (or Outlook configured in Internet-only mode of operation) submit their outbound messages to Exchange using SMTP, and Exchange routes (forwards) these messages to their destinations using SMTP. The SMTP protocol is also the standard for mail transport on the Internet. In other words, SMTP servers (or SMTP hosts on UNIX machines running Sendmail) receive outbound mail from clients sending messages and forward these messages to their destinations, usually a POP3 or IMAP4 server.*

Post Office Protocol 3 (POP3). *This is a standard Internet protocol used by Exchange and on the Internet to provide clients with access to incoming mail. POP3 servers receive mail addressed to users, and the users then download their mail using clients, such as Outlook Express, which support the POP3 protocol.*

Internet Message Access Protocol 4 (IMAP4). *This is a standard Internet protocol used by Exchange and on the Internet to provide clients with access to incoming mail. IMAP4 is more recent and includes greater functionality than POP3. For example, IMAP4 clients can read their message headers and then decide which messages they want to download; POP3 clients always download all messages and their headers.*

Network News Transport Protocol (NNTP). *This is a standard Internet protocol used mainly by USENET, a system of newsgroups replicated across the Internet where users can hold discussions.*

Hypertext Transfer Protocol (HTTP). *This is the standard Internet protocol of the World Wide Web. It is also the protocol governing access to Exchange using Web browsers such as Internet Explorer using the Outlook Web Access (OWA) feature of Exchange.*

Virtual Server Identities

Each virtual server running on a specific machine running Exchange must have its own unique identity for client applications to access resources (mailboxes and public folders). The identity of a virtual server usually consists of two parts: an IP address and a TCP port. Each virtual server on an Exchange server must have a unique combination of these two settings.

For example, the default TCP port for SMTP is 25 and the one for HTTP is 80. If the IP address of your Exchange server is 172.16.11.14, then the identity of the default SMTP virtual server is [172.16.11.14:25] that of the default HTTP virtual server is [172.16.11.14:80].

As another example, you could have two HTTP virtual servers running on a single machine, one using the default TCP port 80 and the other enabled for SSL and using the default port 443. Both virtual servers could have the same or different IP addresses—it doesn't matter because they already have distinct TCP ports and therefore unique identities.

NOTE

HTTP virtual servers actually have three parts to their identities: IP address, TCP port, and optional host header name. For more information on host header names, see Administering IIS5 *by Mitch Tulloch and Patrick Santry (McGraw-Hill).*

TIP

If you want to assign different IP addresses to virtual servers on one machine, you'll have to add additional IP addresses on the appropriate connection of your machine. A machine that has many IP addresses assigned to one adapter or connection is called multihomed.

Table 23.1 shows the default TCP port settings for the standard Internet protocols supported by Exchange in SSL and non-SSL configurations.

TABLE 23.1 Default TCP ports (standard and secure) for Internet protocols.

Protocol	Standard port	Secure port
SMTP	25	
POP3	110	995
IMAP4	143	993
NNTP	119	563
HTTP	80	443

Default Virtual Servers

When you install Exchange on a machine, a default virtual server of each type is created and configured. You can reconfigure these virtual servers and create additional ones.

Advantages of Virtual Servers

Why create additional virtual servers on a machine running Exchange? Most of the time you won't need to, but there are certain scenarios where it might be advantageous:

- You might have two different groups of users in your company, each with their own set of security needs, yet only one machine running Exchange. You can set up separate virtual servers for each group of users and configure security settings differently for each virtual server. For example, one group might use OWA to access the company Exchange server from remote locations using the Internet; in this case, you might want to configure their HTTP virtual server to authenticate and encrypt messaging using SSL. Users inside the company who use OWA don't require the extra overhead associated with SSL and can use a virtual server for which SSL is not enabled.
- You might want to use one machine running Exchange to support messaging for two distinct companies. In this case, separate SMTP and POP3 virtual servers could be created and configured on the machine to keep messaging separate for each company. Don't forget that, in this scenario, clients for employees from each company must be configured to point to their appropriate virtual server.

Less Is More

When you install Exchange, five default virtual servers one for each Internet protocol are automatically created, configured, and started. There are times when you may want to disable some of these virtual servers so that you only have a few or perhaps one virtual server running on any given machine running Exchange. For example:

- You could designate one Exchange server as your company's SMTP server for routing outbound mail and another as your IMAP4 or POP3 server for inbound mail. Make sure you configure the MX record in your DNS server's database to point to your SMTP server.
- Taking things a step further, in a large organization you can build fault tolerance into your messaging system by using several machines as SMTP servers. In this case, you need to create an MX record for each server and assign each a priority. If one server goes offline, outbound mail is still routed successfully.

Managing Virtual Servers

The administrative tasks you can perform on Exchange virtual servers depend to some extent on the protocol supported by the server. However, there are several tasks common to all virtual servers on Exchange:

- Starting, stopping, and pausing virtual servers
- Specifying a unique identity for a virtual server
- Controlling inbound connections for virtual servers

We'll now do some walkthroughs for these tasks and use the default virtual servers on Box14 in the Vancouver administrative group of our testbed deployment. Begin by opening System Manager on Box14 and navigating through the console tree: Organization (root) node → Administrative Groups → Vancouver → Servers → Box14 → Protocols (Figure 23.1).

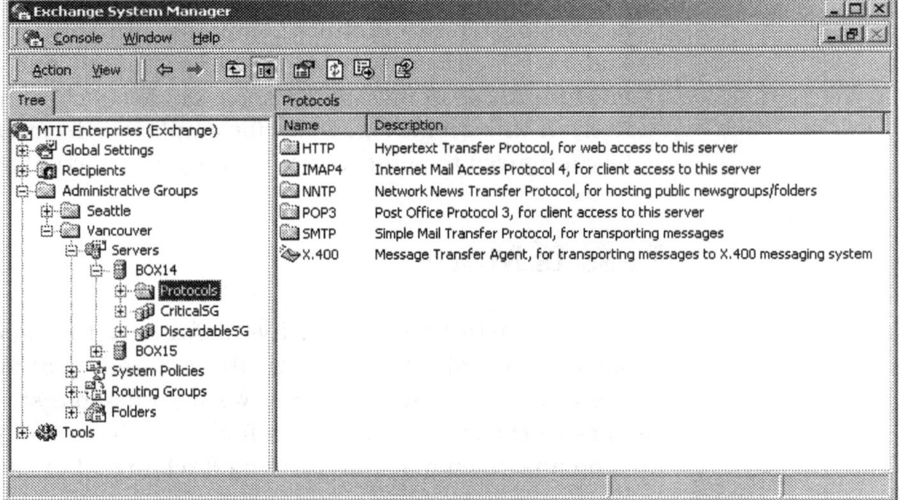

Figure 23.1 The Protocols container for Box14 in Vancouver.

The Protocols container for each Exchange server in System Manager contains nodes for each of the five types of virtual server that Exchange can host. Each of these five nodes (HTTP, IMAP4, NNTP, POP3, and SMTP) is actually a container itself and holds the default virtual server of that type plus any additional virtual servers created for it. These five containers have no configurable settings—you configure the virtual servers within them independently of one another.

NOTE

There is a sixth node in the Protocols container, namely the X400 node. This node represents the Exchange MTA, which is similar to the X400-based MTA in Exchange 5.5 and is used for message transfer and routing in mixed-mode deployments of Exchange when interoperability between Exchange 2000 and Exchange 5.5 is required. The MTA is also used when X400 connectors are installed for connectivity between an Exchange organization and a foreign X400 messaging system. The MTA settings, which are accessed by opening the Properties Sheet for the X400 node, are used to specify credentials for authenticating with X400-based messaging systems, convert X400-formatted messages to format compatible with MAPI clients, and specify connection retry values and message reliability values. For more information on X400 concepts and operation, see my earlier book, Administering Exchange Server *(McGraw-Hill).*

Stopping, Starting, and Pausing Virtual Servers

Walkthrough

Virtual servers can be stopped, started, paused, and resumed like actual servers. For example, to stop and then restart the default IMAP virtual server, right-click on the IMAP4 container under the Protocols container in System Manager and select Stop or click the Stop button on the toolbar. Stopping the default IMAP virtual server has no effect on the state of operation of any other virtual server on the machine, including other IMAP4 virtual servers (if you had created some). To restart, right-click on the virtual server and select Restart.

TIP

If you want to change the configuration settings on a virtual server, you can pause instead of stop it. Pausing the virtual server prevents any new connections from being formed with client applications but doesn't terminate the sessions of clients that are currently connected. Stopping a virtual server prevents new connections from being formed and terminates any existing connections, which might result in connected users losing work.

NOTE

If you have more than one virtual server of the same type on a machine, you can stop or start all of them simultaneously by using the Services console in Administrative Tools. For example, stopping the SMTP service will stop all SMTP virtual servers on the machine. You can also stop all *virtual servers of a given type by stopping the Microsoft Exchange IMAP4 service, the Microsoft Exchange POP3 service, or the World Wide Web Publishing service using the Services console.*

Specifying a Unique Identity for a Virtual Server

Walkthrough

As mentioned earlier, each virtual server, regardless of type, on any machine running Exchange needs to have a unique identity. This identity usually consists of an IP address and a TCP port.

Let's examine the identity of the default IMAP4 virtual server we worked with in the previous walkthrough. Right-click on the Default IMAP4 Virtual Server node under the IMAP4 container and select Properties. This opens the Default IMAP4 Virtual Server Properties Sheet, where the virtual server's current identity is displayed on the General tab (Figure 23.2).

Figure 23.2
Identity of the default IMAP4 virtual server.

Default IMAP4 Virtual Server Properties
General | Access | Message Format
Default IMAP4 Virtual Server
IP address:
(All Unassigned)
Advanced...
Limit number of connections to:
Connection time-out (minutes):
30
Include all public folders when a folder list is requested
Enable fast message retrieval
OK
Cancel
Apply
Help

The IP address is currently displayed as All Unassigned. This setting means that the virtual server will respond on all IP addresses that are currently unassigned to other IMAP4 virtual servers. For example, if we had five different IP addresses bound to the network adapter on the machine and a custom IMAP4 virtual server assigned one of these IP addresses, the default IMAP virtual server would respond to client requests for any of the four other addresses.

Box14 is currently multihomed and has two IP addresses assigned to its adapter, namely 172.16.11.14 and 172.16.11.24 (if your server only has one address, then add another using Local Area Connection in Network and Dialup Connections in Control Panel). Let's assign this IP address the identity of the default IMAP4 virtual server. Click the drop-down arrow at the right of the IP Address listbox shown in Figure 23.2 and select 172.16.11.14 as the IP address for the virtual server.

By default, the TCP port for all IMAP4 virtual servers is set to the well-known port 143 (or 993 if SSL is enabled). To view this, click the Advanced button on the General tab to display the dialog box (Figure 23.3). By clicking Edit, you can change the TCP port or SSL port for the virtual server or select another IP address.

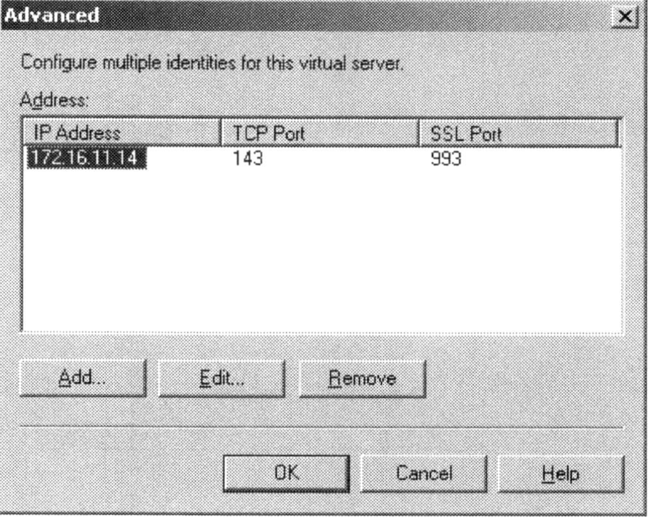

Figure 23.3 Advanced identity settings for default IMAP4 virtual server.

Controlling Inbound Connections for Virtual Servers

Common to the administration of SMTP, POP3, and IMAP4 virtual servers is the ability to control incoming connections to those virtual servers. Let's look at the four methods with which this can be done by examining the default IMAP4 virtual server further. The first three methods are configured by using the buttons on the Access tab of the Properties Sheet for these virtual servers (Figure 23.4), and the fourth uses the settings on the General tab (Figure 23.2).

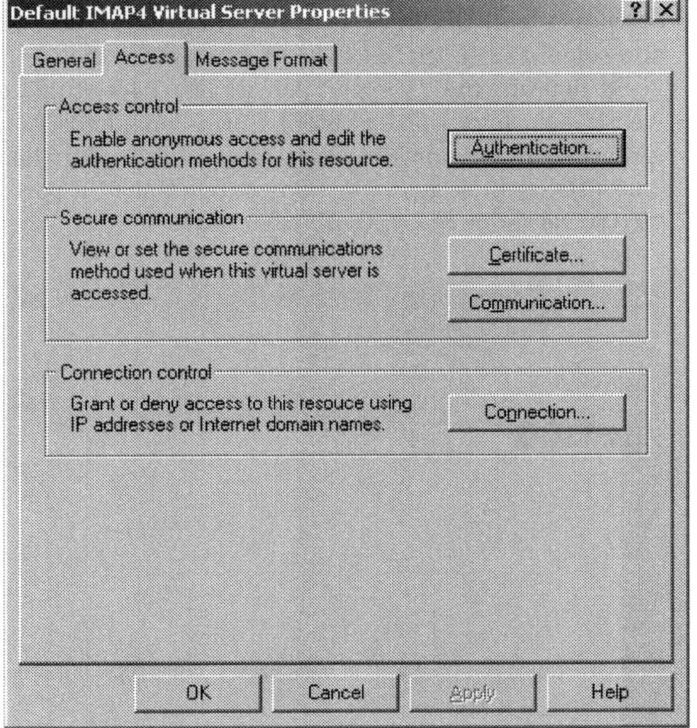

Figure 23.4 Access tab on the Properties Sheet for the default IMAP4 virtual server.

- *Access control.* This method allows you to control access to the virtual server by requiring that incoming connections be properly authenticated. You configure this setting using the Access Control button on the Access tab of the Properties Sheet for the virtual server. There are three possible authentication methods:

- *Anonymous access*. All incoming connections are accepted as authenticated; that is, no authentication of connections occurs. Only SMTP virtual servers support this form of authentication and it is enabled by default.
- *Basic authentication*. Connections are authenticated by using a username and password that are passed across the connection in clear text and therefore not secure. Virtual servers for three protocols (SMTP, POP3, and IMAP4) support this form of authentication and it is enabled by default. SMTP takes it a step further by allowing basic authentication sessions to be encrypted using TLS encryption, a variant of SSL.
- *Integrated Windows authentication*. The logon credentials of the currently logged-on user are used for authentication purposes, and the credentials are hashed during transmission to ensure their security. Virtual servers for these three protocols support this form of authentication and it is enabled by default.

TIP

You might consider disabling basic authentication to ensure greater security by forcing integrated Windows authentication to authenticate incoming connections, but this might not work because integrated Windows authentication normally doesn't work through a corporate firewall if it proxies connection requests. Furthermore, for Exchange servers used internally, you may want to disable anonymous access for SMTP virtual servers for greater security, but bridgehead servers connected to the Internet most likely require that anonymous access be enabled for SMTP to allow the servers to communicate with other SMTP hosts on the Internet.

- *Secure communication*. This method allows you to configure secure communications for your virtual server using X509 certificates on the Certificate and Communication buttons on the Access tab. This subject is beyond the scope of this book.
- *Connection control*. This method allows you to grant or deny access to the virtual server for individual IP addresses, subnets of IP addresses, or DNS domain names. To access this setting, open the Properties Sheet for the virtual server, switch to the Access tab, and click the Connection button to open the Connection dialog box (Figure 23.5). You can grant access to all clients except those with specific IP or DNS restrictions or deny access to all clients and allow access on a case-by-case basis. By default, all IP addresses and domains are allowed access to the virtual server.

Connection control is particularly useful for preventing unsolicited commercial email (spam). If you determine the IP address of the client sending the unwanted messages, deny that address access to your virtual server.

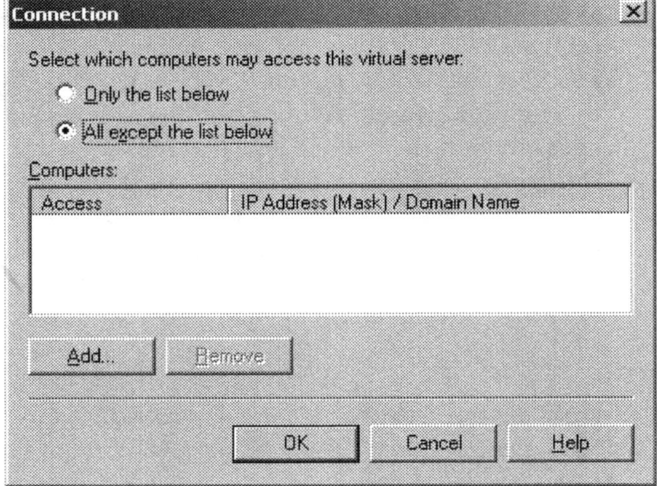

Figure 23.5 Controlling access to a virtual server by IP address or DNS domain.

It's generally best not to deny access on the basis of DNS domain name because Exchange must perform a reverse DNS lookup on every connection attempt to determine whether the connection should be allowed, and this can quickly consume your server resources and affect your server's performance.

- *Connection limits and time-outs*. This method lets you limit the number of simultaneous incoming connections that the virtual server will support and the amount of idle time before a connection is automatically terminated. You configure these settings using the General tab of the virtual server's Properties Sheet.

If clients inform you that they have been disconnected while downloading messages with large attachments, you may need to increase the time-out value for POP3 or IMAP4 virtual servers.

Creating a New Virtual Server

Walkthrough

Let's create an additional IMAP4 virtual server on Box14 as an example. Right-click the IMAP4 container under the Protocols container for Box14 and select New → IMAP4 Virtual Server. This starts the New IMAP4 Virtual Server Wizard (Figure 23.6).

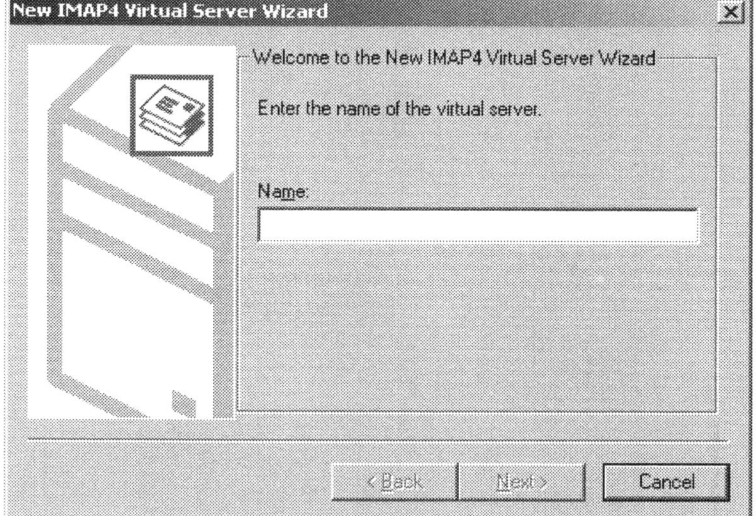

Figure 23.6 Creating a new IMAP4 virtual server.

Name the new virtual server "Alternate IMAP4 Virtual Server" and click Next. Select the IP address 172.16.11.24 from the dropdown listbox and click Finish. The new virtual server appears in the IMAP4 container in System Manager.

We now have two IMAP4 virtual servers on Box14, the default with IP address 172.16.11.14 and the alternate with address 172.16.11.24. Both virtual servers use the standard IMAP4 TCP port 143. We'll test our setup by using Outlook Express (OE) on Box16, which we configured in a previous walkthrough. Log on to Box16 as Administrator, start OE, and select Tools → Accounts to open the Internet Accounts box. Select the Mail tab and open the Properties Sheet for the default mail account. Then switch to the Servers tab on this Properties Sheet to view the current configuration of the account (Figure 23.7).

On the Servers tab, the incoming mail server is an IMAP4 server and this IMAP4 server is specified as box14.mtit.com. Let's skip the DNS configuration of these virtual servers, which would involve creating resource records for our new virtual server on the DNS server, and simply change the specified IMAP4 server to 172.16.11.14, the IP address of the default IMAP4 virtual server (enter 172.16.11.14 in the Incoming Mail field). Click OK and then close and you will be prompted to refresh the folder list. Click Yes and the folder list will be downloaded, after which your mail folders and all public folders should be displayed as expected in the folder tree window of OE.

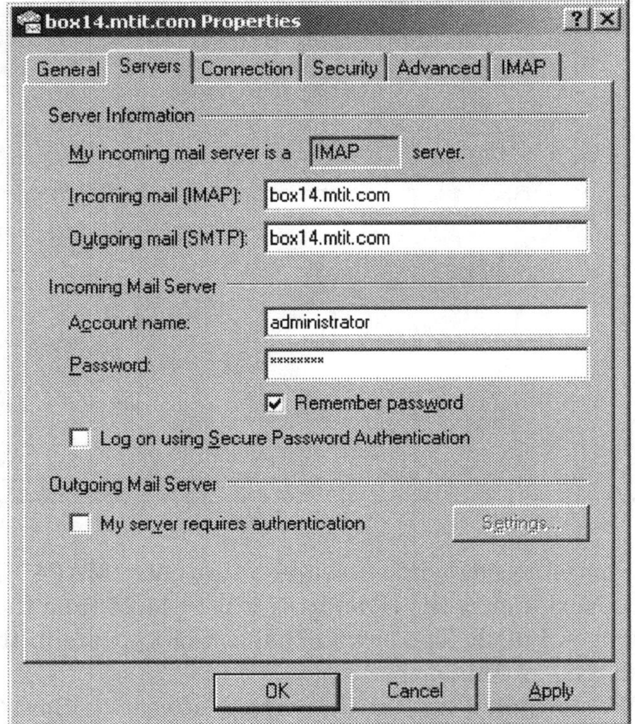

Figure 23.7 Servers tab of mail account for Outlook Express.

Open the Servers tab again for the mail account and this time specify 172.16.11.24 as the IP address for the Incoming Mail (IMAP4) server. Click OK, then Close, then Yes, and the folder information should download as expected. We can see that we can access our mailbox on Box14 using our IMAP4 client (OE) through any virtual server configured on Box14.

Now go to Box14 and stop the alternate IMAP4 virtual server (the one whose IP address is 172.16.11.24) in System Manager. Return to OE on Box16 and select Tools → IMAP Folders from the menu to display the Show/Hide IMAP Folders box. Click the Reset List button to refresh the list of IMAP folders. An error should appear saying "The server has refused the connection." Close and then open OE again on Box16. A series of error messages should be displayed when you restart the client, indicating that it could not access its mail folders on Box14 using IMAP.

Close OE on Box16 and restart the alternate IMAP4 virtual server on Box14 to finish the exercise.

Display Current Sessions for a Virtual Server

Walkthrough

Let's play with our alternate IMAP4 virtual server a little more. Our OE client on Box16 is still configured to use 172.16.11.24 as its IMAP server. Start OE on Box16 again. Now switch to Box14 and select the Current Sessions node under Alternate IMAP4 Virtual Server in System Manager (Figure 23.8).

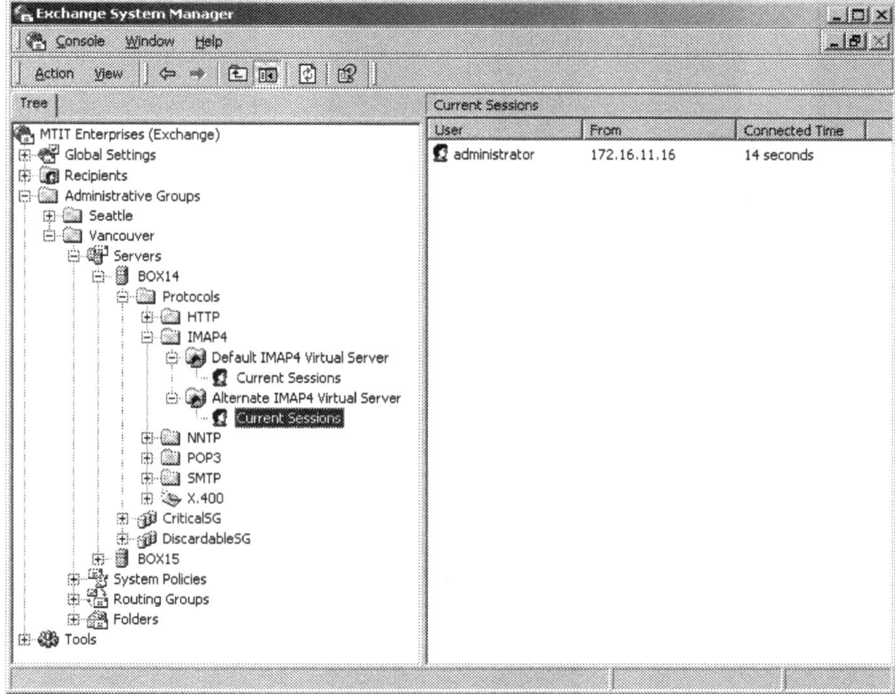

Figure 23.8 Displaying current sessions for a virtual server.

In the Details pane, we see that user Administrator is currently connected to the alternate IMAP4 virtual server on Box14, that this user is running the IMAP4 client program on the machine with IP address 172.16.11.16, and that the user has been connected to the virtual server for at least 14 seconds (click **F5** to refresh the System Manager console).

Terminating Current Sessions for a Virtual Server

Walkthrough

What if you decide that user Administrator is unauthorized to connect to alternate IMAP4 virtual server on Box14? Right-click on the user in the Details pane of System Manager and select Terminate to end the user's session. The session disappears from the Details pane. Go back to Box16 where OE is still running and select Tools → IMAP4 Folders. The folder list is downloaded successfully, and clicking F5 in System Manager on Box14 shows that a new session has been created for the user. This simply shows that terminating the user was a "soft," not a "hard," action; that is, the user is disconnected but can reconnect if there are no other restrictions.

TIP

You can also terminate all user sessions for a virtual server, but this is not recommended except in an emergency because users may lose their work.

Default SMTP Virtual Server

Let's examine one particular virtual server in more detail, namely the default SMTP virtual server. This virtual server is particularly important because SMTP is the underlying message delivery mechanism in Exchange and the message transport mechanism for the Internet. We won't cover it in exhaustive detail but simply point out some highlights of its configuration.

NOTE

You can create additional SMTP virtual servers on an Exchange server, but in most cases this will not be required unless you are hosting multiple domains on a single Exchange server, an advanced topic that is beyond the scope of this book.

Configuring the Default SMTP Virtual Server

Walkthrough

Open System Manager on Box14 and select the SMTP container under the Protocols container for Box14. This displays a node representing the Default SMTP virtual server in the Details pane. Open the Properties Sheet for this virtual server. Let's examine some of these settings:

- *General tab.* We've covered IP address, connection limit, and connection time-out settings earlier in this chapter. The only new setting concerns protocol logging for the virtual server, which we'll discuss in Chapter 24.
- *Access tab.* We've covered the first three portions of this tab earlier in this chapter. The only new thing here is Relay Restrictions, which lets you control whether the virtual server can be used by external mail systems to relay messages to third parties. Click the Relay button to display the Relay Restrictions box (Figure 23.9). By default, mail relaying is disabled except for remote servers that successfully authenticate with your server. You can grant or deny relaying to all remote hosts and then deny or grant this privilege according to IP address, subnet, or DNS domain.

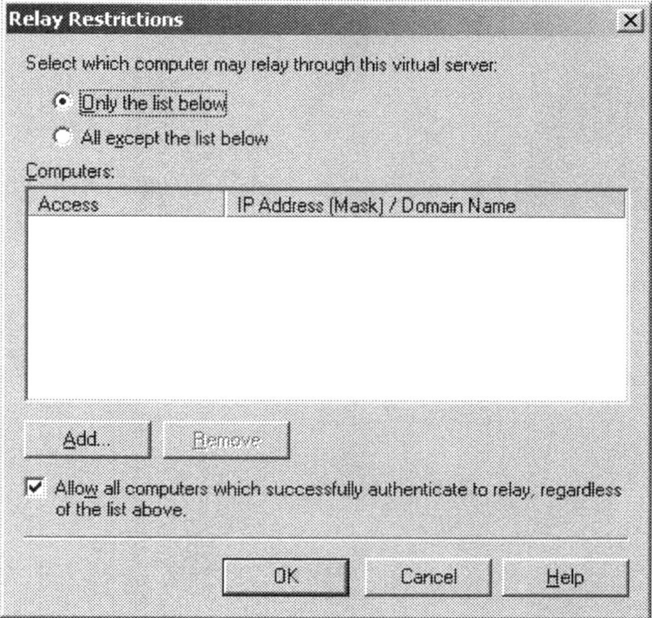

Figure 23.9 Configuring relay restrictions for an SMTP virtual server.

- *Messages tab.* You can specify maximum message size, maximum session size, maximum number of messages per session, and maximum number of recipients per message for all messages and sessions handled by this virtual server (Figure 23.10). You can also specify how undeliverable mail is handled by sending copies of all NDRs to a specified email address (usually an administrator or the postmaster account for the organization), a Badmail directory where undeliverable messages are placed when the NDRs they generate can't reach the sender (for example, when spammers generate messages with phony IP addresses), and you can forward all incoming mail with unresolved recipients to another mail server in your organization that can handle it.

NOTE

Message size limits configured here apply to incoming mail only.

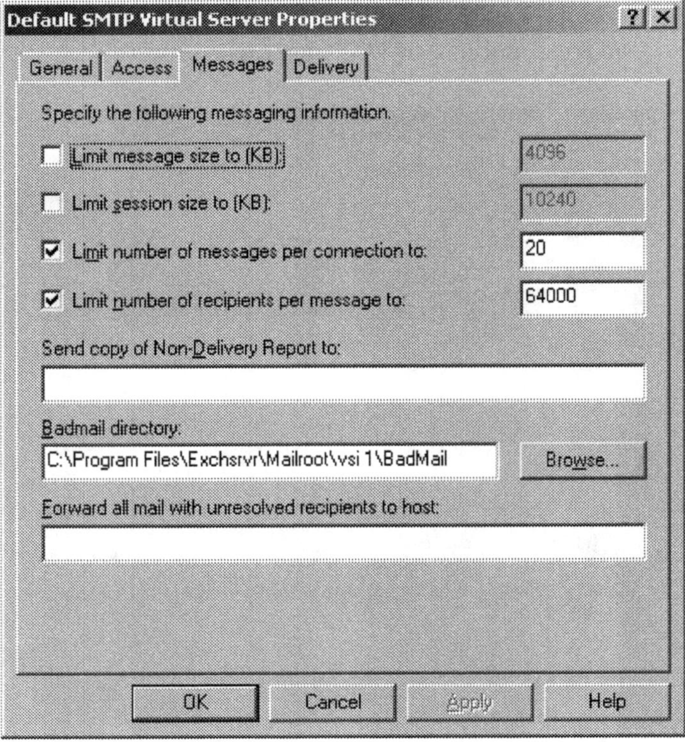

Figure 23.10 Configuring message limits and handling of undeliverable mail for a SNTP virtual server.

TIP

Make sure the Limit Session Size setting is at least several times larger than the Limit Message Size setting.

TIP

Remember that message size limits can be configured at other levels besides that of a specific SMTP virtual server. For example, you can use the Exchange General tab on a user's Properties Sheet in Active Directory, Users and Computers, to configure this setting for an individual user's mailbox. Or you can configure this setting for all users in the entire organization by using the Message Delivery node under Global Settings under the Organization (root) node in System Manager.

- *Delivery tab*. This tab (Figure 23.11) lets you configure retry intervals for outbound mail, delay notification for local and outbound mail, expiration time-out for local and outbound mail, outbound security settings for routing mail to remote SMTP hosts (anonymous access is the only method that is enabled by default), limits for outbound connections (number of connections and time-out values for idle connections), maximum hop count for outbound messages (so that messages caught in routing loops won't loop around forever), a masquerade domain (replaces the actual domain in the Mail From lines of the header of outbound messages), the fully qualified domain name (FQDN) of the SMTP virtual server (which should be used in MX records on DNS servers), a smart host (to forward all outbound mail for further handling), enable DNS reverse lookups on incoming messages (bad idea), specify a list of DNS servers to be used by the virtual server for resolving domains in recipient email addresses, and other settings. A full discussion of these various settings is beyond the scope of this introductory book, but the default settings will work in most cases for simpler Exchange deployments. Here are a few tips:
  - If users complain of too many NDRs, try increasing the Hop count (click Advanced, as shown in Figure 23.11). Before you do this use the `tracert` and `pathping` commands to test the network connection between your local servers and the remote servers from which NDRs are being generated (in case the NDRs are being caused by flaky routers along the way).
  - Configure only basic or integrated Windows Authentication for a virtual server if it delivers all email to a specific server in a different domain. Otherwise, leave outbound security set at anonymous access.

– If your WAN connection is unreliable, try increasing the time-out value for idle outbound connections (click Outbound Connections as shown in Figure 23.11) to increase the probability of successful delivery.

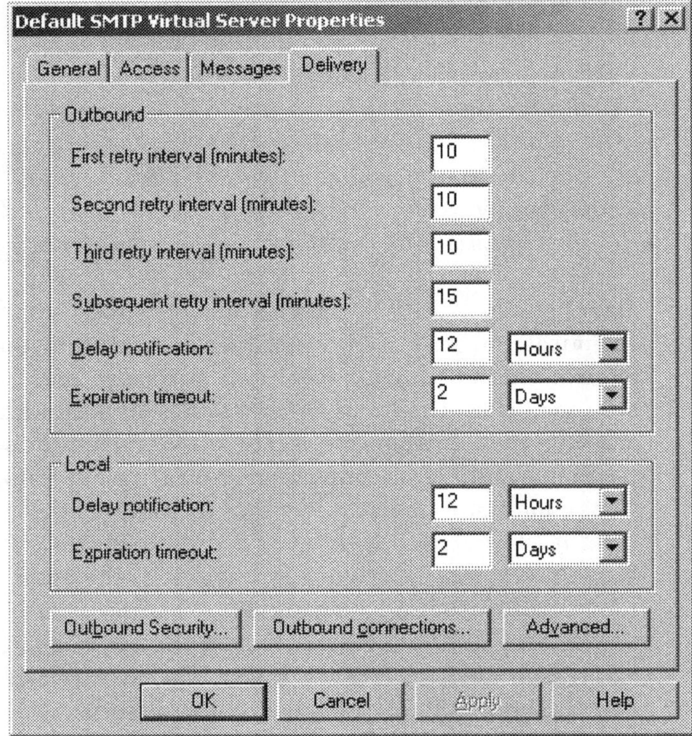

Figure 23.11 Configuring delivery settings for an SMTP virtual server.

NOTE

You can configure SMTP policies that apply globally to all SMTP virtual servers in your organization by right-clicking on Internet Message Formats under Global Settings in System Manager and selecting New → Domain. Give your policy a name, specify the SMTP domain for outgoing mail to which the policy applies, and configure message format and other settings for the policy. The default SMTP policy applies to all domains and is represented by an asterisk (*) in the Details pane when Internet Message Formats is selected in the console tree. This default policy is usually sufficient, can be configured as desired, and applies to all SMTP virtual servers in the organization.

Front-end and Back-end Servers

We'll end this chapter with a brief look at the front-end and back-end architecture that can be implemented using Exchange 2000. This new architecture allows Exchange deployments to scale virtually unlimited numbers of users.

The architecture assigns Exchange servers to two separate groups:

- A group of *front-end servers* that receive all incoming requests for connections from clients. These servers do not host mailboxes or public folders. Instead, when a client attempts a connection to access a mailbox, the front-end server uses LDAP to query Active Directory for the name of the back-end server on which the client's mailbox is located and then proxies (forwards) the connection request to the appropriate back-end server.
- A group of *back-end servers* that host all mailboxes and public folders for an organization. Clients cannot connect directly with these back-end servers; they must use front-end servers as proxies.

UNDER THE HOOD

Exchange and IIS

I haven't explained how Exchange supports virtual servers and front-end/back-end architecture. In Exchange 2000, the message store and protocol engine are separated from one another. Specifically, the SMTP, POP3, IMAP4, NNTP, and HTTP protocols are now handled exclusively by Internet Information Services (IIS) instead of Exchange. IIS has supported virtual servers for several versions, and this feature is available in Exchange 2000. Further, the front-end/back-end architecture for Exchange is enabled by front-end servers running IIS but having no message stores and back-end servers hosting message stores but not running IIS.

Advantages of Using a Front-end/Back-end Architecture

The advantages of using the front-end/back-end architecture apply mainly to environments where OWA is the messaging client:

- The architecture is extremely scalable. For example, if users have trouble connecting to their mailboxes because of too many connections on the front-end servers, simply add another front-end server to handle the load.

- Front-end servers can provide public-folder referrals for IMAP clients, thereby simplifying the process of accessing public folders in a large organization.
- Front-end servers can present a single namespace to clients, allowing all clients to access Exchange resources using a single URL. Changes made at the back end (such as moving mailboxes between servers) have no effect on how clients connect to their mailboxes.
- If SSL is being used to secure messaging communications, all encryption and decryption is performed by front-end servers, freeing back-end servers from some of the load.
- To protect user data even further, front-end servers can be placed beyond the firewall in the DMZ and back-end servers are kept safely behind the firewall.

Configuring a Front-end Server

Walkthrough

Designating an Exchange server as a front-end server is fairly straightforward (but see below). As an example, we'll designate Box16 as a front-end server. Open System Manager, right-click on the node representing Box16, and select Properties. Select the checkbox labeled "This is a front-end server" (Figure 23.12). Click OK and reboot the server. That's it. Now you need to configure your OWA clients to connect to the front-end server to access their mailboxes and all public folders. I'll leave it to you, the reader, to devise a test to prove that Box16 is now a front-end server.

Of course, things are never that simple. The actual procedure for implementing this architecture in an Exchange deployment is more like this:

1. Install your back-end servers first and create storage groups, data stores, mailboxes, and public folders on them.
2. Install the Network Load Balancing component on the Windows 2000 servers you plan to use as front-end servers (recommended).
3. Now install Exchange on your soon-to-be front-end servers. Dismount all mailbox and public stores on these servers and remove them. Designate them as front-end servers using the procedure in the walkthrough above and then reboot them.
4. Configure your DNS servers with resource records for your front-end servers.

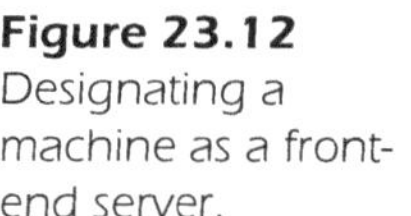

Figure 23.12 *Designating a machine as a front-end server.*

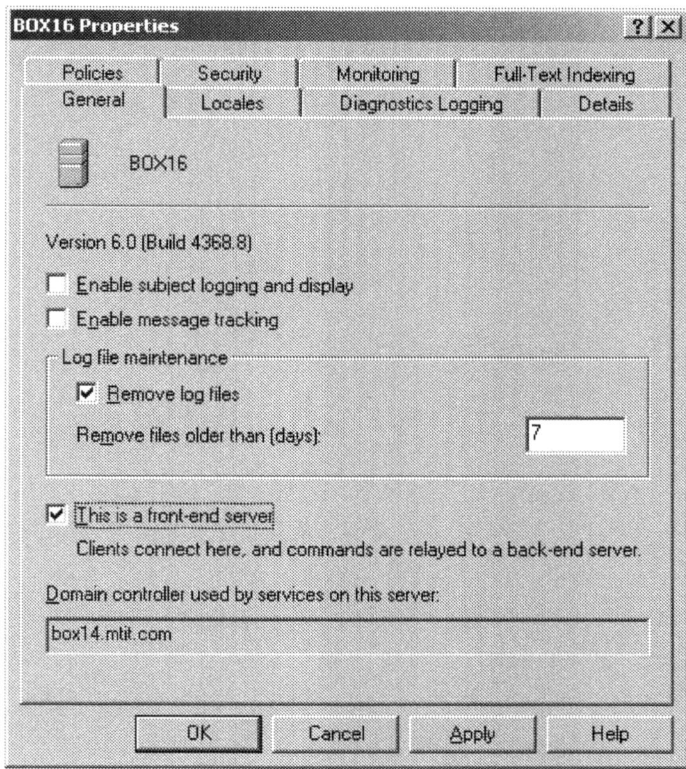

We won't go into detail about such planning issues in this book. A recommended book for a fuller treatment of this topic is *Exchange 2000 Server Resource Kit* (Microsoft Press).

Summary

So far, we've covered many of the tasks relating to day-to-day administration of Exchange 2000. Chapter 24 covers monitoring and maintaining Exchange servers, an essential part of an administrator's job.

CHAPTER 24

Monitoring and Maintenance

This chapter covers monitoring and maintaining Exchange servers with respect to monitors, notifications, logging, message tracking, queues, and disaster recovery. All of these tasks are important for the day-to-day operations of an Exchange organization, and many of them can be used in troubleshooting situations when problems arise.

There are eight walkthroughs in this chapter:

- Viewing server and connector status
- Enabling and configuring monitors
- Enabling and configuring notifications
- Enabling and configuring protocol logging
- Enabling and configuring diagnostic logging
- Enabling and configuring message tracking
- Managing SMTP queues
- Backing up Exchange

Monitoring Exchange

Exchange 2000 includes a number of features and tools for monitoring the health of an Exchange organization and troubleshooting problems when issues arise. In this section, we'll discuss:

- *Server and connector status*. With System Manager you can view the current status of Exchange servers and connectors in your organization.
- *Monitors*. You can enable and configure monitors to show CPU utilization, free disk space, virtual memory availability, Windows 2000 and Exchange services, and other resources.
- *Notifications*. You can enable and configure scripts to run or email notifications to be sent to administrators when issues arise with servers or connectors.
- *Protocol logging*. You can enable and configure logging of SMTP, NNTP, and HTTP services to troubleshoot issues relating to these protocols.
- *Diagnostic logging*. You can enable and configure different levels of diagnostic logging to troubleshoot issues relating to Exchange services.
- *Message tracking*. You can use the Message Tracking Center to track the flow of messages into and through your organization when problems arise or for collecting usage information.

- *Queues.* You can monitor message queues and manipulate messages in these queues, including deleting messages and freezing queues.

We'll examine each of these monitoring and troubleshooting techniques and learn how to back up and restore Exchange in preparation for disaster recovery. To begin, let's look at how to view the current status of an Exchange server or connector using System Manager.

Viewing Server and Connector Status

Walkthrough

You can use System Manager to view the current status of any Exchange server or connector in your organization. Start System Manager and navigate through the console tree: Organization (root) node → Tools → Monitoring and Status → Status. When the Status container is selected in the left pane, the status of your servers and connectors is displayed in the right pane (Figure 24.1).

Figure 24.1 Viewing the status of servers and connectors.

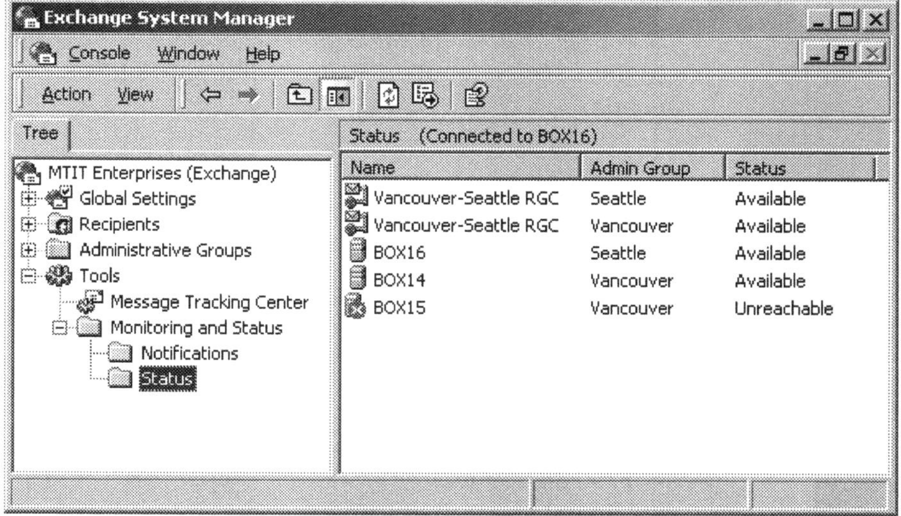

Exchange regularly polls servers throughout the organization and displays their current status in that pane. Possible values for the Status field include:

- *Available.* The server is available on the network and its Exchange services are running properly.

- *Critical: Service not running.* The server is available on the network but one or more of its core Exchange services is not running.
- *Unreachable.* The remote server is down or disconnected from the network.

Special icons next to the name of the server or connector are also used to convey information concerning their status:

- *Red "X".* This indicates that a server or connector is in critical state or unreachable. It is also used to indicate that a monitor configured on the server has reached critical condition (Exchange monitors are discussed later in this chapter).
- *Yellow "!".* This indicates that a monitor configured on the server has reached warning condition.

TIP

If you double-click on a server in the Status container, a Properties Sheet opens, displaying the status of resources being monitored on the server. This Properties Sheet is the same as the Monitors tab on the Properties Sheet for a server in the Servers container of an administrative group in System Manager. We'll look at this again when we consider Exchange monitors.

Monitors

Exchange monitors (or any monitor) provide a way of automatically monitoring the condition of services and system resources on Exchange servers. You can set up monitors to watch:

- CPU utilization
- Free disk space
- Virtual memory usage
- Exchange and Windows 2000 services
- Message queues

Monitors can be configured, enabled, disabled, and removed. When you configure a monitor, you specify a warning or critical level (or both) for some resource. The following conditions can result when these levels are exceeded:

- *Warning condition.* This indicates that a specified threshold has been crossed in the usage of some resource, and you should address the issue as soon as possible.
- *Critical condition.* This indicates that an even higher threshold has been crossed in the usage of the resource, and performance of the server is likely to be severely affected until the situation is corrected. Administrators can specify what they think are suitable warning and critical levels for triggering monitors.

When a warning or critical condition occurs, the appropriate icon (red "X" or yellow "!") appears next to the server's icon in the Status container. You may also configure notifications to indicate what action (sending a message or running a script) should be taken when a monitor reaches warning or critical condition (notifications are discussed in a later section).

NOTE

When configuring monitors, make sure that you specify a higher threshold for critical conditions than for warning conditions.

You can also perform the following administrative tasks using the Status container under the Monitoring and Status container under the Tools container in System Manager:

- Right-clicking on Status container → Connect To lets you select which Exchange server in your organization will display information about monitors.
- Right-clicking on Status container → Custom Filter lets you specify which servers and connectors should be displayed in the Status container, which is useful in a large organization with many servers.

Enabling and Configuring Monitors

Walkthrough

Let's set up some monitors on Box16, our Exchange server in Seattle. Navigate in the console tree of System Manager: Organization (root) node → Administrative Groups → Seattle → Servers → Box16. Open the Properties Sheet for Box16 and switch to the Monitoring tab (Figure 24.2).

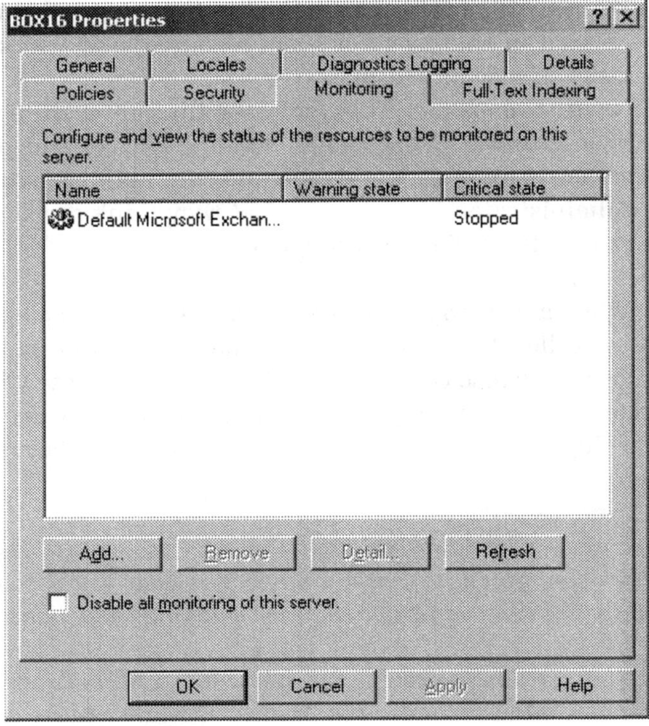

Figure 24.2 Monitoring tab on a server's Properties Sheet.

By default, when you install Exchange, a monitor called Default Microsoft Exchange Services is automatically configured and enabled. This monitors a number of core Microsoft Exchange services:

- Microsoft Exchange Information Store
- Microsoft Exchange MTA Stacks
- Microsoft Exchange Routing Engine
- Microsoft Exchange System Attendant
- Simple Mail Transport Protocol (SMTP)
- World Wide Web Publishing Service

Once the monitor is configured, its state changes to critical condition if any of these services stops running, which causes the red "X" to appear on the server's icon in the Status container.

Let's create a new monitor for CPU utilization on Box16. Click Add (Figure 24.2) to display a dialog box showing a list of resources that can be monitored (Figure 24.3). We need to monitor these resources and suggested threshold values because:

- *Available virtual memory.* If virtual memory becomes low, then system performance degrades and processing of messages suffers. If this situation becomes critical, you need to increase available virtual memory or (preferably) add more RAM. Suggested choices of threshold values are 10 percent available virtual memory for warning state and 5 percent for critical state. You can also specify the number of minutes during which a threshold value is exceeded before triggering the monitor.
- *CPU utilization.* If your CPU utilization becomes too high then message processing will suffer. Also, CPU utilization near 100 percent for an extended period may indicate hardware or driver problems that need to be addressed. Suggested choices of threshold values are 95 percent utilization for warning state and 100 percent for critical state. You can also specify the number of minutes during which a threshold value is exceeded before triggering the monitor.
- *Free disk space.* Exchange needs sufficient disk space for its databases, transaction logs, and other log files. If disk space runs low, then Exchange services may stop and data may be lost, so be sure to configure monitors to watch this resource. Suggested choices of threshold values are 100 MB free disk space for warning state and 25 MB for critical state. You must also specify which logical drive is monitored (create multiple monitors for multiple drives, in particular for the C: drive, where the Exchange system files are located and the M: drive, where IFS is installed).
- *SMTP queue growth.* If the number of messages in SMTP queues is continuously increasing, a connector or network link may have failed. Use this monitor to watch this resource. Suggested choices of threshold values are 10 minutes of continuous queue growth for warning state and 20 minutes for critical state.
- *Windows 2000 service.* You can monitor the condition (running or stopped) of any Windows 2000 service on the server including Exchange services. The entire group of services specified for any given monitor can trigger the monitor into warning or critical state when one or more of these services stops running. You can create multiple service monitors for different groups of services and give each monitor a unique name.
- *X400 queue growth.* A steady increase in the number of messages in a queue may indicate a connector or network link failure. Suggested choices of threshold values are 10 minutes of continuous queue growth for warning state and 20 minutes for critical state.

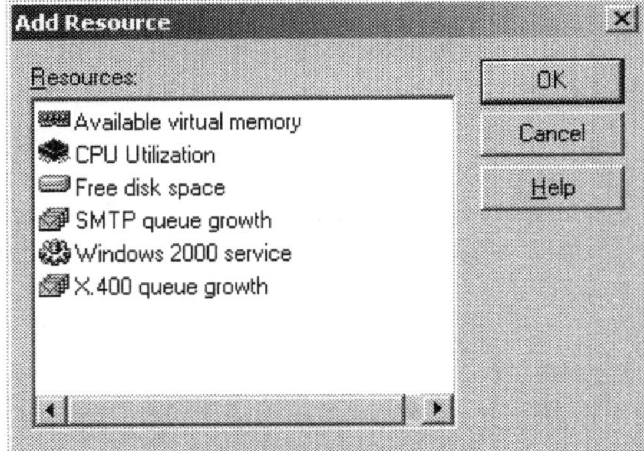

Figure 24.3 Resources that can be monitored on Exchange.

Select CPU Utilization from the dialog box and click OK. This opens the CPU Utilization Thresholds dialog box (Figure 24.4). Enter 5 minutes as the duration that will trigger the monitor when a threshold is exceeded. Select Warning state and specify 95 percent, and then select Critical state and specify 100 percent. Click OK to create the new monitor and return to the Monitoring tab of the server's Properties Sheet.

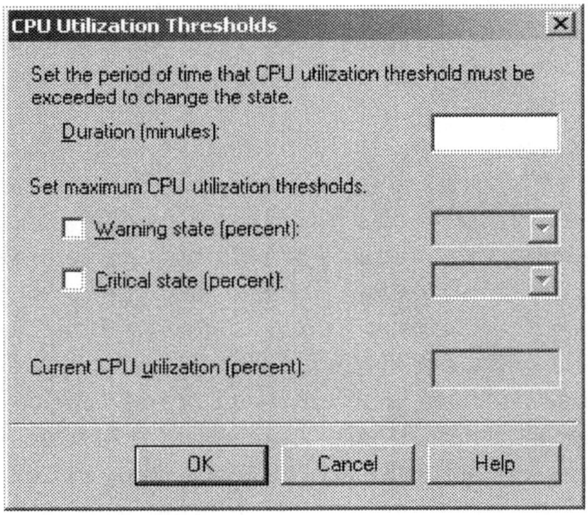

Figure 24.4 Creating a new CPU utilization monitor.

On the Monitoring tab, select the CPU Threshold monitor you created and click the Details button and view the current CPU utilization for the server. Close the dialog box. Experiment by adding monitors and creating conditions that will trigger them.

NOTE

The checkbox "Disable all monitoring of this server" at the bottom of the Monitoring tab can be used to turn off monitoring for a server so that you can bring the server down for repairs or maintenance without generating endless notifications of problems.

TIP

If you have several monitors configured for one server and the icon representing the server in the Status container displays a problem (warning or critical) symbol, double-click on that server in the Status container to display the Monitoring Properties Sheet. This sheet will list the different monitors configured for that server and will display the appropriate problem symbol beside the triggered monitor.

Notifications

When a monitor triggers a problem, a symbol (red "X" or yellow "!") appears beside the server's icon in the Status container (under Tools → Monitoring and Status) in System Manager. Of course, you don't want to watch this container continuously for signs of problems with your Exchange servers! Instead, configure the notifications to alert you when a problem occurs or take some immediate action to correct the issue. Exchange lets you configure two different types of notification:

- *Email*. A message is sent to an administrator when the monitor enters warning or critical state. Once the administrator receives the message and becomes aware of the problem, corrective action can be taken.
- *Script*. A script is run when the monitor enters warning or critical state. For example, you could run a script to reboot the server when CPU utilization reaches a critical value of 100 percent for a certain period.

Enabling and Configuring Notifications

Walkthrough

Let's create a new email notification for the monitors we created on Box16. Select the Notifications container under the Monitoring and Status container under Tools in System Manager. Right-click the Notifications container and select E-mail Notification to open a Properties Sheet for this new notification (Figure 24.5). Now click the Select button and choose Box14 as the server that will monitor Box16.

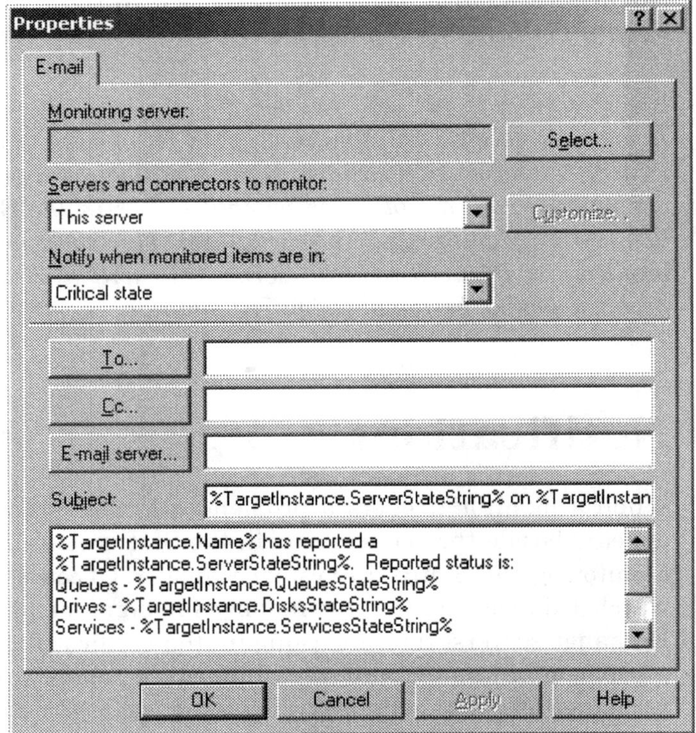

Figure 24.5 Creating a new email notification.

The Servers and Connectors to Monitor listbox specifies which servers and connectors will be monitored by the server we just specified. The choices are:

- This server (Box14 monitors itself)
- All servers
- Any server in the routing group
- All connectors
- Any connector in the routing group
- Custom list of servers
- Custom list of connectors

Select Custom List of Connectors, click the Customize button, and add Box16 as the server you want Box14 to monitor. Specify whether the notification message will be sent when the monitors watching Box16 go into warning or critical state. Specify the recipients (To) and alternate recipients (Cc) who will receive the notification and the email server that will generate the message (select Box14). You can leave the Subject field as is or specify a custom message subject. The bottom listbox uses replaceable variables to specify the contents of the notification message body (this cannot be edited).

As an exercise, see if you can find a simple way of driving your CPU utilization to 100 percent for an extended period to trigger the monitor and then check the result.

Click OK to create the new notification and view this notification in the Notifications container in System Manager. You can modify or delete the notification using the shortcut menu.

NOTE

Script notifications are somewhat simpler to create. You specify the monitoring server, the servers and connectors to monitor, the state (warning or critical) that triggers the notification, the path to the script or executable file, and any command-line options needed by the script or executable file.

Protocol Logging

Protocol logging keeps track of the interaction between clients and virtual servers on Exchange. The feature is supported only for SMTP, HTTP, and NNTP virtual servers and supports four different log file formats:

- *W2C Extended Log File Format (default)*. Creates a space-delimited ASCII log following the W3C logging conventions.
- *Microsoft IIS Log File Format*. Creates a tab-delimited ASCII file following a convention first defined in earlier versions of IIS.
- *NCSA Common Log File Format*. Creates a space-delimited ASCII file following the National Center for Supercomputing Applications (NCSA) logging conventions.
- *ODBC Logging*. Allows logging to an ODBC-compliant database file.

NOTE

For more details on the four log file formats and on how to interpret them, see Administering IIS5 *by Mitch Tulloch and Patrick Santry (McGraw-Hill).*

Table 24.1 shows some of the more important fields in these log files relating to Exchange protocol logging.

TABLE 24.1
Important fields in Exchange Protocol log files.

Property	Field	Description
Bytes received	cs-bytes	Number of bytes received by the server
Bytes sent	sc-bytes	Number of bytes sent by the server
Client IP address	c-ip	IP address of the client making the request
Date	date	Date when connection occurred
Method	cs-method	Protocol command sent by the client
Protocol status	sc-status	Protocol reply code
Server IP address	s-ip	IP address of the virtual server generating the log entry
Server name	s-computername	Name of the server generating the log entry
Service name	s-sitename	The name of the service that processed the protocol command sent by the client
Time	time	Time when connection occurred
Time taken	time-taken	Time in milliseconds for the server to process the protocol command sent by the client
User name	cs-username	Authenticated user account used in the connection
Win32 status	sc-status	Error code (zero means success)

Enabling and Configuring Protocol Logging

Walkthrough

Let's enable protocol logging for the default SMTP virtual server on Box16. Navigate in the console tree in System Manager: Organization (root) node → Administrative Groups → Seattle → Servers → Box16 → Protocols → SMTP. Right-click on Default SMTP Virtual Server in the Details (right) pane and select Properties. On the General tab, select the Enable Logging checkbox and leave the Active Log Format set at W3C Extended Log File Format. Click OK to enable protocol logging on this virtual server.

As another exercise, go to a client machine and start Outlook Express and connect to a mailbox on Box16. Send some mail. Then use Windows Explorer to find the protocol logging files on Box16, which are located in a subdirectory of \System32\Logfiles. Open the log files using a text editor such as Notepad or import them into Excel to examine the information logged from your exercise.

TIP

Although monitors and notifications are standard methods for monitoring servers in an Exchange organization and should be liberally implemented, protocol logging and diagnostic logging are generally used only in troubleshooting situations because these two forms of logging are resource-intensive activities on servers and can affect server performance if left configured for extended periods.

Diagnostic Logging

Diagnostic logging is another form of logging you can enable on Exchange servers. This feature is used primarily to troubleshoot problems with Exchange services and generates entries in the Windows 2000 Event logs. Table 24.2 lists the different Exchange services on which diagnostic logging can be enabled, together with their Event Source names, which identify these events in the Event logs.

TABLE 24.2 Event source names for Exchange services.

Event Source	Exchange Service
IMAP4Svc	Microsoft Exchange IMAP4
LME-GWIZE	Microsoft Exchange Connector for Novell GroupWise
LME-Notes	Microsoft Exchange Connector for Lotus Notes
MSExchangeDX	Microsoft Exchange Directory Synchronization
MSExchangeCCMC	Microsoft Exchange Connector for Lotus cc:Mail
MSExchangeFB	MS Schedule+ Free-Busy Connector
MSExchangeGWRtr	Microsoft Exchange Router for Novell GroupWise
MSExchangeIS	Microsoft Exchange Information Store
MSExchangeMSMI	MS Mail Connector Interchange
MSExchangeSA	Microsoft Exchange System Attendant
MSExchangeSRS	Microsoft Exchange Site Replication Service
MSExchangeTransport	Microsoft Exchange Routing Engine
MSExchangeMTA	Microsoft Exchange MTA Stacks
POP3Svc	Microsoft Exchange POP3

Levels of Diagnostic Logging

There are four levels of diagnostic logging that can be configured. These levels are distinguished by the level of detail that they provide on the activity of Exchange services and the performance hit they produce on the server when enabled. As a result of this performance issue, you should enable diagnostic logging only when troubleshooting problems involving Exchange services and not for general monitoring of server health. The four diagnostic logging levels supported are:

- *None (default level).* Only significant events relating to Exchange services are recorded in Event logs. Use this level during normal operation of Exchange.
- *Minimum.* Exchange services record an event for each major action they perform, but this information is logged in summary form only in Event logs. Use this level to identify the problem when troubleshooting issues relating to Exchange services.
- *Medium.* Exchange services record an event for each major action they perform and for each step in these tasks, and this information is logged in detailed form in Event logs. Use this level to dig deeper when troubleshooting issues relating to Exchange services.
- *Maximum.* Audits all actions of Exchange services in detail and records this information in Event logs. Use this level as a last resort because the volume of information and level of detail produced can be enormous and difficult to interpret.

TIP

Before enabling diagnostic logging, make sure your Event logs are configured with a maximum log size sufficient to hold the information being collected and make sure you have sufficient disk space.

Enabling and Configuring Diagnostic Logging

Walkthrough

We'll enable diagnostic logging for the information store on Box16 at the Maximum level and see what happens when a user logs on to his or her mailbox using Outlook Web Access (OWA). First open Event Viewer on Box16 and clear all events in the Application and System logs. Now open System Manager and open the Properties Sheet for Box16 under the Servers container in the Seattle administrative group. Switch to the Diagnostic Logging tab (Figure 24.6).

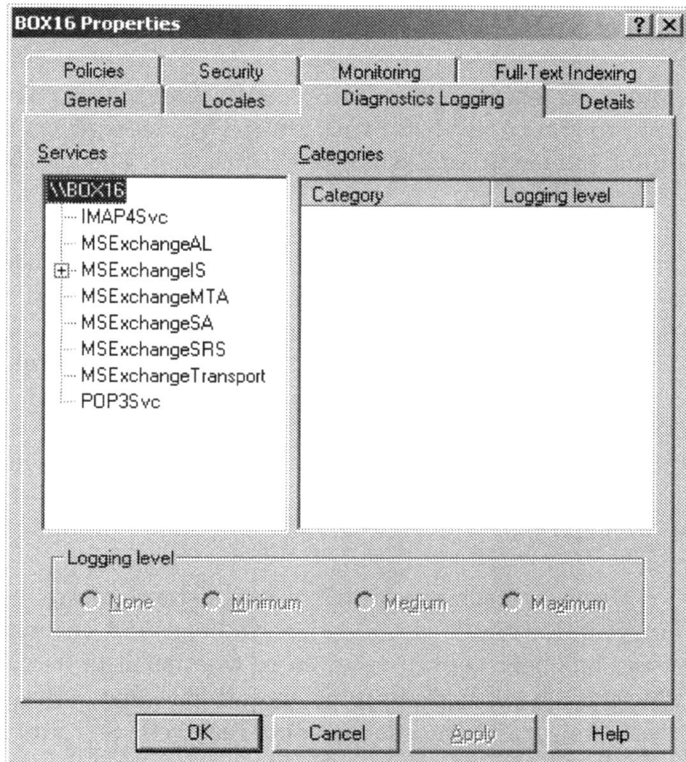

Figure 24.6 Configuring diagnostic logging on server Box16.

Expand MSExchangeIS under Services and select Private to display a list of categories you can log for diagnostic purposes. In the Categories listbox, select Logons and change the Logging Level from None to Maximum. Click OK to apply the changes and close the Properties Sheet.

Start OWA for user seauser whose mailbox is located on Box16 in Seattle by opening the URL http://box16/exchange/seauser. Enter the user's credentials to open the mail folders. Now switch to Event Viewer and refresh the view for the Application log and you should see a number of Success Audit events. Some of these are system events but a few should relate directly to our exercise.

Go back and change the diagnostic logging setting to None again.

Message Tracking

Message tracking is a feature of Exchange that, when enabled, allows you to track the actual paths taken by messages as they move through, into, and out of an Exchange organization. This can be useful for several reasons:

- If users are complaining about NDRs, you can use message tracking to troubleshoot the problem, which might be a failed connector or network link.
- By tracking postings to public folders you can gauge the usage of these resources in your organization, which can be helpful for planning.
- Big Brother might want to keep close tabs on what's going on in the company messaging system, and message tracking is one way of doing this.

Message tracking can tell you the status of any message transferred in your Exchange organization: you can find out whether a given message has been sent or received or whether it is still queued for delivery. Message tracking maintains special logs that contain selected information concerning messages sent, received, or routed by the server on which message tracking is enabled.

Message tracking must be enabled on a Exchange server if you want to track messages sent, received, or routed by that server. In general, you will enable message tracking on either:

- All servers in the organization.
- All servers in a given routing group.

Levels of Message Tracking

There are two different levels of message tracking that can be configured on a specific Exchange server:

- *Standard.* This logs the date, time, message ID, sender, and recipient of every message sent, received, or routed by the server.
- *Extended.* This adds subject, message headers, and other information to the message tracking logs generated by Standard message logging.

Enabling and Configuring Message Tracking

To configure message tracking on Box16, open the Properties Sheet for Box16 under the Servers container in the Seattle administrative group. On the General tab, there are two checkboxes relating to message tracking (Figure 24.7):

- *Enable message tracking*. Selecting this checkbox enables Standard message logging.
- *Enable subject logging and display*. Selecting this checkbox (and the previous one) enables Extended message logging.

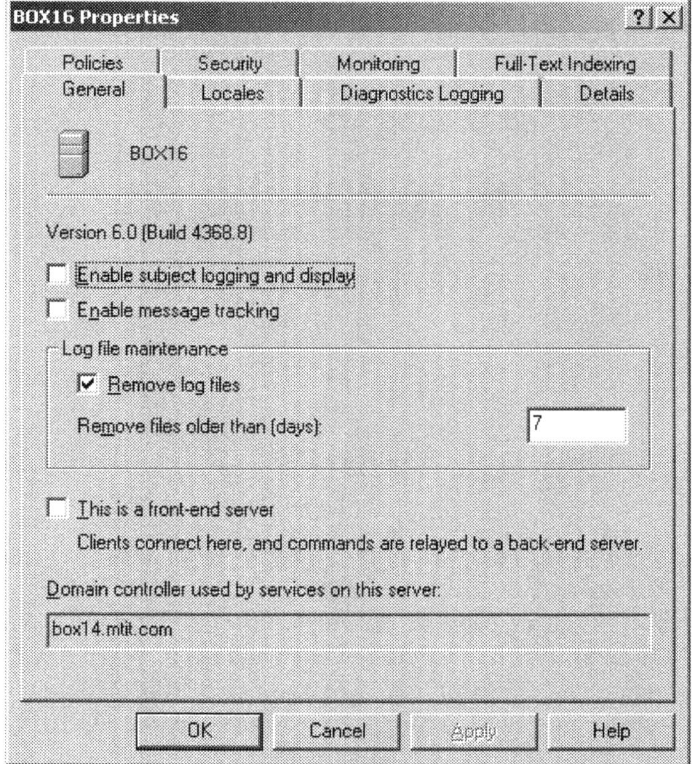

Figure 24.7 Enabling message tracking for server Box16.

Select both checkboxes and close the Properties Sheet. Configure message tracking on the other Exchange servers in the testbed deployment you are working with. Then log onto various mailboxes using different clients and send messages between these clients to generate information for the message tracking logs. As a simple example, I sent a message from seauser@mtit.com in Seattle to vanuser@mtit.com in Vancouver.

To track this message, right-click on Message Tracking Center (under Tools in System Manager) and select Track Message from the shortcut menu (Figure 24.8). This opens the Message Tracking Center, which is used to collect information from the tracking logs on servers on which message tracking is enabled and display this information in a readable form to allow you to track specific messages as they move through your organization.

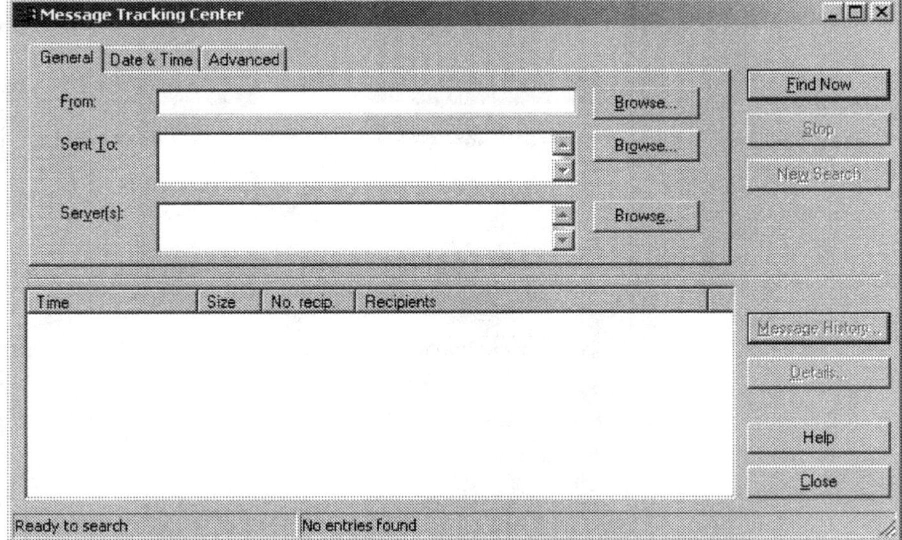

Figure 24.8
The Message Tracking Center.

In the From field, click Browse and select seauser from Active Directory and then vanuser in the Sent To field. Select all servers in your organization in the Servers field. Now click Find Now to read all information concerning the message from the tracking logs on each server and combine this information into a history of the route taken by the message through your organization. Possible message(s) should be displayed in the bottom listbox of the Message Tracking Center window. Select the desired message from the list and click Message History to display the tracking details of the message (Figure 24.9). You can select any step in the message history and click Details to obtain more information.

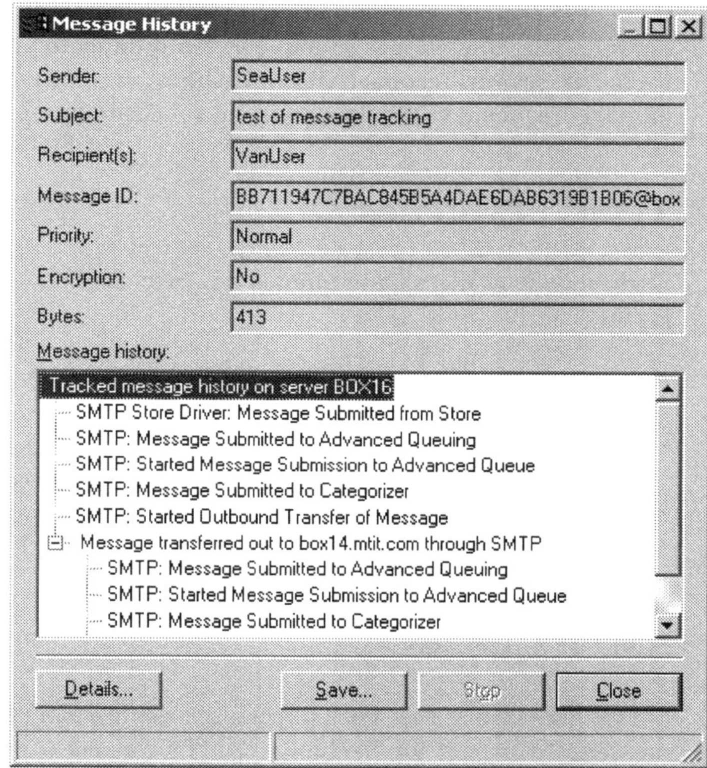

Figure 24.9 Displaying the message history of a selected message.

TIP

Make sure you have lots of free disk space on the servers when you enable message tracking on them. On the General tab of the Properties Sheet for a server under Log File Maintenance (Figure 24.7), you can specify how long information in message tracking log files is maintained on the server before being purged. Make sure this setting is enabled and a period specified during which message tracking or log files may grow until the server stops functioning due to lack of available disk space.

Queues

Another essential aspect of monitoring an Exchange organization is monitoring of message queues. These queues are used to temporarily store messages while they are waiting to be processed and routed to their destinations. In the section on monitors, we learned that increasing numbers of messages in a queue could indicate problems with a connector or network connectivity, but there are many more ways you can manage queues and the messages within them, as we will see shortly.

Types of Queues

Exchange 2000 messaging queues can be classified into one of two categories:

- *System queues*. These include queues for SMTP messaging (default transport for Exchange), X400 MTA (used for transferring messages with foreign X400 messaging systems), and MAPI (used for Lotus Notes, Lotus cc:Mail, and Novell GroupWise connectors).
- *Link queues*. These are instantiated when Exchange has to route multiple messages to the same destination.

SMTP Queues

SMTP queues are the most important because SMTP is the underlying message transport for Exchange. SMTP queues exist on a per-virtual-server basis in Exchange, with a separate set of queues for each SMTP virtual server. The different types of SMTP queues are (Figure 24.10):

- *Pre-Submission*. This queue contains messages that have been received by the SMTP virtual server but have not yet been processed for delivery.
- *Local delivery*. This queue contains messages being routed for delivery to a mailbox in the local machine's information store.
- *Messages awaiting directory lookup*. This queue contains messages whose recipients have not yet had their addresses resolved from Active Directory.
- *Messages waiting to be routed.* This queue contains messages ready for routing to a remote server by passing them to the appropriate link queue.
- *<Connector_Name>*. This queue contains messages queued for delivery through the specified connector.
- *Final destination currently unreachable*. This queue contains messages that cannot be routed because their destination domains cannot be resolved.

Managing SMTP Queues

Walkthrough

We'll examine the queues for the default SMTP virtual server on Box16. Navigate through the console tree in System Manager as follows: Organization (root) node → Administrative Groups → Seattle → Servers → Box16 → Protocols → SMTP → Default SMTP Virtual Server → Queues (Figure 24.10).

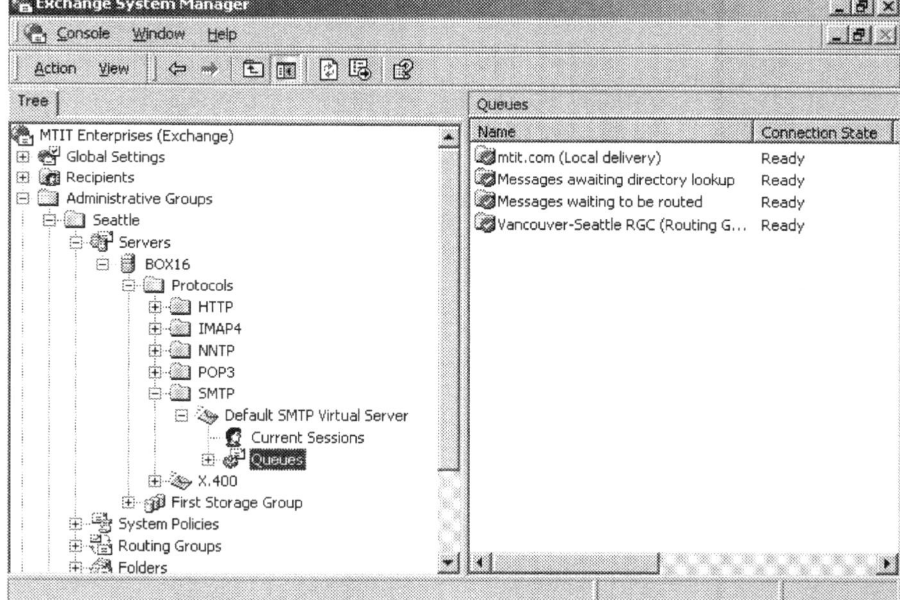

Figure 24.10 Viewing the queues for the default SMTP virtual server on Box16.

There are a number of fields displayed in the Details (right) pane when the Queues node is selected in the Tree (left) pane of System Manager. These fields include:

- *Name.* The name of the queue as described previously.
- *Connection state.* The current state of the queue, which can be:
  - *Active.* The queue currently contains messages that are being passed to the appropriate link queue for outbound routing.
  - *Frozen.* The queue can receive messages but cannot route or deliver them.
  - *Ready.* The queue is ready to receive messages for routing and delivery.

- *Remote.* The queue is waiting for the remote SMTP host to issue a TURN/ETRN command to initiate dequeuing of its messages.
- *Retry.* The queue has attempted to deliver or route messages, has failed, and is waiting to try again.
- *Scheduled.* The queue is waiting for a scheduled connection time for routing or delivering messages.

- Time of Submission of Oldest Msg. When the oldest messages was submitted to the queue by a client.

TIP

If Time of Submission of Oldest Msg is a few days or more, a message delivery or routing problem such as a failed connector, a network link down, or a remote SMTP host offline may have occurred.

- *Total # of Msgs.* This indicates the total number of messages waiting for delivery or routing in the queue.
- *Total Msg Size (KB).* The total size of all queued messages. If this becomes too large, it could fill available disk space and bring messaging to a standstill.
- *Time of Next Connection Retry.* When the queue is in a Retry state, this field will indicate when the next attempt will be made to form a connection with the remote SMTP host and route the message to its destination.

Below is a summary of some of the tasks that an administrator can perform on SMTP queues using System Manager and when they should be done:

- *Enabling and disabling connections.* You can enable or disable connections for all queues on a given SMTP virtual server by right-clicking the Queues node and selecting Enable | Disable All Connections. When queues are disabled, they cannot route or deliver messages to their destinations. You might do this if you are having problems with your server and plan to troubleshoot.
- *Forcing a connection.* You can force a queue to change to Active state by right-clicking on the queue in the Details pane and selecting Force Connection. You might do this to force delivery of messages in a queue whose current state is Retry or Scheduled.
- *Enumerating messages in a queue.* Enumerating messages causes individual messages to be displayed in a given queue. To enumerate messages 100 at a time for a particular queue, right-click on the

queue and select Enumerate 100 Messages. Repeat to enumerate additional messages, or right-click and select Re-enumerate to refresh the current list. You can also create a custom filter for enumerating specific types of messages in the queue.

- *Freezing and unfreezing a queue.* You can freeze a queue by right-clicking on the queue and selecting Freeze All Messages. This prevents messages from leaving the queue but allows new messages to enter the queue. You might do this if the WAN link is down and you want to prevent NDRs from being generated while the link is under repair. You can also freeze individual messages in a queue by first enumerating the messages in the queue and then right-clicking on the desired message in the queue and selecting Freeze.
- *Deleting messages from queues.* Once messages are enumerated and displayed in a queue, you can delete selected messages by right-clicking and selecting either:
  - *Delete All Messages (No NDR).* Deletes all messages in the queue and does not send NDRs to senders.
  - *Delete All Messages (Send NDR).* Deletes all messages in the queue and sends NDRs to senders.

  You can also selectively delete individual messages in the queue and return or not return an NDR to the sender.

Try this: disable the network connection (pull the LAN plug) between Box16 and the other servers in your testbed deployment. Start OWA on Box16 and log on to seauser's mailbox. Send a message to vanuser@mtit.com. Then enumerate the queues for the default SMTP virtual server on Box16. In which queue is the message? Delete the message from the queue.

Backup and Restore

A crucial aspect of maintaining an Exchange organization is regularly backing up the Exchange servers so that you can recover when a disaster occurs. For backup, you can use the Windows 2000 Backup utility or a third-party tool designed for Exchange 2000. This section assumes you have some familiarity with the concepts and issues relating to backing up and restoring Windows 2000 servers; the following walkthrough focuses on using Windows 2000 Backup.

Backing Up Files

To make a full backup of an Exchange server, you need to back up the following items:

- *Exchange user data.* This includes mailbox stores, public-folder stores, and transaction logs.
- *Exchange configuration information.* This information is drawn from several sources including the Exchange directory database DIR.EDB, Active Directory, and the system registry.
- *Operating system and Exchange directories.* In general, you should back up the C: drive, which contains Windows 2000 operating system files and Exchange 2000 application files, and the M: drive, where the Exchange Installable File System is installed.
- *System state data.* This consists of files essential for recovering the operating system on a machine.

NOTE

By default, Windows 2000 Backup performs an online backup of Exchange, which allows the servers to continue to operate. Nevertheless, it is best to make backups during off-peak hours, such as 2 to 4 AM, because doing so is more efficient.

NOTE

It's critical that transaction logs and data stores are backed up to ensure full recoverability of user data up to the time of the previous backup. When Exchange is configured to use standard logging (which it is by default) rather than circular logging, you can make weekly full backups of Exchange servers and daily incremental (or differential) backups, and can restore the information store using these backup sets. If circular logging is enabled (and this is not recommended), you must perform full backups each night to recover the store.

Scope of Backup and Restore

When you backup Exchange, you can back up one or more than one storage group in the organization. In other words, storage groups are the smallest unit of backup in Exchange. For example, on an Exchange server you can choose to back up:

- A single storage group
- Multiple storage groups
- The entire information store

Alternatively, you can restore individual data stores within storage groups. In other words, data stores are the smallest unit of restore in Exchange. For example, when restoring an Exchange server, you can choose to restore:

- A single data store within a storage group
- Multiple data stores within a storage group
- A single storage group
- Multiple storage groups
- The entire information store

NOTE

Windows 2000 Backup does not include the functionality of restoring individual mailboxes within data stores. However, it is possible with Exchange 2000 to create data stores that host a single mailbox, and then you can restore this mailbox using Windows 2000 Backup if required.

Backing up Exchange

Walkthrough

We'll finish this chapter by performing a backup of Box14 in Vancouver. Start the Windows 2000 Backup utility by selecting Start → Programs → Accessories →System → Backup (Figure 24.11).

NOTE

You can also start Backup by using the `ntbackup` *command from the command line or opening Computer Management → System Tools → System Information → select Tools menu → Windows → Backup.*

You can use the Backup Wizard or switch to the Backup tab and configure the backup manually. We'll use the wizard for this walkthrough. Click the Backup Wizard button to start it. When the welcome screen appears, click Next. Select "Back up selected files, drives, or network data" and click Next.

On this screen of the wizard, you specify which files to back up (Figure 24.12). Table 24.3 shows different scenarios for backing up Exchange user data files.

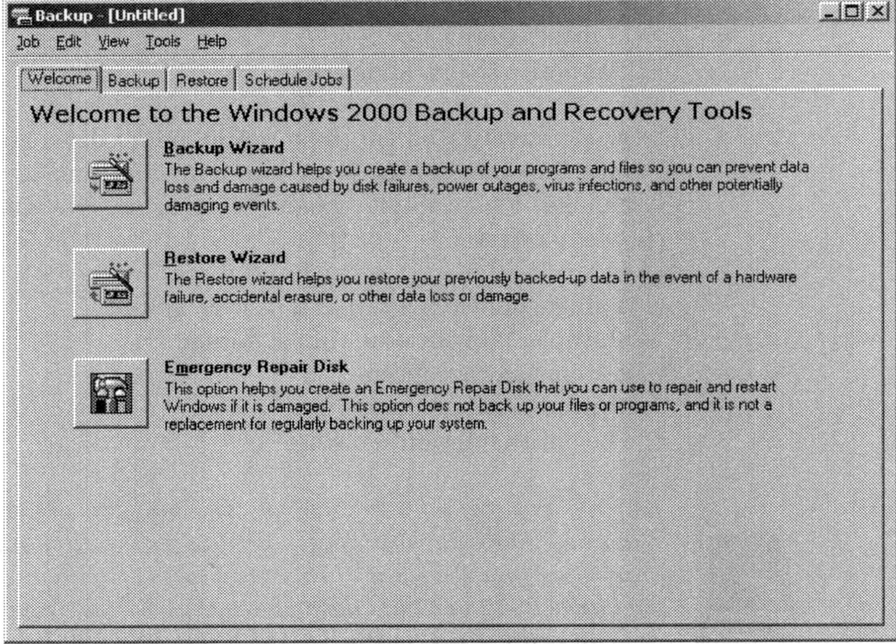

Figure 24.11 The Windows 2000 backup utility.

TABLE 24.3 Backup scenarios for Exchange user data files when using the items to back up screen of the Windows 2000 Backup wizard.

What to back up	How to back up
Full backup of all Exchange servers in an organization	Select the Microsoft Exchange Server node
Full backup of specific Exchange servers	Expand the Microsoft Exchange server node and select the servers to back up
Back up all user data but not configuration data on a specific Exchange server	Expand the Microsoft Exchange server node and select the Information Store node
Back up specific storage groups on one specific Exchange server	Expand the Microsoft Exchange server node, expand the node for the desired server, and select the storage groups

Once you've selected which Exchange user data files to back up, you should also make sure that you back up Exchange configuration information. To do this, select the C: and M: drives. To make sure that you also back up system state information on the machine, select System State.

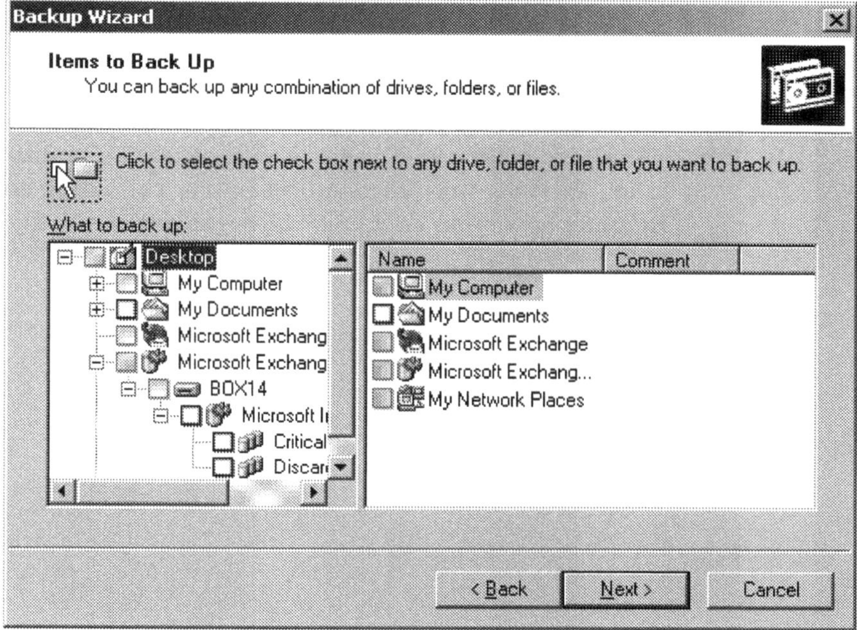

Figure 24.12 Selecting files to back up.

Now click Next and select the Backup Media Type. Select File to backup Exchange to a network share or select the appropriate type of tape drive or other removable storage device.

Click Advanced if you want to change the default settings for compression and verification. Choose to append the backup to the previous backup set or replace the data on the medium. Specify a backup label and medium label if required, give your backup job a name, and then run the backup job immediately or schedule it for later (if you schedule it for later, you must enter the credentials of a user with appropriate privileges for running the job, usually someone belonging to the Backup Operators group).

Try experimenting with backing up Exchange as follows: Do a full backup on one of your testbed Exchange servers. Then delete a mailbox from one of the mailbox stores. Run the Restore wizard and restore only the mailbox store containing the missing mailbox. Test that the user can access his or her mailbox after the restoration.

Summary

In this chapter we've looked at a number of administrative tasks relating to monitoring and maintaining an Exchange organization. This completes our overview of basic Exchange 2000 administrative tasks. However, for the sake of completeness, the final chapter deals with upgrading existing Exchange 5.5 organizations to Exchange 2000.

CHAPTER 25

Upgrading from Exchange 5.5

This chapter covers upgrading from Exchange 5.5 to Exchange 2000. General procedures for upgrades are discussed, after which a walk-through of an upgrade is performed.

There are five walkthroughs in this chapter:

- Upgrading Exchange 5.5 to Windows 2000
- Installing the Active Directory Connector (ADC)
- Preparing the forest using ForestPrep
- Configuring a connection agreement
- Preparing the domain using DomainPrep
- Upgrading Exchange 5.5 to Exchange 2000

Upgrading to Exchange 2000

As mentioned in the Introduction, the focus of this book has been the day-to-day administration of Exchange 2000. To learn the basic administrative tasks, we've focused on a pure Exchange 2000 environment, but in real life many companies will be upgrading from earlier versions of Exchange or migrating from other messaging systems such as Lotus Notes or Novell GroupWise. A full discussion of upgrading and migrating to Exchange 2000 could fill a book, and there are several books on the market dealing specifically with this topic, such as the *Microsoft Exchange 2000 Server Resource Kit* from Microsoft Press. Such books are generally weak, however, in covering the day-to-day administration of Exchange 2000, which is the reason I wrote this book. However, this book would not be complete without a brief discussion of upgrading to Exchange 2000.

Exchange 2000 and Previous Versions of Exchange

If you plan to upgrade from a previous version of Exchange, you need to know which versions can be upgraded successfully. Here is the relevant information:

- Exchange 4.0 and 5.0 *cannot* be upgraded to Exchange 2000 because Exchange 2000 runs only on Windows 2000, not on Windows NT, and Exchange 4.0 and 5.0 cannot run on Windows 2000. However, you can successfully have Exchange 4.0 and 5.0 coexist with Exchange 2000 in an Exchange organization, provided you have installed the latest versions of services packs for these earlier versions. Coexistence between Exchange 2000 and Exchange 4.0/5.0 is not recommended because you would have to administer the older versions separately. Furthermore, if any of the Exchange 4.0/5.0 servers are Windows NT domain controllers, then your Windows 2000 domain would have to be running in mixed mode and therefore could not use features such as universal groups to simplify the administration of your enterprise.

- Exchange 5.5 *can* be successfully upgraded to Exchange 2000, provided you have Exchange 5.5 Service Pack 3 (X5.5 SP3) installed. This service pack is necessary for using the ADC to migrate Exchange 5.5 directory information to Windows 2000's Active Directory. Exchange 2000 can coexist with Exchange 5.5 servers running only Service Pack 1 or 2, but it's recommended that Service Pack 3 be installed on all Exchange 5.5 servers, especially if you plan to upgrade them to Exchange 2000 and not just have them coexist with Exchange 2000 servers.

NOTE

Actually, in an Exchange 5.5 organization with multiple sites, you need only one Exchange 5.5 running X5.5 SP3 on each site. You can use each such server to replicate that site's directory information to Active Directory using the ADC. However, you might want to upgrade all your Exchange 5.5 servers to X5.5 SP3 to simplify the process.

Planning an Upgrade

This section provides a step-by-step look at planning an upgrade from Exchange 5.5 to Exchange 2000. The walkthroughs in this chapter provide some details on this process.

The first thing to note is that Exchange 2000 can be installed only on a machine running Windows 2000 Server or Windows 2000 Advanced Server and in Windows 2000 where Active Directory is installed and configured. Planning and implementing Active Directory in an enterprise is beyond the scope of this book, but it is important for deploying Exchange 2000 because of the close ties between Exchange 2000 and Active Directory (previous versions of Exchange maintained their own directory database of Exchange configuration data, but Exchange 2000 stores this information in Active Directory).

NOTE

In fact, the machine on which you want to install Exchange 2000 must also be running Windows 2000 Service Pack 1 (W2K SP1) because it contains various hot fixes necessary to support Exchange 2000. Not only must this machine have W2K SP1 installed on it, but all domain controllers in that domain must also have W2K SP1 installed.

The complexity of your Active Directory forest (number of domain trees and number of domains in each tree) determines how you roll out Exchange 2000. The more complex the forest, the more preparatory work must be done before installing Exchange.

Another factor to consider is whether your Windows 2000 domains are running in native mode (Windows 2000 domain controllers only) or mixed mode (interoperability with downlevel Windows NT backup domain controllers). It's best if your Windows 2000 domains are running in native mode because it allows Exchange 5.5 distribution lists (DLs) to be migrated to Windows 2000 distribution groups.

You also should cast the roles your various Exchange 5.5 servers will play in your existing messaging system. You may have several Exchange 5.5 servers deployed as general-purpose servers with mailboxes, public folders, and one or two connectors, or you may be using dedicated mailbox servers, public-folder servers, and connector servers. During the upgrade process, you may want to maintain these different roles for your servers or you may want to merge some of the roles by consolidating multiple Exchange 5.5 servers into single Exchange 2000 servers.

Another decision you need to make is upgrading the entire system in one shot (simpler in theory but if something goes wrong it could be a very long weekend for you) or gradually by having Exchange 2000 and Exchange 5.5 servers coexist during the upgrade process. This decision is important because Exchange 2000 servers running in mixed, not native, mode can interoperate and coexist with downlevel Exchange 5.5 servers within the same organization. Exchange 2000 servers running in mixed mode seem the same as downlevel Exchange 5.5 (and 5.0 and 4.0) servers, and Exchange 2000 administrative groups are mapped directly to Exchange 5.5 (and 5.0) sites. However, when Exchange 2000 is running in mixed mode, you cannot move servers between administrative groups, which limits your ability to reconfigure the administrative topology of your organization. Also, routing groups map directly to administrative groups in mixed mode, which limits your ability to reconfigure the routing topology of your organization. In mixed mode, Exchange 2000 servers communicate with Exchange 5.5 and earlier servers on the same site using remote procedure calls (RPCs) instead of SMTP, and RPCs use more overhead and have less tolerance for connection unreliability and latency than SMTP does, so LAN and WAN connectivity is another factor to consider.

NOTE

Remember that we are talking about Exchange 2000 native/mixed-mode operations, not Windows 2000 native/mixed-mode operations, which is something different. In Exchange, mixed-mode administrative and routing groups are essentially identical and are viewed by downlevel Exchange servers as sites.

As long as you have downlevel (5.5 or earlier) Exchange servers in your organization, you cannot switch Exchange 2000 servers from native mode to mixed mode. So you may want to upgrade your entire system simultaneously but in a way that provides full recovery in case something goes wrong. We'll look at several upgrade strategies in a moment.

Another issue to consider if you plan to maintain coexistence between Exchange 2000 and downlevel versions of Exchange is exchange of directory information between the two systems. You will need to install the ADC and create connection agreements between the Exchange 5.5 sites and Active Directory to unify the directory information between Active Directory and earlier versions of Exchange. We'll learn how to do this later in this chapter.

Maintaining coexistence between new and old Exchange servers also makes administration more complex because each system is administered with different tools: Exchange Administrator for Exchange 5.5 and System Manager for Exchange 2000. And once you have at least one Exchange 2000 installed and connection agreements configured, you must use Active Directory, Users and Computers to manage users' mailboxes, not User Manager For Domains (even if some of your downlevel Exchange servers are still running on Windows NT).

As you can see, the upgrade process involves a number of issues and steps and requires careful planning, especially in a large organization with many sites. Although a full treatment of this subject is beyond the scope of this book, let's look at three basic ways of upgrading Exchange 5.5 servers to Exchange 2000: in-place, move mailbox, and swing.

In-place Method

With this approach, Exchange 2000 is installed on machines currently running Exchange 5.5 SP3. This is fairly straightforward and not much can go wrong if you plan things carefully, but you need to make sure that your machine's hardware can support Exchange 2000, which has considerably higher hardware requirements than Exchange 5.5. Also, your Exchange servers will be down during the time it takes to upgrade (often this means a nice weekend at the office).

The advantage of this method is its simplicity and its cost (no extra machine is required because existing ones are used). However, you should make a full (and verified) backup of your server before upgrading it; if something goes wrong during the upgrade, you'll have to use the backup data.

Move-mailbox Method

If the hardware in your Exchange 5.5 servers can't support Exchange 2000 (or can't be easily upgraded to support it), then you can use the move-mailbox method:

1. Install Exchange 2000 on a brand new machine running Windows 2000.
2. Join the new Exchange 2000 server to an existing Exchange 5.5 site.
3. Move mailboxes and public folders from the existing Exchange 5.5 site to the new Exchange 2000 server.
4. Disconnect the Exchange 5.5 servers from the network and store them for a rainy day (or redeploy them immediately if something goes wrong with the upgrade).

The move-mailbox method is somewhat more complicated than the in-place method but it has two advantages:

- If something goes wrong with the upgrade, you still have the Exchange 5.5 servers to fall back on and redeploy, which is faster and easier than restoring from backup media.
- You can migrate mailboxes from Exchange versions as early as 4.0 using this method. With in-place upgrades, you first have to upgrade Exchange 4.0 servers to Exchange 5.5 SP3.

TIP

The move-mailbox method is recommended by Microsoft for upgrading Exchange 5.5 organizations that have dedicated mailbox servers and public-folder servers.

Swing Method

A variant of the move-mailbox method is the swing method:

1. Install Exchange 2000 on a brand new machine running Windows 2000.
2. Join the new Exchange 2000 server to the existing Exchange 5.5 site.
3. Move mailboxes and public folders from the existing Exchange 5.5 site to the new Exchange 2000 server.
4. Delete Exchange 5.5 from the servers, upgrade their hardware, install Windows 2000 and then Exchange 2000 on them, and return to step 2 to upgrade all the sites.

The advantages and disadvantages of this method are fairly obvious, given the previous discussion of the other two methods.

Steps for Upgrading

The rest of this chapter has walkthroughs for a basic in-place upgrade. We will be using a new testbed scenario with two machines:

- *Box81*. This machine is the root Windows 2000 domain controller for the mtit.com domain (downlevel domain name MTIT) and has Windows 2000 SP1 installed. The domain is running in Windows 2000 native mode to support universal groups for migration of Exchange 5.5 DLs.
- *Box82*. This machine is a member server in the MTIT domain and is running Exchange 5.5 SP3 over Windows NT 4.0 Server SP4. A number of mailboxes, DLs, and public folders have been created on this machine, and test messages have been sent and items posted using a client computer running Outlook 2000.

Our upgrade procedure, which will upgrade the Exchange 5.5 machine directly to Exchange 2000, will be as follows:

- Upgrade from Windows NT to Windows 2000 SP1 on Exchange 5.5 server Box82.
- Install an ADC on Box81 to migrate Exchange 5.5 configuration and recipient information to Active Directory.
- Run ForestPrep to prepare the forest for Exchange 2000 by updating the schema.
- Configure a connection agreement using the ADC console.
- Run DomainPrep to prepare the domain for Exchange 2000.
- Finish the process by running Exchange 2000 Setup on Box82 to upgrade it from Exchange 5.5 to Exchange 2000.

This simple upgrade scenario will be used to illustrate the various tasks and steps that may be involved in upgrading an existing Exchange 5.5 organization to Exchange 2000. For more information, see Appendix 1 for a list of white papers and other resources from Microsoft that explain in detail the different kinds of upgrades.

Upgrading Exchange 5.5 to Windows 2000

Walkthrough

This procedure is straightforward. The only real issue is whether the hardware of your existing Windows NT machine can support Windows 2000. If your existing hardware can support Windows 2000, simply insert the Windows 2000 Advanced server CD or connect to a shared distribution point on the network, run Setup, select the Upgrade option, and follow the prompts. Then install Windows 2000 SP1 on the machine, which is required before installing Exchange 2000. Use Outlook from the client computer to test that users can still connect to their Exchange 5.5 mailboxes on Box82 and send mail.

Installing the ADC

Walkthrough

Switch to Box81, the forest root domain controller in our testbed forest. Log on using the default Administrator account for the mtit.com domain (this account has the necessary privileges to complete the walkthrough). We're going to install the ADC to establish interoperability between the Exchange 5.5 directory on Box82 and Active Directory on Box81 (see Under the Hood).

Insert the Exchange 2000 CD into Box81, open a command prompt, switch to the \ADC\I386 directory on the CD, and run Setup.exe. The ADC Installation Wizard should start (Figure 25.1).

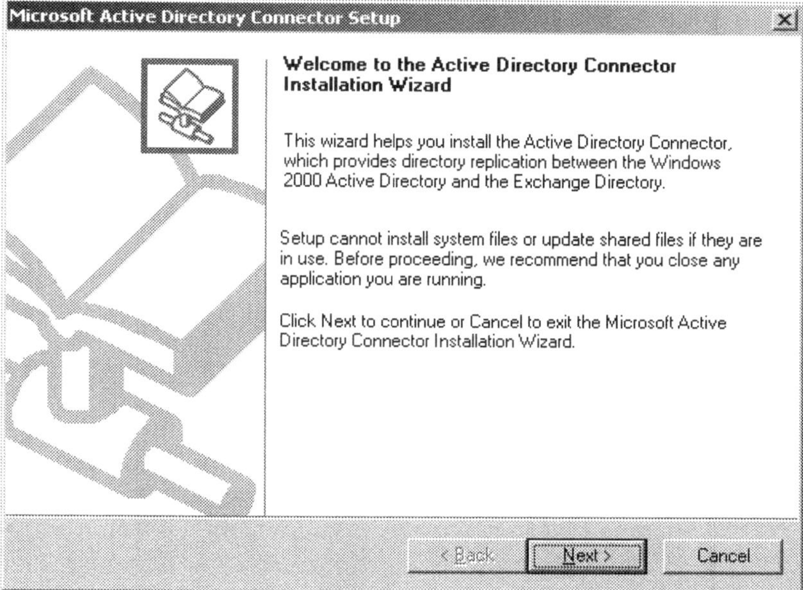

Microsoft Active Directory Connector Setup
Welcome to the Active Directory Connector Installation Wizard
This wizard helps you install the Active Directory Connector, which provides directory replication between the Windows 2000 Active Directory and the Exchange Directory.
Setup cannot install system files or update shared files if they are in use. Before proceeding, we recommend that you close any application you are running.
Click Next to continue or Cancel to exit the Microsoft Active Directory Connector Installation Wizard.
< Back
Next >
Cancel

Figure 25.1 The Active Directory Connector Installation Wizard.

Click Next to open the Component Selection screen of the wizard. Select Install for both components:

- Microsoft Active Directory Connector Service component
- Microsoft Active Directory Connector Management components

Click Next and accept the default installation location or specify another one. Click Next and accept the default ADC service account or another one and enter the password for that account.

TIP

The default ADC service account is your current logon account. If you prefer, you can select any another domain account or you can start Active Directory Users and Computers and create a new account.

Click Next and the installation process continues as files are copied to your system. This will take some time because ten files are processed that update the Active Directory schema on your Schema Master domain controller.

TIP

Installation of the first ADC will take even longer if you don't install it directly on the domain controller/global catalog server that is running in Schema Master operations role. Subsequent installations of additional ADCs are faster because the schema no longer needs to be updated.

Once installation is complete, click Finish and proceed to the next walkthrough. In real life, you would wait a while first before continuing to give your enterprise time for the schema updates to replicate to all domain controllers in the forest. This can take longer if you have many Windows 2000 sites configured for remote locations.

UNDER THE HOOD

ADC and Related Concepts

The ADC is essential for coexistence between Exchange 5.5 and Exchange 2000 and for upgrading Exchange 5.5 to Exchange 2000. The ADC replicates and synchronizes the directory information contained within the Exchange 5.5 directory database with Windows 2000's Active Directory (AD). This is required because Exchange 2000 does not have its own dedicated directory as Exchange 5.5 did; instead, Exchange 2000 uses AD as its directory to store configuration information and recipient properties. If you have an Exchange 5.5 organization that you want to upgrade to Exchange 2000, it is necessary to install and configure ADCs before installing the first Exchange 2000 server because Exchange 2000 has no access to the Exchange 5.5 directory.

ADC can be used to perform one-way replication of Exchange 5.5 directory information to AD before an upgrade from Exchange 5.5 to 2000. Alternatively, if the two versions are to coexist, ADC can be configured to synchronize information between the two directories. ADC uses Lightweight Directory Access Protocol (LDAP) for performing such replication and synchronization between the two directories. ADC is implemented as a Windows 2000 service and can be stopped and started like any other service.

Microsoft recommends that ADCs be installed on Windows 2000 member servers because of the drain on system resources that can occur when ADCs are run. You should freeze changes to configuration and recipient properties on your Exchange 5.5 servers before running the ADC and be sure that Exchange 5.5 SP3 is installed on the Exchange 5.5 servers that will have their information replicated to AD using the ADC.

ADCs are managed using a console called the Active Directory Connector Manager (ADCM). This console is used to create and configure connection agreements. A connection agreement *specifies the servers whose directory information will be replicated, the classes of objects to replicate, the target containers where these objects will be replicated to, and the replication schedule. Connection agreements are typically created between Exchange 5.5 servers and Windows 2000 domain controllers running as global catalog servers. You can define multiple connection agreements for a single ADC, typically to synchronize AD with multiple Exchange sites using one server per site.*

There are two types of connection agreements: user connection agreements, which replicate recipient properties, and configuration connection agreements, which replicate Exchange server configuration information. User connection agreements must be manually configured, whereas configuration connection agreements are established automatically by ADC.

Installing Exchange 2000 on a machine also installs the component called Site Replication Services (SRS). *SRS supports the operation of ADC by enabling an Exchange 2000 server to emulate an Exchange 5.5 server (from the viewpoint of the Exchange 5.5 servers). SRS is actually a modified Exchange 5.5 directory service that installs on Exchange 2000 servers to support interoperability with downlevel Exchange 5.5 servers in mixed-mode environments.*

NOTE

There are two versions of the ADC: one comes with Windows 2000 Server and an enhanced version comes with Exchange 2000. Be sure to use the enhanced version when establishing coexistence between Exchange 5.5 and 2000 or when upgrading to Exchange 2000.

Preparing the Forest Using ForestPrep

Walkthrough

We're now ready to prepare our Windows 2000 forest for installing Exchange 2000. To prepare the forest, we'll use a utility called ForestPrep that is included on the Exchange 2000 CD. This utility prepares AD for Exchange 2000 by extending the schema using information specific to Exchange 2000, creating new classes and attributes for objects specific to Exchange 2000, and granting permissions for new Exchange 2000 administrator accounts.

NOTE

We are upgrading an existing Exchange 5.5 server to Exchange 2000. If you are joining your first Exchange 2000 server to an existing Exchange 5.5 organization, you must install Exchange 5.5 SP3 and the ADC before running ForestPrep, and you will need to supply the name of an existing Exchange 5.5 server in your organization and its Exchange site service account while running the utility.

To run ForestPrep on a Windows 2000 machine, a user needs privileges equivalent to those of Exchange 2000 Full Administrator. In other words, the user running the utility must belong to the following Windows 2000 security groups:

- Enterprise Admins group
- Schema Admins group
- Local computer Administrator group

You must also have network connectivity with the Windows 2000 domain controller that has the schema master role for your forest. This is typically the first domain controller you install in your forest (that is, the forest root domain controller).

NOTE

ForestPrep only needs to be run once for the forest (and is an irreversible action), whereas DomainPrep needs to be run later for each domain in which Exchange 2000 servers are installed (and preferably for all domains in the forest).

If you are migrating an existing Exchange 5.5 organization to Exchange 2000, you also need to specify an existing Exchange 5.5 server when running ForestPrep. This server must be online and you need to know the password for the Exchange service account in the site where this Exchange 5.5 server is located.

NOTE

Why didn't we run ForestPrep before we installed our first Exchange 2000 server in Chapter 1? Actually, we did! If you are deploying a pure Exchange 2000 organization with no existing downlevel Exchange 5.5 servers, you can simply run Setup from the Exchange 2000 CD, and the ForestPrep and domain prep utilities are automatically run during installation (provided the user account of the individual running

Exchange 2000 Setup is a member of the Enterprise Admins and Schema Admins groups in the forest and the first Exchange 2000 server is installed in the same domain in which the domain controller running the Schema Master role is located). Of course, including these utilities in Setup is what made the installation of our first Exchange 2000 server in Chapter 1 such a slow process—it took some time for ForestPrep to upgrade the schema of AD. Separating ForestPrep from Exchange 2000 Setup, as we are doing here, has two main advantages: less continuous down time during installation, and the ability to separate tasks like running ForestPrep that require broad, enterprisewide privileges because they change AD and thus the entire enterprise from tasks like installing Exchange 2000 on a machine that requires fewer privileges because failure has a less serious impact on the enterprise.

Therefore, in a large company, a typical scenario would be for a high-level senior administrator to prepare the forest using ForestPrep and install the first Exchange 2000 server, delegate various Exchange 2000 administrative roles using the Exchange Administration Delegation Wizard, and have more junior administrators install and configure the remaining Exchange 2000 servers and prepare the individual domains using DomainPrep.

The ForestPrep utility is run by running Exchange 2000 Setup using the `/forestprep` switch. Log on to Box81, the root domain controller in our testbed forest, using the default Administrator account, which has the necessary privileges for running this utility, insert the Exchange 2000 CD, open a command prompt window, and type:

```
<CD-drive>\Setup\I386\Setup /forestprep
```

The welcome screen for the Exchange 2000 Installation Wizard will appear (Figure 25.2).

Walk through the wizard by accepting the EULA, entering the 25-digit product ID code, and accepting the default Component Selection screen (this cannot be modified and indicates only that ForestPrep is being executed). You can change the location of the ForestPrep files, but it is not necessary.

The next screen prompts you to create a new Exchange organization or join/upgrade an existing one (Figure 25.3). Select the latter option (join/upgrade) and click Next.

Microsoft Exchange 2000 Installation Wizard
Welcome to the Microsoft Exchange 2000 Installation Wizard.
This wizard helps you install Microsoft Exchange 2000.
Setup cannot install system files or update shared files if they are in use. Before proceeding, we recommend that you close any application you are running.
Click Next to continue or Cancel to exit the Microsoft Exchange 2000 Installation Wizard.
< Back
Next >
Cancel

Figure 25.2 Running ForestPrep.

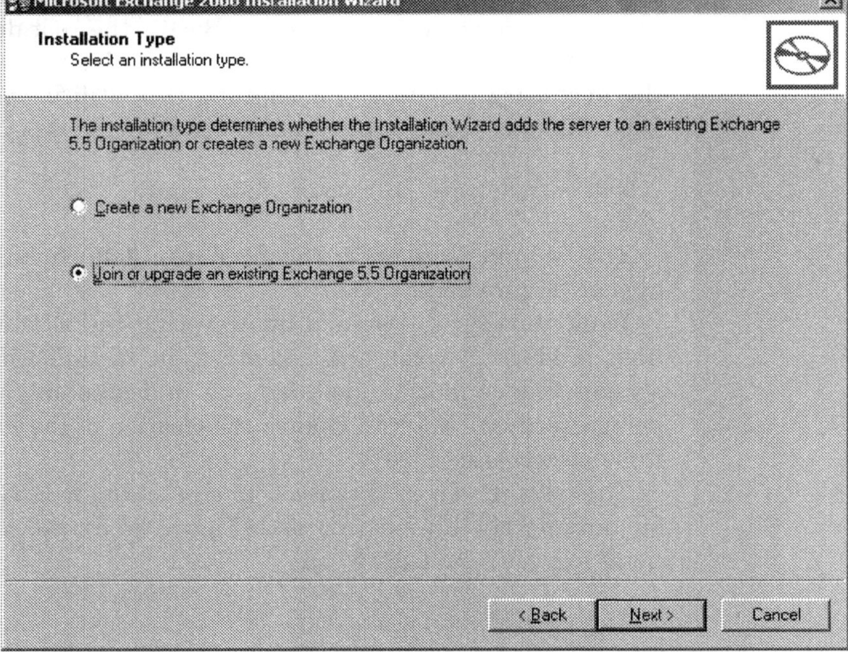
Microsoft Exchange 2000 Installation Wizard
Installation Type
Select an installation type.
The installation type determines whether the Installation Wizard adds the server to an existing Exchange 5.5 Organization or creates a new Exchange Organization.
Create a new Exchange Organization
Join or upgrade an existing Exchange 5.5 Organization
< Back
Next >
Cancel

Figure 25.3 Select the second option for this walkthrough.

The next screen prompts you for the name of an Exchange 5.5 server in your existing Exchange 5.5 organization, so type Box82 here and click Next. Make sure that Box82 is online and can be pinged from Box81 before proceeding. It may take a moment for ForestPrep to contact Box82, after which a dialog box will appear "Setup will now test some prerequisite conditions—this may take a few minutes." Click OK to continue.

The next screen prompts you to specify a valid Windows 2000 domain account that will be assigned the privileges necessary for it to install Exchange 2000 in your forest. The current logon account is displayed by default, which we'll accept by clicking Next.

The next screen displays the site service account for the Exchange 5.5 server we specified earlier (Figure 25.4). Type the password for this account and click Next.

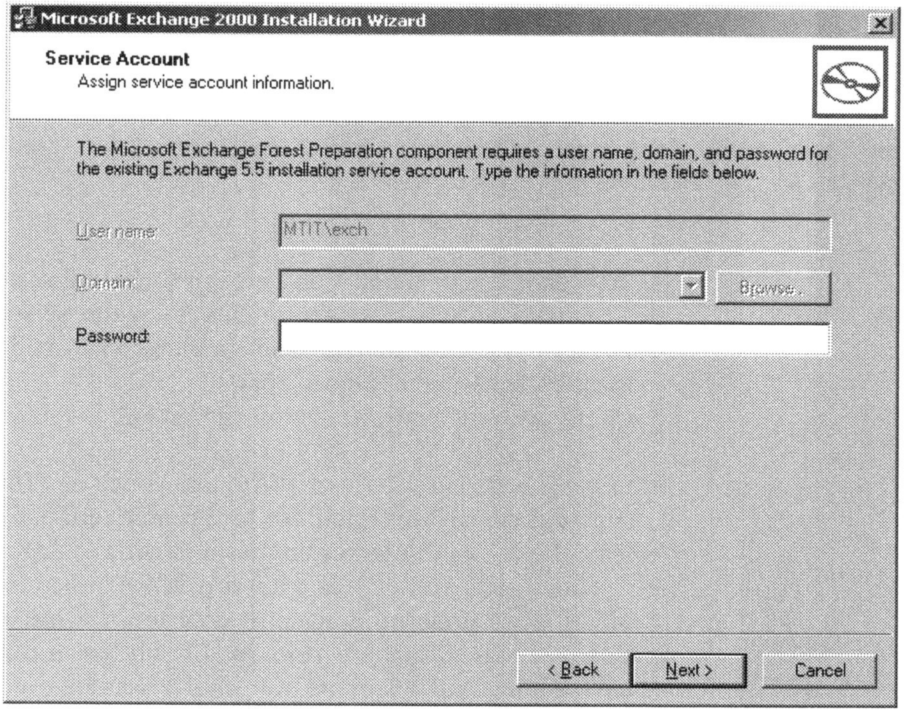

Figure 25.4
Specify the Exchange 5.5 service account for BOX82.

ForestPrep now modifies the AD schema to prepare the forest for Exchange 2000. Once this is completed, click Finish and continue with the next walkthrough.

Configuring a Connection Agreement

Walkthrough

We now need to establish a connection agreement between AD on Box81 and the Exchange 5.5 directory on Box82. To do this, open the ADC console under Administrative Tools on Box81 (Figure 25.5).

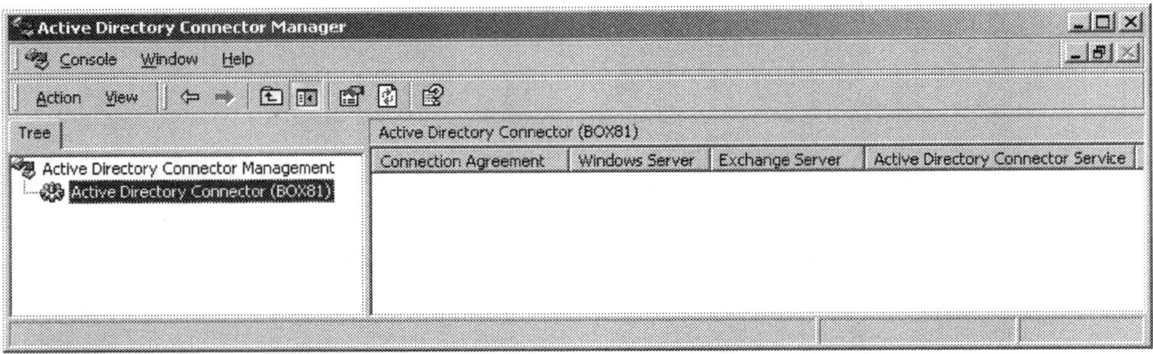

Figure 25.5 The Active Directory Connector console.

To create a new connection agreement for migrating mailbox properties to AD, right-click on Active Directory and select New → Recipient Connection Agreement. This opens a blank Properties Sheet for the new connection agreement (Figure 25.6).

Configure your new connection agreement as follows:

- *General tab.* Enter a descriptive name such as "Toronto to AD," leave the replication direction set to From Exchange To Windows, and leave Box81 as the server on which to run the ADC service.
- *Connections tab.* Click the top Modify button and select the MTIT\Administrator account as the one that will access AD on Box81. Then click the bottom Modify button and select the site service account for the Toronto site where Exchange server Box82 resides, which is the account that will access the information in the Exchange 5.5 directory on Box82 (you need an account that has Read and Write access to this directory). Make sure that the Windows Server information Server is specified as Box81 and the Exchange Server information Server is specified as Box82 (see Figure 25.7).

Figure 25.6 Creating a new connection agreement.

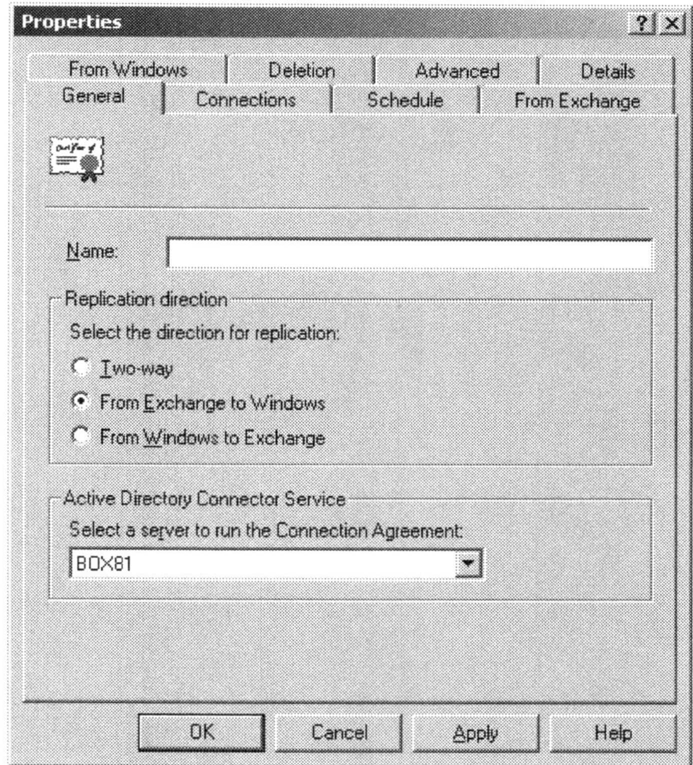

NOTE

The default LDAP port on the Exchange 5.5 bridgehead server is 389. If this conflicts with a port on Windows 2000 (this can happen if the Exchange 5.5 server was a Windows NT domain controller before being upgraded to Windows 2000), then change it to something else (see TechNet for further information).

- *Schedule tab*. By default, connection agreements are scheduled to run early in the morning, but for purposes of this walkthrough select Always and also the checkbox "Replicate the entire directory the next time the agreement is run" at the bottom of the sheet (this last step is actually unnecessary because the entire directory is replicated the first time the connection agreement is run).
- *From Exchange*. Click Add and select the default Recipients container in the Toronto site of the Exchange 5.5 organization MTIT. This will

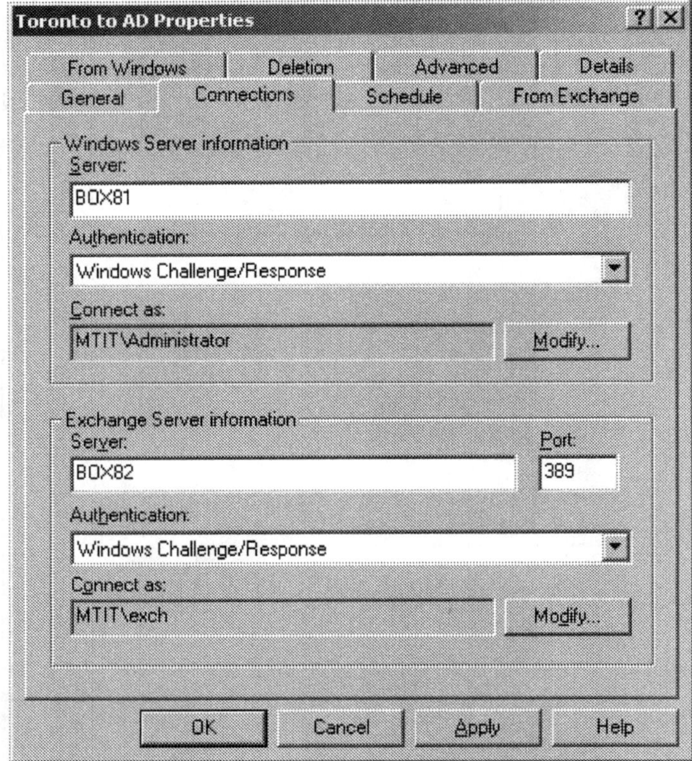

Figure 25.7 Configuring the Connections tab for the connection agreement.

replicate properties of all recipients on Box82 to AD. Then click the Modify button to specify the container in AD that the mailboxes properties will be migrated to. The From Exchange tab looks something like Figure 25.8, depending on your selections.

- *From Windows tab*. This tab doesn't need to be configured unless you are replicating directory information both ways (for instance, if you were planning on having the two versions of Exchange coexist for some time on your network).
- *Deletion tab*. Lets you decide what to do with mailboxes for deleted user accounts. Leave these at their defaults settings.
- *Advanced tab*. Leave these at their defaults settings, which are sufficient in most cases.

Now click OK to create the new connection agreement. A dialog box will appear indicating that two new security groups, Exchange Enterprise Servers and Exchange Domain Servers, have been created in AD.

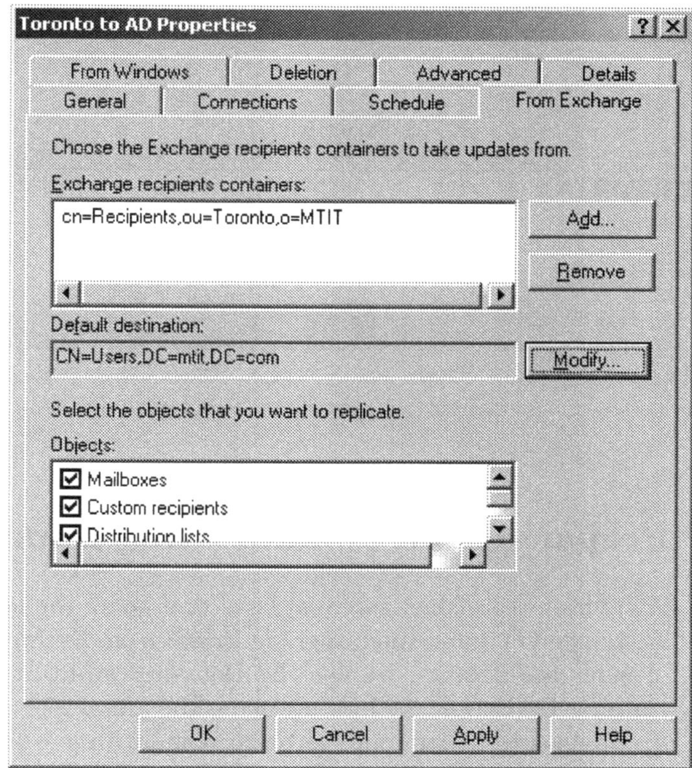

Figure 25.8 Configuring the From Exchange tab for the connection agreement.

The new connection agreement should now be visible in the ADC console (Figure 25.9).

The connection agreement may take a few minutes to run, so take a coffee break. When you return, open Active Directory Users and Computers on Box81 and open the Properties Sheet for one of the users whose mailbox properties were migrated to AD. The user account should now have several additional tabs showing (they weren't there before—trust me!), namely the Exchange General and E-mail Addresses tabs. We now have Exchange 2000 mailboxes for our users—at least their properties—because the actual mailbox folders won't be created until Exchange 2000 is installed on Box82.

TIP

If the mailbox properties don't show up, right-click on the connection agreement in the ADC console and select Replicate Now to force an immediate replication.

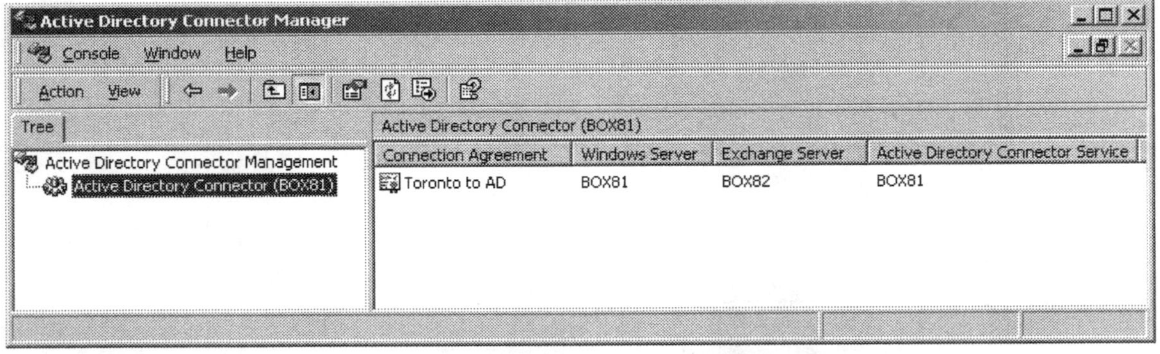

Figure 25.9 The new connection agreement displayed in the ADC console.

Preparing the Domain Using DomainPrep

We're almost finished—we just have to prepare the mtit.com domain for Exchange 2000 and then upgrade Box82 from Exchange 5.5 to 2000. To prepare the domain, we use the DomainPrep utility, which is run by running Exchange 2000 Setup using the `/domainprep` switch. DomainPrep needs to be run once for each domain that will contain Exchange 2000 servers or will host Exchange 2000 recipients such as mailbox-enabled user accounts. DomainPrep creates security groups and permissions necessary for Exchange servers to modify user attributes as required.

Log on to Box81 with an account that belongs to the Domain Admins group (we'll use the default domain Administrator account again). Insert the Exchange 2000 CD, open a command prompt window, and type <CD-drive>\Setup\I386\Setup /domainprep.

The welcome screen for the Exchange 2000 Installation Wizard appears once again. Walk through the steps of the wizard the way you did for ForestPrep. This should be pretty quick.

Actually, running DomainPrep in our testbed scenario was superfluous because ForestPrep created the two new security groups (Exchange Domain Servers and Exchange Enterprise Servers) that DomainPrep would have created.

Upgrading Exchange 5.5 to Exchange 2000

Let's do an in-place upgrade of our Exchange 5.5 SP3 server Box82 to Exchange 2000. Before you begin, check to make sure that Internet Information Services (IIS) is installed on the machine, including the SMTP and NTTP services. If not, select Control Panel → Add/Remove Programs → Add/Remove Windows Components → select Internet Information Services → Next → insert Windows 2000 SP1 CD and Windows 2000 Advanced Server CD as prompted → OK to install all the IIS services required by Exchange 2000. This extra step will be needed if your original Windows NT server BOX82 did not have IIS installed on it.

Insert the Exchange 2000 CD in Box82 and run `Setup` from the \Setup\I386 directory to start the Exchange 2000 Installation Wizard. On the Component Selection screen of the wizard, certain components will be preselected and displayed as having Upgrade status—this cannot be altered, but components can be added if needed.

Click Next and specify the password for the Exchange 5.5 site service account on Box82. Continue through the wizard using the defaults until Exchange 2000 is installed. Then complete the walkthrough by using Outlook on a client computer to connect to a user's mailbox and send mail.

Summary

The procedures outlined in this chapter for upgrading an existing Exchange 5.5 organization are not meant to be complete but simply illustrative of the steps involved in such a process. For a fuller treatment of upgrades and migrations, see the *Microsoft Exchange 2000 Server Resource Kit* from Microsoft Press.

APPENDIX A

EXCHANGE RESOURCES ON THE WEB

There are a great many useful sites for Microsoft Exchange on the Internet. These sites range from independent to vendor affiliated, from online communities to links pages, from news sources to collections of step-by-step tutorials. Most of these sites now include coverage of Exchange 2000, and a few are devoted exclusively to it. This appendix is a sampler of twelve different sites that I have found useful for the administration and development of Exchange solutions. A brief description of each site is included with the relevant URL.

Swynk

www.swynk.com

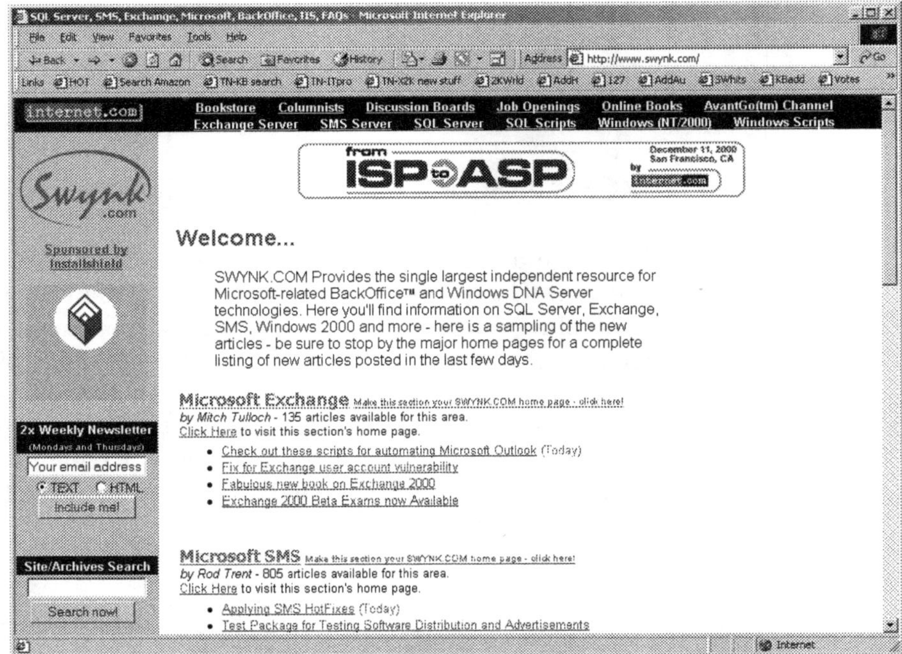

Figure A.1 Swynk, an online community of experts in Exchange and other BackOffice products.

Describing itself as "the single largest independent resource for Microsoft-related BackOffice and Windows DNA Server technologies," Swynk lives up to its name by providing numerous valuable resources including:

- An active online community of columnists who are experienced IT professionals and who write articles of all types including tutorials, troubleshooting tips, security alerts, book and product reviews, news bulletins, and administration scripts.
- Biweekly email newsletter that includes links to all the latest articles on the subject.
- Discussion boards and list servers for posting questions for others to read and answer.
- Job boards advertising positions needing to be filled.
- Searchable knowledge base of articles contributed by columnists.

- AvantGo channel for wireless access to Swynk information.

The Exchange section on Swynk can be found at *www.swynk.com/exchange.*

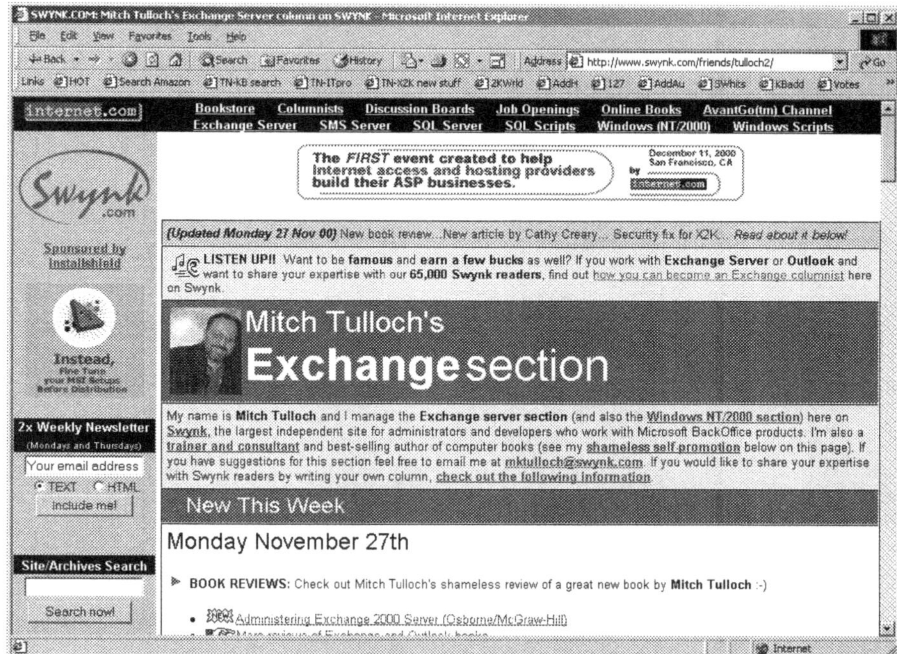

Figure A.2
My own home page on Swynk.

You can also find the home page of the manager of the Exchange section on Swynk (yours truly, of course) from www.swynk.com/mitch. My own home page provides links to other columnists' pages, timely articles, security bulletins, book reviews (including my own books), news, links, and lots more stuff. As you can see, I'm quite shameless in promoting myself!

Slipstick Systems

www.slipstick.com

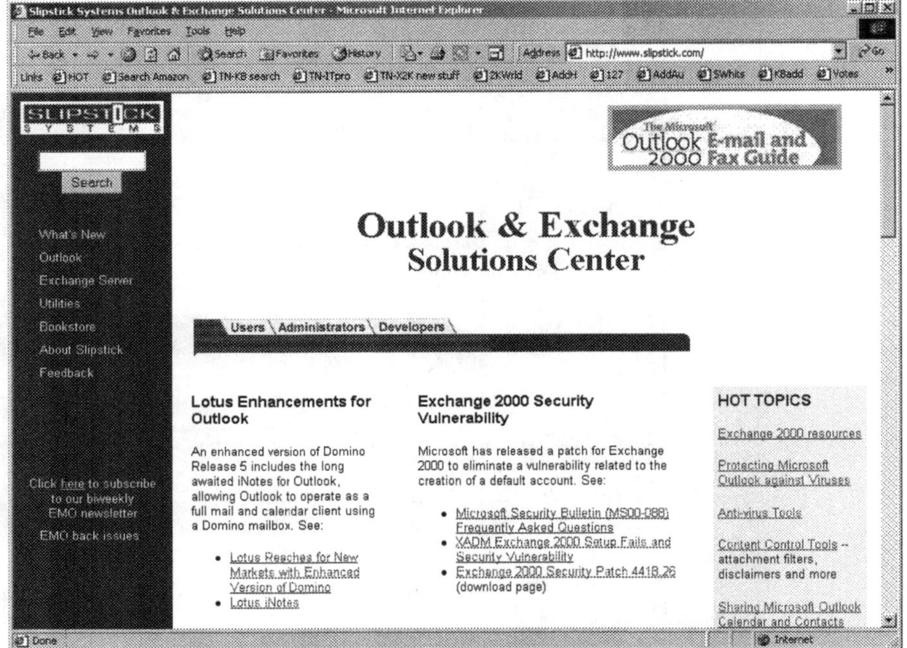

Figure A.3
Slipstick Systems, a solutions center and portal for Exchange and Outlook information.

Billing itself as the "Outlook & Exchange Solutions Center," Slipstick Systems is run by Sue Mosher, a veteran Microsoft MVP, and specializes in researching and solving problems with Microsoft Outlook and Microsoft Exchange Server. The Web site acts as a portal for other Exchange–centric sites on the Internet and provides the following resources:

- News about Exchange support issues with links to bulletins on Microsoft's web site and other sites.
- Links to white papers, security bulletins, download sites for service packs and fixes, discussion boards, books, and more.
- Comprehensive list of third-party add-ons for Exchange together with brief descriptions.
- Biweekly EMO newsletter full of timely and useful information.

Msexchange.org

www.msexchange.org

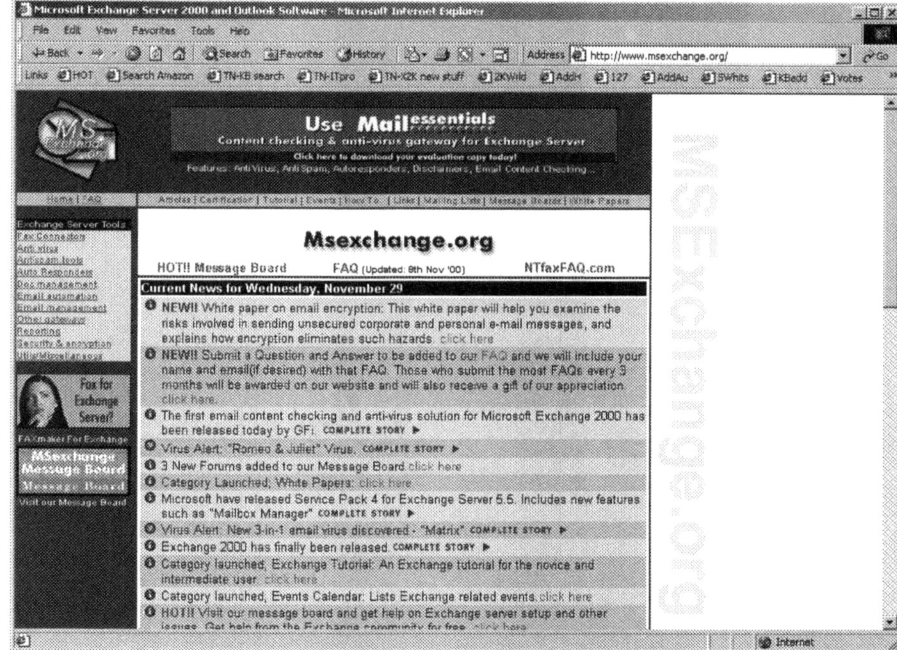

Figure A.4 Msexchange.org, a site with third party product listings, news, tutorials, FAQs, message boards, and more.

This site is dedicated to Microsoft Exchange and Outlook, with third-party product listings, news, articles, FAQs, message boards, and more. The discussion boards are particularly busy at this site.

Exchange-mail.org

www.exchange-mail.org

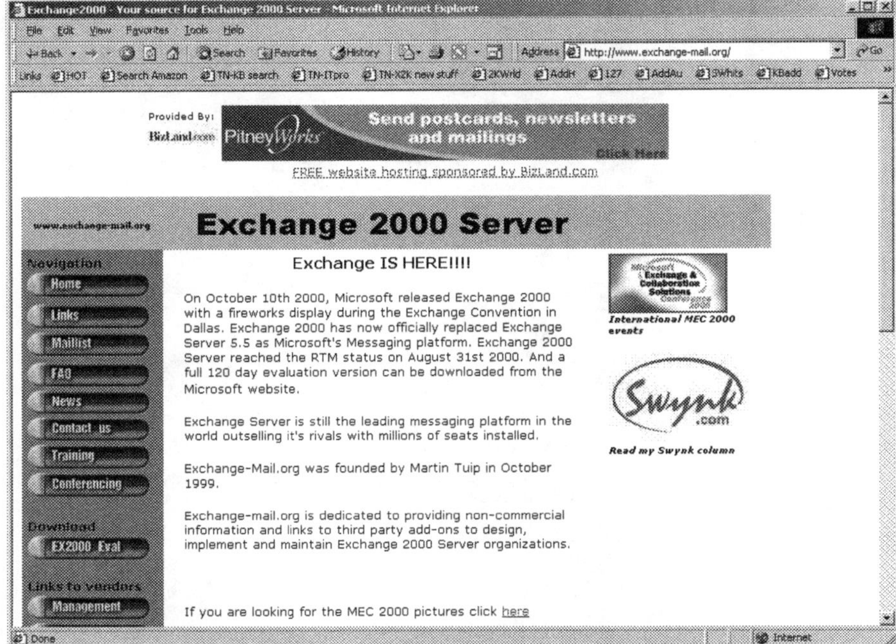

Figure A.5
Exchange-mail.org, a site providing information and links on Exchange 2000.

This site was founded by Martin Tuip and is dedicated to providing non-commercial information and links to third-party add-ons to design, implement, and maintain Exchange 2000 Server organizations. It includes FAQs, mailing lists, news bulletins, and links to white papers, books, vendor sites, and other information specifically relating to Exchange 2000.

Microsoft TechNet

www.microsoft.com/technet/exchange/

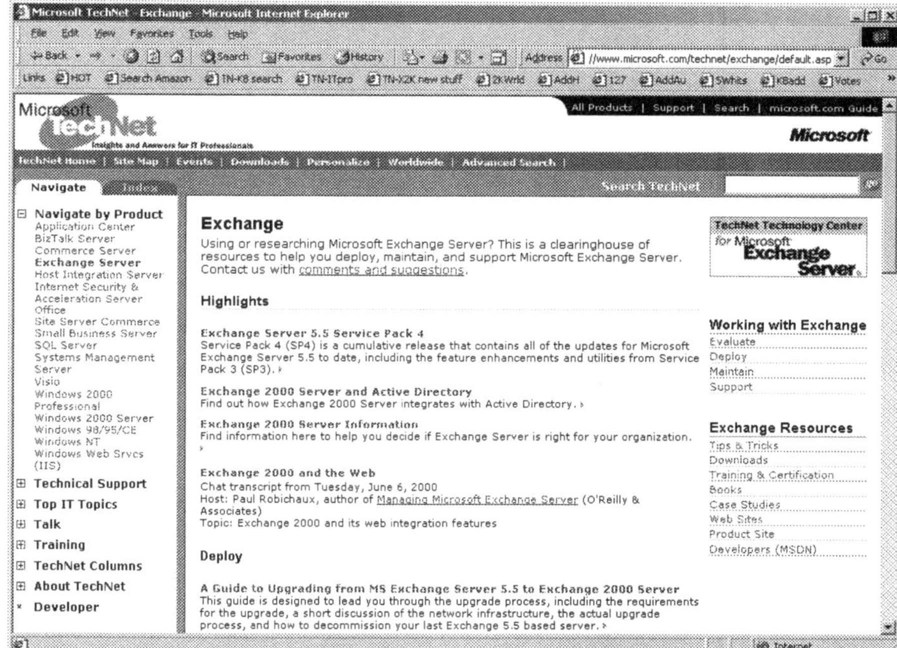

Figure A.6 The Exchange section on Microsoft TechNet.

The official support site for Exchange-related issues, this site has news, downloads, and links to white papers and other resources on all aspects of Exchange. This is an invaluable site for all professionals who work with Exchange, but you have to take the marketing hype with an occasional grain of salt.

Microsoft Exchange Internals

www.exinternals.com

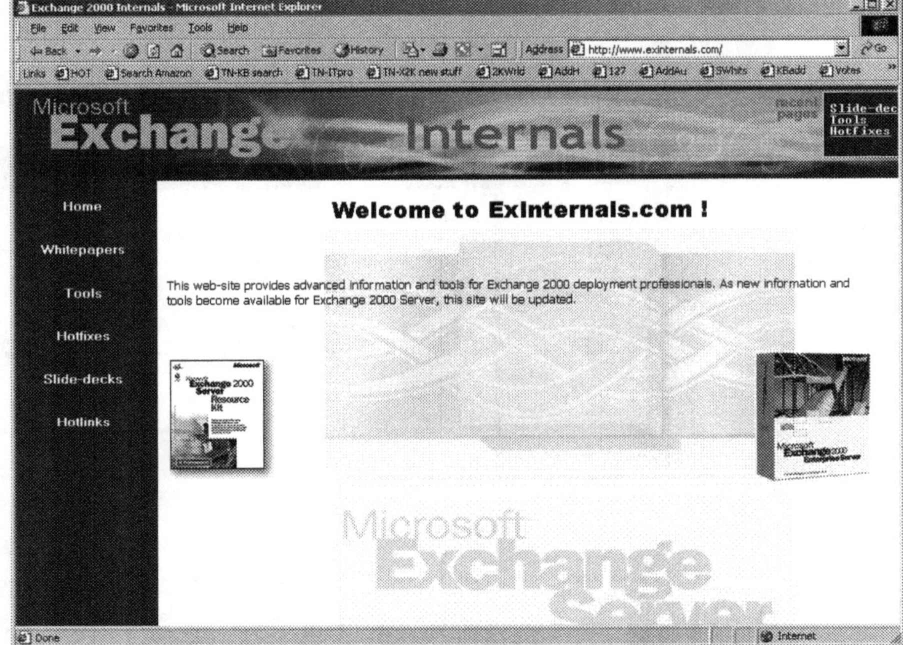

Figure A.7 The Microsoft Exchange Internals site.

This site includes a number of resources specific to Exchange 2000 including white papers from Microsoft's Exchange Server Product Unit, unsupported troubleshooting tools from Microsoft, downloads for service packs and hotfixes needed by Exchange 2000, PowerPoint slide presentations from TechWeek and other conferences, and links to other Exchange 2000–centric resources on the Web.

DevX Exchange and Outlook

exchange.devx.com

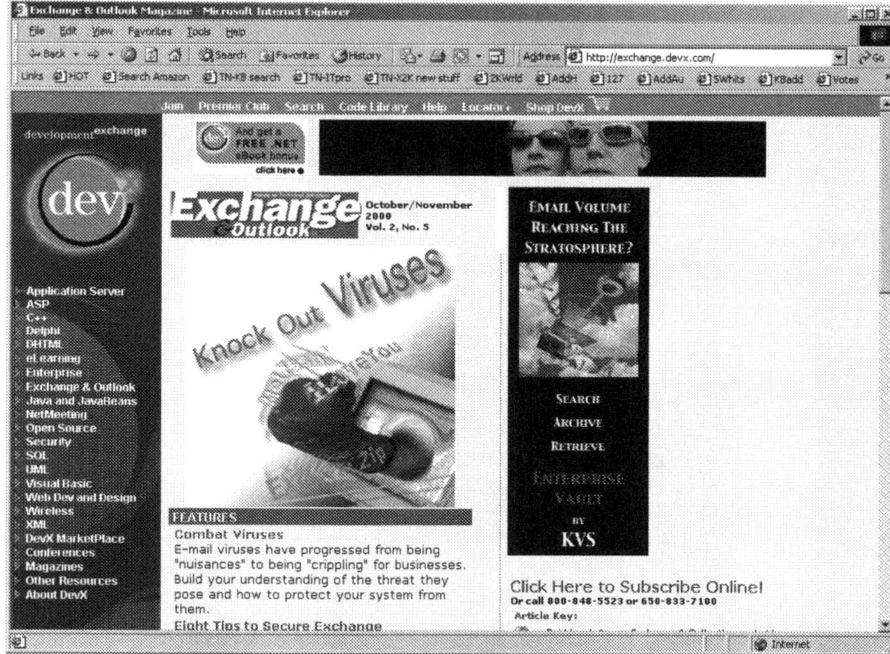

Figure A.8 The DevX Exchange & Outlook section.

Billing itself as "the leading independent commercial site for IT development information," DevX includes many useful resources for Exchange/Outlook developers including:

- Online subscription to *Exchange & Outlook* magazine
- News bulletins and announcements
- Exchange *Update* email newsletter
- Developer-related discussion groups
- Ask The Exchange Pro FAQ, which allows you to get help by submitting your questions
- Catalog of useful Exchange and Outlook third-party products
- An online demo Exchange 2000 showcase site

Microsoft Exchange Home

www.microsoft.com/exchange

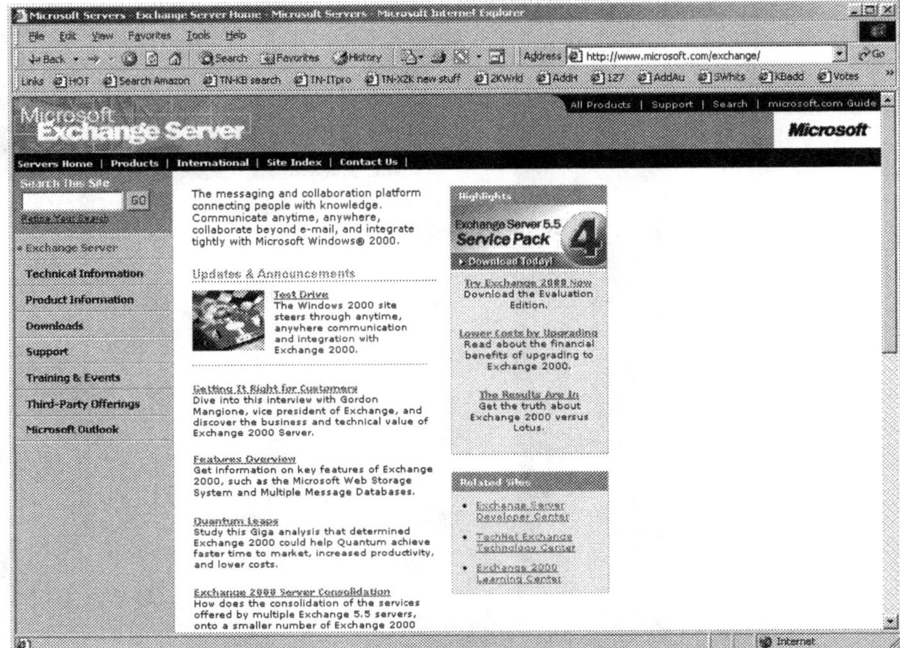

Figure A.9 Microsoft Exchange Home.

As the official home page for Microsoft Exchange, this site has a number of useful resources including:

- Feature sheets on the various versions of Exchange, including licensing and pricing information
- Marketing studies comparing Exchange with other messaging systems (some hype but mostly right on)
- White papers on all aspects of Exchange planning, deployment, installation, upgrades, migration, administration, monitoring, maintenance, troubleshooting, and so on
- Downloads of service packs, fixes, add-ons, and utilities from Microsoft
- A support center with FAQs, online documentation, searchable knowledge base (from TechNet), and so on
- Scheduled Microsoft-sponsored training events focused on Exchange
- Links to third-party vendors and their products
- Tips on integrating Microsoft Outlook with Exchange

Exchange Administrator

www.exchangeadmin.com

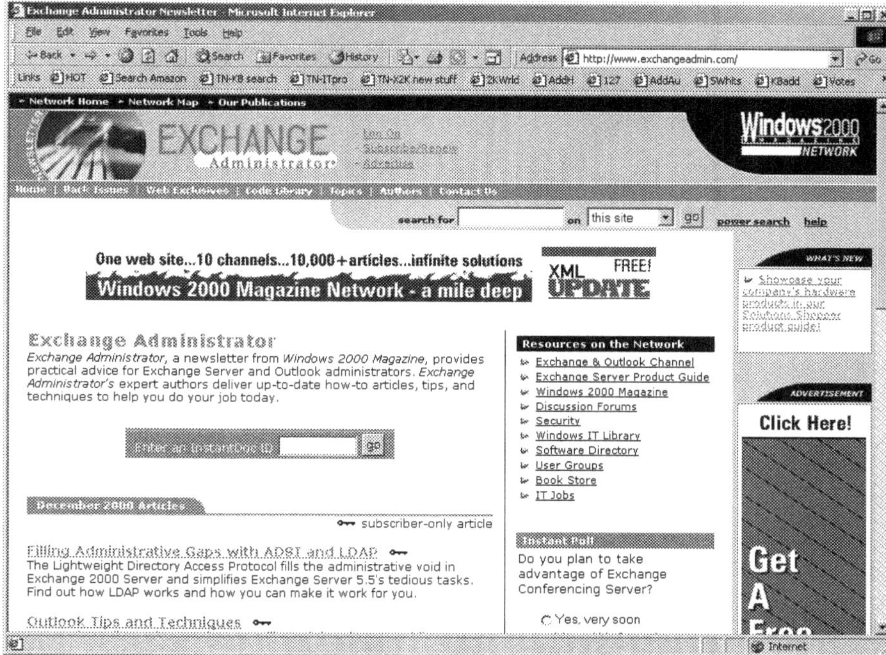

Figure A.10 Exchange Administrator from Windows 2000 Magazine.

This newsletter and Web site from *Windows 2000 Magazine* is targeted specifically to administrators who work with Exchange. The site bills itself as delivering "up-to-date how-to articles, tips, and techniques to help you do your job today." The site includes:

- A subscriber-based online magazine with valuable articles for Exchange administrators
- Free sample articles and web-based exclusives
- Free *Exchange Administrator Update* email newsletter
- Exchange Server product guide
- Exchange and Outlook channel with articles and online forums

JustExchangeJobs.com

www.justexchangejobs.com

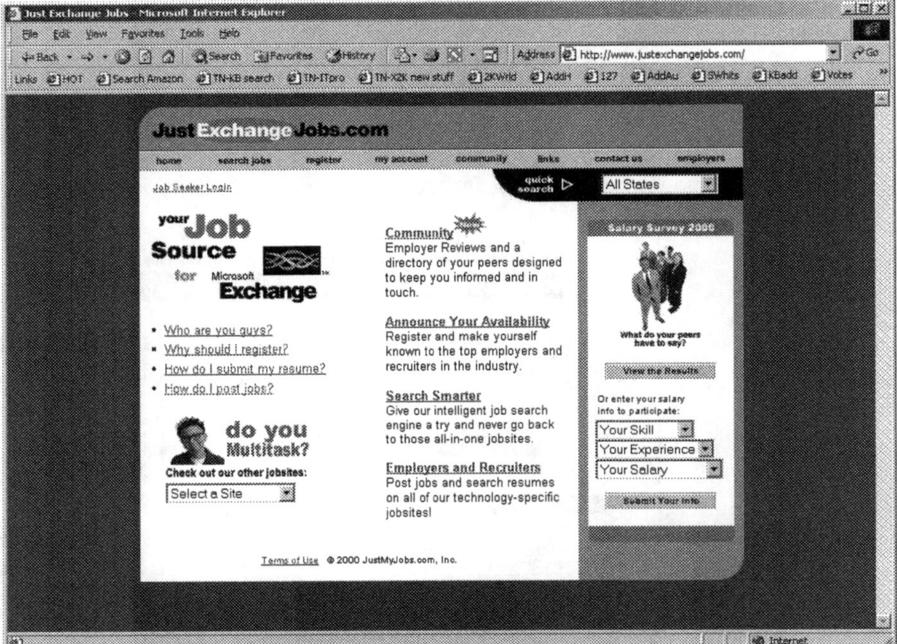

Figure A.11 Online site for Exchange-related job listings.

Part of the JustComputerJobs.com umbrella jobsite for IT professionals, justexchangejobs.com lets you search for Exchange-related jobs and post your resume to advertise your talents to the corporate community. A quick search came up with more than 100 available positions in the United States alone. You can register with the site to receive notification when registered companies show an interest in your online resume.

MSDN Online Exchange Server Development Center

msdn.microsoft.com/exchange/

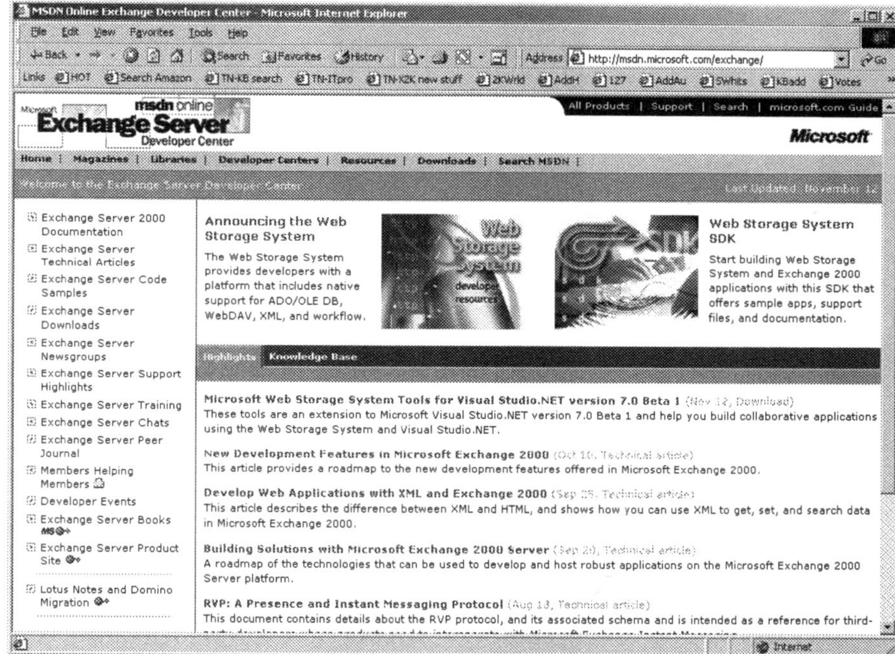

Figure A.12 MSDN Exchange site for developers.

Familiarity with this site is essential for those developing custom solutions based on Exchange and Outlook. The site is a treasure trove of code, tutorials, news, links, chat rooms, peer forums, reviews, and more.

APPENDIX B

THIRD-PARTY PRODUCTS FOR EXCHANGE

A number of valuable third-party tools and add-ons for Exchange 2000 are available or about to hit the market. This appendix reviews two such products concerning data protection that I've used and several other products that I have not been able to review. Check out my Exchange column on Swynk (www.swynk.com/mitch) regularly for other product reviews by me and other Exchange section columnists on Swynk.

Veritas Backup Exec 8.5

www.veritas.com

Backup Exec is a popular backup and recovery tool for the Windows NT and 2000 platforms, and includes backup agents for the full line of Microsoft BackOffice applications including Exchange 2000 and SQL 2000. Use this product to protect the data on your Exchange servers and to recover quickly from a disaster.

Product Review

Installation of this product is straightforward, but some preparatory planning is helpful. You can install Backup Exec and Backup Exec Agent for Microsoft Exchange Server directly on the Exchange server you want to back up. Alternatively, you can install Backup Exec on a designated backup server (a server with attached archival storage devices such as tape drives) and the Backup Exec Agent for Exchange on the Exchange servers on your network, but the service account you create for Backup Exec must be a member of the local administrators group on your Exchange servers and the Exchange administration tools must be installed on your designated backup server. You also have the option during Setup of installing Backup Exec Remote Agent on remote servers and workstations to allow remote backup and restoration of Windows 2000 features on these machines. Be sure to reboot your machine after installing Backup Exec or any of its components.

Installing the Exchange agent on your Exchange servers is not as intuitive. If you insert the Backup Exec CD into your Exchange server and try to select only the Exchange agent for installation, you are prompted to install the full product and not allowed to proceed. Instead you have to exit the installation program and use Add/Remove Programs in Control Panel to install the agent on the machine. Note also that the printed manual included with the product actually contains several manuals including the Options Manual that explain how to install the Exchange Agent and other agents. Each section has its own index, which was a bit confusing: I flipped to the back of the book, looked up Microsoft Exchange, and then couldn't find the references listed there until I finally realized the printed book was actually two books in one! This should be clearly stated on the cover of the book.

When you first run the VERITAS Backup Exec application, several wizards walk you though the process of configuring backup hardware, media overwrite protection, and automatic virus scanning. The Backup Exec Assistant window then appears (Figure B.1), from which you can create, schedule, and monitor backup jobs, initiate restores, configure backup devices and media pools, and perform related tasks using these wizards.

Backing up jobs is intuitive and easy using the assistant. The manual included with the product fills in the gaps when the job is not so intuitive. Alternatively, you can close the assistant and perform tasks manually using the Backup Exec administrative console (Figure B.2). Note that this is not an MMC, so this version (8.5) of Backup Exec is not 100 percent integrated into the Windows 2000 design environment (although it is fully functional in every way).

You can back up the entire information store, individual storage groups, or data stores on an Exchange server or individual mailboxes, folders, or messages. If you want to do the latter, you first have to create a mailbox for the Backup Exec service account by mailbox-enabling the account using Active Directory Users and Computers, and you need a MAPI email client such as Outlook installed on the backup server. Back-

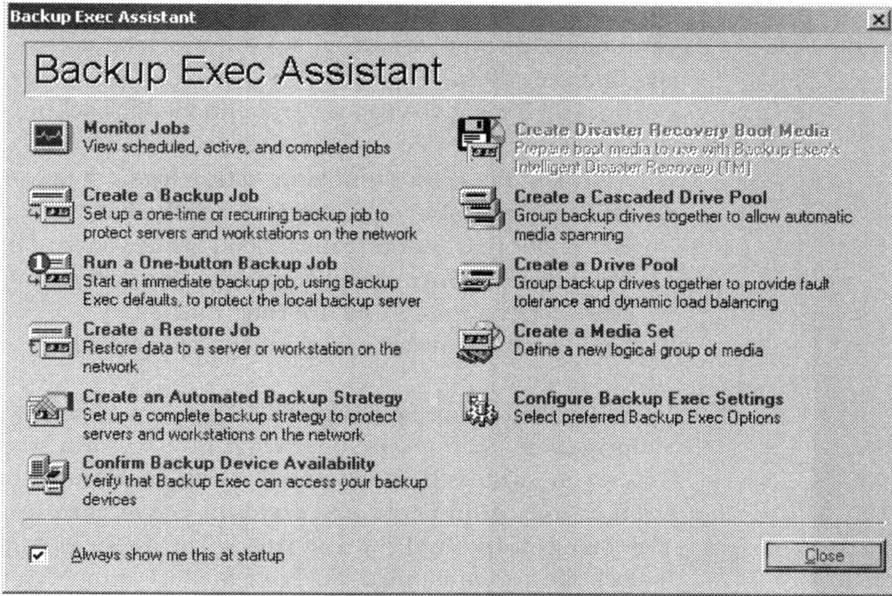

Figure B.1 The Backup Exec Assistant.

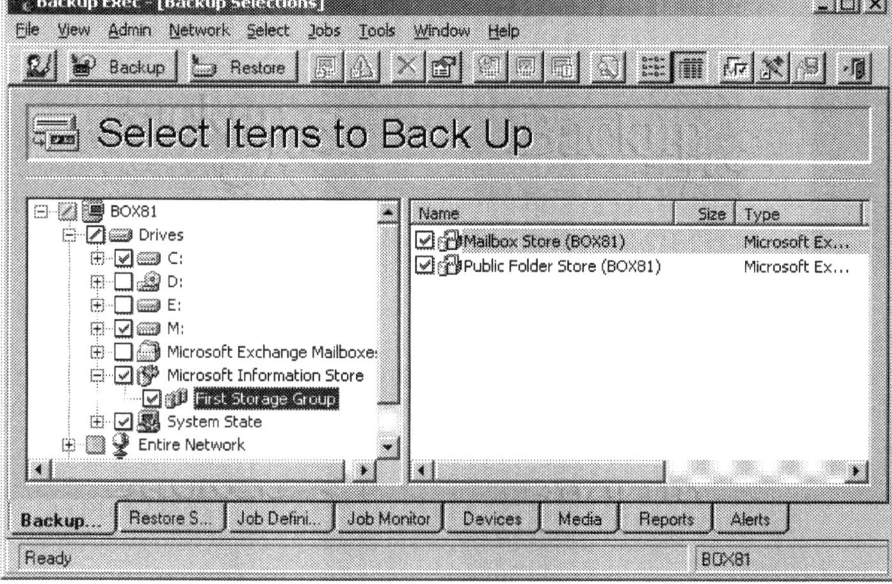

Figure B.2 The Backup Exec administrative console.

ing up individual mailboxes, folders, or messages actually takes longer and has a greater impact on system performance, so you probably won't do this very often.

Backup Exec gives you several options for backing up Exchange:

- *Full.* Database files and transaction logs are backed up, and logs that have all transactions committed are flushed.
- *Copy.* Databases and transaction logs are backed up.
- *Incremental.* Only transaction logs are backed up: logs that have all transactions committed are then flushed.
- *Differential.* Only transaction logs are backed up.

When restoring Exchange data, you can choose to restore the entire information store or specific storage groups, data stores, mailboxes, folders, or messages. If the restored messages already exist in the destination folder, duplicates are created. Some care must be taken when restoring individual data stores within a storage group: if you don't select the recommended No Loss Restore option, you can lose transaction logs for the entire storage group. Otherwise, things are fairly intuitive when working with this product.

CommVault Galaxy 2.5.0 with iDataAgent for Exchange

www.commvault.com

CommVault Galaxy is a suite of powerful storage management tools for backing up, managing, and restoring data across an enterprise. It consists of three sets of components:

- CommServer Storage Manager, which coordinates storage management
- MediaAgents, which transfer data to backup media libraries
- DataAgents or Intelligent Data Agents, which enable host computer systems to have their data backed up

I was particularly interested in the iDataAgent for Exchange, which lets you restore online the Exchange information store down to the level of a single message with all its Outlook properties, date/time stamp, message ID, attachments, and other settings intact. You can also recover individual mailboxes or just a single folder or subfolder within a mailbox. You can also implement storage policies with Galaxy for implementing data management strategies across your enterprise. And you can perform these administrative tasks using an MMC or remotely using browser-based tools.

Product Review

This product has one of the best collections of manuals I've seen in a while. There are well-written Quick Start Guides that walk you step by step through the installation process, and administration guides that cover the different iDataAgents that are used to backup, manage, and restore the Windows 2000 File System, Exchange 2000 information store, and so on.

Installation of Galaxy has several stages. First make sure that DNS is configured properly for your network because it is used by Galaxy for name resolution (although hosts files can be used in a small environment). Configure your tape library ahead of time.

The first Galaxy component you install is the CommServe software, preferably on a clean Windows 2000 server with 2 GB of free disk space because SQL Server 7.0 also is installed. Installation took some time and several reboots were required. The installation creates a storage framework called Galaxy CommCell, which when completed will consist of CommServe Storage Manager, one or more MediaAgents managing storage libraries, and one or more iDataAgents, specifically Windows File System agent for backing up Windows 2000 file systems and possibly other agents such as the Exchange agent for backing up Exchange server data.

The second step in the procedure is to install the MediaAgent software on the server that has the connected tape library or other removable media library. Installation is straightforward and supports a variety of media devices. Make sure the CommServe server is running when you install MediaAgent on your media server.

Once this is complete, you install the default client software, the iDataAgent for Windows File System, on the servers for which you plan to back up data. This is a prerequisite for installing other agents such as the Exchange agent because Exchange uses the Windows 2000 file system APIs for data storage.

At this stage, you have a working CommCell and should be able to back up file systems on the servers running the iDataAgents (iDAs). You can do this by logging on to the CommServe machine and opening the Galaxy CommCell MMC from the Galaxy programs group in the Start menu (Figure B.3). Use this console to create and schedule backup jobs, restore, generate reports, manage media and security, create storage policies, and so on. Note that you log on to the CommCell using the cvadmin account created during installation (the password for this account is *cvadmin*). You cannot log onto the console using Windows 2000 accounts, even the Administrator account.

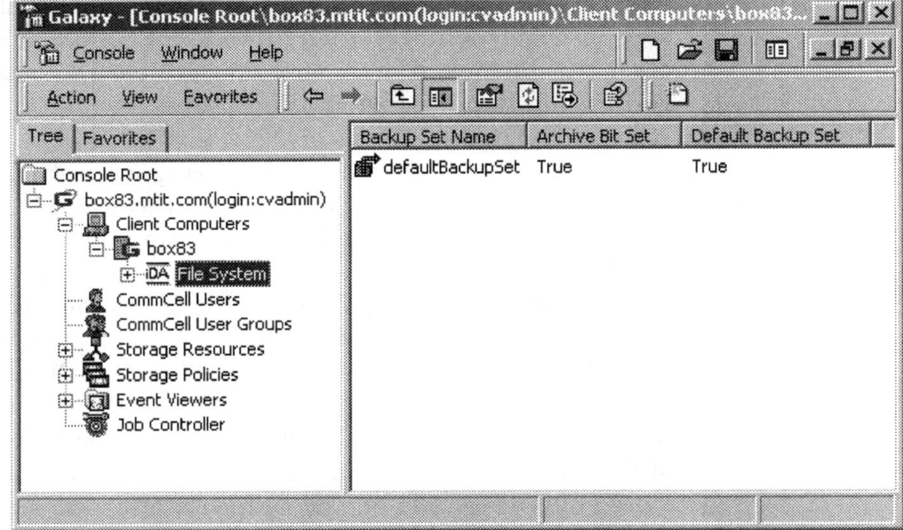

Figure B.3 The Galaxy CommCell Snap-in for MMC.

To back up the Exchange information stores, you need to install the iDA for Exchange on your Exchange servers (there are different versions for Exchange 5.5 and Exchange 2000, so get the right one). The iDA for Windows File System should be installed on these machines, but it can be installed with the iDA for Exchange. Before you install the iDA for Exchange, you need to create a Galaxy Administrator mailbox-enabled user using Active Directory Users and Computers and allow enough time for Active Directory to replicate this information to other domain controllers. Make sure this account has a non-null password; I found that I couldn't install the Exchange agent until I had changed the password to something non-null. The Client Quick Start Guide for Microsoft Exchange 2000 Server outlines all the steps clearly. Then you log onto your Exchange server as an administrator and install the iDA for

Exchange Mailbox, after which you install the iDA for Exchange Database. Make sure you reboot your Exchange server after installing the iDA even though you won't be prompted to do so.

The CommServe Console will have the additional functionality of backing up Exchange 2000 mailboxes and databases. Figure B.4 shows the Java version of the CommCell administrator tool, which is started through Internet Explorer. Note that the CommServe Java Runtime Environment must be installed on a remote machine running Internet Explorer.

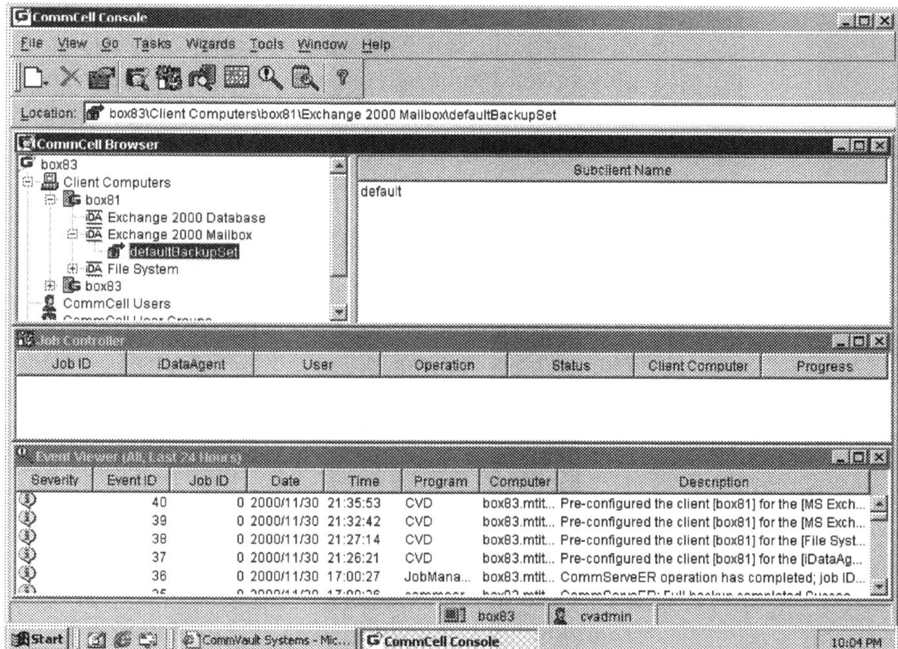

Figure B.4
The Galaxy CommCell Console for Java GUI.

IXOS-ExchangeARCHIVE

www.ixos.com

IXOS-ExchangeARCHIVE is an add-on for Exchange that frees up space in the information store by archiving messages and attachments to optical storage media or some other location. As a result, a user mailbox configured with a 20-MB storage limit can effectively store 1 GB or more of data. All that remains in the mailbox are links to the messages or attachments, and these links take up less than 1.0 kB of space. Archiving can be configured two ways:

- Automatic archiving according to the size and age of items
- Manual archiving on the client by simply dragging the item into a small desktop Window called the ExchangeARCHIVE Archive Form

When an Outlook user double-clicks on an archived message or attachment, the utility automatically retrieves the item from the archive medium and displays it.

The main benefit of this process is that the load on the data storage components on the Exchange servers is reduced. As a result, you can deploy fewer Exchange servers, which can save money and ease administration.

abridean Provisor

www.abridean.com

Abridean Provisor was designed for Application Server Providers (ASPs) to provide clients with customized Exchange 2000–based messaging and collaboration solutions. Provisor was designed to make the application provisioning process fast and simple by using intuitive Wizard-driven and MMC based management interfaces. Using abridean Provisor, an ASP can quickly provision Exchange 2000 for many companies together with integrated metering, and the billing features of SQL 7.0 Server is used for the billing database.

A single Exchange 2000 server can securely host many companies by using Provisor's proprietary Customer Partitioning feature, and it takes only a few mouse clicks to set up a new company using the ASP Admin tools. Customers can manage messaging and collaboration services hosted by the ASP and administer these services. For companies that want to outsource their messaging and collaboration from an ASP, abridean Provisor may be the solution.

The ASP administrators use the management console to create and configure top-level organizational units representing companies belonging to different customers. These customers are also provided with their own versions of the management console for customizing their provisioned Exchange 2000 services (Figure B.5). Using this console, customers can easily create and configure their own organizational units, users, groups, and contacts, change passwords, delegate administrative responsibilities over organizational units and their contents to specific users, and perform other common management tasks.

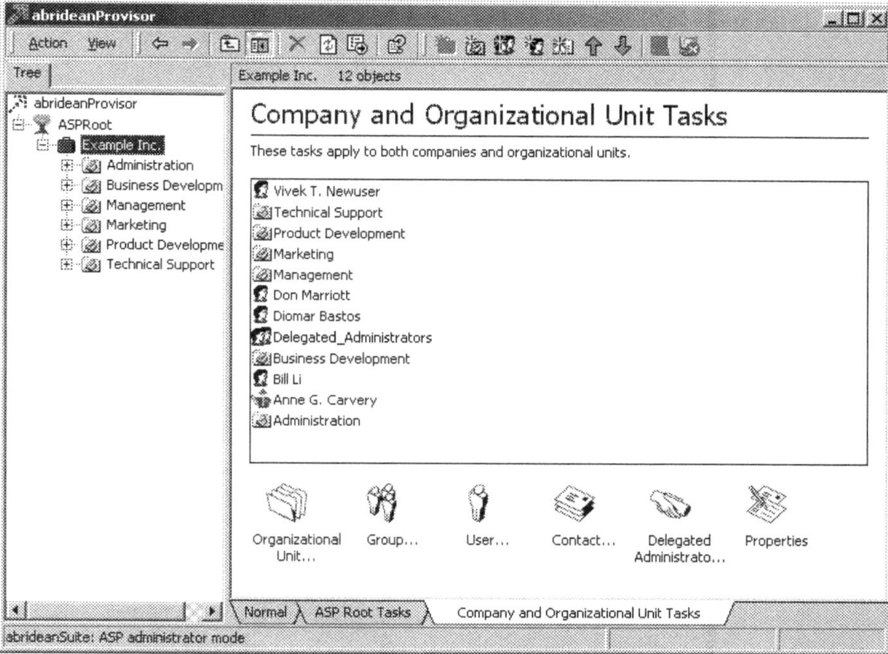

Figure B.5 abridean Provisor management console (reprinted with permission from Abridean Inc.)

Hardware and software requirements for Provisor are basic, so any ASP wanting to provide it for customers with Exchange 2000 services should be able to get it up and running quickly. Recommended requirements include one Active Directory domain controller, one SQL 7.0 server, one or more Exchange 2000 servers, and a broadband Internet connection.

INDEX

Note: Boldface numbers indicate illustrations; italic t indicates a table.

D

N

O

P

S

T

www.ingramcontent.com/pod-product-compliance
Lightning Source LLC
Chambersburg PA
CBHW080132060326
40689CB00018B/3758

* 9 7 8 0 0 7 2 1 2 7 0 8 9 *